Lecture Notes in Computer Science 910

Edited by G. Goos, J. Hartmanis and J. van Leeuwen

Advisory Board: W. Brauer   D. Gries   J. Stoer

Andreas Podelski (Ed.)

Constraint Programming: Basics and Trends

1994 Châtillon Spring School
Châtillon-sur-Seine, France, May 16-20, 1994
Selected Papers

 Springer

Series Editors

Gerhard Goos
Universität Karlsruhe
Vincenz-Priessnitz-Straße 3, D-76128 Karlsruhe, Germany

Juris Hartmanis
Department of Computer Science, Cornell University
4130 Upson Hall, Ithaca, NY 14853, USA

Jan van Leeuwen
Department of Computer Science, Utrecht University
Padualaan 14, 3584 CH Utrecht, The Netherlands

Volume Editor

Andreas Podelski
Max-Planck-Institut für Informatik
Im Stadtwald, D-66123 Saarbrücken, Germany

CR Subject Classification (1991): D.1.m, D.3.2-3, D.1.3, I.2.8

ISBN 3-540-59155-9 Springer-Verlag Berlin Heidelberg New York

CIP data applied for

© Springer-Verlag Berlin Heidelberg 1995
Printed in Germany

Typesetting: Camera-ready by author
SPIN: 10485618   06/3142-543210 - Printed on acid-free paper

Foreword

The set of papers presented in this volume corresponds to lectures given at the 22nd Spring School in Theoretical Computer Science in Châtillon-sur-Seine (France) from May 16th to May 20th 1994.

This series of Spring Schools was initiated in 1973 by Maurice Nivat and his colleagues at the Laboratoire d'Informatique Théorique et Programmation (LITP). Since then a school has been organized every year on a different subject in a different location, with a preference for very small French towns deep in the countryside, which provide a pleasant atmosphere propitious to scientific discussions. It is attended by the speakers who agree to present the subjects benevolently to an audience more than half of whom are very young research students.

This time we found the same enthusiastic lecturers as usual and I must thank them heartily for having written the present texts, many of which are surveys we hope will be useful to a number of researchers, be they confirmed ones or younger ones who wish to enter the field.

I would also like to thank Maurice Nivat, who asked me to organize the school, and Hassan Aït-Kaci and Patrick Sallé, who helped me build the scientific program and face the numerous organizational problems. The mayor of Châtillon-sur-Seine, by allowing us to use the "salle des fêtes" of the town, was very helpful and I thank him for his kind words of welcome.

Saarbrücken, February 1995   Andreas Podelski

Introduction

Constraint Logic Programming: State of the Art and Research Themes

Gert Smolka

Constraint Logic Programming (CLP) generalizes the conventional Horn clause model into two directions, thus providing for important applications that are outside the scope of Prolog. CLP factorizes logic programming into a parametric construction P(X), where P is a programming scheme applied to a constraint system X. Jaffar and Lassez formulated and investigated in 1986 the so-called CLP scheme CLP(X), which is a straightforward generalization of the conventional Horn clause model. In CLP(X), SLD-resolution is modified such that it employs constraint solving for the constraint system X rather than unification of terms. The conventional Horn clause model is obtained as the instance CLP(Herbrand), where Herbrand is the finite tree constraint system. There are other programming schemes than CLP(X), most prominently among them several versions of Saraswats Concurrent Constraint Programming Scheme cc(X). While CLP(X) requires an incremental test for satisfiability of constraints, cc(X) requires in addition an incremental test for entailment of constraints.

Research in CLP is concerned with the design, foundation, and implementation of constraint programming languages. Major research topics are particular constraint systems (e.g., numbers, booleans, and trees) and possible programming schemes P(X). While research on particular constraint systems has reached a certain maturity, research on possible programming schemes is still at an early stage.

CLP has been driven by practical language designs. The first CLP language was Colmerauer's Prolog II, designed and implemented in the early 1980s. Prolog II's constraint system is based on possibly infinite trees (thus eliminating the need for the occurs check) and employs equations and disequations as constraints. Prolog II also introduced a new control facility called freeze, which allows goals to be delayed until given variables are bound to nonvariables. Delaying control was developed further by Lee Naish and is now present in most state-of-the-art Prolog implementations. Providing delay facilities requires that the purely sequential control of early Prologs is replaced by a concurrent control regime.

In the mid-eighties several researchers realized that by providing the right constraint systems in a Prolog-like language, many important applications that where outside the reach of Prolog could be attacked. In Marseille, Prolog III was designed, which has linear constraints over rational numbers (solved by an incremental simplex algorithm), Boolean constraints including all truth functions (solved by a resolution-based method), and constraints over lists and trees. Nonlinear arithmetic constraints are delayed until they become linear.

At ECRC in Munich the CLP language CHIP was designed. Like Prolog III, CHIP has linear constraints over rational numbers and full Boolean constraints. Different constraint solving methods for Boolean constraints were explored, among them Boolean unification. But in retrospect most importantly, CHIP has finite domain constraints, which provide full integer arithmetic for variables a priori constrained to finite sets of integers. Finite domain constraints are at the heart of many combinatorial search problems arising in applications like scheduling. Due to their many important applications, constraint techniques for finite domains had been investigated by researchers in Artificial Intelligence since the 1970s. Now logic programming was recognized as the natural programming paradigm for constraint programming.

Checking satisfiability of finite domain constraints is an NP-complete problem. Thus applying the CLP scheme will be useless in practice since it requires a complete constraint solver. Rather, CHIP employs an incomplete solver and different possibilities to program constraint propagation. The search for the right programming scheme P(FD) to be used with finite domain constraints is not settled yet, but important progress has been made. Among the programming constructs under discussion are committed choice (Saraswat's ask), cardinality, and constructive disjunction. Van Hentenryck and others have proposed two different versions of a framework cc(FD), one of them featuring meta-constraints called indexical.

Other important CLP languages are CLP(R), CLP(BNR), and LIFE. CLP(R) processes linear constraints over floating point numbers, which is in contrast to CHIP and Prolog III, which employ rational numbers with infinite precision. LIFE, the successor of Login, computes with record-like descriptions, called psi-terms, providing benefits for applications in computational linguistics and knowledge representation. A recent rational reconstruction reveals psi-terms as fine-grained constraints over so-called feature trees, generalizing equational constraints over conventional rational constructor trees.

The most prominent constraint domains under investigation are finite domains, rational numbers, feature trees, and Boolean algebras. There is also research on constraints over real and complex numbers (employing methods from Computer Algebra), pseudo-boolean constraints (employing methods from Operations Research), lists, and finite sets, among others.

There is an intimate connection between Constraint and Concurrent Logic Programming due to the fact that programming constraint propagation requires a concurrent control regime. The central programming construct of concurrent logic programming, committed choice, is equally useful for constraint logic programming. A logic analysis of committed choice modeling guard satisfaction as constraint entailment was given by Maher as early as 1987. Saraswat took committed choice as the central notion of his concurrent constraint framework (he speaks of ask clauses) and clarified the connections with models of concurrent computation such as Milner's CCS. Primitive forms of committed choice are CHIP's demons and functional residuation in LIFE.

AKL and Oz are two language designs trying to provide within one uniform language both for concurrent (as in multi-agent) and constraint logic programming. They both provide for deep guards and encapsulated search. Both also provide novel communication primitives to support concurrent objects. While AKL still adheres to the idiosyncrasies of Prolog, Oz is a higher-order language whose setup is closer to modern functional programming languages.

Many of the European key players in CLP are cooperating in the ESPRIT Basic Research Action ACCLAIM (Advanced Concurrent Constraint Languages: Applications, Implementation, and Methodology). The principal investigators of ACCLAIM are Philippe Codognet (INRIA), Alain Colmerauer (Marseille), Bart Demoen (Leuven), Seif Haridi (SICS), Manuel Hermenegildo (Madrid), Hoon Hong (RISC), Ugo Montanari (Pisa), Andreas Podelski (MPI), and Gert Smolka (DFKI).

CLP is a very active field. It is present at all major (logic) programming conferences. Besides this book, the following references can serve as entry points to literature on CLP.

Frédéric Benhamou and Alain Colmerauer, *Constraint Logic Programming: Selected Research.* MIT Press, Cambridge, Mass., 1993.

Joxan Jaffar & Michael J. Maher, Constraint Logic Programming: A Survey, *Journal of Logic Programming* 19 & 20, 503–581, 1994.

Thom Frühwirth, Alexander Herold, Volker Küchenhoff, Thierry Le Provost, Eric Monfroy, and Mark Wallace, *Constraint Logic Programming – An Informal Introduction.* In: G. Comyn, N. E. Fuchs and M. J. Ratcliffe (eds.), Logic Programming in Action: Proceedings of LPSS '92, Springer-Verlag LNCS 636, 3–35, 1992.

Special Issue on Constraint Logic Programming, *Journal of Logic Programming* 16:3&4, 1993.

Contents

Contents

Interval Constraint Logic Programming

Frédéric Benhamou

Laboratoire d'Informatique Fondamentale d'Orléans
LIFO, Université d'Orléans
Rue Léonard de Vinci
B.P. 6759 45067 ORLEANS Cedex 2, France
<benhamou@chaborel.univ-orleans.fr>

Abstract. In this paper, we present an overview on the use of interval arithmetic to process numerical constraints in Constraint Logic Programming. The main principle is to approximate n-ary relations over $\Re$ with Cartesian products of intervals whose bounds are taken in a finite subset of $\Re$. Variables represent real values whose domains are intervals defined in the same manner. Narrowing operators are defined from approximations. These operators compute, from an interval and a relation, a set included in the initial interval. Sets of constraints are then processed thanks to a local consistency algorithm: pruning at each step step values from initial intervals. This algorithm is shown to be correct and to terminate, on the basis of a certain number of properties of narrowing operators. We focus here on the description of the general framework based on approximations, on its application to interval constraint solving over continuous and discrete quantities, to establish a strong link between approximations and local consistency notions and show that arc-consistency is an instance of the approximation framework. We finally describe related work on different variants of the initial algorithm proposed by John Cleary and developed by W. Older and A. Vellino which have been proposed in this context. These variants feature four particular points: generalization of the computation, improvement of domain reduction, efficiency of the computation and finally, cooperation with other solvers. Some open questions are also identified.

1   Introduction

The use of intervals in Constraint Logic Programming has been investigated by several authors in the last few years. The field was pioneered by J. Cleary [12] and the main ideas were extended and implemented by W. Older and A. Vellino [42, 43] in their system BNR-Prolog. A number of systems followed, among which one can cite CLP(BNR)[5, 41], Interlog [23], Newton [9], ICTP [50], Echidna [46], CIAL [41], ICS [4], PRINCE [8]. All these systems have in common a programming language based on a relational form of interval arithmetic and the use of a fixpoint algorithm to process networks of constraints. As we establish in this paper, this last method is closely related to arc-consistency, a well-known concept in Artificial Intelligence [35, 36]. This is not the only connection with Artificial Intelligence, since interval constraint solving has been studied by several authors

Interval Constraint Logic Programming

Frédéric Benhamou

Laboratoire d'Informatique Fondamentale d'Orléans
I.I.I.A., Université d'Orléans
, Rue Léonard de Vinci
B.P. 6759 45067 ORLEANS Cedex 2 France
`<benhamou@chambord.univ-orleans.fr>`

Abstract. In this paper, we present an overview on the use of interval arithmetic to process numerical constraints in Constraint Logic Programming. The main principle is to approximate n-ary relations over $I\!R$ with Cartesian products of intervals whose bounds are taken in a finite subset of $I\!R$. Variables represent real values whose domains are intervals defined in the same manner. Narrowing operators are defined from approximations. These operators compute, from an interval and a relation, a set included in the initial interval.Sets of constraints are then processed thanks to a local consistency algorithm pruning at each step values from initial intervals. This algorithm is shown to be correct and to terminate, on the basis of a certain number of properties of narrowing operators. We focus here on the description of the general framework based on approximations, on its application to interval constraint solving over continuous and discrete quantities, we establish a strong ling between approximations and local consistency notions and show that arc-consistency is an instance of the approximation framework. We finally describe recent work on different variants of the initial algorithm proposed by John Cleary and developped by W. Older and A. Vellino which have been proposed in this context. These variants address four particular points: generalization of the constraint language, improvement of domain reductions, efficiency of the computation and finally, cooperation with other solvers. Some open questions are also identified.

1 Introduction

The use of intervals in Constraint Logic Programming has been investigated by several authors in the last few years. The field was pioneered by J. Cleary [12] and the main ideas were extended and implemented by W. Older and A. Vellino [42, 43] in their system BNR-Prolog. A number of systems followed, among which one can cite CLP(BNR)[5, 44], Interlog [28], Newton[6], ICHIP [36], Echidna [46], CIAL [11], ICE [8], PRINCE [9]. All these systems have in common a constraint language based on a relational form of interval arithmetic and the use of a fixpoint algorithm to process networks of constraints. As we establish in this paper, this last method is closely related to arc-consistency, a well-known concept in Artificial Intelligence [39, 38]. This is not the only connection with Artificial Intelligence, since interval constraint solving has been studied by several authors to address temporal reasoning ([2]) or Constraint Satisfaction Problems([29, 25, 34]). As it is developped in this paper, this common theoretical and algorithmic platform addresses a number of issues previously pointed out in Prolog and in CLP. The first issue concerns numerical computations in Logic programming. The original Prolog way of tackling numbers (pre-defined relations tested after evaluation of ground numerical terms using floating point operations) was lacking both correctness and relationality. The introduction of the CLP paradigm [30, 13, 32, 3] and the design and implementation of CLP languages such as CLP($\Re$) [31], CHIP [19, 48] and Prolog III [13] provided an elegant and general framework to augment Prolog with a relational treatment of various algebras, leading to the processing of constraints over real and rational numbers closely akin to the general philosophy of the language.

Nevertheless, numbers in constraint systems are either represented with floating point numbers (e.g. CLP($\Re$)) or infinite precision numbers (e.g. Prolog III). In the first case, correctness of the computations is not guaranteed, since floating point numbers lack most of the very basic properties of the real numbers, like associativity and ditributivity. The infinite precision representation guarantees correctness for rational number in the linear case. A third approach, inherited from interval analysis [40, 1] consists in representing any real number with an ordered pair of real numbers representing its lower and upper bounds. Operations are then processed on these bounds, with the guarantee that computations over the theoretical real numbers coincides with the actual computations, at least in the sense that theoretical values always lie in the corresponding interval. A first implementation of interval arithmetic in Prolog was proposed in [10].

Besides providing a framework for correct and relational numerical computations, CLP(Intervals) moves a step forward the basic improvements of CLP over Prolog both on expressiveness and efficiency. In effect, CLP(Intervals) handle constraints marginally studied in a CLP context, namely non-linear constraints over the reals[1]. Furthermore, the general theoretical framework on top of CLP(Intervals) provides a unified description of constraint solving over various domains formerly handled in completely separate "black boxes" (Booleans, integers, real numbers). This framework describes as well some built-in constraints developped for efficiency reasons (e.g. the cardinality operator introduced in [50]). This uniformity gives, for instance, the ability to process systems made of real, Boolean or finite domain constraints and sharing the same variables.

The key concept in Interval Constraint Logic Programming is *approximation*. Intuitively, approximations are functions that maps relations to boxes, built from the Cartesian product of their projections. Approximations define *narrowing operators,* contracting functions that map boxes into smaller boxes, thus reducing the domain of possible values for some contrained variables. Local consistency notions are built from fixedpoints of narrowing operators and are implemented

---

[1] Exception are of course the well-known delay-based treatment of non-linear constraints implemented in CLP($\Re$) and Prolog III discussed in details in [14], and also the implementation of a CLP language prototype on top of algorithms developped in computer algebra ([22]).

with propagation techniques. Finally, possible solutions of constraint systems are separated with branch and bound or divide and conquer mrthods. Apart from defining these notions, this paper attempt to summarize a relevant amount of work carried out recently in the direction of generalizing and/or improving these crucial aspects of Interval Arithmetic in a CLP context.

More precisely, the rest of the paper is organized as follows: section 2 defines *approximation* and *narrowing* and generalizes two convexity results. Section 3 introduces the definition of local consistency notions from narrowing operators, makes the explicit connexion with arc-consistency and describes the corresponding generic algorithm. Section 4 describes the application of these results to the definition of interval-based constraint solving over the real numbers. Section 5 addresses the natural extension of the CLP(Intervals) framework to handle discrete constraints over the Booleans, Pseudo-Booleans and integers. Section 6 provides a few examples and briefly describe classical benchmarks used in the field. Section 7 presents recent improvements and experiments in various areas and discuss possible further directions and Section 8 concludes the paper.

2 Approximation and Narrowing

Following the work presented in [12, 43, 35], the notions of approximation and narrowing, applied to constraints over real numbers, integers and Booleans, were introduced by W. Older and the author in [5]. Recently, it was shown independently by A. Colmerauer in [15] and M. Van Emden in [47] that the scheme could be generalized to any domain under certain conditions. The present section gives the general definitions of approximation and narrowing and generalizes a certain number of results presented in [5].

2.1 Approximation

Let D be a set. The powerset of D is denoted $\mathcal{P}(D)$. An approximation function over D is defined as follows:

Definition 1 *Let D be a set. Let $\underline{apx}$ be a function defined from $\mathcal{P}(D)$ into $\mathcal{P}(D)$. The function $\underline{apx}$ is an approximation over D iff the four following properties hold:*

1. $\underline{apx}(\emptyset) = \emptyset$,
2. $\forall \rho \in \mathcal{P}(D), \rho \subset \underline{apx}(\rho)$,
3. $\forall \rho, \rho' \in \mathcal{P}(D), \rho \subset \rho'$ *implies* $\underline{apx}(\rho) \subset \underline{apx}(\rho')$,
4. $\forall \rho \in \mathcal{P}(D), \underline{apx}(\underline{apx}(\rho)) = \underline{apx}(\rho)$.

Approximation functions has the following properties with respect to union and intersection:

Property 1 *Let ρ, ρ' be two elements of $\mathcal{P}(D)$. Then,*

1. $\underline{apx}(\rho \cup \rho') = \underline{apx}(\underline{apx}(\rho) \cup \underline{apx}(\rho'))$,

2. $\underline{apx}(\rho \cap \rho') \subset \underline{apx}(\rho) \cap \underline{apx}(\rho')$.

It is shown in [15] that, given a set D, it is equivalent to define an approximation function over D or to define a subset of $\mathcal{P}(D)$ containing $\{\emptyset, D\}$ and closed under intersection. If $\underline{apx}$ is an approximation function, its approximation set will be denoted $\mathcal{P}_{\text{apx}}(D)$. Furthermore, such sets, partially ordered by set inclusion constitute lattices in which the meet operation is defined by set intersection. The join of sets is defined as the smallest set larger than all of them, i.e. the approximation of their union. Based on this property, a complete lattice theoretic fixpoint semantics for the specific case of real number approximations by Cartesian products of F-intervals is developed in [43].

Approximation over a set D are extended[2] to D^n in the following way:

Definition 2 *Let $\underline{apx}$ be an approximation function over a set D. Let ρ be an n-ary relation over D. Then,*

$$\underline{apx}(\rho) = (\underline{apx}(\pi_1(\rho))) \times \ldots \times (\underline{apx}(\pi_n(\rho)))$$

where $\pi_i(\rho)$, the ith projection of ρ, is defined as follows:

$$\pi_i(\rho) = \{x_i \in D \mid (\exists x_1, \ldots, x_{i-1}, x_{i+1}, \ldots, x_n \in D) \text{ such that } (x_1, \ldots, x_n) \in \rho\}$$

These extensions are approximations, in the sense defined above. Furthermore, we have

$$\mathcal{P}_{\text{apx}}(D^n) = (\mathcal{P}_{\text{apx}}(D))^n,$$
$$\underline{apx}(\pi_i(\rho)) = \pi_i(\underline{apx}(\rho)).$$

2.2 Narrowing

The definition of the narrowing operator associated with an approximation function is at the basis of Relational Interval Arithmetic. Intuitively, given an n-ary relation ρ over a set D, and u an element of $\mathcal{P}_{\text{apx}}(D^n)$, the result of the narrowing function of ρ applied to u is the smallest element of $\mathcal{P}_{\text{apx}}(D^n)$ containing $u \cap \rho$. Here follows the definition and basic properties of narrowing functions:

Definition 3 *Let ρ be an n-ary relation on a set D. The narrowing function of ρ is the function $\overrightarrow{\rho}_{\text{apx}} : I(\mathcal{F})^n \longrightarrow I(\mathcal{F})^n$, such that for every u,*

$$\overrightarrow{\rho}_{\text{apx}}(u) = \underline{apx}(u \cap \rho).$$

In unambiguous cases, $\overrightarrow{\rho}_{\text{apx}}$ will be denoted simply by $\overrightarrow{\rho}$. The narrowing functions are contractant, correct, monotone and idempotent, as expressed by the following theorem (the proof can be found in [5]):

---

[2] For the sake of readability, we use the same notation for approximations and their extensions.

Theorem 1 *For every $\rho \in D$, and every $u, v \in \mathcal{P}_{\text{apx}}(D^n)$,*

$$(1) \qquad \overrightarrow{\rho}(u) \subset u, \qquad \textit{(Contractance)}$$

$$(2) \qquad u \cap \rho = \overrightarrow{\rho}(u) \cap \rho, \qquad \textit{(Correctness)}$$

$$(3) \; u \subset v \; \textit{implies} \; \overrightarrow{\rho}(u) \subset \overrightarrow{\rho}(v), \; \textit{(Monotonicity)}$$

$$(4) \qquad \overrightarrow{\rho}(\overrightarrow{\rho}(u)) = \overrightarrow{\rho}(u). \qquad \textit{(Idempotence)}$$

As we will devellop in further sections, narrowing operators are essential to define local consistency notions and to prove the termination and correctness of the associated propagation algorithms.

2.3 Convexity with respect to approximation

We give here the general definition for convex relations with respect to an approximation $\underline{\text{apx}}$ defined over a set D. We will show in the next sections how this property is used in CLP(Intervals).

Definition 4 *An n-ary relation ρ on D is convex with repect to $\underline{\text{apx}}$, if for every $u \in \mathcal{P}_{\text{apx}}(D^n)$ and every i in $\{1, \ldots, n\}$, $\pi_i(\rho \cap u) \in \mathcal{P}_{\text{apx}}(D)$.*

2.4 Composition theorem

In this section we generalize two results already discussed in [5] which are crucial to devise a narrowing-based operational semantics to CLP(Intervals) languages including non-interval-convex primitives in their constraint language, as shown in the next sections.

Property 2 (Decomposition) *Let ρ and ρ' be two n-ary relations on a set D. Then, for every $u \in \mathcal{P}_{\text{apx}}(D^n)$:*

$$\overrightarrow{\rho \cup \rho'}(u) = \underline{\text{apx}}(\overrightarrow{\rho}(u) \cup \overrightarrow{\rho'}(u)) \tag{1}$$

The corresponding equality in the intersection case does not hold in general although one can show the following inclusion:

$$\overrightarrow{\rho \cap \rho'}(u) \subset \overrightarrow{\rho}(u) \cap \overrightarrow{\rho'}(u)$$

We focus here on the conditions under which the narrowing of the intersection can be sharply computed. We first introduce the notion of dependence.

Definition 5 (Dependence) *An n-ary relation ρ on a set D is dependent on dimension i, ($i \in \{1, \ldots, n\}$), iff, $\forall (x_1, \ldots, x_n) \in D^n, \forall y \in D$,*

$$(x_1, \ldots, x_n) \in \rho \iff (x_1, \ldots, x_{i-1}, y, x_{i+1}, \ldots, x_n) \in \rho$$

Based on the notion of dependencies, the Composition theorem follows:

Theorem 2 (Composition) *Let ρ and ρ' be two n-ary relations on a set D, convex with respect to an approximation $\underline{apx}$, defined over D. If there exists at most one i in $\{1, \ldots, n\}$ such that ρ and ρ' are dependent on dimension i then for every $u \in \mathcal{P}_{\underline{apx}}(D^n)$:*

$$\overrightarrow{\rho \cap \rho'}(u) = \overrightarrow{\rho}(\overrightarrow{\rho'}(u)) \cap \overrightarrow{\rho'}(\overrightarrow{\rho}(u))$$

3 Narrowing-based local consistency

When designing Constraint Programming languages based on the principles defined in the previous section, one has to move from primitive constraints to constraint systems. In the framework presented here, these sets are represented by constraint networks and this processing is based on local consistency algorithms[3] developped in Artificial Intelligence, and more precisely to adaptations of arc-consistency algorithms ([39, 38]).

In the Constraint Satisfaction Problem (CSP) framework, constraint sets over finite domains are represented with graphs whose nodes (denoted with $1, 2, \ldots, n$) represent variables and are associated sets of possible values denoted D_i and whose directed arcs (denoted $R(i, j)$ represent unary and binary relations expressed over these variables. For each arc $\rho(i, j), i \neq j$, there is an arc $\rho(j, i)$ expressing the same property from a symmetric point of view. In such a graph, an arc $\rho(i, j)$ is said to be *arc-consistent* iff for any value $x \in D_i$, there is a value $y \in D_j$ such that $\rho(x, y)$. Arc-consistency has turned out to be a major local consistency property in terms of devising efficient algorithms to solve discrete combinatorial problems.

This framework generalizes easily to n-ary constraints, by representing systems with hyper-graphs. Arc-consistency can then be expressed as follows:

Definition 6 (Arc-Consistency) *Let S be a set. Let $\langle D_1, \ldots, D_n \rangle$ be a sequence of domains, and ρ an n-ary relation over S. The hyper-arc $\rho(i_1, \ldots, i_n)$ is arc-consistent wrt $\langle D_1, \ldots, D_n \rangle$ iff*
$$\forall a_1 \in D_1, \exists a_2 \in D_2, \ldots, \exists a_n \in D_n, \text{ such that } \rho(a_1, \ldots, a_n)\}$$

Moving from hyper-arcs to relations, this definition can be rewritten (and slightly generalized) as follows:

Definition 7 *Let S be a set, let $u = u_1 \times \ldots \times u_n$ be a subset of S^n, and ρ an n-ary relation over S. Then, ρ is arc-consistent wrt $\langle u_1, \ldots, u_n \rangle$ iff*

$$\forall i \in \{1, \ldots, n\}, u_i \subset \pi_i(\rho \cap u)$$

---

[3] These algorithms are also sometimes referred to as local propagation algorithms.

Now, let us consider the identity function over $\mathcal{P}(S)$. It is clearly an approximation function in the sense of Definition 1, and its extension over $\mathcal{P}(S^n)$, as defined in Definition 2 maps every subset of S^n to the Cartesian products of its projections and is denoted $\underline{cp}$.

It follows that if ρ is arc-consistent wrt $\langle u_1, \ldots, u_n \rangle$, we have:

1. $u \subset \underline{cp}(\rho \cap u)$ (Definition 7)
2. $\underline{cp}(\rho \cap u) \subset u$ (Monotonicity of approximations)

Then, we can establish, in terms of fixed point, the following connexion between arc-consistency and narrowing operators:

Theorem 3 *Let S be a set, let $u = u_1 \times \ldots \times u_n$ be a subset of S^n, and ρ an n-ary relation over S. ρ is arc-consistent wrt $\langle u_1, \ldots, u_n \rangle$ iff*

$$\overrightarrow{\rho}(u) = u$$

It follows that local consistency notions used in Interval Constraint Logic Programming only differ from arc-consistency, possibly extended to infinite domains, in the choice of a particular domain, namely $I\!\!R$, and of specialized approximation functions. When the associated approximate domain is finite[4], propagation methods based on AC-3 [38] and described above are correct terminate and are strategy-independant ([43]), due to the correctness, contractance, idempotence and monotonicity properties of narrowing functions, as already presented in Section 2.2.

Here follows the generic narrowing algorithm, adapted from [7]. We assume that relations are exactly represented by constraints defined on variables from $\{v_1, \ldots, v_n\}$. These variables take their values in domains $D_1, \ldots, D_n$. We note $var(C)$ the set of variables occurring in C.

```
fixpoint( in {C₁,...,Cₙ} ; inout {D₁,...,Dₙ} )
begin
      queue := {C₁,...,Cₙ};
      while queue ≠ ∅ do
          C := POP_QUEUE;
          D := C⃗(D₁ × ... × Dₙ);
          if D ≠ Dᵢ then
              Dᵢ := D;
              queue := queue ∪ {Cⱼ | vᵢ ∈ var(Cⱼ)} \ {C}
          endif
      endwhile
end;
```

The rest of the paper is devoted to the application of these principles to constraint solving over the real numbers.

---

[4] Which is of course the case when the initial domain is finite.

4 Interval constraint solving

We describe here the application of this general framework based on approximations to the solving of constraint systems over the real numbers. We recall basic results of Interval Arithmetic, and define the adapted approximation notions.

4.1 Basics of Interval Arithmetic

We consider $I\!R \cup \{-\infty, +\infty\}$, the set of real numbers augmented with the two infinity symbols, and the natural extension of the relation $\leq$ to this set. For every $b, c \in I\!R$ and every $a, d \in I\!R \cup \{-\infty, +\infty\}, a \leq b \leq c \leq d$, we will use the following notations for intervals:

$[b, c] = \{x \in I\!R \mid b \leq x \leq c\}$
$[c, d) = \{x \in I\!R \mid c \leq x < d\}$
$(a, b] = \{x \in I\!R \mid a < x \leq b\}$
$(a, d) = \{x \in I\!R \mid a < x < d\}$

Let $I(I\!R)$ be the set of all intervals. Note that $\Re \subset I(I\!R)$ since for every a in $I\!R$, $[a, a] \in I\!R$. In what follows, $\langle a, b \rangle$ will denote any of the previously defined interval forms. If $\star \in \{+, -, \times, \div\}$ arithmetic operations over $I(I\!R)$ are defined in the following way:

$$< a, b > \star < c, d > = \{x \star y \mid x \in < a, b >, y \in < c, d >\}$$

except for $< a, b > \div < c, d >$ which is not defined if $0 \in < c, d >$.

Here follows an equivalent (and more operational) definition for closed intervals (the general formulae for any intervals can be found for example in [12]):

$[a, b] + [c, d] = [a + c, b + d]$
$[a, b] - [c, d] = [a - d, b - c]$
$[a, b] \times [c, d] = [\min(ac, ad, bc, bd), \max(ac, ad, bc, bd)]$
$[a, b] \div [c, d] = [a, b] \times [\frac{1}{c}, \frac{1}{d}], \text{if } 0 \notin [c, d]$

Other operations over $I(I\!R)$ like $\cos, \sin, \log$, etc. can be defined along the same lines. The main properties of the basic arithmetic operations are:

1. Interval addition and multiplication are both commutative and associative
2. The real number 0 (resp. 1) is an identity for addition (resp. multiplcation)
3. Distributivity does not always hold for interval arithmetic, although it enjoys the *sub-distributivity* law, i.e., for every intervals I, J, K:

$$I \times (J + K) \subset (I + J) \times (I + K)$$

4. Basic arithmetic operations are inclusion monotonic, i.e.
   for all $\star \in \{+, -, \times, \div\}$, for every $I, J, K, L \in I(I\!R), I \subset K, J \subset L$,

$$I \star J \subset K \star L$$

R. Moore show in [40] that for every value x taken in a given interval I, if F is a monotone interval extension of a function f defined over $\Re$, then $f(x)$ lies in the interval $F(I)$. This result is generally refered to as the fundamental theorem of Interval Arithmetic.

4.2   F-Intervals

One of the key points in interval arithmetic is to move from real intervals to rounded intervals, that is to say intervals whose bounds are taken in a finite subset of $I\!R$. This permits to implement an arithmetic based on any finite representation of numbers without losing the correctness of the computations. More formally, let E be a finite subset of $I\!R$,

Definition 8 *Given a set* $F = E \cup \{-\infty, +\infty\}$, *an F-interval is any element* $\langle a, b \rangle$ *of* $I(I\!R)$ *such that* $a \in F$ *and* $b \in F$.

Let $I(\mathcal{F})$ be the set of F-intervals. Set inclusion is a partial ordering on real intervals, and thus on F-intervals. For every real number a the greatest (resp. smallest) element of E less than (resp. greater than) a will be denoted $a{\downarrow}$ (resp. $a{\uparrow}$).

The arithmetic defined for real intervals must be adapted to F-intervals, since in the general case, F is not closed for the basic operations over the reals. Here follows the functional definition of the basic operations over $I(\mathcal{F})$:

$[a, b] + [c, d] = [(a + c){\downarrow}, (b + d){\uparrow}]$
$[a, b] - [c, d] = [(a - d){\downarrow}, (b - c){\uparrow}]$
$[a, b] \times [c, d] = [\min((ac){\downarrow}, (ad){\downarrow}, (bc){\downarrow}, (bd){\downarrow}), \max((ac){\uparrow}, (ad){\uparrow}, (bc){\uparrow}, (bd){\uparrow})]$
Finally, if $0 \notin [c, d]$,
$[a, b] \div [c, d] = [\min((\frac{a}{c}){\downarrow}, (\frac{a}{d}){\downarrow}, (\frac{b}{c}){\downarrow}, (\frac{b}{d}){\downarrow}), \max((\frac{a}{c}){\uparrow}, (\frac{a}{d}){\uparrow}, (\frac{b}{c}){\uparrow}, (\frac{b}{d}){\uparrow})]$.

We have already stated that interval-based CLP languages were based on a relational form of interval arithmetic, although what is described in th litterature concern mainly functional interval arithmetic. The key point here consists in transforming n-ary functions into (n+1)-ary predicates corresponding to the graph of the function. For example:

$$\text{plus} = \{(x, y, z) \in I\!R^3 \mid x + y = z\}$$

Functional notations are generally allowed in Interval CLP systems to preserve the usual syntax, but all the constraints are processed from the relational point of view mentioned above.

4.3   Approximating real numbers

To detail any arithmetic-based constraint processing over the real numbers, it is convenient to introduce two levels of approximations[5]. First, real numbers are approximated with F-intervals. F being closed under intersection, for any real number a, there exists a smaller F-interval containing a.

---

[5] This is not led by any theoretical considerations, since these levels are, in fact, identical, but allows us to distinguish two different aspects: the approximation of real numbers with F-intervals, mainly motivated by the correctness of the representation, and the approximation of arithmetic relations which is the basis of the constraint processing.

Definition 9 *The approximation of any real number a, denoted $\hat{a}$, is the small-est F-interval containing a*

It follows that if $a \in E$ then $\hat{a} = [a, a]$, otherwise $\hat{a}$ is the open[6] F-interval, $\hat{a} = (a{\downarrow}, a{\uparrow})$.

From a practical point of view, when E is a set of floating-point numbers (as described for example in the IEEE standard [27]), this definition corresponds to the representation of real numbers by "machine intervals" [1, 40] or "floating-point intervals" ([12]).

4.4 Approximating n-ary relations over $I\!R$

As just mentioned, in CLP(Intervals) systems, relations over $I\!R^n$ are approximated with Cartesian products of F-intervals called F-boxes. This is achieved in two different and quite opposite ways. On the one hand, in most systems, real subsets are approximated with continuous F-intervals (see for example [12, 43, 5, 6, 28]). On the other hand, another scheme is proposed in [46] which approximates real sets with union of F-intervals. This last technique provides a finer granularity, inherited from the work carried out on finite domain constraints ([48, 49]). In this case, the semantics attached to domain reductions which cannot be translated in terms of domain bounds modifications is more closely approximated. Nevertheless, computations over F-interval unions may lead, in many cases, to combinatorial explosion, avoided when applying the first technique. It remains that serious theoretical and experimental comparisons between the two approaches are still to be performed.

Here follows the definitions for F-interval vectors, F-boxes and the two approximations described above.

A *vector* is any finite sequence $(u_1, \ldots, u_n)$ of subsets of $I\!R$. The ith component of any vector u is denoted by u_i.

An *interval vector* is any vector such that every $u_i \in I(I\!R)$, and an *F-interval vector* is any vector such that every $u_i \in I(\mathcal{F})$. Let $\mathcal{V}$ be the set of all F-interval vectors.

A *box* (resp. *F-box*) is any n-ary relation ρ on $I\!R$ such that there exists an interval vector (resp an F-interval vector) $(u_1, \ldots, u_n)$ verifying $\rho = u_1 \times \ldots \times u_n$. Let $B(\mathcal{F})$ be the set of all F-boxes.

Let $U(\mathcal{F}) = \{D \subseteq I\!R \mid \exists \langle I_1, \ldots, I_n \rangle \in I(\mathcal{F})^n : D = I_1 \cup \ldots \cup I_n\}$.

Both $I(\mathcal{F})$ and $U(\mathcal{F})$ are closed under intersection and contains $\{\emptyset, I\!R\}$. Here follows a definition of their corresponding approximation functions.

---

[6] Following the numerical analysis community, several authors (e.g. [43]) would define F as being a set of closed F-intervals and thus perform a slightly less accurate approximation, although all the principal results still hold in that case. The key difference between these two approaches concerns the introduction of disequations, as it will be developed in further sections.

Definition 10 (Union) *Let r be a subset of* $\mathbb{R}$*. The* union approximation *of r, denoted by* <u>union</u>*(r), is the smallest (w.r.t. the inclusion) element of* $U(\mathcal{F})$ *containing r.*

Definition 11 (Hull) *Let r be a subset of* $\mathbb{R}$*, The* F-interval hull *of r, denoted by* <u>hull</u>*(r), is the smallest F-interval containing r.*

It is easy to show that <u>apx</u> and <u>hull</u> verify the conditions expressed in Definition 1. Clearly, these definitions generalize Definition 9. Furthermore, the following properties hold:

1. $\underline{apx}(r) \subseteq \underline{hull}(r)$,
2. $\underline{hull}(\underline{apx}(r)) = \underline{apx}(\underline{hull}(r)) = \underline{hull}(r)$,
3. $\underline{apx}(\{a\}) = \underline{hull}(\{a\}) = \hat{a}$.

As expected, the final generalization of <u>apx</u> and <u>hull</u> to n-ary relations over $\mathbb{R}$ is achieved by applying Definition 2.

4.5 Narrowing

The narrowing operators are defined as mentioned in the previous section. In this particular case the interpretation of their basic properties can be expresed as follows:

Contractance: the narrowed intervals are smaller than the initial intervals,
Correctness: every valid solution in the theoretical real numbers lies in the narrowed intervals
Monotonicity: the narrowing preserves the inclusion
Idempotence: the narrowed intervals have to be computed but once

4.6 Interval convexity

Interval arithmetic, as presented in [12, 35, 36], restricts the definition of primitives to *interval convex* relations, i.e. relations which are convex with respect to the *hull* approximation.

As far as the processing of unions of interval convex relations is concerned, the choices are either the introduction of explicit backtracking points ([12, 35, 36]) or the application of the composition property (see Section 2.3) applied to <u>union</u> or <u>hull</u>.

For relations which are expressed in terms of intersection of interval-convex relations the usual method is to decompose them and apply the consistency algorithm corresponding to the chosen approximation. Unfortunately, although intervals computed through this method are safe, they are generally bigger than what is expected.

To guarantee the sharp computation of narrowing applied to non-interval-convex primitives, we make use of the composition Theorem (See section 2.3) described in the previous section. In effect, as shown in the next section, most of the usual non interval-convex primitives (e.g. integer, not equal, min, max, etc.) can be expressed in terms of unions and intersections of interval convex relations verifying the theorem conditions.

To give a short example of the application of the theorem, let us consider the realtion min, defined in the following way:

$$\min = \{(x, y, z) \in \Re^3, \min(x, y) = z\}$$

The relation can be expressed as follows, thus leading to the direct application of the decomposition an composition properties:

$$\min = (\{(x, y, z) \in \Re^3, x \le y\} \cap \{(x, y, z) \in \Re^3, z = x\}) \cup$$
$$(\{(x, y, z) \in \Re^3, x > y\} \cap \{(x, y, z) \in \Re^3, z = y\})$$

5   From continuous to discrete domains

Based on the various properties of interval arithmetic, the first interval-based Constraint Logic Programming system, BNR-Prolog, was designed at Bell Northern Research, in the late 80's. It implemented hull-consistency over closed F-intervals, and introduced a myriad of primitives over the real numbers including transcendental functions like $\sin, \cos, \log$, etc.

The general framework presented in the first part of this paper permits to move from continuous to discrete constraints. The key ideas are that, first integer constraints and real constraints are not defined over separate domains. In effect, the set of integers being considered as a relation over $I\!R$, is thus treated with its own narrowing operator, leading, as established in the previous sections to a behaviour similar to local consistency algorithms implemented finite domain oriented languages like CHIP ([19]) or cc(FD) ([49]). As far as Boolean Constraints are concerned, there are processed as 0/1 integer constraints, usual Boolean operators being defined thanks to numerical relations. Finally, the unicity of the constraint domain and the unified treatment of these constraints led us to replace specialized operators, like the cardinality operator or built-in disjunctions simply by making usage of the whole algebraic structure to process different constraint types (e.g. addition, multiplication and comparisons of Boolean quantities, Boolean values representing numerical relations, etc.). This work led to the design of a successor to BNR-Prolog called CLP(BNR) (for Constraint solving over the Boolean the naturals and the reals) described in depth in [5, 3]. Many other systems provide discrete constraint processing on the same basis (Interlog [28], ICE [8], PRINCE [9])

We conclude this short presentation of the current state of the art by the presentation of some simple examples and benchmarks used in CLP(Intervals).

6   Examples

In this section we propose some examples, adapted from actual executions on systems like CLP(BNR) or Newton. To facilitate the reading, the syntax has been adapted to respect as much as possible the usual mathematical notations.

6.1 Simple examples

This example is adapted from [44] and is tranlated from an actual execution on the CLP (BNR) system. The intention here is to give a first feeling of simple inferences computed by the system and show how real numbers and integers are integrated.

Query: $y \in [1,3], y = x^2$.
Answer: $y \in [1,3]$,
$\quad x \in [-1.73205080756888, 1.73205080756888]$

Here is the same relation with both integer arguments; note that y becomes bound:

Query: $x : integer, y : integer, y \in [1,3], y = x^2$.
Answer: $x : integer, y : integer$,
$\quad y = 1$
$\quad x \in [-1,1]$

If x is constrained to be positive, then x also becomes bound to its unique answer:

Query: $x : integer, y : integer, y \in [1,3], y = x^2, x > 0$.
Answer: $y = 1$
$\quad x = 1$

Similar rules apply to general boolean relations:

Query: $b : boolean, 1 = b \wedge (c \vee \neg d)$.
Answer: $b = 1$
$\quad c : boolean$
$\quad d : boolean$

Query: $b : boolean, 1 = b \wedge (c \vee \neg d), 0 = b \wedge c$.
Answer: $b = 1$
$\quad c = 0$

In some cases where an equation has a unique solution, equation solving is automatic:

Query: $1 = x + 2 * y, y - 3 * x = 0$.
Answer: $x \in [0.142857142857143, 0.142857142857143]$
$\quad y \in [0.428571428571429, 0.428571428571429]$

Here is a more interesting example, involving non-linear (including transcendental) equation solving:

Query: $x \geq 0, y \geq 0, \tan(x) = y, x^2 + y^2 = 5$.
Answer: $x \in [1.09666812870547, 1.09666812870547]$
$\quad y \in [1.94867108960995, 1.94867108960995]$

Note that although the upper and lower bounds in these answers print the same at this printing precision, the internal binary forms must differ by at least one bit in the last place, or else the variables would have been bound to the exact answer.

For more complex problems, which may have multiple solutions, there is a "solve" predicate which separates the solutions (by backtracking) and forces convergence. For example, for polynomial root finding :

Query: $x \in [0, 1], 0 = 35x^{256} - 14x^{17} + x, \text{solve}(x)$.
Answer: $x : 0.0$

Answer: $x \in [0.847943660827315, 0.847943660827315]$

Answer: $x \in [0.995842494200498, 0.995842494200498]$

Similarly, for a pair of simultaneous non-linear equations :

Query: $x^3 + y^3 = 2xy, x^2 + y^2 = 1, x \geq 0, \text{solve}(x)$.
Answer: $x \in [0.391018886096038, 0.391085781049752]$
$y \in [-0.920382654506382, -0.92035423172858]$

Answer: $x \in [0.449060394395367, 0.450226789190836]$
$y \in [0.892914239048135, 0.893501405810577]$

Answer: $x \in [0.892906985142645, 0.893513338815017]$
$y \in [0.449036650353057, 0.450241175242194]$

6.2 Non-linear problem over the real numbers

A popular benchmark in the interval Constraint Programming community is the Wilkinson Polynomial initially proposed in [52]. The problem is to solve the following equation:

$$\prod_{i=1}^{20}(X + 1) + EX^{19} = 0.$$

This equation trivially admits 20 real roots when $E = 0$. The point here is to illustrate the fact that a minuscule pertubation can lead to dramatic effects. In this case, the set of real roots of this equation when $E = 2^{-23}$ is reduced to ten values. As related in [11, 9], most interval systems return ten intervals containing the actual solutions of the equation when $E = 2^{-23}$.

6.3 Mixed Boolean/Numerical constraints

Mixed boolean and integer constraints can be used to solve puzzles like the magic series [13, 48]. The problem here is to find a sequence of non-negative integers

$(x_0, ...x_{n-1})$ such that, for every i in $\{0, ..., n-1\}$, x_i is the number of occurences of the integer i in the sequence. In other words, for every $i \in \{0, ..., n-1\}$

$$x_i = \sum_{j=0}^{n-1} (x_j = i),$$

where the value of $(x = y)$ is the integer 1 if $(x = y)$ is true and the integer 0 if $(x \neq y)$ is true. Moreover, it can be shown that the two following properties hold.

$$\sum_{i=0}^{n-1} x_i = n, \sum_{i=0}^{n-1} i\, x_i = n$$

These redundant constraints are generally added to augment the pruning during the enumeration process. The CLP(Intervals) program that expresses the main constraints (redundancies excluded) is as follows[7]:

```
magic(N, L) :-
    |L| = N,
    non_neg_integer(L),
    main_constraints(L),
    enum(L).

main_constraints(L) :- main_constraints(L, 0).

main_constraints(L, |L|).
main_constraints(L, I) :-
    |L'| = I,
    L = L'.[X].L'',
    sum(L, I, X),
    main_constraints(L, I + 1).

sum([], I, 0).
sum([X|L], I, S) :-
    S = (X = I) + S',
    sum(L, I, S').
```

The queries that compute the magic series of length $4, 7, 10$ produce the following results:

Query: magic$(4, L)$
Answer: magic$(4, [1, 2, 1, 0])$
Answer: magic$(4, [2, 0, 2, 0])$

---

[7] For the sake of legibility, constraints are considered as goals and their syntax is kept as "mathematical" as possible. Dot operators stand for list concatenations as in **Prolog III** (see [13] and $|L|$ returns the number of elements of list L. The **non_neg_integer** predicate is not developped

Query: magic(7, L)
Answer: magic(7, $[3, 2, 1, 1, 0, 0, 0]$)

Query: magic(10, L)
Answer: magic(10, $[6, 2, 1, 0, 0, 0, 0, 0, 0, 0]$)

This section concludes the general presentation and we focus in the next section on various studies which are at the frontier of this framework, and which have proven to achieve real improvements to the original approach. We also mention some open questions related to these extensions.

7 Recent work and open questions

7.1 Global constraint processing

As already discussed, most systems decompose complex constraints in sets of primitive constraints for which the narrowing operators are easy to compute. One exception to this rule is Newton([5]), a language in which a certain class of complex constraints are processed more globally. These constraints are of the form $f(x_1, \ldots, x_n) \diamond 0$, where f is a continuous, derivable function and $\diamond$ a relation symbol taken in $\{=, \geq\}$. The key idea behind the processing of such constraints is to treat separately projections of such constraints and to define a relaxation of arc-consistency, called box-consistency. Without presenting the technical details in depth, the intuition behind box-consistency is to remove the existential quantification from the arc-consistency definition and to replace variables by their domains using constraint extension. This is expressed by the following definition:

Definition 12 *A projection constraint $\pi_i(c)$ is box-consistent with respect to the sequence of domains $\langle D_1, \ldots, D_n \rangle$ if and only if:*

$$D_i = hull(D_i \cap \{a_i \in I\!R \mid \langle D_1, \ldots, D_{i-1}, \overrightarrow{a_i}, D_{i+1}, \ldots, D_n \rangle \in \overrightarrow{C}\}).$$

where $\overrightarrow{C}$ denotes the interval extension of the relation associated to the constraint C.

The whole point in defining such a consistency is to give a declarative meaning to the implementation of techniques coming from Interval analysis. In Newton, box-consistency is enforced by combining an Interval Newton method and a local splitting procedure. Other implementation can be envisaged, including the implementation of Krawczyck and Hansen operators. For a precise discussion on these methods one should refer for example to [1].

Experimental results on several benchmarks show dramatic improvements in terms of efficiency when compared to systems relying on constraint decomposition into primitive relations. A related approach mixing splitting strategies and in the Krawczyck method is proposed in [23] to improve the computation of safe starting regions[8] for non-linear problems.

---

[8] A safe starting region is a box containing exactly one solution and such that iterative methods initialized in any point of the box are guaranted to converge.

7.2 Integration with other Constraint solvers

Although implementing efficiently in the same framework constraint solving over real numbers, Booleans and integers as well as mixed numerical/Boolean constraints, the methods discussed here show their limits when dealing with rational linear constraints and symbolic constraints[9].

Concerning linear constraints, it is well known that efficient complete algorithms like Gaussian elimination and Simplex have been implemented with success in CLP systems like CLP($\Re$)[31] or Prolog III[13]. Interval methods relying on local consistency algorithms show themselves quite inefficient over the same problems. The explanation comes mainly from the fact that the crucial information that identical variables refer to identical values is lost in the narrowing process which replaces variables with intervals corresponding to their ranges.

Nevertheless, it should be noted that the pivot operations which are performed in the Simplex, for example, correspond to symbolic transformations computing redundant constraints. In an interval setting, due to the correctness of the computations, these redundancies can be added safely to the system, leading to better accuracy.

Another approach consists in incorporating a separate solver for linear equations in the unification machinery and to define the cooperation mechanisms between the two solvers. This leads to two main difficulties.

First, by essence, the actual numbers manipulated in linear constraint systems are rational numbers. When implemented, they are best represented with pairs of infinite precision integers or approximated by floating point numbers. In both cases, these numbers will have to live with interval representations of the same quantities. There are basically three solutions to this problem: drastically separate the two constraint worlds, implementing an interval-based Simplex method, or devising an interval system in which (some) bounds are coded with infinite precision. In the first two cases, the main issue is the definition of constants, both syntactically and semantically. In the last case, the termination of the fixpoint algorithm cannot rely on the finiteness of the set in which interval bounds take their values.

Finally, from an operational point of view, it seems crucial to make use of each solver to improve the efficiency of the other, that is to say to design information exchanges protocols. It seems that two main solutions can be envisaged: exchanging the values of those variables whose domains are constant-like and exchanging bound modifications. In the first case, one has to give a precise definition of constant-like, which could include, for example, intervals whose bounds are consecutive floating points. In the second case, as described in [8], the key issue might be to replace the tableau Simplex of CLP($\Re$) and Prolog III with a simplex on bounded variables.

---

[9] Boolean constraints are not considered here as symbolic constraints since their processing is essentially numerical. The term Boolean was kept to illustrate the strong relationship that exists with the same type of constraints in various CLP languages, but naming them 0/1 constraint would have been more appropriate in this context.

Concerning the cooperation with symbolic constraint solvers, besides the usual possible integration of the interval solver in a Prolog system taking care of the constraint solving over rational trees, some amount of work has been carried out (see for example [47])in the direction of generalizing the approximation and narrowing concepts to other algebraic structures like Herbrand universes, symbolic finite domains or set constraints.

7.3 Symbolic transformations

Finally, let us mention that, following some preliminary ideas expressed in [40] a certain number of symbolic transformations can be applied before entering the narrowing process. Some of these techniques are implemented in an interval system described in [26]. More generally, the study of the possible combinations of Computer Algebraic and Numerical Analysis techniques is already well-established in the culture of mathematical-oriented computer science. Interval methods being mainly numerical in nature, the same approach applied to Interval Constraint Logic Programming is, at least theoretically, a promising topic of research in the area.

8 Conclusion

We have presented in this paper a certain number of recent contributions to the relatively young and very active field of Interval Constraint Logic Programming. We have attempted to stress out the importance and generality of the key concepts of approximation and narrowing which give a framework in which further improvements and alternate approaches to Constraint Solving might fit, especially when dealing with algebras for which incomplete algorithms are the only practical tools available. We have tried to explicit the strong links with well-established research both in Artificial Intelligence and in Numerical Analysis. Finally, we have attempted to provide a brief overview of recent improvements made to the initial ideas expressed by J. Cleary and then by W. Older and A. Vellino. These improvement follow different paths: the enrichment of the algebraic structures, the partial globalization of primitive constraint, the use of symbolic methods inherited from computer algebra and finally the integration with other solvers. Although a certain number of experiments have been carried out through the use of the CLP(BNR) system, a section on industrial applications is missing, since the widespread availability of interval based systems is still ahead. The first results are very encouraging, but on this point, the final verdict will come from the outside world.

References

1. G. Alefeld and J. Herzberger. *Introduction to Interval Computations.* Academic Press, 1983.
2. J. Allen. Maintaining Knowledge about Temporal Intervals. *Communications of the ACM*,26, pp842–843, 1983.
3. F. Benhamou and A. Colmerauer (eds.) *Constraint Logic Programming: Selected Research,* MIT Press, 1993.
4. F. Benhamou and J.L. Massat. Boolean Pseudo-Equations in Constraint Logic Programming, *Proceedings of ICLP'93*, MIT Press, pp 517–531, Budapest, Hungary, 1993
5. F. Benhamou and W. Older. Applying Interval Arithmetic to Real, Integer and Boolean Constraints. *Journal of Logic Programming*, 1994. (Submitted).
6. F. Benhamou, W. Older and A. Vellino. Interval Constraint Solving. *INTERVALS '94, collection of abstracts*, St Petersburgh, Russia, 1994.
7. F. Benhamou, D. MacAllester and P. Van Hentenryck. CLP(Intervals) revisited. *Proceedings of ILPS'94*, Ithaca, NY, USA, 1994.
8. H. Beringer, B. De Backer Combinatorial problem solving in Constraint Logic Programming with cooperating Solvers. In *Logic Programming : Formal Methods and Practical Applications*, C. Beierle and L. Plumer eds., Elsevier Science Publishers, 1994.
9. P. Bouvier, J.L. Massat, S. N'Dong,Touraivane, E. Vetillard Performance Evaluation of the Prince Prototype Deliverable WP2-3/R6, Esprit Project PRINCE 5246, 1994.
10. A. Bundy. A generalized interval package and its semantic checking. *ACM Trans. on Mathematical Systems*, 10 (4), p 397–409, 1984.
11. C.K. Chiu and J.H.M. Lee. Towards Practical Interval Constraint Solving in Logic Programming. *Proceedings of ILPS'94*, Ithaca, NY, USA, 1994.
12. J.G. Cleary. Logical Arithmetic. *Future Generation Computing Systems*, 2(2), p 125–149, 1987.
13. A. Colmerauer. An Introduction to Prolog III. *Communications of the ACM*, 33(7):69, 1990.
14. A. Colmerauer. Naive Solving of Non-linear Constraints, *Constraint Logic Programming: Selected Research*, F. Benhamou and A. Colmerauer (eds.), MIT Press, pages 89–112, 1993.
15. A. Colmerauer. Résolution approchée de contraintes par produits cartésiens d'ensembles privilégiés. Working paper, 1994.
16. A. Colmerauer. A legal framework for discussing approximate solving of Constraints. *INTERVALS '94, collection of abstracts*, St Petersburgh, Russia, 1994.
17. E. Davis. Constraint Propagation with Interval Labels. *Artificial Intelligence*, 32:281–331, 1987.
18. J.E. Dennis and R.B. Schnabel. *Numerical Methods for Unconstrained Optimization and Nonlinear Equations.* Prentice Hall, Englewood Cliffs, New Jersey, 1983.
19. M. Dincbas, H. Simonis and P. Van Hentenryck Extending Equation Solving and Constraints Handling in Logic Programming. *Proc. Colloquium CREAS MCC*, Austin, Texas, 1987.
20. E.R. Hansen and R.I. Greenberg. An Interval Newton Method. *Appl. Math. Comput.*, 12:89–98, 1983.
21. E.R. Hansen and S. Sengupta. Bounding Solutions of Systems of Equations Using Interval Analysis. *BIT*, 21:203–211, 1981.

22. H. Hong. RISC-CLP(Real):Logic programming with Non- linear constraints over the Reals *Constraint Logic Programming: Selected Research,* F. Benhamou and A. Colmerauer, eds. MIT Press, 1993.

23. H. Hong and V. Stahl. Safe Starting Regions by Fixed Points and Tightening. Submitted for Publication, November 1993.

24. E. Hyvönen. Constraint Reasoning Based on Interval Arithmetic. . In *Proceedings of 11th IJCAI,* pp 193–198, Morgan–Kaufmann publishers, 1989.

25. E. Hyvönen. Constraint Reasoning Based on Interval Arithmetic. The Tolerance Propagation Approach. *Artificial Intelligence,* 58, pp 71–112, 1992.

26. E. Hyvönen, S. De Pascale and A. Lehtola. Interval Constraint Programming in C++. *Constraint Programming,* B. Mayoh, E. Tyugu and J. Penjam eds., NATO ASI series, Series F, Vol. 1, Springer-Verlag, pp 350–366, 1994.

27. IEEE Standard for Binary Floating-point Arithmetic. *ANSI/IEEE Std 754-1985,* Institute of Electrical and Electronics Engineers, NYC, NY, USA.

28. INTERLOG 1.0: User's guide (in french). *Dassault Electronique, 55 Quai M. Dassault, 92214 Saint Cloud, France.*

29. Constraint Propagation with Interval Labels. *Artificial Intelligence,* 32, pp 281–331, 1987.

30. J. Jaffar and J.L. Lassez, Constraint Logic Programming. *Proc. POPL,* ACM, 1987.

31. J. Jaffar, S. Michaylov, P. J. Stuckey and R. H. C. Yap, The CLP($\Re$) Language and System *ACM Transactions on Programming Languages and Systems,* Vol. 14, no 3, pages 339–395, 1992.

32. J. Jaffar and M. Maher, Constraint Logic Programming: a Survey *Journal of Logic Programming,* Vol. 19/20, pages 503–581, 1994.

33. R. Krawczyk. Newton-Algorithmen zur Bestimmung von Nullstellen mit Fehlerschranken. *Computing,* 4:187–201, 1985.

34. P.B. Ladkin and A. Reinefeld. Effective Solution of Qualitative Interval Constraint Problems. *Artificial Intelligence,* 57, pp 107–124, 1992.

35. J.H.M. Lee and M.H. van Emden. Adapting CLP($\Re$) to Floating-Point Arithmetic. *Proceedings of FGCSC,* Tokyo, Japan, 1992.

36. J.H.M. Lee and M.H. van Emden. Interval Computation as Deduction in CHIP. *Journal of Logic Programming,* 16(3-4):255–276, 1993.

37. O. Lhomme. Consistency Techniques for Numeric CSPs. *Proceedings of the 13th IJCAI,* 1993.

38. A.K. Mackworth. Consistency in Networks of Relations. *Artificial Intelligence,* 8(1):99–118, 1977.

39. U. Montanari. Networks of Constraints : Fundamental Properties and Applications to Picture Processing. *Information Science,* 7(2):95–132,1974.

40. R.E. Moore. *Interval Analysis.* Prentice-Hall, Englewood Cliffs, NJ, 1966.

41. J.J. More and M.Y. Cosnard. Numerical Solution of Nonlinear Equations. *ACM Transactions on Mathematical Software,* 5:64–85, 1979.

42. W. Older and A. Vellino, "Extending Prolog with Constraint Arithmetic on Real Intervals", in *Proceedings of the Canadian Conference on Electrical and Computer Engineering,* 1990.

43. W. Older and A. Vellino. *Constraint Arithmetic on Real Intervals.* In *Constraint Logic Programming: Selected Papers,* F. Benhamou & A. Colmerauer eds., The MIT Press, Cambridge, MA, 1993.

44. W. Older and F. Benhamou. Programming in CLP(BNR). In *PPCP'94,* Newport, RI (USA), 1993.

45. L.B. Rall. *Automatic Differentiation: Techniques and Applications.* Springer Lectures Notes in Computer Science, Springer Verlag, New York, 1981.
46. G. Sidebottom and W. havens. Hierarchical Arc Consistency Applied to Numeric Processing in Constraint Logic Programming. *Computational Intelligence*, 8(4), 1992.
47. M.H. Van Emden The Compatibility Operator for Real Intervals, Herbrand Universes and Finite Domains *Research Report*, University of Victoria, Canada, 1994.
48. P. Van Hentenryck. *Constraint Satisfaction in Logic Programming* MIT Press, Cambridge, 1989.
49. P. Van Hentenryck, V. Saraswat, and Y. Deville. The Design, Implementation, and Evaluation of the Constraint Language cc(FD). Technical Report, Brown University, December 1992.
50. P. Van Hentenryck and Yves Deville. The Cardinality Operator: A new Logical Connective for Constraint Logic Programming *Constraint Logic Programming: Selected Research,* F. Benhamou and A. Colmerauer (eds.), MIT Press, pages 383–403, 1993.
51. W. Walster. Philosophy and practicalities of Interval Arithmetic. *Reliability in Computing*, pp 309–323, Academic Press, 1988.
52. J.H. Wilkinson. *The algebraic Eigenvalue Problem*, Oxford University Press, 1965.
53. J. Zhou. Approximate Solving of $y = cos(x)$ and Other Real Constraints by Cartesian Product of Intervals. Technical Report, LIM, University of Marseilles, 1994.

Solving Pseudo-Boolean Constraints*

Alexander Bockmayr

Max-Planck-Institut für Informatik, Im Stadtwald, D-66123 Saarbrücken,
bockmayr@mpi-sb.mpg.de

Abstract. Pseudo-Boolean constraints are equations or inequalities between integer polynomials in 0-1 variables. On the one hand, they generalize Boolean constraints, on the other hand, they are a restricted form of finite domain constraints. In this paper, we present special constraint solving techniques for the domain $\{0,1\}$ originating from mathematical programming. The key concepts are the generation of strong valid inequalities for the solution set of a constraint system and the notion of branch-and-cut.

1 Introduction

Pseudo-Boolean constraints are a generalization of Boolean constraints and combine Boolean algebra with arithmetic. A *pseudo-Boolean function* is an integer-valued function

$$f : \{0,1\}^n \to \mathbb{Z}$$

of 0-1 variables. Any such function can be written as a multilinear polynomial in 0-1 variables with integer coefficients.

Example 1. The pseudo-Boolean function $f : \{0,1\}^2 \to \mathbb{Z}$ with $f(1,1) = 1, f(1,0) = -2, f(0,1) = 3, f(0,0) = -5$ can be represented as $f(x,y) = 1 \cdot xy - 2 \cdot x(1-y) + 3 \cdot (1-x)y - 5 \cdot (1-x)(1-y) = -5xy + 3x + 8y - 5$.

A *pseudo-Boolean constraint* is an equation or an inequality between pseudo-Boolean functions. Pseudo-Boolean constraints can be linear or non-linear. For example, the non-linear constraint $x \cdot y + y \cdot z + x \cdot z \geq 1$ and the linear constraint $x + y + z \geq 2$ have the same set of 0-1 solutions. In this paper, we will study mainly linear pseudo-Boolean constraints.

Boolean functions are special pseudo-Boolean functions with codomain $\{0,1\} \subset \mathbb{Z}$. The logical connectives $^-, \wedge, \vee, \oplus$ can be expressed by the arithmetic operations $+, -, \cdot$ using the identities

$$\overline{x} \equiv 1 - x,$$
$$x \oplus y \equiv x + y - 2 \cdot x \cdot y,$$
$$x \wedge y \equiv x \cdot y,$$
$$x \vee y \equiv x + y - x \cdot y.$$

---

* This work was supported by the German Ministry for Research and Technology (BMFT) (contract ITS 9103), the ESPRIT Basic Research Project ACCLAIM (contract EP 7195) and the ESPRIT Working Group CCL (contract EP 6028).

A set C of *propositional clauses* of the form

$$x_1 \vee \ldots \vee x_m \vee \overline{y}_1 \vee \ldots \vee \overline{y}_k$$

can be translated into a system of *clausal inequalities* of the form

$$x_1 + \cdots + x_m + (1 - y_1) + \cdots + (1 - y_k) \geq 1 \qquad \text{or}$$
$$x_1 + \cdots + x_m \quad - y_1 \; - \cdots \cdots \quad - y_k \; \geq 1 - k.$$

The set C is satisfiable if and only if the corresponding system of linear inequalities has a 0-1 solution. In particular, deciding the satisfiability of a set of pseudo-Boolean constraints is in general an *NP*-hard problem.

A constraint logic programming language CLP($\mathcal{PB}$) for logic programming with pseudo-Boolean constraints was introduced in [9, 10]. Pseudo-Boolean constraints generalize Boolean constraints. On the other hand, they are a restricted form of finite domain constraints, where all domains are equal to $\{0, 1\}$. Schematically, we have the inclusions

$$\text{CLP}(\mathcal{B}) \subset \text{CLP}(\mathcal{PB}) \subset \text{CLP}(\mathcal{FD}).$$

This implies that one can use finite domain techniques to solve pseudo-Boolean constraints. For the Boolean case, it was shown in [13, 14] that a finite domain approach can be both simple and efficient. However, finite domain methods, which are based on local consistency and constraint propagation, cannot exploit the special mathematical structure of 0-1 problems. Moreover, finite domain solvers are usually not complete. A set of constraints may be locally consistent although it does not admit a global solution. In order to achieve completeness, the values in the domains have to be enumerated by an additional backtracking mechanism (`labeling` procedure).

In this paper, we present techniques for complete pseudo-Boolean constraint solving that exploit the special mathematical structure of the domain $\{0, 1\}$. The general problem in constraint solving is to compute a *solved form* representing all the solutions of a given constraint set. In many practical applications, one is moreover interested in selecting a solution that is *optimal* with respect to some objective function. In our case, this is again a pseudo-Boolean function. Therefore, we propose to study the following problems:

Solving pseudo-Boolean constraints: Given a set C of pseudo-Boolean constraints, compute a solved form $\mathcal{S}(C)$ which represents the solution set. In particular, decide whether this set is empty or not.

Pseudo-Boolean optimization: Optimize a pseudo-Boolean function subject to a set of pseudo-Boolean constraints.

The pseudo-Boolean optimization problem has been studied for many years in mathematical programming and operations research. Pseudo-Boolean functions arise naturally when modeling yes/no decisions. Many classical *combinatorial optimization problems* can be formulated very naturally as linear or non-linear pseudo-Boolean optimizations problems.

Example 2. Suppose there is a vessel with capacity w and goods g_i with weight w_i and value v_i for $i = 1, \ldots, n$. The task is to determine a most valuable cargo. We introduce 0-1 variables x_i indicating whether g_i is loaded on the vessel or not. The cargos that do not exceed the capacity of the vessel are described by the linear pseudo-Boolean constraint

$$w_1 \cdot x_1 + \cdots + w_n \cdot x_n \leq w.$$

To find a most valuable cargo, we have to solve a *knapsack problem*, that is a linear pseudo-Boolean optimization problem with one linear inequality constraint:

$$\max \{ v_1 \cdot x_1 + \cdots + v_n \cdot x_n \mid w_1 \cdot x_1 + \cdots + w_n \cdot x_n \leq w, x \in \{0, 1\}^n \}.$$

2 Solving Pseudo-Boolean Constraints

Consider a system of linear pseudo-Boolean constraints

$$
\begin{matrix}
a_{11}x_1 + \ldots + a_{1n}x_n \geq b_1 \\
\vdots \qquad\qquad\qquad \vdots \\
a_{m1}x_1 + \ldots + a_{mn}x_n \geq b_m
\end{matrix}
\quad \Leftrightarrow Ax \geq b
$$

with a matrix $A \in \mathbb{Z}^{m \times n}$, a vector $b \in \mathbb{Z}^m$, and 0-1 variables $x_1, \ldots, x_n \in \{0, 1\}$.

- What does it mean to solve such a system ?
- What should the solved form look like ?

The solved form should provide a simple and concise description of the solution set. In particular, it should indicate whether this set is empty or not. The problem is that there exists a large number of possibilities to describe a given set of 0-1 vectors. It is not clear which of them should be chosen. First, we may distinguish

- equational descriptions and
- inequality descriptions

of the solution set.

2.1 Equational Descriptions

The most natural way to describe the solutions of a pseudo-Boolean constraint system is to use *families of solutions* like

x_1	x_2	x_3	x_4	x_5
0	0	–	–	–
0	1	1	–	–
1	0	1	–	–

Such a representation may be useful for systems with a small number of variables but it is not suitable for larger systems. Also, this is a disjunctive representation. It is equivalent to the logical formula

$$(x_1 = 0 \wedge x_2 = 0) \vee (x_1 = 0 \wedge x_2 = 1 \wedge x_3 = 1) \vee (x_1 = 1 \wedge x_2 = 0 \wedge x_3 = 1).$$

In the context of constraint logic programming, disjunction in the solved form of a constraint set means that we introduce an additional level of indeterminism during program execution. Backtracking has to be done not only at the programming level but also within the constraint solving procedure. This leads to a blow-up of the search space which we want to avoid.

A second approach is therefore to compute a parametric solution or a *most general pseudo-Boolean unifier* [10]

$$x_1 = t_1[y_1, \ldots, y_k]$$
$$\vdots$$
$$x_n = t_n[y_1, \ldots, y_k],$$

where $t_1, \ldots, t_n$ are pseudo-Boolean terms containing new variables $y_1, \ldots, y_k$. This corresponds to one of the most common approaches in Boolean constraint solving [12]. The advantage of this approach is that we capture all the solutions of the constraint set by a conjunctive formula, which in addition can be seen as an idempotent substitution. However, practical experience already in the Boolean case has shown that these most general unifiers involve very complex pseudo-Boolean terms. Therefore, they seem to be useful only for special problem classes, for example in circuit verification.

2.2 Inequality Descriptions

Instead of computing an explicit representation of the solution set using equalities, we may also compute an implicit representation based on *inequalities*. This is particularly useful in the context of optimization because it allows us to use powerful methods from operations research. Given a constraint system $C : Ax \geq b$, the idea is to compute a solved form $S(C) : \overline{A}x \geq \overline{b}$ which is again a system of linear inequalities. Since we want to simplify our problem, $S(C)$ should be "simpler" than C. But, what does this mean? There are many possibilities to compare linear inequality descriptions $Ax \geq b$ of a 0-1 set S. In particular, we may consider

- the size of the system $Ax \geq b$ depending on the number of inequalities and the size of their coefficients.
- the strength of the inequalities in the system $Ax \geq b$.

Example 3. Consider the linear pseudo-Boolean inequality

$$3x_1 + 2x_2 + x_3 + x_4 + x_5 \geq 5. \tag{1}$$

The set of 0-1 solutions is

$$
\begin{aligned}
S = \{ \ &(0,1,1,1,1), (1,0,0,1,1), (1,0,1,0,1), (1,0,1,1,0), \\
&(1,0,1,1,1), (1,1,0,0,0), (1,1,0,0,1), (1,1,0,1,0), \\
&(1,1,0,1,1), (1,1,1,0,0), (1,1,1,0,1), (1,1,1,1,0), \\
&(1,1,1,1,1) \ \}.
\end{aligned}
\tag{2}
$$

Using clausal inequalities, which correspond to clauses in propositional logic, this set can be represented as the solution set of the constraint system

$$
\begin{aligned}
x_1 + x_2 \geq 1, \quad x_1 + x_3 \geq 1, \quad x_1 + x_4 \geq 1, \quad x_1 + x_5 \geq 1, \\
x_2 + x_3 + x_4 \geq 1, \quad x_2 + x_3 + x_5 \geq 1, \quad x_2 + x_4 + x_5 \geq 1.
\end{aligned}
\tag{3}
$$

Instead of classical clauses, we may also use extended clauses $L_1 + \cdots + L_m \geq d$ stating that at least d out of m literals $L_1, \ldots, L_m$ have to be true (see Def. 5)

$$
\begin{aligned}
x_1 + x_2 \geq 1, \quad x_1 + x_3 \geq 1, \quad x_1 + x_4 \geq 1, \quad x_1 + x_5 \geq 1, \\
x_1 + x_2 + x_3 + x_4 \geq 2, \quad x_1 + x_2 + x_3 + x_5 \geq 2, \quad x_1 + x_2 + x_4 + x_5 \geq 2.
\end{aligned}
\tag{4}
$$

Representation (3) is smaller in size than representation (4). In particular, the right-hand side in (3) is always 1, whereas it is 1 or 2 in (4). On the other hand, the inequalities in representation (4) are stronger than those in (3), according to the next definition.

Definition 4. Let $Q, X \subseteq \mathbb{R}^n$. An inequality $\alpha x \geq \beta$ is *valid* for Q iff $\alpha x_0 \geq \beta$, for all $x_0 \in Q$. An inequality $\alpha x \geq \beta$ is *stronger than* $\gamma x \geq \delta$ *with respect to* X iff

$$
\{x \in X \mid \alpha x \geq \beta\} \subseteq \{x \in X \mid \gamma x \geq \delta\}.
$$

The inequality is *strictly stronger* iff the inclusion is strict.

2.3 Constraint Solving as Constraint Strengthening

The basic idea of the constraint solving methods presented in this paper is to compute "better" descriptions of the 0-1 solution set S of a given constraint set by adding strong valid inequalities for S. Constraint solving thus means incremental strengthening of the current constraint set. Depending on the set X in Def. 4, there are several possibilities to strengthen a given inequality system. We may compare inequalities with respect to their

- 0-1 solutions, i.e. $X = \{0, 1\}^n$, or
- real solutions, i.e. $X = \mathbb{R}^n$.

This leads to two different approaches for pseudo-Boolean constraint solving, which will be described in the next sections:

- Computing prime inequalities, i.e. strongest inequalities for $X = \{0, 1\}^n$.
- Computing facet-defining inequalities, i.e. strongest inequalities for $X = \mathbb{R}^n$.

3 Prime Extended Clauses

A first approach for solving a system of pseudo-Boolean constraints [3, 6] is to compute an equivalent set of *prime extended clauses*.

3.1 Extended Clauses

Definition 5. An *extended clause* is a linear pseudo-Boolean inequality of the form

$$L_1 + \cdots + L_m \geq d, \tag{5}$$

where $d \geq 1$ is a positive integer number and $L_i, i = 1, \ldots, m$, is either a *positive literal* x_i or a *negative literal* $\overline{x}_i = 1 - x_i$. The intuitive meaning of (5) is that at least d out of the m literals L_i have to be true. Classical clauses or clausal inequalities correspond to the case $d = 1$. If $x_i, i = 1, \ldots, l$, are the positive literals and $\overline{y}_j, j = 1, \ldots, k$, are the negative literals, then the extended clause (5) can also be written in the form

$$x_1 + \cdots + x_l - y_1 - \cdots - y_k \geq d - k. \tag{6}$$

A *prime extended clause* with respect to a set $S \subseteq \{0, 1\}^n$ is a strongest valid extended clause for S, i.e. a valid extended clause for S such that there is no other valid extended clause for S which is strictly stronger with respect to $\{0, 1\}^n$. By $\Pi(C)$ we denote the set of all prime extended clauses for the 0-1 solution set S of a pseudo-Boolean constraint system C.

Classical and extended clauses: In many cases, extended clauses give a more compact representation of a set $S \subseteq \{0, 1\}^n$ than classical clauses. For example, the extended clause $L_1 + \cdots + L_m \geq d$ is equivalent to the conjunction $\bigwedge_{I \subseteq \{1, \ldots, m\} : |I| = m - d + 1} \sum_{i \in I} L_i \geq 1$ of $\binom{m}{m - d + 1}$ classical clauses.

Implication of extended clauses: A classical clause $L_1 + \cdots + L_m \geq 1$ implies another clause $L_1' + \cdots + L_k' \geq 1$ if and only if $L = \{L_1, \ldots, L_m\} \subseteq L' = \{L_1', \ldots, L_k'\}$. A similar result holds for extended clauses. Abbreviate an extended clause $L_1 + \cdots + L_m \geq d$ by $L \geq d$ and view L as a set of literals $\{L_1, \ldots, L_m\}$ of cardinality $|L| = m$. Then $L \geq d$ implies $L' \geq d'$ (equivalently $L \geq d$ is stronger than $L' \geq d'$ with respect to $\{0, 1\}^n$) if and only if $|L \setminus L'| \leq d - d'$. This means that the implication problem for extended clauses is easy, while for arbitrary linear 0-1 inequalities it is *NP*-hard.

3.2 Generalized Resolution

Given a set of linear pseudo-Boolean constraints C, the set of prime extended clauses $\Pi(C)$ can be computed in two steps:

1. Transform C into a set of extended clauses $\mathcal{E}(C)$.
2. Compute from $\mathcal{E}(C)$ the set of prime extended clauses $\Pi(C)$.

The first transformation is not described here and can be found in [4, 5]. To compute a set of prime extended clauses for a set of extended clauses $\mathcal{E}$ one can use *generalized resolution* [18, 20]. This deductive system is based on the following inference rules:

Resolution: $\mathcal{E} \vdash \mathcal{E} \cup \{R\}$ if there exist classical clauses C_1 and C_2 each implied by some extended clause in $\mathcal{E}$ such that R is a classical resolvent of C_1 and C_2 and R is not implied by some extended clause in $\mathcal{E}$.

Diagonal Sum: $\mathcal{E} \vdash \mathcal{E} \cup \{DS\}$ if there exist m extended clauses

$$
\begin{aligned}
\Box \;\; L_2 + L_3 + \cdots + L_{m-1} + L_m &\geq d \\
L_1 \;\; \Box \;\; + L_3 + \cdots + L_{m-1} + L_m &\geq d \\
&\vdots \\
L_1 + L_2 + L_3 + \cdots + L_{m-1} \;\; \Box &\geq d
\end{aligned}
$$

each implied by some extended clause in $\mathcal{E}$ such that DS is the extended clause

$$L_1 + L_2 + L_3 + \cdots + L_{m-1} + L_m \geq d + 1$$

and DS is not implied by some extended clause in $\mathcal{E}$.

Here, the symbol $\Box$ is used to indicate a missing literal.

Simplification: $\mathcal{E} \cup \{C\} \vdash \mathcal{E}$ iff C is implied by some extended clause in $\mathcal{E}$.

Given a set of extended clauses C, applying the rules **Resolution, Diagonal Sum, Simplification** as long as possible yields the set $\Pi(C)$ of prime extended clauses for the 0-1 solution set S of C. The main properties of the solved form $\Pi(C)$ are the following:

- C is unsatisfiable if and only if $0 \geq 1 \in \Pi(C)$.
- An extended clause $L \geq d$ is implied by C if and only if it is implied by some prime extended clause $L' \geq d'$ in $\Pi(C)$.

Thus, given the set of prime extended clauses $\Pi(C)$, testing satisfiability and entailment becomes very easy. The set $\Pi(C)$, on the other hand, can be very large. Therefore, $\Pi(C)$ has to be seen as an *ideal solved form*. This means that, in practice, only an approximation of $\Pi(C)$ will be computed. We generate just as many extended clauses as are needed to answer the current questions on satisfiability or entailment.

4 Facet-Defining Inequalities

If we drop the condition $x \in \{0, 1\}^n$, then a system of linear pseudo-Boolean inequalities

$$
\begin{matrix}
a_{11}x_1 + \cdots + a_{1n}x_n \geq b_1 \\
\vdots \qquad\qquad \vdots \quad \vdots \\
a_{m1}x_1 + \cdots + a_{mn}x_n \geq b_m
\end{matrix}
\quad \Leftrightarrow Ax \geq b, \tag{7}
$$

with $A \in \mathbb{Z}^{m \times n}$, $x \in \{0,1\}^n$ and $b \in \mathbb{Z}^m$ becomes a system of *linear arithmetic constraints* over the real numbers, which defines a *polyhedron* P in $\mathbb{R}^n$ (for the basic theory of polyhedra see [22, 24]). The set of 0-1 solutions $S = P \cap \{0,1\}^n$ corresponds to the set of 0-1 points lying within P (see Fig. 1a).

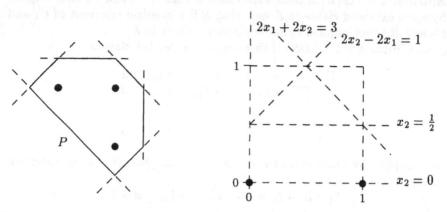

Fig. 1. a) Polyhedron P defined by six linear inequalities containing three 0-1 points b) Three linear 0-1 inequality descriptions of $S = \{(0,0), (1,0)\}$

There is an important difference between linear inequality descriptions of the real polyhedron P and the 0-1 set S. Call a system $Ax \geq b$ over $\mathbb{R}^n$ (resp. $\{0,1\}^n$) *irredundant* if no constraint $\alpha x \geq \beta$ can be removed without changing the solution set P (resp. S). For a full-dimensional polyhedron P there is up to multiplication of inequalities by a positive real number a unique representation of P by an irredundant system of inequalities $Ax \geq b$. The inequalities in $Ax \geq b$ are in a 1-1 correspondence with the facets of P. An inequality defines a *facet* of an n-dimensional polyhedron P if it is valid for P and if moreover there are n affinely independent points in P for which it is satisfied at equality.

For a 0-1 set S, however, there are many different representations by irredundant systems. For example, the irredundant constraint sets $\{x_2 \leq 0\}$, $\{2x_2 \leq 1\}$, and $\{2x_1 + 2x_2 \leq 3, 2x_2 - 2x_1 \leq 1\}$ all define the same 0-1 set $S = \{(0,0), (1,0)\} \subseteq \mathbb{R}^2$ (see Fig. 1b).

4.1 The Convex Hull of the 0-1 Solution Set

From a polyhedral point of view, the best linear inequality description of the 0-1 set

$$S = \{x \in \{0,1\}^n \mid Ax \geq b\}$$

is a linear inequality description of the *convex hull*

$$conv(S) = \{x \in \mathbb{R}^n \mid \tilde{A}x \geq \tilde{b}\}$$

by a system $\Gamma(C) : \tilde{A}x \geq \tilde{b}$ of facet-defining inequalities. While prime extended clauses are strongest inequalities with respect to $X = \{0,1\}^n$, facet-defining inequalities are strongest inequalities with respect to $X = \mathbb{R}^n$. $\Gamma(C)$ is the *ideal solved form* from the polyhedral point of view. The key property of this solved form is that it allows us to reduce 0-1 problems to linear arithmetic problems, for which efficient techniques from mathematical programming are available. More precisely, for any $c \in \mathbb{R}^n$

$$\max\{cx \mid x \in S \subseteq \{0,1\}^n\} = \max\{cx \mid x \in conv(S) \subseteq \mathbb{R}^n\}.$$

The first problem is a *discrete* linear optimization problem over the 0-1 set $S \subseteq \{0,1\}^n$, while the second problem is a *continuous* linear optimization problem over the real polyhedron $P = conv(S) \subseteq \mathbb{R}^n$. The objective function cx attains its maximum value on P in a vertex x^* of P. Since P is the convex hull of a set of 0-1 points, x^* must be a 0-1 point. Therefore, x^* is also an optimal solution to the 0-1 problem. This means that, in principle, we can solve a linear 0-1 optimization problem over the 0-1 set S by computing (e.g. with the Simplex algorithm) a basic optimal solution for the corresponding linear optimization problem over the convex hull $conv(S)$.

It is not necessary to have the complete description $\Gamma(C)$ of $conv(S)$, which might be extremely complex. That is why $\Gamma(C)$, like $\Pi(C)$, is called an ideal solved form. It is enough to have an approximation of $conv(S)$, which can be computed by the generation of cutting planes. We start with the *linear relaxation* $P = \{x \in \mathbb{R}^n \mid Ax \geq b, 0 \leq x \leq 1\}$ of the original problem. Then we add new inequalities which are satisfied by all points in S but which cut off at least one fractional vertex of P. These are called *cutting planes*. This is repeated until a 0-1 vertex is obtained, which belongs to the 0-1 solution set S of C (see Fig. 2).

It is crucial for this approach that the cutting planes which are generated are strong with respect to $\mathbb{R}^n$. In the best case, they should define facets of $conv(S)$ or at least faces of sufficiently high dimension. Traditional *Chvátal-Gomory* cuts [16] do not have this property. They converge much too slowly in order to be practically useful. For special problems (knapsack, set covering, traveling salesman etc.) strong valid inequalities have been found by analyzing the specific problem structure. For general 0-1 problems, strong valid inequalities are very hard to obtain. An early strong cutting plane approach for general 0-1 problems was presented in [15]. The cutting planes used there are facet-defining inequalities for the knapsack polytope generated by an individual 0-1 constraint. This approach has been particularly successful in the case of large-scale 0-1 problems with a sparse coefficient matrix and with no apparent special structure. In this case, the constraints do not interact very much, so that one can expect that strong valid inequalities for the knapsack polytope of an individual 0-1 constraint will also be strong for the 0-1 polytope of the full problem. The mixed integer optimizer MINTO [21] is based on these ideas. They are also used in the new version of the commercial mixed integer package CPLEX 3.0.

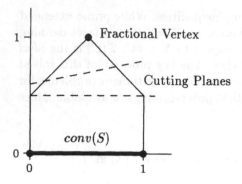

Fig. 2. Approximating the convex hull of S by cutting planes

4.2 The Lift-and-Project-Method

We present here a promising new method to find strong cutting planes for general 0-1 problems, namely the *lift-and-project* method for mixed 0-1 optimization [2, 1]. This approach was able to solve several previously unsolved problems and is competitive with state-of-the-art commercial mixed integer optimizers. In several cases, the procedure even outperformed specialized algorithms on the class of problems for which these algorithms were designed.

The starting point of the lift-and-project method is a *sequential convexification* theorem. Suppose

$$P = \{x \in \mathbb{R}^n \mid Ax \geq b, 0 \leq x \leq 1\} \stackrel{\text{def}}{=} \{x \in \mathbb{R}^n \mid \tilde{A}x \geq \tilde{b}\}, \qquad (8)$$

with $A \in \mathbb{R}^{m \times n}, b \in \mathbb{R}^m$, is a polyhedron in $\mathbb{R}^n$. If

$$R_j(P) = conv(P \cap \{x \in \mathbb{R}^n \mid x_j \in \{0,1\}\}), \quad \text{for } j = 1, \ldots, n, \qquad (9)$$

is the convex hull of those points in P for which $x_j = 0$ or $x_j = 1$, then

$$R_1(R_2(\ldots R_n(P))) = conv(S), \qquad (10)$$

where as usual $S = P \cap \{0,1\}^n$. This sequential convexification property is typical for the domain $\{0,1\}$ and does not hold for larger domains like $\{0,1,-1\}$. The idea of [2, 1] is to use facets of $R_j(P)$ as strong cutting planes for S. By lifting the problem into a higher-dimensional space one can show that $R_j(P) = \{x \in \mathbb{R}^n \mid \alpha x \geq \beta \text{ for all } (\alpha, \beta) \in R_j^*(P)\}$ where $R_j^*(P)$ is the set of those $(\alpha, \beta) \in \mathbb{R}^{n+1}$ for which there exist vectors $u, v \in \mathbb{R}^{m+2n}$ and $u_0, v_0 \in \mathbb{R}$ satisfying

$$
\begin{aligned}
\alpha - u\tilde{A} - u_0 e_j & & = 0 \\
\alpha & - v\tilde{A} - v_0 e_j & = 0 \\
u\tilde{b} & & = \beta \\
& v\tilde{b} + v_0 & = \beta \\
& u, v \geq 0,
\end{aligned}
\qquad (11)
$$

where e_j is the j-th unit vector in $\mathbb{R}^n$. If P is full-dimensional, $P \cap \{x \mid x_j = 0\} \neq \emptyset$ and $P \cap \{x \mid x_j = 1\} \neq \emptyset$, then for any constant $\beta \neq 0$, $\alpha x \geq \beta$ defines a facet of $R_j(P)$ iff (α, β) is an extreme ray of the polyhedral cone $R_j^*(P)$. To compute such extreme rays one can solve a linear program of the form

$$\max\{\beta - x^*\alpha \mid (\alpha, \beta) \in R_j^*(P) \cap T\} \tag{12}$$

where x^* is the fractional vertex of P that should be cut off, and T is a normalization set that truncates the cone $R_j^*(P)$. Several choices of T are possible. For example, one can use $T = \{(\alpha, \beta) \mid -1 \leq \alpha_i \leq 1, i = 1, \ldots, n\}$ or $T = \{(\alpha, \beta) \mid \sum_{i=1}^n |\alpha_i| \leq 1\}$. In some cases, one can also choose the truncation $\beta = 1$ or $\beta = -1$.

Example 6. Consider the set of 0-1 constraints

$$C = \{-2x_1 - 2x_2 \geq -3, \ 2x_1 - 2x_2 \geq -1\}.$$

The linear relaxation P is given by the system of linear inequalities $\tilde{A}x \geq \tilde{b}$, where

$$\tilde{A}^T = \begin{pmatrix} -2 & 2 & 1 & 0 & -1 & 0 \\ -2 & -2 & 0 & 1 & 0 & -1 \end{pmatrix} \quad \text{and} \quad \tilde{b}^T = (-3 \ -1 \ 0 \ 0 \ -1 \ -1).$$

To cut off the fractional vertex $(\frac{1}{2}, 1)$ of P we solve the linear program

$\max -\frac{1}{2}\alpha_1 - \alpha_2 + \beta$ subject to

$$
\begin{array}{lllllll}
\alpha_1 & +2u_1 & -2u_2 & -u_3 & & +u_5 & -u_0 = 0 \\
\alpha_2 & +2u_1 & +2u_2 & & -u_4 & +u_6 & = 0 \\
\alpha_1 & +2v_1 & -2v_2 & -v_3 & & +v_5 & -v_0 = 0 \\
\alpha_2 & +2v_1 & +2v_2 & & -v_4 & +v_6 & = 0 \\
& -3u_1 & -u_2 & & & -u_5 -u_6 & = \beta \\
& -3v_1 & -v_2 & & & -v_5 -v_6 +v_0 & = \beta
\end{array}
$$

$$-1 \leq \alpha_1, \alpha_2 \leq 1$$
$$u_1, u_2, u_3, u_4, u_5, u_6, v_1, v_2, v_3, v_4, v_5, v_6 \geq 0.$$

We get the optimal solution $\alpha_1 = 0, \alpha_2 = -1, \beta = -\frac{1}{2}$, which corresponds to the facet $x_2 \leq \frac{1}{2}$ of $R_1(P)$. In the same way, we can compute the facets $x_1 + \frac{1}{2}x_2 \leq 1$ and $x_1 - \frac{1}{2}x_2 \geq 0$ of $R_2(P)$, which cut off the vertices $(1, \frac{1}{2})$ and $(0, \frac{1}{2})$ respectively (see Fig. 3). In this example, we really compute facets of $R_j(P)$. Note however that, due to the truncation T, this needs not always be the case.

4.3 Polyhedral Cutting Planes for Pseudo-Boolean Constraints

Next we give a polyhedral cutting plane algorithm for solving pseudo-Boolean constraints [11]. Implicitly, it computes a *solved form* of a given constraint set $C : Ax \geq b, x \in \{0, 1\}^n$.

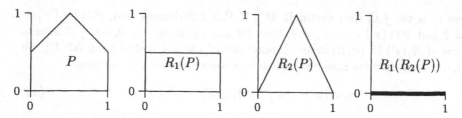

Fig. 3. Convexification of $P = \{x \in [0,1]^2 \mid -2x_1 - 2x_2 \geq -3, \ 2x_1 - 2x_2 \geq -1\}$.

Polyhedral Cutting Plane Algorithm.

Initialization: Let $t := 1$; $C^1 := \{Ax \geq b, 0 \leq x \leq 1\}$,
Iteration t: 1. Solution of the linear relaxation: Optimize a linear function g^t over the relaxation

$$P^t = \{x \in \mathbb{R}^n \mid x \text{ is a solution of } C^t\}.$$

2. Infeasibility test: If $P^t = \emptyset$, stop, C is unsolvable.
Otherwise let the vertex $x^t \in P^t$ be an optimal solution.
3. Feasible 0-1 solution: If $x_j^t \in \{0,1\}$, for $j = 1,\ldots,n$, stop,
x^t is a feasible 0-1 solution of C,
C^t is the *solved form* of C.
4. Cut generation: For $j \in \{1,\ldots,n\}$ with $0 < x_j^t < 1$ generate a
j-cut $\alpha^j x \geq \beta^j$ by solving

$$\max\{\beta - \alpha x^t \mid (\alpha, \beta) \in R_j^*(P^t) \cap T\}. \tag{13}$$

Define C^{t+1} by adding the j-cuts $\alpha^j x \geq \beta^j$ to the constraint set
C^t.
Simplify C^t considered as a set of linear arithmetic constraints.
5. Let $t := t + 1$ and goto 1.

The basic tool in this polyhedral cutting plane algorithm is linear optimization, which is used to compute a vertex of the current relaxation and to generate a separating cutting plane. If a j-cut is added, the corresponding linear optimization problems change only slightly. We get a new row in the constraint matrix of the first problem and two new columns in the constraint matrix of the second problem. The rest remains unchanged.

Example 7. We illustrate the polyhedral cutting plane algorithm with the linear 0-1 inequality

$$3x_1 + 2x_2 + x_3 + x_4 + x_5 \geq 5 \tag{14}$$

from Example 3. For most objective functions, linear optimization over the corresponding linear relaxation yields immediately a 0-1 solution. Minimizing the objective function $x_1 + x_4 + x_5$ yields the fractional vertex $x_1 = 2/3, x_2 = x_3 = 1, x_4 = x_5 = 0$. Now, the cutting plane procedure generates the 1-cut

$x_1 + x_4 + x_5 \geq 1$. Adding this cut to the linear relaxation and re-optimizing yields the optimal 0-1 solution $x_1 = x_2 = x_3 = 1, x_4 = x_5 = 0$. This means that the solved form for this example is

$$3x_1 + 2x_2 + x_3 + x_4 + x_5 \geq 5, x_1 + x_4 + x_5 \geq 1.$$

The ideal solved form of (14) is much larger. The facet-defining inequalities of the convex hull of the 0-1 solution set S are

$$x_1 + x_2 \geq 1, \quad x_1 + x_3 \geq 1, \quad x_1 + x_4 \geq 1, \quad x_1 + x_5 \geq 1,$$
$$2x_1 + x_2 + x_3 + x_4 \geq 3, \quad 2x_1 + x_2 + x_3 + x_5 \geq 3, \quad 2x_1 + x_2 + x_4 + x_5 \geq 3,$$
$$3x_1 + 2x_2 + x_3 + x_4 + x_5 \geq 5$$
$$x_1 \leq 1, \quad x_2 \leq 1, \quad x_3 \leq 1, \quad x_4 \leq 1, \quad x_5 \leq 1.$$

For a specialized version of the polyhedral cutting plane algorithm, which uses a relaxation of P^t during cut generation, one can prove that for any constraint set $C : Ax \geq b, x \in \{0,1\}^n$ the algorithm either finds a feasible 0-1 solution or detects that C is unsolvable [11].

The polyhedral cutting plane algorithm can also be used for *optimization* and *entailment*. If we want to compute an optimal solution to the linear 0-1 optimization problem $\min\{cx \mid Ax \geq b, x \in \{0,1\}^n\}$, we choose $g^t(x) = cx$, for all $t = 1, 2, \ldots$. If the algorithm stops with a solution $x^* \in \{0,1\}^n$, then this solution is optimal. In order to check whether a constraint $cx \geq d$ is entailed by a constraint set $Ax \geq b$, we can minimize the objective function cx subject to $Ax \geq b, x \in \{0,1\}^n$. As soon as we find an optimal solution x^t for the linear relaxation P^t such that $cx^t \geq d$, the constraint is entailed. If $cx^* < d$, for an optimal solution x^* of the 0-1 problem, the constraint is not entailed.

5 Branch-and-Cut

It is a general experience with cutting plane algorithms that the effect of the cutting planes on the objective function value is more significant at the beginning than at the end. In order to move away from the current optimal solution when the cuts become shallow, the cutting plane algorithm can be combined with classical branch-and-bound.

5.1 Branch-and-Bound

The idea of *branch-and-bound* is to divide the set of feasible solutions into subsets, to compute bounds for the objective function on these subsets, and to use these bounds to discard some of the subsets from further consideration. In the case of 0-1 optimization, the splitting of the set of feasible solutions is usually done by fixing a variable to the values 0 and 1.

Example 8. Consider the linear 0-1 optimization problem

$$\max\{x_1 + x_2 + x_3 \mid x_1 - x_2 \geq 0, \; x_1 - x_3 \geq 0, \; x_2 + x_3 \geq 1, x \in \{0,1\}^3\}.$$

The branch-and-bound tree is given in Fig. 4. It contains only 7 instead of possibly 15 nodes. The linear relaxation of S^0 is infeasible. The sets S^{110} resp. S^{111} contain only one point with value 2 resp. 3. For S^{10} we get the upper bound 2 which is smaller than 3. Therefore, this node needs not be expanded and $(1, 1, 1)$ is the optimal solution with optimal value 3.

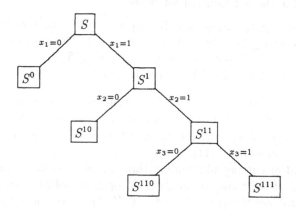

Fig. 4. Branch-and-bound tree

5.2   Branch-and-Cut

Branch-and-bound is the standard technique used in finite domain constraint solvers in case an optimal solution of the given constraint set has to be found. It was also very popular in operations research until it became clear that bounds computed by solving the linear relaxation could be considerably improved by generating suitable cutting planes. Better bounds in turn reduce the size of the branch-and-bound search tree. Approaches that combine branch-and-bound with cutting plane generation are called *branch-and-cut*.

In a first period, cutting planes were generated only at the root node of the branch-and-bound tree in order to improve the initial formulation given by the linear relaxation. This had already remarkable effects as is illustrated by the following example.

Example 9. Consider the standard benchmark p0033 of the mixed integer programming library MIPLIB [7]. This is a linear 0-1 minimization problem consisting of 33 0-1 variables and 15 constraints. If standard branch-and-bound is applied without adding cuts, the best solution found after 1000 nodes has value 3095, and the tree still contains 163 active nodes. If branch-and-bound is applied after generating 20 cuts (in 6 iterations), then a solution of value 3095 is found at node 17, and an optimal solution of value 3089 is found at node 65. Optimality is proved at node 77 [22, p.466].

In a second step, cutting planes were used not only at the root node of the branch-and-bound tree but also for the rest of the tree [23]. The crucial point now is that the cutting planes that are generated at one node are not only valid for the descendants of the this node but for all other nodes in the tree. This means that one has to compute coefficients for the variables that have been fixed before. Cutting planes generated by the lift-and-project method have this crucial property. They can be *lifted* from one node in the branch-and-bound tree to all other nodes [2, 1, 11]. Therefore, the polyhedral cutting plane algorithm for pseudo-Boolean constraint solving given before can be embedded into a branch-and-cut procedure, which usually converges much faster.

We sketch a branch-and-cut procedure for solving the problem $\min\{cx \mid Ax \geq b, x \in \{0,1\}^n\}$ [2, 23]. For $F_0, F_1 \subseteq \{1,\ldots,n\}, F_0 \cap F_1 = \emptyset$, and $C : Ax \geq b, 0 \leq x \leq 1$ let $LP(c, C, F_0, F_1)$ denote the linear optimization problem

$$\min\{cx \mid Ax \geq b, 0 \leq x \leq 1, \ x_i = 0, \text{for } i \in F_0, \ x_i = 1, \text{for } i \in F_1\}.$$

Branch-and-Cut Procedure.

1. **Initialization:** Let $\mathcal{L} = \{(\emptyset, \emptyset)\}$, $C = \{Ax \geq b, 0 \leq x \leq 1\}$, $UB = \infty$.
2. **Node Selection:** If $\mathcal{L} = \emptyset$, then stop.
   Otherwise choose an ordered pair (F_0, F_1) and remove it from $\mathcal{L}$.
3. **Lower Bound:** Solve the linear relaxation $LP(c, C, F_0, F_1)$.
   If the problem is infeasible, goto Step 2, otherwise let $\overline{x}$ denote its optimal solution.
   If $c\overline{x} \geq UB$ goto Step 2.
   If $\overline{x}$ is integer let $x^* = \overline{x}, UB = c\overline{x}$ and goto Step 2.
4. **Branching-Cutting-Decision:** Should cutting planes being generated? If yes, goto Step 5, else goto Step 6.
5. **Cut Generation:** Generate lift-and-project cutting planes $\alpha x \geq \beta$ violated by $\overline{x}$.
   Lift the cuts so that they are valid for the whole branch-and-cut tree.
   Add the resulting cuts to C and goto Step 3.
6. **Branching:** Pick an index $j \in \{1,\ldots,n\}$ such that $0 < \overline{x}_j < 1$.
   Generate the subproblems corresponding to $(F_0 \cup \{j\}, F_1)$ and $(F_0, F_1 \cup \{j\})$ and add them to $\mathcal{L}$. Goto Step 2.

When the algorithm stops, the problem is either infeasible or x^* is an optimal solution. C is the solved form of the constraint set $Ax \geq b$. Note that in spite of branching the solved form does not involve disjunction. This property, which is very important in the context of constraint logic programming, is obtained by the cut lifting process.

5.3 Logic-Based Branch-and-Cut

For classical clauses, there exist close parallels between branch-and-bound and the well-known Davis-Putnam procedure for the satisfiability problem in propositional logic [19]. Both methods are based on implicit enumeration. In the Davis-Putnam algorithm, unit resolution is applied at each node of the enumeration tree to simplify the current clause set. In branch-and-bound, the linear relaxation is solved in order to obtain a new bound for the objective function. These two techniques are also closely related. In [8] it is shown that a set of clauses has a unit refutation if and only if the linear relaxation of the corresponding system of clausal inequalities has no real solution.

In standard branch-and-cut, one computes strong valid inequalities with respect to $X = \mathbb{R}^n$. The same can be done also for $X = \{0,1\}^n$. This leads to *logic-based branch-and-cut* for 0-1 optimization as proposed in [17]. *Logic cuts* are strong valid inequalities with respect to $\{0,1\}^n$. Instead of the linear relaxation a suitable *discrete relaxation* is solved. A logic-based branch-and-cut method for pseudo-Boolean constraint solving is developed in [6].

6 Conclusion

In this paper we have presented two approaches for pseudo-Boolean constraint solving. Both are based on the idea of solving a constraint system by strengthening the underlying constraints, either with respect to their 0-1 solutions or with respect to their real solutions. The strengthening is done by computing strong valid inequalities or cutting planes, which can be either logical or polyhedral. Strong cutting planes may drastically reduce the search space of implicit enumeration algorithms. For the domain $\{0,1\}$, they can be an important improvement of existing finite domain constraint solvers.

Acknowledgement

The author would like to thank Peter Barth and Thomas Kasper for reading a draft of this paper and for many fruitful discussions.

References

1. E. Balas, S. Ceria, and G. Cornuéjols. A lift-and-project cutting plane algorithm for mixed 0-1 programs. *Mathematical Programming*, 58:295 – 324, 1993.
2. E. Balas, S. Ceria, and G. Cornuéjols. Solving mixed 0-1 programs by a lift-and-project method. In *Symposium on Discrete Algorithms, SODA, Austin, Texas*. ACM - SIAM, 1993.
3. P. Barth. A complete symbolic 0-1 constraint solver. In *3rd Workshop on Constraint Logic Programming, WCLP'93, Marseille*, March 1993.
4. P. Barth. Linear 0-1 inequalities and extended clauses. In *Logic Programming and Automated Reasoning, LPAR'93, St. Petersburg*, Springer, LNCS 698, 1993.
5. P. Barth. Linear 0-1 inequalities and extended clauses. Technical Report MPI-I-94-216, Max-Planck-Institut für Informatik, Saarbrücken, April 1994.
6. P. Barth. *Logic-based 0-1 constraint solving in constraint logic programming*. PhD thesis, Fachbereich Informatik, Univ. des Saarlandes, 1994. In preparation.

7. R. E. Bixby, E. A. Boyd, and R. Indovina. MIPLIB: A test set for mixed integer programming problems. *SIAM News 25*, page 16, 1992.

8. C. E. Blair, R. G. Jeroslow, and J. K. Lowe. Some results and experiments in programming techniques for propositional logic. *Computers & Operations Research*, 13(5):633–645, 1986.

9. A. Bockmayr. Logic programming with pseudo-Boolean constraints. Technical Report MPI-I-91-227, Max-Planck-Institut für Informatik, Saarbrücken, 1991.

10. A. Bockmayr. Logic programming with pseudo-Boolean constraints. In F. Benhamou and A. Colmerauer, editors, *Constraint Logic Programming. Selected Research*, chapter 18, pages 327 – 350. MIT Press, 1993.

11. A. Bockmayr. Cutting planes in constraint logic programming. Technical Report MPI-I-94-207, Max-Planck-Institut für Informatik, Saarbrücken, February 1994.

12. W. Büttner and H. Simonis. Embedding Boolean expressions in logic programming. *Journal of Symbolic Computation*, 4(2):191–205, 1987.

13. P. Codognet and D. Diaz. Boolean constraint solving using clp(FD). In *Logic Programming. Proceedings of the 1993 International Symposium, ILPS'93, Vancouver*. MIT Press, 1993.

14. P. Codognet and D. Diaz. clp(B): Combining simplicity and efficiency in Boolean constraint solving. In *Programming Language Implementation and Logic Programming, PLILP'94, Madrid*. Springer, LNCS 844, 1994.

15. H. Crowder, E. J. Johnson, and M. Padberg. Solving large-scale 0-1 linear programming problems. *Operations Research*, 31(5):803–834, 1983.

16. R. E. Gomory. Outline of an algorithm for integer solutions to linear programs. *Bull. AMS*, 64:275 – 278, 1958.

17. J. Hooker. Logic-based methods for optimization: A tutorial. Working Paper 1994-05, GSIA, Carnegie-Mellon-University, 1994.

18. J. N. Hooker. Generalized resolution and cutting planes. *Annals of Operations Research*, 12:217 – 239, 1988.

19. J. N. Hooker. A quantitative approach to logical inference. *Decision Support Systems*, 4:45 – 69, 1988.

20. J. N. Hooker. Generalized resolution for 0-1 linear inequalities. *Annals of Mathematics and Artificial Intelligence*, 6:271–286, 1992.

21. G. Nemhauser, M. W. P. Savelsbergh, and G. Sigismondi. MINTO, a Mixed INTeger Optimizer. *Operations Research Letters*, 15:47 – 58, 1994.

22. G. L. Nemhauser and L. A. Wolsey. *Integer and Combinatorial Optimization*. John Wiley, 1988.

23. M. Padberg and G. Rinaldi. A branch-and-cut algorithm for the resolution of large-scale symmetric traveling salesman problems. *SIAM Review*, 33(1):60 –100, 1991.

24. A. Schrijver. *Theory of Linear and Integer Programming*. John Wiley, 1986.

Enhancing the constraint-solving power of clp(FD) by means of path-consistency methods

Philippe Codognet
INRIA – Rocquencourt
Domaine de Voluceau, 78153 Le Chesnay (France)
Philippe.Codognet@inria.fr

Giuseppe Nardiello[1]
Dipartimento di Matematica – Università di Padova
Via Belzoni 7, 35131 Padova (Italy)
giuseppe@hilbert.math.unipd.it

Abstract. We consider methods for handling constraints over finite domains based on the notion of *path consistency*. We show that these methods can be easily integrated in the *glass-box* constraint-solver of the clp(FD) system. Besides the clp(FD) *indexical constraints* encoding (partial) arc-consistency methods, we introduce new primitive constraints, that we call *m-constraints*, which encode path-consistency methods. These new constraints increase the constraint-solving power and the extensibility of the clp(FD) language.

1 Introduction

During recent years there has been a growing interest for the integration of constraints and constraint-handling techniques in Logic Programming (LP) [21]. The theoretical foundation for the Constraint Logic Programming paradigm resulting from this integration has been given in [19, 20]. The practical value of this approach has been proved by the wide range of real-world applications developed in CLP languages like CHIP [2, 10, 12, 35], CLP(R) [22] and PrologIII [5].

In this paper we focus our attention on the constraint domain of Finite Domains (FD) as introduced in LP by the CHIP language [35, 10]. In FD constraints are stated on variables ranging over *finite domains* of natural numbers, that in the following we will call *fd-variables*. They are handled by means of *local consistency methods* developed in AI for solving Constraint Satisfaction Problems [23, 33].

The basic idea of the local consistency methods is to refine finite domains by removing local inconsistencies, that is values that do not satisfy a subset of the

---

[1] This work is an extended and revised version of [9]. It has been carried out while the second author was visiting INRIA-Rocquencourt, France.

problem constraints. Constraint-solving algorithms based on local consistency methods work by enforcing local consistency and propagating the obtained domain refinements. The efficiency of the backtracking search procedure can be improved by integrating local consistency methods [17]. Indeed, the "active" use of constraints [35] for refining the domains leads to an *a priori* pruning of the search space.

In CHIP, constraint-handling procedures are based on particular local consistency methods known as *arc-consistency* methods [35, 10]. Arc-consistency methods refine finite-domains by removing values which do not satisfy a single constraint. The constraint-handling phase is interleaved with the tree-search phase by means of clause selection and partial enumeration, i.e. instantiation of fd-variables by their allowed values (this is also called *labeling* of fd-variables).

The clp(FD) language integrates arc-consistency methods in a very clean and effective way. The basic idea of clp(FD) is to have a single primitive constraint *X in r*, called *indexical constraint*. The expression *r*, called *range*, specifies the allowed values for the fd-variable *X* in terms of the allowed values for other fd-variables. The range can be seen as encoding the local consistency methods used for solving constraints over FD. More complex constraints such as linear equations and inequalities are then defined in terms of this primitive constraint. Moreover, the *X in r* expressions provide a language for expressing constraint-handling methods in a way that is not allowed in languages like CHIP. Indeed, in clp(FD) is possible to define high-level constraints and to specify the constraint-solving scheme to be used in terms of the indexical constraints. This approach to constraint solving has been called *glass-box* in opposition to a *black-box* approach to constraint solving adopted by other languages. This idea is originally due to [38] and could be summarized in the slogan *"declarative constraint solving"*.

Indexical constraints have also been proved to be a good basis for extending the WAM to an abstract machine for FD where some global optimizations can be easily performed. This approach has been demonstrated to be effective: the clp(FD) system is about four time faster than CHIP on average, with peak speedup reaching eight [6, 7]. Moreover, indexical constraints can be specialized for the particular FD of the boolean values, obtaining also in this case a simple and efficient constraint-solver system [8].

Since arc-consistency methods remove only values that are inconsistent with respect to a *single* constraint, they may fail to detect (and remove) global inconsistencies. The following example illustrates that this may be the case even for a very simple problem.

Example 1. Consider the problem constituted by the constraints $X \neq Z$, $Z \neq Y$ and $Y \neq X$, where X, Y and Z are fd-variables ranging respectively over the finite domains $D_X = D_Y = D_Z = \{0, 1\}$. By enforcing arc-consistency we do not remove any value from the domain. However, in this case there are no consistent assignment of values to the fd-variables that could satisfy all the constraints.

The fact that globally inconsistent values are not ruled out has bad consequences

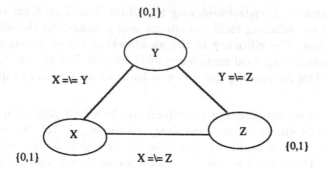

Fig. 1.

on the efficiency of the search procedure. Indeed, the inconsistencies will be detected only later on in the search after some labelings of fd-variables have taken place.

These facts suggest that it could be useful to provide constraint logic languages dealing with constraints over finite domains with stronger constraint-handling methods. In particular, in this paper we will discuss the possibility of integrating methods that refine finite domains by removing values that are inconsistent with respect to more than a single constraint. More precisely, we will consider local consistency methods based on the notion of *path-consistency*. For example, by enforcing path-consistency the global inconsistency of the problem shown in the example 1 would be detected because all the values would be removed from the domains. Of course, the greater domain-refinement power of path-consistency methods has to be measured with the fact that they are computationally more expensive (but still polynomial as the arc-consistency methods: see [26, 27, 33]).

In the following we discuss how to embed methods based on the notion of path-consistency in the constraint logic language clp(FD). As we will show, the integration of path-consistency methods in the clp(FD) system can be realized in a way that conforms to the glass-box approach. Besides the indexical constraints X *in* r, we will consider another primitive constraint $[X, Y]$ *in* m that we call *m-constraint*, whose range m encodes path-consistency methods. These new constraints increase the constraint-solving power and the extensibility of the clp(FD) language. We will also show that the clp(FD) architecture can be minimally extended to accommodate these new constraints.

Plan of the paper. The paper is organized as follows. The next two sections provide the formal framework for the integration of path-consistency methods in clp(FD). More precisely, in the next section 2 we recall basis notions about constraint satisfaction, in particular that of path-consistency; then, in section 3 we formalize the path-consistency refinement method, by using the formalism given by Montanari [28]. In section 4 we introduce the new clp(FD) primitive constraints and we discuss some issue related to their definition and use. The next section 5 is devoted to show how to extend the clp(FD) language by means of the m-constraints. Finally, section 6 concludes by discussing future work.

2 Constraint satisfaction

In this section we revisit some basic notions concerning constraint satisfaction methods. In particular, we focus our attention on the notion of path-consistency. A good reference to this topic is [33] (see also [23] for a shorter overview).

2.1 Consistency satisfaction problems

A *consistency satisfaction problem* (CSP for short) consists of a set of *fd-variables*[2] $X_1, \ldots, X_n$, allowed to take values in *finite domains* $D_{X_1}, \ldots, D_{X_n}$, and of a set of *constraints* $C_1, \ldots, C_e$. Every constraint C_k is defined on some fd-variables $var(C_k) = \{X_1, \ldots, X_{l_k}\}$, where l_k is the *arity*, as a subset of $D_{X_1} \times \ldots \times D_{X_{l_k}}$. Solving a CSP means finding one or all the assignments of values to the fd-variables such that all the constraints are satisfied.

CSPs can be depicted by means of a *constraint hypergraph* (sometimes also called *constraint network*) where nodes represent fd-variables and hyperarcs represent constraints. Here we represent an *n*-ary constraint C by n directed hyperarcs denoted $C_{X_1 X_2 X_3 \ldots X_n}, C_{X_2 X_1 X_3 \ldots X_n}, \ldots, C_{X_n X_1 X_2 \ldots X_{n-1}}$, where $var(C) = \{X_1, \ldots, X_n\}$. Therefore, in the following we will use "(hyper)arc" and "(hyper)path" as synonymous respectively of "directed constraint" and "sequence of directed constraits".

2.2 Local Consistency

CSPs are in general NP-complete (see [33, 23]). Several *local consistency* techniques have been designed in AI to prune the search space of CSPs. As said in the introduction, local consistency techniques work by considering a subproblem of the original one, that is a subcollection of fd-variables and constraints, and by enforcing local consistency on it. Enforcing local consistency means refining the domains of these fd-variables by removing from their domain the values that are inconsistent with these constraints. In particular, the notions of *arc-consistency* and *path-consistency* have been introduced [28, 24, 25].

$$\forall\, a \in D_X \,\exists\, b \in D_Y$$

such that $C_{XY}(a, b)$ holds

---

[2] In the CSP context they are simply called variables. Here we use a different terminology to distinguish them from the logical variables ranging over the (infinite) Herbrand Universe.

Applying the *arc-consistency refinement* (AC-Revise) procedure [24] to a constraint consists in removing from the domains of its fd-variables all the values that cannot make the constraint arc-consistent. Enforcing arc-consistency on a constraint network consists in repeatedly applying the AC-Revise procedure to each constraint until no further refinement is obtained [24, 33].

The AC-Revise procedure is at the basis of the algorithms for enforcing arc-consistency on a CSP: AC-1 [28], AC-2 and AC-3 [24], AC-4 [27] and the specialized algorithms AC-5 [37] and AC-6 [3].

The generalization of this notion for n-ary constraints ($n \geq 2$) is immediate. An hyperarc $C_{X,Y_1,\dots,Y_{n-1}}$ is *(hyper)arc-consistent* if:

$$\forall \, a \in D_X \; \exists \, (b_1, \dots, b_{n-1}) \in (D_{Y_1} \times \dots \times D_{Y_{n-1}})$$

$$\text{such that } C_{XY_1 \dots Y_{n-1}}(a, b_1, \dots, b_{n-1})$$

Besides *full* AC-Revise procedures, also *partial* AC-Revise (PAC-Revise) procedures have been designed. Partial methods do not necessarily remove all the (arc-)inconsistent values from the domains of the fd-variables. For example, PAC-Revise procedures can be obtained by considering the fd-variables Y as ranging over the interval approximation $I_Y = \{b \mid min(D_Y) \leq b \geq max(D_Y)\}$ of their real domains D_Y [35]. An example of these partial procedures is provided by the *sup-inf* method used in CHIP for handling linear (in)equalities over natural numbers [35]. It has been shown that in many cases such weaker, but cheaper, methods can be as effective as the full AC-Revise method in pruning the search space [35, 12].

2.3 Path-consistency

As above, we first give the definition of path-consistency in the simpler case of binary constraints and then in the general case.

An $(m-1)$-length path of arcs $(C_{Z_1 Z_2}, \dots, C_{Z_{m-1} Z_m})$ is *path-consistent* if [28, 24]:

$$\forall \, (b_1, b_m) \in (D_{Z_1} \times D_{Z_m}) \text{ such that } C_{Z_1 Z_m}(b_1, b_m) \text{ holds}$$

$$\exists \, (b_2, \dots, b_{m-1}) \in (D_{Z_2} \times \dots \times D_{Z_{m-1}})$$

$$\text{such that } C_{Z_i Z_{i+1}}(b_i, b_{i+1}) \text{ holds } \forall \, i \in \{1, \dots, m-1\}$$

The constraint on the pairs of values for the fd-variables Z_1 and Z_m expressed by this formula is referred to as the *induced constraint*. We denote it $C_{Z_1 Z_m}^{path(Z_2 \dots Z_{m-1})}$.

The *path-consistency refinement* (PC-Revise) procedure applied to the path $(C_{Z_1 Z_2}, \dots, C_{Z_{m-1} Z_m})$ consists in inducing the constraint $C_{Z_1 Z_m}^{path(Z_2 \dots Z_{m-1})}$, that is in removing those pairs of values for the fd-variables Z_1 and Z_m such that the constraints along the path cannot be satisfied by assigning values to the fd-variables $Z_2, \dots, Z_{m-1}$. Enforcing path-consistency consists in repeatedly applying PC-Revise to each possible path until no more refinements are obtained [28, 24, 33].

The PC-Revise procedure is at the basis of the algorithms for enforcing path-consistency on a CSP: PC-1 [28], PC-2 [24], PC-3 and PC-4 [27, 18].

Montanari proved that for attaining path-consistency it is sufficient to consider the notion of *2-length* path-consistency [28]. This result is reported by [24] as "Montanari's theorem": "If every path of length 2 of a network with a complete graph is path-consistent the network is path consistent". Notice that the assumption that the constraint graph is complete is not restrictive, insofar the constraint network can always be completed by means of "true" constraints. Therefore, achieving path-consistency may modify the structure of the original constraint network. Nevertheless, in the following we consider also with paths of length *more* than two. In section 4 we will account for the choice of keeping a general definition of path-consistency.

Let us now consider the general definition of path-consistency for n-ary constraints ($n \geq 2$). We first introduce some useful notation and terminology.

A *(hyper)path* is specified by a sequence of hyperarcs $C_1, \ldots, C_m$ such that $var(C_i) \cap var(C_{i+1}) \neq \emptyset \ \forall \, i \in \{1, \ldots, m-1\}$ and by a sequence of fd-variables $Z_1, \ldots, Z_m$ such that $Z_1 \in var(C_1)$, $Z_m \in var(C_m)$ and $Z_j \in (var(C_j) \cap var(C_{j+1})) \ \forall \, j \in \{2, \ldots, m-1\}$. We will refer to $C_1, \ldots, C_m$ as to the *path-constraints* and to $Z_1, \ldots, Z_m$ as to the *path-fd-variables*. Given a (hyper)path, in order to single out path-fd-variables Z_i and Z_{i+1} in a path-constraint C from the other fd-variables $\tilde{W}_{i,j} = var(C) \setminus \{Z_i, Z_{i+1}\}$, we let $C_{Z_i Z_j \tilde{W}_{i,j}}$ denote C.

Let C be an m-ary constraint and let $\tilde{W} = \{W_1, \ldots, W_l\} \subseteq var(C)$. An *fd-substitution* is standard substitution whose domain and range are fd-variables. We let $\Theta(\tilde{W})$ be the set of all the (ground) fd-substitutions $\{W_1/c_1, \ldots, W_l/c_l\}$ such that $(c_1, \ldots, c_l) \in (D_{W_1} \times \ldots \times D_{W_l})$. Let $\theta \in \Theta(\tilde{W})$. We let $C\,\theta$ the application of θ to C. In particular, we will consider fd-substitutions $\theta \in \Theta(\tilde{W}_{i,j})$ instantiating all but two of the fd-variables of a constraint $C_{Z_i Z_j \tilde{W}_{i,j}}$.

Now we can give the general definition of path-consistency.

Intuitively, a (hyper)path $(C_{Z_1 Z_2 \tilde{W}_{1,2}}, \ldots, C_{Z_{m-1} Z_m \tilde{W}_{m-1,m}})$ is (hyper)path-consistent if for each pair of values for Z_1 and Z_m there is at least one assignment of values to all the path-fd-variables $\{Z_2, \ldots, Z_{m-1}\}$ *as well as* to all the others fd-variable $W_1, \ldots, W_l$ involved in the path-constraints and in $C_{Z_1 Z_m \tilde{W}_{1,m}}$) such that all these constraints are satisfied. Hereafter follows the formal definition.

An (hyper)path $(C_{Z_1 Z_2 \tilde{W}_{1,2}}, \ldots, C_{Z_{m-1} Z_m \tilde{W}_{m-1,m}})$ is *(hyper)path consistent* if:

$$\forall \, (b_1, b_m) \in (D_{Z_1} \times D_{Z_m})$$
$$\exists \, \theta \in \Theta(\{Z_2, \ldots, Z_{m-1}\} \cup \{W_1, \ldots, W_l\})$$

such that

$$C_{Z_1 Z_m \tilde{W}_{1,m}} \, \theta \ \text{holds, and}$$
$$C_{Z_i Z_{i+1} \tilde{W}_{m-1,m}} \, \theta \ \text{holds} \ \forall \, i \in \{1, \ldots, m-1\}$$

Notice that, since a path-fd-variable Z_k may be also a *non*-path-fd-variable for other constraints, we have that $\tilde{W}_{1,2} \cup \ldots \cup \tilde{W}_{m-1,m} \cup \tilde{W}_{1,m} \subseteq \{W_1, \ldots, W_l\} \cup \{Z_1, \ldots, Z_m\}$.

Before ending this section, it is worth noticing that, as for the AC-Revise procedure it is possible to define *partial* (in opposition to *full*) PC-Revise (PPC-Revise) procedures. These partial procedures would not necessarily remove all the (path-)inconsistent pairs of values but could be useful in some cases to achieve path-consistency at a cheaper price.

For example a possible PPC-Revise could by defined by considering the fd-variables Z as ranging over the interval approximation I_Z of their real domains D_Z. Seemingly, this interesting point has not yet been investigated. In section 4 we will discuss furtherly this point.

3 Constraint satisfaction methods

In this section we formalize the local consistency methods presented in the previous section, and in particular the PC-Revise method, by making use of the formalism introduced by Montanari in his seminal paper [28].

3.1 Operators for binary constraints

As usual, first we restrict to consider binary constraints and then we discuss the general case.

A binary relation (constraint) C_{XY} between two fd-variables X and Y can be represented as $(N \times M)$-matrix 0-1 matrix, N and M being respectively the size of the corresponding finite domains D_X and D_Y. This matrix, that we denote $m[C_{XY}]$, is defined as follows: the element of row r and column s, denoted $m[C_{XY}][r, s]$, is 1 if $C_{XY}(r, s)$ holds, 0 otherwise. Notice that $m[C_{YX}] = m[C_{XY}]^T$, that is the matrix representing the inverse relation is the transposed matrix of the ones representing the direct relation. By $m[D_Z]$ we denote the square matrix representing the domain of the fd-variable Z that is the matrix defined as $m[D_Z][r, r] = 1$ if $r \in D_Z$ and 0 everywhere else. Moreover, by $m[D_{XY}]$ we denote the matrix defined as $m[D_{XY}][r, s] = 1$ if $r \in D_X$ and $s \in D_Y$, 0 everywhere else.

Montanari defined some operators on binary constraints [28] that provide a convenient formalism for expliciting local consistency conditions.

Let $m[C'_{XZ}]$ and $m[C''_{XZ}]$ be two matrices representing respectively the two constraints C'_{XZ} and C''_{XZ}, between X and Z. We define the operations (and corresponding operators) on constraints (on their matricial representation) of *negation* ($\ominus$), *disjunction* ($\oplus$) and *conjunction* ($\otimes$) as follows:

$$\ominus(m[C_{XZ}])[r, s] = \neg m[C_{XZ}][r, s]$$

$$(m[C'_{XZ}] \oplus m[C''_{XZ}])[r, s] = m[C'_{XZ}][r, s] \vee m[C''_{XZ}][r, s]$$

$$(m[C'_{XZ}] \otimes m[C''_{XZ}])[r, s] = m[C'_{XZ}][r, s] \wedge m[C''_{XZ}][r, s]$$

The *empty constraint* $false_{XZ}$ disallowing any pair of values is represented by the matrix $\emptyset_{XZ}$ defined as $\emptyset_{XZ}[r, s] = 0$. The *universal constraint* $true_{XZ}$ allowing any pair of values is represented by the matrix U_{XZ} defined as $U_{XZ}[r, s] =$

1. As said, if in the constraint graph there is not an arc between two nodes X and Z, the constraint between C_{XZ} them is implicitly $true_{XZ}$[3].

Let $m[C_{XZ}]$ and $m[C_{ZY}]$ be two matrices representing respectively the constraints C_{XZ} and C_{ZY}. We define the operation (and corresponding operator) of *composition* ($\odot$) as follows:

$$(m[C_{XZ}] \odot m[C_{ZY}])[r,s] = \bigvee_t (m[C_{XZ}][r,t] \wedge m[C_{ZY}][t,s])$$

This operation is the standard *row by column* matrix product when the result is normalized to 1. Composition is associative but it is not distributive over intersection, that is in general $M_{XZ} \odot (M'_{ZY} \otimes M''_{ZY}) \neq (M_{XZ} \odot M'_{ZY}) \otimes (M_{XZ} \odot M''_{ZY})$ (see [28]).

The PC-Revise method can be formalized by translating, by a straightforward way, the path-consistency condition for binary constraints in terms of matrices and the above-described operators. Indeed, since fd-variables range over finite domains, existential and universal quantifications in the corresponding formulas are replaced respectively by disjunction and conjunction.

PC-Revise The PC-Revise procedure for an m-length path of binary constraints $(C_{Z_1 Z_2}, C_{Z_{m-1} Z_m})$ can be written as follows [28, 33]:

$$m[C_{Z_1 Z_m}^{path(Z_2,\ldots,Z_{m-1})}] = m[C_{Z_1 Z_m}] \otimes (m[C_{Z_1 Z_2}] \odot$$
$$m[D_{Z_2}] \odot m[C_{Z_2 Z_3}] \odot$$
$$\odot \ldots \odot$$
$$\odot m[D_{Z_{m-1}}] \odot m[C_{Z_{m-1} Z_m}])$$

As it is easy to see the worst-case time complexity of the PC-Revise procedure for an $(m-1)$-length path is polynomial: $\mathcal{O}(md^3)$, d being the maximal size of the finite domains (see also [28, 27, 33]). Notice that time complexity of the AC-Revise procedure for binary constraints is $\mathcal{O}(d^2)$ (or even less for PAC-Revise procedures: the sup-inf method is $\mathcal{O}(d)$).

---

[3] It is possible (see [28]) to define the partial ordering relation $\sqsubseteq$ between constraints as the set inclusion, that is in terms of their matricial representation: $C'_{XZ} \sqsubseteq C''_{XZ}$ iff $m[C'_{XZ}][r,s] < m[C''_{XZ}][r,s] \; \forall s,t$. Constraints between two fd-variables X and Z form a complete lattice with greatest element represented by U_{XZ} and least element represented by $\emptyset_{XZ}$ where the operations of *glb* and *lub* coincide with conjunction and disjunction respectively on their matricial representation.

3.2 Approximating n-ary constraints by means of binary constraints

Till now we have dealt with binary constraints. As noticed by Montanari, it would be possible to extend the formalization to n-ary constraint ($n \geq 2$) in a straightforward way but this it would be unlikely worthwhile given the cost of representing and manipulating them [28]. Therefore, following [28], we approximate n-ary constraints by means of binary constraints.

In order to define this approximation we introduce some others operators on relations. Let C be an n-ary constraint and let $var(C) = \{W\} \cup \{Z_1, \ldots, Z_{n-1}\}$. We define the *variable-elimination operator* $\exists_W$ as follows:

$$\exists_W(C) = \{(b_1, \ldots, b_{n-1}) \in (D_{Z_1}, \ldots, D_{Z_{n-1}}) \mid \exists\, \theta \in \Theta(\{W\})$$

$$\text{such that } C\, \theta(b_1, \ldots, b_{n-1}) \text{ holds}\}$$

The result of applying $\exists_W$ to C is an $(n-1)$-ary relation obtained by C allowing the fd-variable W to take any possible value. This operation corresponds to take in the look-up table representation of C only the columns corresponding to the fd-variables *other than* W and merging repeated tuples. Composition of variable-elimination operators is commutative:

$$\exists_{W_2}(\exists_{W_1}(C)) = \exists_{W_1}(\exists_{W_2}(C))$$

Therefore we denote $\exists_{W_l}(\ldots(\exists_{W_1}(C))\ldots)$, where $W_i \in var(C)\ \forall\, i \in \{1, \ldots, l\}$, by $\exists_{W_1 \ldots W_l}(C)$. Now let C be an n-ary constraint and let $var(C) = \{W_1, \ldots, W_l\} \cup \{Z_1, \ldots, Z_{n-l}\}$. We define the *projection operator* $\pi_{Z_1 \ldots Z_{n-l}}$ as follows:

$$\pi_{Z_1 \ldots Z_{n-l}}(C) = \exists_{W_1 \ldots W_l}(C)$$

Thus, binary constraints approximating the n-ary constraint C are those obtained by considering all the possible projections to two of its fd-variables[4]:

$$\{C'_{ij} \mid C'_{ij} = \pi_{Z_i Z_j} C \text{ where } Z_i, Z_j \in var(C)\}$$

If n-ary constraints are approximated by means of binary constraints, the path-consistency formula for a path $(C_{Z_1 Z_2 \tilde{W}_{1,2}}, \ldots, C_{Z_{m-1} Z_m \tilde{W}_{m-1,m}})$ (refer to section 2.3) can be written as follows:

$$\forall\, (b_1, b_m) \in (D_{Z_1}, D_{Z_m}$$

$$\exists\, \theta \in \Theta(\{Z_2, \ldots, Z_{m-1}\})$$

$$\text{such that}$$

$$\exists\, \theta_{1,m} \in \Theta(\tilde{W}_{1,m}) \text{ such that } C_{Z_1 Z_m \tilde{W}_{1,m}} \theta_{1,m} \theta \text{ holds, and}$$

$$\exists\, \theta_{i,i+1} \in \Theta(\tilde{W}_{i,i+1}) \text{ such that } C_{Z_i Z_{i+1} \tilde{W}_{m-1,m}} \theta_{i,i+1} \theta \text{ holds } \forall\, i \in \{1, \ldots, m-1\}$$

---

[4] Montanari showed that by applying this approximation to a constraint we obtain a minimal (with respect to $\subseteq$) network between those representing the original one [28].

Therefore we are first approximate the n-ary constraints by binary constraints and then we consider the satisfaction of these binary constraints. Visually, this can be seen as moving the existential quantifiers over the fd-variables that are not path-fd-variables down to the conjuncts in the formula expressing the path-consistency condition. Thus, the fact that in this way we obtain a weaker path-consistency condition can be easily understood by considering that the formula $\exists (p(X) \wedge q(X))$ implies $\exists p(X) \wedge \exists q(X)$ but the vice-versa does not.

PC-Revise The PC-Revise procedure for a path of constraints

$$(C_{Z_1 Z_2 \tilde{W}_{1,2}}, \ldots, C_{Z_{m-1} Z_m \tilde{W}_{m-1,m}})$$

can be written as follows:

$$m[C^{path(Z_2 \ldots Z_{m-1})}_{Z_1 Z_m}] = m[\pi_{Z_1 Z_m}(C_{Z_1 Z_m \tilde{W}_{1,m}})] \otimes (\, m[\pi_{Z_1 Z_m}(C_{Z_1 Z_m \tilde{W}_{1,m}})] \odot$$

$$\odot \, m[D_{Z_2}] \odot m[\pi_{Z_2 Z_3}(C_{Z_2 Z_3 \tilde{W}_{2,3}})] \odot$$

$$\odot \ldots \odot$$

$$m[D_{Z_{m-1}}] \odot m[\pi_{Z_{m-1} Z_m}(C_{Z_{m-1} Z_m \tilde{W}_{m-1,m}})] \,)$$

where the matrix corresponding to the binary constraint $\pi_{Z_i Z_j}(C_{Z_i Z_j \tilde{W}_{i,j}})$ can be defined in as follows:

$$m[\pi_{Z_i Z_j}(C_{Z_i Z_j \tilde{W}_{i,j}})] = \bigoplus_{\theta \in \Theta(\tilde{W}_{i,j})} m[C_{Z_i Z_j \tilde{W}_{i,j}} \; \theta]$$

Therefore, in the following we can consider only binary constraints, possibly obtained by projecting n-ary constraints.

4 Defining M-constraints: $[X, Y]$ in m

As anticipated in the introduction, methods for enforcing path-consistency can be made available in clp(FD) by defining new primitive constraints, that we call *m-constraints*. In this section we introduce these new constraints and discuss some issues related to their definition and use. A formal definition of the m-constraints will be given in the next section when we will describe how to embed these new primitive constraints in the clp(FD) system.

4.1 Indexical constraints

As said in the introduction, in the clp(FD) language the only primitive constraints are the indexical constraints X in r, that here we will call shortly *i-constraints*. The range r is an expression (see [6] for the syntax) which encodes (partial) arc-consistency conditions. For example the constraint $X = Y + 1$ can be handled by using either *partial* or *full* arc-consistency methods. The corresponding arc-consistency conditions for updating the domain of X (the ones for Y being similar) are

$$\forall \, a \in D_X \; \exists \, b \in D_Y \text{ such that } a = b + 1$$

and

$$\forall\, a \in D_X \ \exists\, b \in I_Y \text{ such that } a = b + 1$$

They can be encoded respectively as follows:

$$X \ in \ dom(Y) + 1$$

and

$$X \ in \ min(Y) + 1..max(Y) + 1$$

The i-constraint X *in* r specifies the allowed values for the *constrained fd-variable* X when the arc-consistency condition encoded in r is computed. That is, if r_X is the range obtained by computing the expression r, the refined domain D'_X of X is:

$$D'_X \ \leftarrow \ r_X \cap D_X$$

Three cases may occur when computing an i-constraint: a *failure* if $D'_X = \emptyset$; an *OK-check* if $D'_X = D_X$; otherwise, a *domain-refinement* and a consequent *propagation* of this refinement to i-constraints referring the fd-variable X in their range. In the two last cases the i-constraint is also *suspended*, that is it is not removed from the store so to be possibly reconsidered again. Actually, the mechanism for waking suspended i-constraints is more sophisticated: if in the range of an i-constraint X occurs as $min(X)$ (resp. as $max(X)$) then the i-constraint is reconsidered only if the minimum (resp. the maximum) value allowed for X is changed.

The range of i-constraints can also encode *delaying mechanisms*. For example the i-constraint:

$$X \ in \ val(Y) + 1$$

is executed only when the fd-variable Y has a definite (i.e. unique) value.

4.2 M-constraints

In order to introduce path-consistency methods in clp(FD) we exploit the same idea used for embedding arc-consistency methods. That is, we define new primitive constraints $[X, Y]$ *in* m that we call *m-constraints* (standing for *matrix constraints*). The "range" m of an m-constraint is an expression encoding path-consistency conditions. Range expression for m-constraints are built over matrices representing relations and over the operators introduced in section 3. The formal syntax of m-constraints will be given in section 5.

Intuitively, $[X, Y]$ *in* m specify the allowed values for the pair of *constrained fd-variables* $[X, Y]$ when the path-consistency condition encoded in m is computed. That is, if m_{XY} is the "range" obtained by computing the expression m, the refined domain D_{XY} of $[X, Y]$ is:

$$D'_{XY} \ \leftarrow \ m_{XY} \cap D_{XY}$$

Since the result of computing the range will be a matrix m_{XY}, the matrix $m[D'_{XY}]$ representing the refined domain for $[X, Y]$ is:

$$m[D'_{XY}] \ \leftarrow \ m_{XY} \otimes m[D_{XY}]$$

Initially, the domain D_{XY} is given by all the possible pairs of allowed values for X and Y, that is it is represented by the matrix U_{XY}. As for i-constraints, three cases may occur when an m-constraint is computed: if $D'_{XY} = \emptyset$ then *failure*; if $D'_{XY} = D_{XY}$ then *OK-check*; otherwise, a *refinement* of D_{XY} and a consequent *propagation* of the refinement to m-constraints referencing the domain of $[X, Y]$ in their range. In the last two cases, the m-constraint is *suspended*. In particular, if D_{XY} when is refined becomes a singleton then the fd-variables X and Y get instantiated and propagation also to i-constraints referring to them in their range occurs. This mechanism provides one side of the interface between fd-variables and pairs of fd-variables. The other side of the interface is provided by the propagation of the domain refinements for X and Y to m-constraints constraining at least one of these fd-variables.

In the following we show some examples that should clarify how m-constraints can be defined and computed.

First of all, we want to show how refining the domain for a pair of fd-variables by computing an m-constraint codifying a path-consistency condition corresponds to inducing in the constraint graph the constraint obtained by enforcing this path-consistency condition.

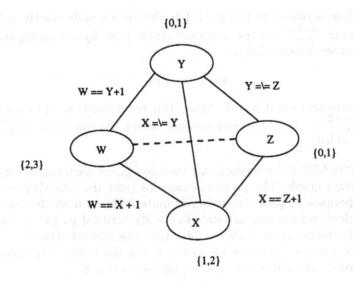

Fig. 2.

Example 2. The problem consisting of the constraints $W = X + 1$, $X = Z + 1$, $Z \neq Y$, $X \neq Y$ and $W = Y + 2$ and of the finite-domains $D_X = \{1, 2\}$, $D_Y = D_Z = \{0, 1\}$ and $D_W = \{2, 3\}$ is unsatisfiable[5]. The (global) inconsistency of

---

[5] Notice that in this case the problem is unsatisfiable whatever are the domains of the variables and even if the constraint $X \neq Y$ is removed.

the problem can be detected by enforcing path-consistency but not by enforcing arc-consistency.

Let us now consider the m-constraints

$$[Z, W] \ in \ m[Z = X - 1] \odot m[D_X] \odot m[X = W - 1]$$

and

$$[X, W] \ in \ m[X = W - 1] \otimes (m[X = Z + 1] \odot m[D_Z] \odot m[D_{ZW}])$$

and suppose that before computing these m-constraints the domain for $[Z, W]$ and $[X, W]$ was the initial domain represented by U_{ZW} and U_{XW}, respectively. Then, by computing the second m-constraint m-constraint we get

$$m_{XW} = \begin{vmatrix} 1 & 0 \\ 0 & 1 \end{vmatrix}$$

and D_{XW} is refined to $\{\langle 1, 2 \rangle, \langle 2, 3 \rangle\}$. By computing the first m-constraint, we obtain the following matrix:

$$m_{ZW} = \begin{vmatrix} 0 & 1 \\ 1 & 0 \end{vmatrix}$$

and thus D_{ZW} is refined to $\{\langle 1, 2 \rangle, \langle 0, 3 \rangle\}$. This corresponds exactly to inducing the constraints $C_{ZW}^{path(X)}$ in the constraint graph. Now, by computing the second m-constraint we obtain a failure:

$$m_{XW} = \emptyset_{XW}$$

i.e. the inconsistency is detected. Again, this corresponds to inducing the constraint $C_{XW}^{path(Z)}$ in the constraint network where the constraint $C_{ZW}^{path(X)}$ was previously added.

As said, in CSP PC-x methods are used to enforce path-consistency on the whole (binary) graph. The previous examples (and the following ones) show that our approach to path-consistency is quite different from the one adopted in CSP. Indeed, we use m-constraints to specify "critical paths" of constraints where path-consistency methods are intended to be applied. Therefore, the user is allowed/requested to use the knowledge about the problem to specify these "critical paths". We will return on this point in section 5.

As mentioned in the previous section we do not restrain our attention on 2-length paths. The following example should clarify our choice.

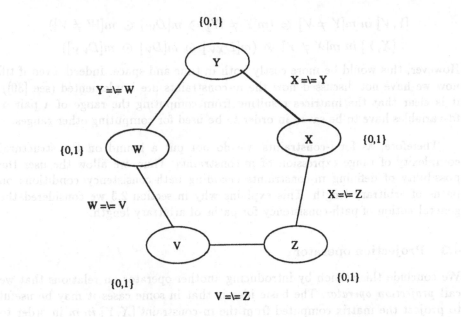

Fig. 3.

Example 3. Consider the problem consisting of the constraints $X \neq Z$, $Z \neq V$, $V \neq W$, $W \neq Y$, $Y \neq X$ and the finite-domains $D_X = D_Z = D_V = D_W = D_Y = \{0, 1\}$. It is unsatisfiable and, again, the (global) inconsistency of the problem can be detected by enforcing path-consistency but not by enforcing arc-consistency.

Let us consider the m-constraint

$$[X, Y] \text{ in } m[X \neq Y] \otimes (m[X \neq Z] \odot m[D_Z] \odot m[Z \neq V] \odot m[D_V] \odot$$

$$\odot m[V \neq W] \odot m[D_W] \odot m[W \neq Y])$$

Computing this m-constraint corresponds to inducing $C_{XY}^{path(ZVW)}$ by enforcing path-consistency on the 5-length path $(C_{XZ}, C_{ZV}, C_{VW}, C_{WY})$. Indeed, by computing it we obtain a failure:

$$m_{XY} = \emptyset_{XY}$$

so detecting the inconsistency. As mentioned in section 2, algorithms for enforcing path-consistency would enforce path-consistency on all possible 2-length paths until quiescience (no more refinements) or failure is reached. Therefore, inconsistency could be detected by enforcing $C_{XV}^{path(XZV)}$, inducing $X \neq V$, $C_{YV}^{path(YVW)}$, inducing $Y \neq V$, and finally $C_{XY}^{path(XVY)}$. This would correspond in our approach to computing the following m-constraints:

$$[X, V] \text{ in } m[X \neq V] \otimes (m[X \neq Z] \odot m[D_Z] \odot m[Z \neq V])$$

$$[Y, V] \ in \ m[Y \neq V] \otimes (m[Y \neq W] \odot m[D_W] \odot m[W \neq V])$$
$$[X, Y] \ in \ m[X \neq Y] \otimes (m[D_{XV}] \odot m[D_V] \odot m[D_{VY}])$$

However, this would be more costly both in time and space. Indeed, even if till now we have not discussed how the m-constraints are implemented (see [30]), it is clear that the matrices resulting from computing the range of a pair of fd-variables have to be saved in order to be used for computing other ranges.

Therefore, as for i-constraints, we do not put a bound on the structural complexity of range expression of m-constraints. Thus, we allow the user the possibility of defining m-constraints encoding path-consistency conditions on paths of arbitrary length. This explains why in section 2.3 we considered the general notion of path-consistency for paths of arbitrary length.

4.3   Projection operator

We conclude this section by introducing another operator on relations that we call *projection operator*. The basic idea is that in some cases it may be useful to project the matrix computed from the m-constraint $[X, Y]$ *in* m in order to propagate the inferred information directly to the domains D_X and D_Y of the fd-variables. The following example illustrates this point.

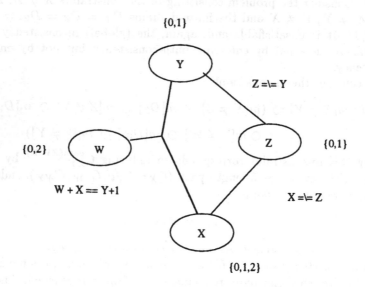

Fig. 4.

Example 4. Consider the problem consisting of the constraints $X \neq Z$, $Z \neq Y$, $W + X = Y + 1$ and of the finite-domains $D_X = \{0, 1, 2\}$, $D_Y = D_Z = \{0, 1\}$ and

$D_W = \{0, 2\}$. Again the problem is unsatisfiable and while this can be detected by enforcing path-consistency, it cannot by enforcing arc-consistency.

Let us consider the m-constraint

$$[X, Y] \ in \ m[\pi_{XY}(W + X = Y + 1)] \otimes (m[X \neq Z] \odot m[D_Z] \odot m[Z \neq Y])$$

which corresponds to inducing $C_{XYW}^{path(Z)}$. Notice that $\pi_{XY}(W + X = Y + 1) \equiv (X \neq Y)$. By computing it, we obtain the matrix

$$m_{XY} = \begin{vmatrix} 0 & 0 \\ 0 & 0 \\ 1 & 1 \end{vmatrix}$$

that is we get the domain for $[X, Y]$ refined to $\{\langle 2, 0 \rangle, \langle 2, 1 \rangle\}$. Here we see that the only allowed value for X is 2. This information could be extracted by *projecting* the computed matrix on the domains of the constrained fd-variables.

Therefore, we introduce the *range projection operator* $\textcircled{\pi}$ and allow the range of an m-constraint to be $\textcircled{\pi}(m)$. Computing $[X, Y] \ in \ \textcircled{\pi}(m)$ amounts in this case to computing D'_{XY} and performing the following projection operations on the constrained fd-variables:

$$D'_X \leftarrow \pi_X \ D'_{XY}$$

$$D'_Y \leftarrow \pi_Y \ D'_{XY}$$

This way we realize a tighter interface between fd-variables and pairs of fd-variables, and hence, a more powerful interaction between m-constraints and i-constraints.

The following example shows how the two kinds of primitive constraints in clp(FD) can be effectively used in combination.

Example 5. The problem consisting of the constraints $X \neq Z$, $Z \neq Y$, $Y \neq X$, $W > X$ and $W = Y + 2$ and of the finite-domains $D_X = \{0, 1, 2\}$, $D_Y = D_Z = \{0, 1\}$, $D_W = \{2, 3\}$ admits only one solution. No domain would be refined by enforcing arc-consistency procedure. On the contrary inconsistent assignments are ruled out by enforcing path-consistency.

By computing the m-constraint

$$[X, Y] \ in \ \textcircled{\pi}(m[X \neq Y] \otimes (m[X \neq Z] \odot m[D_Z] \odot m[Z \neq Y]))$$

we obtain

$$m_{XY} = \begin{vmatrix} 0 & 0 \\ 0 & 0 \\ 1 & 1 \end{vmatrix}$$

that is, that $D_X = \{2\}$. On the contrary, by computing

$$[X, Y] \ in \ \textcircled{\pi}(m[X \neq Y] \otimes (m[X < W] \odot m[D_W] \odot m[W = Y + 2]))$$

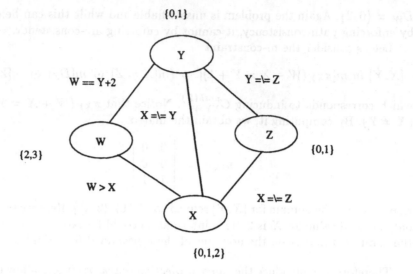

Fig. 5.

we obtain

$$m_{XY} = \begin{vmatrix} 0 & 1 \\ 1 & 0 \\ 0 & 1 \end{vmatrix}$$

and no domain refinement.

Let us now compute the m-constraint

$$[X, Y] \text{ in } m[X \neq Y] \otimes (m[X \neq Z] \odot m[D_Z] \odot m[Z \neq Y]) \otimes$$

$$\otimes (m[X < W] \odot m[D_W] \odot m[W = Y + 2])$$

encoding $m[C_{XY}^{path(Z)}] \otimes m[C_{XY}^{path(W)}]$, conjuction of the conditions encoded by the previous two m-constraints, we obtain

$$m_{XY} = \begin{vmatrix} 0 & 0 \\ 0 & 0 \\ 0 & 1 \end{vmatrix}$$

that is, $D_X = \{2\}$ and $D_Y = \{1\}$. However, since m-constraints can be very costly it is better to use them thriftly to trigger a possibly suspended computation without having to start labeling fd-variables and to rely on i-constraints for the propagation. For example in this specific problem an i-constraint of the kind

$$Y \text{ in } - val(X)$$

would instantiate as Y as a side-effect of the propagation of the refinement for D_X.

A final remark concerns the policy to be adopted for waking suspended constraints. Indeed, since m-constraints are computationally more costly than i-constraints, it is better to wake up first i-constraints and then m-constraints. This way, m-constraints are used as triggers of constraint-solving phases avoiding possibly labeling phases and the propagation of the domain reductions relies primarily on i-constraints.

5 Embedding m-constraints in the clp(FD) system

In the previous section we discussed the definition of new primitive constraints of the form $[X, Y]$ *in* m as a way to embed path-consistency methods in clp(FD). Here we show how to extend the clp(FD) system to accommodate the new constraints. We also analyze a simple user-defined constraint in terms of both i-constraints and m-constraints and we discuss its use for a concrete example.

As described in the previous section, the integration of path-consistency methods can be made in conformity with the glass-box approach adopted in clp(FD). Therefore, the user is allowed to specify by means of m-constraints, *and* of i-constraints, new high-level constraints and to tailor the application of the available constraint-solving methods to the specific problem at hand.

The following table shows the syntax of m-constraints. The predicate p can be any well-defined relation on natural numbers (either a binary predicate or an n-ary predicate projected on two of its fd-variables). The table shows also the possibility of defining m-constraints encoding *partial* path-consistency methods by treating finite domains like intervals.

The expressions $min(X)$, $max(X)$ and $minmax(X)$ have an operational meaning: as in the case of i-constraints, they are used to wake m-constraints depending on the domain of the variable X respectively when the minimum, the maximum or one of these two is modified. It could also possible to enrich the language by defining val(X) delaying the computation of the range until the value of the fd-variable is defined (i.e. unique).

The integration of m-constraints in the clp(FD) increases the expressiveness and the power of the language. Indeed, high-level constraints can be defined in terms of i-constraints and m-constraints, so exploiting their combined constraint-solving and propagation power. As an example, we consider the user-defined constraint all_different(X,Y,Z) enforcing disequality constraints between three FD-variables.

```
all_different(X,Y,Z) :-
        different(X,Y),
        different(Y,Z),
        different(Z,X),
        [X, Y] in matrix(arg1 =/= arg2) conjm (matrix(dom([X,Z]))
        compm matrix(dom(Z)) compm matrix(dom([Z,Y]))),
```

$$
\begin{array}{lll}
C & ::= [X,Y] \text{ in } m_{XY} & range \\
& | \ [X,Y] \text{ in } \textcircled{\tiny T} \ m_{XY} & projected\ range \\[1em]
m_{X,Y} & \quad m_{XY} \oplus m_{XY} & disjunction \\
& | \ m_{XY} \otimes m_{XY} & conjunction \\
& | \ m_{XZ} \odot m_{ZY} & composition \\
& | \ \ominus m_{XY} & negation \\
& | \ \mathtt{matrix}[r_{XY}] & matrix \\
& | \ \mathtt{matrix}[r_{XX}] & square\ matrix \\[1em]
r_{XX} & ::= \mathtt{dom(X)} & domain \\
& | \ \mathtt{min(X)} \\
& | \ \mathtt{max(X)} \\
& | \ \mathtt{minmax(X)} \\[1em]
r_{XY} & ::= \mathtt{dom(X,Y)} & domain \\
& | \ \mathtt{p(X,Y)} & binary\ relation \\
& | \ \pi_{X,Y} \ \mathtt{p(\ldots,X,\ldots,Y,\ldots)} & n\text{-}ary\ relation
\end{array}
$$

Table 1. Syntax of m-constraints

```
[Y, Z]  in matrix(arg1 =/= arg2)  conjm (matrix(dom([Y,X]))
compm matrix(dom(X))  compm matrix(dom([X,Z])),
[Z, X]  in matrix(arg1 =/= arg2)  conjm (matrix(dom([Z,Y]))
compm matrix(dom(Y))  compm matrix(dom([Y,X]))).
```

where

```
different(X, Y) :-
        X in - val(Y),
        Y in - val(X).
```

encodes the condition that the allowed values for X have to be different from
the (definite) value of Y (and viceversa).

Let us analyze how this constraint is handled (refer to the semantics of m-
constraints given in section 3). Initially the matrices representing the domains of
the pair are the unit matrices U. Therefore, the first time the m-constraints are
computed the "ranges" of the pairs are set to the matrix representing the relation
$\neq$, i.e. the matrix having zeros on the main diagonal. Then, each time one of the
fd-variables whose domain occur in the right-hand-side of an m-constraint (e.g.
Z in the first one) gets its domain refined, the m-constraint is woken and the
domain of the corresponding pair (e.g. $[X,Y]$) is updated. Possibly, this leads to
a propagation to the other two m-constraints. In particular, if the "range" of a
pair of fd-variables gets refined to only one value, a propagation to the indexical

constraints (as well as to the m-constraints) depending on the domain of these fd-variables takes place.

In this way, even if the domain of the fd-variables has not been reduced to only one value (so that the indexical constraints could be used), still some refinement of the domains of the (pairs of) fd-variables could be performed. As mentioned in the introduction and in section 4, this may allow the detection of some global inconsistencies without having to resort to labelings. Now the question is whether the higher computational cost of the m-constraints is compensated by the additional constraint-solving power gained by using them. Indeed, it is well known in the CSP community that the embedding of PC-Revise in the backtracking procedure does not pay up. However, we argue that our approach to the integration of path-consistency methods is effective in practical problems.

A simple example of the use of m-constraints is provided by a general scheduling problem where a renewable resource is shared among a certain number of tasks, possibly sharing other resources. Only one task at time can use this resource. This problem can be modeled by considering an fd-variable for each task. The domain of the fd-variable represents the time points allowed for executing the tasks, and hence for using the resource. The fd-variables are constrained by disequalities. For simplicity sake, we consider only three tasks (and corresponding variables X_1, X_2 and X_3).

The situation is depicted in the figure, where the shadowed (possibly overlapping) areas of the constraint graph represent the subproblems sharing the resource.

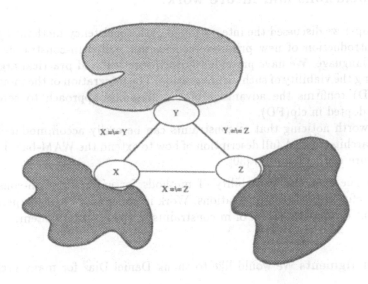

Fig. 6. A scheduling problem

Now, as already said, a constraint-handling based only on arc-consistency methods encoded in indexical constraints may fail to remove some inconsistencies, and, thus, to detect the inconsistency of the whole problem (see example 1) or to instantiate some fd-variables (see example 4). Consequently, the search could proceed – possibly uselessly – until a labeling procedure would eventually be activated. Notice that an (ad hoc) labelling heuristics would not be helpful in this respect.

On the contrary, the search for solutions might benefit from the early pruning operated by path-consistency methods. As said, this has a computational cost. However, the bigger is the size of the problem (i.e., in our example, of the subproblems for the three tasks sharing the resource), the more the cost of enforcing path-consistency on *some* fd-variables (i.e., on X_1, X_2 and X_3) would be less relevant. Therefore, in this problem the use of an user constraint like all_different(X_1, X_2, X_3) defined also in terms of m-constraints would be quite appropriate.

This simple example shows that in our extended clp(FD) language the user is provided a way of encoding in the constraint-solver the knowledge that some specific parts of the problem under consideration may deserve a special treatment. This should also clarify the emphasis we put on the importance of integrating path-consistency methods in a language adopting the *glass-box* approach to constraint solving. Indeed, only in this case the user is allowed to design a constraint solver tailored to the specific problem.

6 Conclusions and future work

In this paper we discussed the integration of path-consistency methods by means of the introduction of new primitive constraints, called m-constraints, in the clp(FD) language. We have presented both theoretical and practical arguments supporting the viability of such an integration. The integration of the m-constraints in clp(FD) confirms the advantage of the glass-box approach to constraint-solving adopted in clp(FD).

It is worth noticing that m-constraints can be easily accommodated in the clp(FD) architecture. A full description of how to extend the WAM-based clp(FD) architecture can be found in [30].

We argue that the availability of methods for enforcing path-consistency can be useful in practical applications. Work is under way on the experimental assessment of the integration of m-constraints in the clp(FD) system.

Acknowledgments We would like to thank Daniel Diaz for many useful discussions.

References

1. H. Aït-Kaci. *Warren's Abstract Machine.* The MIT Press, (1991).
2. A. Aggoun and N. Beldiceanu. Overview of the CHIP Compiler System. In Proc. Eighth Int. Conf. on Logic Programming (ICLP'91), Paris, France, The MIT Press, pp. 775-789 (1991). Also in *Constraint Logic Programming: selected research* (A. Colmerauer and F. Benhamou eds.), The MIT Press, (1993).
3. C. Bessière. Arc-consistency and arc-consistency again. Art. Int. 65, pp. 179-190, (1984).
4. P. Boizumault, Y. Delon, L. Péridy. Solving a Real-life Planning Exams Problem using Constraint Logic Programming. In *Constraint Processing – Proc. of the Int. WS at CSAM'93* (M. Meyer ed.), DFKI Research Report 93-39, pp.106-112, August (1993).
5. A. Colmerauer. An Introduction to Prolog III. ACM Comm., 33(7), pp. 70-90, July (1990).
6. D. Diaz and Ph. Codognet. A Minimal Extension of the WAM for clp(FD). In Proc. Tenth Int. Conf. on Logic Programming (ICLP'93), Budapest, Hungary, The MIT Press, pp.774-790 (1993).
7. Ph. Codognet and D. Diaz. Compiling Constraints in clp(FD). Tech. Rep. INRIA (1993).
8. Ph. Codognet and D. Diaz. Local Propagation Methods for Solving Boolean Constraints in Constraint Logic Programming. Tech. Rep. INRIA (1993).
9. Ph. Codognet and G. Nardiello. Path consistency in clp(FD). Proceedings of CCL'94 - 1st International Conference on Constraint in Computational Logics, Munich, LNCS 845 (J.-P. Jouannaud ed.), Springer-Verlag (1994).
10. CHIP User's Guide. Version 4.0 Revision A. COSYTEC SA, June 11, France (1993).
11. M.C. Cooper. An Optimal k-Consistency Algorithm. Art. Int. 41, pp. 89-95, (1989/90).
12. M. Dincbas, M. Simonis, and P. Van Hentenryck. Solving Large Combinatorial Problems in Constraint Logic Programming. Journal of Logic Programming, 8(1-2), pp. 75-93, (1990).
13. R. Dechter, I. Meiri and J. Pearl. Temporal constraint networks. Art. Int. 49, pp. 61-95 (1991).
14. M. Dincbas, P. Van Hentenryck, M. Simonis, A. Aggoun, T. Graf, F. Berthier. The Constraint Logic Programming Language CHIP. In Proc. Int. Conf. on Fifth Generation Computer System (FGCS'88), Tokyo, Japan, December, pp. 693-702 (1988).
15. E.C. Freuder. Synthesizing constraint expressions. Communications of the ACM, 21, pp. 958-966, (1978).
16. E.C. Freuder. A Sufficient Condition for Backtrack-Free Search. Journal of the ACM, 29(1), pp. 24-32, (1982).
17. R.M. Haralick and G.L. Elliott. Increasing Tree Search Efficiency for Constraint Satisfaction Problems. Art. Int. 14, pp. 263-313, (1980).
18. C.-C. Han and C.H. Lee. Comments on Mohr and Henderson's Path Consistency Algorithm. Art. Int. 36, pp. 125-130, (1988).
19. J. Jaffar and J.-L. Lassez. Constraint Logic Programming. Tech. Rep. 86/73, Monash University, Victoria, Australia, June (1986).
20. J. Jaffar and J.-L. Lassez. Constraint Logic Programming. In Proc. 14th ACM Conf. on Priciples of Programming Languages (POPL'87), Munich, January, pp. 111-119 (1987).

21. J. Jaffar and M.J. Maher. Constraint Logic Programming: A Survey. J. Logic Programming, *to appear*, (1994).
22. J. Jaffar, S. Michaylov, P.J. Stuckey and R.H.C. Yap. The CLP($\mathcal{R}$) Language and System. ACM Trans. on Prog. Lang. and Systems, vol. 14(3), pp. 339-395, (1992).
23. V. Kumar. Algorithms for Constraint-Satisfaction Problems: A Survey. AI Magazine, pp. 32-44, Spring (1992).
24. A.K. Mackworth. Consistency in Network of Relations. AI Journal, 8(1), pp.99-118, (1977).
25. A.K. Mackworth. The logic of constraint satisfaction. AI Journal, 58(1-3) (special volume on Constraint Based Reasoning), pp.3-20, (1992).
26. A.K. Mackworth and E.C. Freuder. The Complexity of Some Polynomial Network Consistency Algorithms for Constraint Satisfaction Problems. Art. Int. 25, pp.65-74, (1985).
27. R. Mohr and T.C. Henderson. Arc and Path Consistency Revisited. Artificial Intelligence, 28, pp.225-233, (1986).
28. U. Montanari. Networks of Constraints: Fundamental Properties and Applications to Picture Processing. Information Sciences 7, pp. 95-132, (1974).
29. B.A. Nadel. Constraint Satisfaction Algorithms. Computational Intelligence, 5, pp. 188-224, (1989).
30. G. Nardiello. The clp(FD)++ system: its Language and Implementation. *draft*, July, (1994).
31. W. Older and A. Vellino. Constraint Arithmetic on Real Intervals. In *Constraint Logic Programming* (F. Benhamou and A. Colmerauer eds.), pp. 175-195, The MIT Press, (1993).
32. B.M. Smith. How to solve the zebra problem or path-consistency the easy way. Proc. ECAI'92, pp. 36-37, (1992).
33. E. Tsang. *Foundations of Constraint Satisfaction*. Academic Press, (1993).
34. P. van Beek. On the minimality and decomposability of constraint networks. Proc. AAAI'92, pp. 447-452, (1992).
35. P. Van Hentenryck. *Constraint Satisfaction in Logic Programming*. The MIT Press, (1989).
36. P. Van Hentenryck and Y. Deville. The Cardinality Operator: A new Logical Connective for Constraint Logic Programming. In Proc. Eighth Int. Conf. on Logic Programming (ICLP'91), The MIT Press, Paris, France, (1991).
37. P. Van Hentenryck, Y. Deville and C.-M. Teng. A generic arc-consistency algorithm and its specializations. Artificial Intelligence 57, pp 291-321, (1992).
38. P. Van Hentenryck, V.A. Saraswat and Y. Deville. Constraint processing in cc(FD). Draft (1991)

Constraints in Term Algebras
An Overview of Constraint Solving Techniques

Hubert Comon

CNRS and LRI
Université de Paris Sud
Bat. 490
91405 ORSAY cedex, France.
E-mail comon@lri.lri.fr

Abstract. We will give a very brief overview on three methods for solving constraints over term algebras, namely formula rewriting, automata techniques and combination techniques. For results which illustrate the specific methods, we give literature pointers (which may be indirect ones, i.e., to more extensive surveys).

1 Introduction

Constraint systems come in three parts: a set of formulas (the syntax), a structure in which these formulas are interpreted (the semantics) and an algorithm which decides the satisfaction of a formula in the given structure. Constraint systems are used in various fields of computation. In particular, they are used in connection with logic languages, because they allow to express easily some problems in the specific domain of their interpretation. When the specific domain of interpretation is a term algebra (we will call hereafter such constraints *symbolic*), constraints systems allow to describe easily large or even infinite sets of formulas. Many applications of symbolic constraints in automated deduction have been pointed out recently (see the chapter on constraints and automated deduction by H. Kirchner).

A typical example of symbolic constraints is Presburger arithmetic. Formulas are first-order formulas build (e.g.) on the function symbols $+, 0, 1$ and the relational symbols $=, \geq$. These formulas are interpreted in the natural numbers, with the expected meaning of the functional and relational symbols. This domain of interpretation can also be seen as a term algebra over $+, 0, 1$ where $+$ is associative and commutative and 0 is a neutral element. In other words, the domain of interpretation is the quotient of $T(\{+, 0, 1\})$ by the congruence generated by the three axioms $x + y = y + x$; $x + (y + z) = (x + y) + z$; $x + 0 = x$. Presburger arithmetic is decidable and there are several decision methods such as quantifier elimination, Büchi theorem or model-theoretic methods.

Our aim here is precisely to give an overview of symbolic constraint solving techniques which will be illustrated by many results which can be found in the literature.[12] Besides model-theoretic techniques, there are three well-identified constraint solving methods: formula rewriting, automata techniques, combination techniques. They are successively shortly described below.

2 Formula rewriting

The idea is very simple and can be summarized into a slogan:

Solve   =   Reduce to Solved Forms.

More precisely, we distinguish a particular set of formulas called *solved forms* which are always trivially satisfiable or trivially unsatisfiable. Then we design a set of (scheme of) rewrite rules on formulas which is proved correct (i.e. they rewrite formulas in equivalent formulas w.r.t. the given interpretation structure), terminating (no infinite reduction sequence) and such that every irreducible formula is a solved form. This, of course, provides one or several constraint solving algorithms. These techniques are presented in more details in [5, 6].

A typical example is *unification*. Unification is the process of solving equations in a term algebra $T(F, X)/_{=_E}$. More precisely, constraints are conjunctions of equations $s = t$ where s, t are terms formed out of a set of function symbols F and a set of variables X. Some of the variables may be existentially quantified. The interpretation structure is given by a set of (implicitly universally quantified) equations E between terms of $T(F, X)$, which gives the interpretation of equality. In particular, when $E = \emptyset$, the function symbols are freely interpreted and we get classical unification problems which are used in e.g. logic programming and automated deduction. In this case, there are several possible definitions of solved forms which yield more or less efficient unification algorithms such as the *tree solved forms* and *DAG solved forms* of [16]. Tree solved form also correspond to *most general unifiers*: they are either $\perp$ or formulas of the form

$$x_1 = s_1 \wedge \ldots \wedge x_n = s_n$$

where $x_1, \ldots, x_n$ are distinct variables which do not occur in the terms $s_1, \ldots, s_n$.

It is now classical to present unification as a process of applying rewrite rules until a solved form is reached, because, on one hand, this does not depend on the particular data structure which is used to represent terms or equations, on the other hand, this clearly separates correctness proofs from termination and completeness respectively and leaves more flexibility for the control (see [16]).

There are other examples of constraint solving techniques using this method. Quantifier elimination techniques can be seen as an instance of the formula

---

[1] We don't aim at giving a complete bibliography. We refer instead to some other surveys such as [20, 5, 16, 10, 11].

[2] W.r.t. constraint solving in general, we should emphasize that we are only interested here in *global satisfaction* of the constraints.

rewriting approach. For example, the classical decidability results of Presburger arithmetic or real number theory as reported in [20]. More recently, this method was used in [9] showing the decidability of the theory of finite trees (this was already shown by Mal'cev in [19]). In [18], it can be found another proof of the same result, which actually correspond to another choice of solved forms. Similar methods are used in [8] where the first-order theory of finite terms is studied in presence of a congruence relation $=_E$. Formula rewriting is again used in membership constraint solving [7] and for feature logic [1].

The advantages of such methods are manyfold:

1. They separate the constraint solving rules from the control. This has several consequences and, in particular, allows to design several constraint solving algorithms at the same time, each of them being obtained by strengthening the control which has been used in the termination proof.
2. They are simple: each rule is an instance of some axiom of the domain of computation.
3. They are incremental: solved forms can be re-used for further constraint satisfaction problems as the result of former computations.
4. Explicit solutions (or an enumeration of the solutions) are easily obtained from the solved forms.

Such advantages are discussed in more details in [5, 6].

For many other constraint systems (if not all other constraint system), formula rewriting is used as a "preprocessor", simplifying the formulas that have to be solved by the actual constraint solver and detecting straightforward inconsistencies.

3 Automata techniques

These techniques originate in another slogan:

$$\text{Formulas} \quad = \quad \text{Automata}$$

which is at the basis of Büchi's theorem in the sixties (See again [20] for more details, or [23])

More precisely, each formula ϕ with free variables $x_1, \ldots, x_n$ is associated with an automaton $\mathcal{A}$ (of an appropriate class of automata) in such a way that the tuples of terms (or trees, or words) $t_1, \ldots, t_n$ that satisfy ϕ are exactly the tuples of terms (or trees or words) that are accepted by $\mathcal{A}$. As an example, consider Presburger arithmetic. Each natural number n can be seen as a word on the alphabet $\{0, 1\}$ which denotes the binary representation of n (read from right to left for technical reasons). It is easy to construct a two-states word automaton on $\{0, 1\}^3$ which accepts the triples of words (w_1, w_2, w_3) such that w_3 is the binary representation of the sum of w_1 and w_2. (In such a situation, triples of words are coded into a single word over the alphabet $\{0, 1\}^3$ taking as a fist letter the triple of first letters of each word, etc ...).

Then each logical connective correspond to an operation on languages recognized by automata of the given class. For example $\wedge$ correspond to the intersection of languages. In this context, decision problems for constraints are equivalent to decision problems for automata. For example satisfiability correspond to the emptyness problem.

It is out of the scope of this note to develop the theory of automata and logic. There are excellent surveys on this topics, such as [23]. Concerning constraint solving and automata, the reader is referred to [11].

Besides Presburger arithmetic, automata techniques have been recently used in several areas of symbolic constraint solving. Let us cite *encompassment constraints* [4] which provides in particular with a very elegant decision proof for ground reducibility. Automata techniques are also used in several *set constraints* solving methods [13, 14] and in membership constraint solving [7].

Here, instead of solved forms, the solutions of a constraint are described by means of automata, which is sometimes more convenient. These techniques are also incremental.

4 Combination techniques

The problem of combining symbolic constraint solving was first considered in the unification case: assume that we are given two sets of equations E and E' (which can be empty) and which do not share any function symbol. Assume moreover that we know unification algorithms for both these theories. How to combine them into a unification algorithms in the union $E \cup E'$? As an instance of this problem E can consist of the associativity and commutativity of a symbol (say, $+$) and E' is empty. Then the question becomes: how is it possible to design a unification algorithm over $T(F \cup \{+\})$, i.e. adding free function symbols to the AC theory of $+$?

General techniques in the unification case are due to M. Schmidt-Schauß [22] and A. Boudet [3]. They consist mainly in guessing in advance the relationships between terms that occur in the constraint. Then, using suitable abstractions, the constraint is decomposed into *pure systems* which are solved in each theory separately. This has been further exploited to find the complexity of AC unification [17] or for more general constraint solving combination problems [21].

Actually, it appears that the same methods also work for other constraint systems. This has been demonstrated for symbolic ordering constraint solving. The formulas of such constraint systems consist of (existentially quantified) conjunctions of equations and inequalities $s > t$ between terms. $=$ is interpreted as the syntactic equality on $T(F, X)$ and $\geq$ is interpreted as a *recursive path ordering* on terms. This kind of constraints is used in automated deduction (see the chapter on constraints in automated deduction). More details and references are given in the survey on symbolic ordering constraints solving [10]. The idea is again to guess a total ordering on terms that appear in the constraint and to remove some trivially unsatisfiable situations.

Combination techniques are actually similar to "Branch and Bound" techniques in finite domains constraint solving. They inherit the same drawbacks: inefficiency. That is why they are used in practice in combination with rewriting techniques, which solve most of the unsatisfiability situations.

5 Other methods

In principle, any method which has been developed in mathematical logic for proving the completeness of a theory can be used, together with a complete deduction system for first-order logic, as a constraint solving method. For example, the completeness of a (recursive) axiomatization of feature logic with arity constraints has been shown using Ehrenfeucht-Fraïssé games [2]. However, such methods cannot be very efficient in practice.

6 Conclusion

After this very brief review of some methods for constraint solving over term algebras, we complete this note with a more extensive bibliography on constraint solving. Again, we don't aim at giving a complete bibliography, and refer instead to some other surveys such as [20, 5, 16, 10, 11].

References

1. R. Backofen and G. Smolka. A complete and recursive feature theory. Research Report RR–92–30, DFKI, Saarbrücken, Sept. 1992. To appear in Theoretical Computer Science.
2. R. Backofen and R. Treinen. How to win a game with features. In J.-P. Jouannaud, editor, *Proc. Int. Conf. on Constraints in Computational Logics*, volume 845 of *Lecture Notes in Computer Science*, pages 320–335. Springer-Verlag, Sept. 1994.
3. A. Boudet. Combining unification algorithms. *Journal of Symbolic Computation*, 16:597–626, 1993.
4. A.-C. Caron, J.-L. Coquidé, and M. Dauchet. Encompassment properties and automata with constraints. In C. Kirchner, editor, *Proc. 5th. Int. Conf. on Rewriting Techniques and Applications*, Lecture Notes in Computer Science, vol. 690, Montreal, Canada, 1993. Springer-Verlag.
5. H. Comon. Disunification: a survey. In J.-L. Lassez and G. Plotkin, editors, *Computational Logic: Essays in Honor of Alan Robinson*. MIT Press, 1991.
6. H. Comon. Constraints in term algebras (short survey). In T. R. M. Nivat, C. Rattray and G. Scollo, editors, *Proc. Conf. on Algebraic Methodology and Software Technology*, Univ. of Twente, 1993. Springer Verlag, series Workshop in Computing. Invited talk.
7. H. Comon and C. Delor. Equational formulae with membership constraints. *Information and Computation*, 112(2):167–216, Aug. 1994.
8. H. Comon, M. Haberstrau, and J.-P. Jouannaud. Syntacticness, cycle-syntacticness and shallow theories. *Information and Computation*, 111(1), May 1994.

9. H. Comon and P. Lescanne. Equational problems and disunification. *Journal of Symbolic Computation*, 7:371–425, 1989.
10. H. Comon and R. Treinen. Ordering constraints on trees. In S. Tison, editor, *Proc. CAAP 94, LNCS*, Edinburgh, Apr. 1994. Springer Verlag. (Invited Lecture).
11. M. Dauchet. Rewriting and tree automata. In H. Comon and J.-P. Jouannaud, editors, *Proc. Spring School on Theoretical Computer Science: Rewriting*, Lecture Notes in Computer Science, to appear, Odeillo, France, 1994. Springer-Verlag.
12. T. Frühwirth. Constraint simplification rules. Technical report, ECRC Munchen, 1992.
13. R. Gilleron, S. Tison, and M. Tommasi. Solving systems of set constraints using tree automata. In *Proc. 10th Symposium on Theoretical Aspects of Computer Science, Würzburg, LNCS*, 1993.
14. R. Gilleron, S. Tison, and M. Tommasi. Solving systems of set constraints with negated subset relationships. In *Proc. 34th Symposium on Foundations of Computer Science*, pages 372–380, Palo Alto, CA, Nov. 1993. IEEE Computer society press.
15. J.-P. Jouannaud, editor. *Constraints in Computational Logics*, volume 845 of *Lecture Notes in Computer Science*. Springer-Verlag, 1994.
16. J.-P. Jouannaud and C. Kirchner. Solving equations in abstract algebras: A rule-based survey of unification. In J.-L. Lassez and G. Plotkin, editors, *Computational Logic: Essays in Honor of Alan Robinson*. MIT-Press, 1991.
17. D. Kapur and P. Narendran. Double-exponential complexity of computing a complete set of ac-unifiers. In *Proc. 7th IEEE Symp. Logic in Computer Science, Santa Cruz*, June 1992.
18. M. J. Maher. Complete axiomatizations of the algebras of finite, rational and infinite trees. In *Proc. 3rd IEEE Symp. Logic in Computer Science, Edinburgh*, pages 348–357, July 1988.
19. A. Mal'cev. On the elementary theories of locally free algebras. *Soviet Math. Doklady*, 1961.
20. M. Rabin. Decidable theories. In J. Barwise, editor, *Handbook of Mathematical Logic*, pages 595–629. North-Holland, 1977.
21. C. Ringeissen. Combinaison de résolutions de contraintes. Thèse de Doctorat, Université de Nancy I, France, Dec. 1993.
22. M. Schmidt-Schauß. Unification in a combination of arbitrary disjoint equational theories. *Journal of Symbolic Computation*, 1990. Special issue on Unification.
23. W. Thomas. Automata on infinite objects. In J. van Leeuwen, editor, *Handbook of Theoretical Computer Science*, pages 134–191. Elsevier, 1990.

Constructive negation by pruning and optimization higher-order predicates for CLP and CC languages

François Fages

LIENS CNRS*, Ecole Normale Supérieure, 45 rue d'Ulm, 75230 Paris Cedex 05.
E-mail: fages@dmi.ens.fr

Abstract. We survey several forms of negation in constraint logic programming following the program's completion approach. We show that a new scheme called constructive negation by pruning provides a generic operational semantics which is correct and complete w.r.t. Kunen's three-valued logic semantics. We emphasis a full abstraction result which permits to go beyond the theorem proving point of view and to completely characterize the operational behavior of CLP programs with negation. We derive from these results a complete scheme for optimization higher-order predicates in CLP languages, and an operational semantics for concurrent constraint (CC) languages extended with negation and optimization higher-order agents.

1 Introduction

The amalgamation of constraint programming, logic programming and concurrent programming results in a very powerful model of computation that is conceptually simple and semantically elegant [13] [23].

Several constraint logic programming (CLP) systems and concurrent constraint (CC) systems have been developed over the last decade. These systems have been proved successful in complex problem modeling and combinatorial optimization problems across a variety of application domains, ranging from digital and analog circuits analysis and synthesis, to options trading and financial planning, job-shop scheduling, crew management, etc. [14].

In these realizations the real components of the problem at hand are modeled by relations over interface variables. These relations are defined with primitive constraints, recursively defined predicates, conjunctions and disjunctions. Relational models can thus be arbitrarily assembled with the CLP and CC programs constructors.

Extending the CLP and CC classes of languages with a negation operator is a major issue as it allows the user to express arbitrary logical combination of relational models. The full power of expression of first-order logic is then

---

* This work has been partially supported by MESR contracts 92 S 0777 and PRC AMN 93 S 0051.

accessible. In this way we obtain a framework to express also optimization and preferred solutions [10].

However negation in logic programming is known to be a delicate problem which raises many difficulties. Simply inferring negative information from a positive logic program is already a form of non-monotonic inference that shows essential differences between the two main approaches to the model theoretic semantics of logic programs: namely the *standard model* approach and the *program's completion* approach [1].

From a programming language point of view the standard model approach is not viable because it is highly undecidable. However from a knowledge representation point of view standard models correspond naturally to the intended semantics of programs. Therefore the challenge is to provide constructs which capture the essential aspects of standard models, in a recursively enumerable setting.

In this article we survey in a progressive manner the program's completion approach to CLP programs with negation. We introduce a new principle called constructive negation by pruning which is correct and complete w.r.t. the three-valued logical consequences of the program's completion. We emphasize a full abstraction result which permits to go beyond the theorem proving point of view and to completely characterize the operational behavior of normal CLP programs. These results are based on [8].

Then we show how constructive negation by pruning allows to define optimization higher-order predicates for CLP programs. We show that in this context the operational semantics specializes into an efficient branch and bound like procedure proved correct and complete in a full first-order setting.

Finally we study the fundamental extension of the class CC of concurrent constraint logic languages [23] with a negation operator. We show that the principle of constructive negation by pruning can be applied in this context. We derive from this principle an operational semantics for CC languages extended with negation and optimization higher-order agents.

2 Preliminaries on definite Constraint Logic Programs

A language of constraints is defined on a signature Σ of constants, function and predicate symbols (containing *true*, *false* and $=$), and on a denumerable set V of variables. A *primitive constraint* is an atom of the form $p(t_1, ..., t_n)$ where p is a predicate symbol in Σ and the t_i's are Σ, V-terms. A *constraint* is a conjunction of primitive constraints. The set of free variables in an expression e is denoted by $FV(e)$.

CLP programs are defined using an extra set of predicate symbols Π disjoint from Σ. An *atom* has the form $p(t_1, ..., t_n)$ where $p \in \Pi$ and the t_i's are Σ, V-terms. A *literal* is an atom or a negated atom $\neg A$.

A *definite CLP program* is a finite set of clauses of the form:

$$A \leftarrow c | A_1, ..., A_n$$

where $n \geq 0$, A is an atom, called the head, c a constraint, and the A_i's are atoms (the sequence is denoted by $\Box$ if $n = 0$). The *local variables* of a program clause is the set of free variables in the clause which do not occur in the head. A *definite goal* is a clause of the form

$$\leftarrow c|A_1, ..., A_n$$

where the A_i's are atoms (resp. literals). In the rest of this paper we shall assume that all atoms in programs and goals contain no constant or function symbol. Of course this is not a restriction as any program or goal can be rewritten in such a form by introducing new variables and equality constraints with terms. For instance $p(x + 1) \leftarrow p(x)$ should be read as $p(y) \leftarrow y = x + 1|p(x)$.

A $CLP(\mathcal{A})$ program is a CLP program given with a Σ-structure $\mathcal{A}$ which fixes the interpretation of constraints. An $\mathcal{A}$-valuation for a Σ-expression is a mapping $\theta : V \rightarrow \mathcal{A}$ which extends by morphism to terms and constraints. A constraint c is $\mathcal{A}$-solvable iff there exists an $\mathcal{A}$-valuation θ, s.t. $\mathcal{A} \models c\theta$.

We shall not suppose that $\mathcal{A}$ is solution compact [13], we suppose only that the constraints are decidable in $\mathcal{A}$, so that $\mathcal{A}$ can be presented by a first-order theory $th(\mathcal{A})$, satisfying:

1. (soundness) $\mathcal{A} \models th(\mathcal{A})$,
2. (satisfaction completeness) and for any constraint c, either $th(\mathcal{A}) \models \exists c$, or $th(\mathcal{A}) \models \neg \exists c$.

$CLP(\mathcal{A})$ programs are interpreted operationally by a simple transition system on goals, $\rightarrow \in \mathcal{G} \times \mathcal{G}$, defined by the following CSLD resolution rule:

$$CSLD : \frac{(p(X) \leftarrow d|\beta) \in P \quad \mathcal{A} \models \exists(c \wedge d)}{c|\alpha, p(X), \alpha' \rightarrow c \wedge d|\alpha, \beta, \alpha'}$$

In such a transition, $p(X)$ is called the *selected* atom. A *CSLD derivation* is a sequence of transitions. A derivation is *successful* if it is finite and ends with a pure constraint goal containing no atom. A *computed answer constraint* (abbrev. c.a.c.) for a goal G is a constraint c such that there exists a successful derivation from G to $c|\Box$. A (CSLD) *derivation tree* for a goal G is the tree of all derivations from G obtained by fixing a selected atom in each node. The result of independence of the selection rule [17] states that all CSLD derivation trees of a given goal have the same set of computed answer constraints.

From a programming language point of view, computed answer constraints constitute a natural notion of observation which is finer than the simple existence of a successful derivation for a goal, characterized by ground success set semantics [13]. In this paper two programs will be said operationally equivalent if they have the same sets of c.a.c. (see [4] for other notions of observations). We shall thus consider formal semantics of CLP programs which permit to characterize computed answer constraints [18], [12], instead of ground semantics which, outside the case of pure logic programs over the Herbrand domain [2], generally do not suffice to modelize the operational behavior of CLP programs.

The c.a.c. for a composite goal can be retrieved from the c.a.c. for the atoms which appear in the goal (and-compositionality lemma 1), therefore the operational semantics of a $CLP(\mathcal{A})$ program is defined as a set of constrained atoms which gives the set of c.a.c. for unconstrained atomic goals solely:

Lemma 1 (And-compositionality lemma). *Let P be a $CLP(\mathcal{A})$ program. d is a computed answer constraint for the goal $c|A_1, ..., A_n$ if and only if there exist computed answer constraints $d_1, ..., d_n$ for the goals $true|A_1, ..., true|A_n$ respectively such that $d = c \wedge \bigwedge_{i=1}^{n} d_i$.*

Definition 2. The operational semantics of a CLP program P is the set $\mathcal{O}(P) = \{c|p(X) \mid p \in \Pi, \ c \text{ is a c.a.c. for the goal } true|p(X)\}$.

The corresponding logical semantics of a definite $CLP(\mathcal{A})$ program is given by the logical consequences of the clauses of the program together with the theory of the structure, whereas the algebraic semantics is defined by the truth in all $\mathcal{A}$-models of P.

Definition 3. The logical semantics of a $CLP(\mathcal{A})$ program P is the set

$$\mathcal{L}(P) = \{c|p(X) \mid p \in \Pi, \ P, th(\mathcal{A}) \models \forall (c \rightarrow p(X)) \wedge \exists (c)\}.$$

The algebraic semantics of P is the set

$$Alg(P) = \{c|p(X) \mid p \in \Pi, \ P, \mathcal{A} \models \forall (c \rightarrow p(X)) \wedge \exists (c)\}.$$

The equivalence between the semantics can be expressed by inclusion and by several covering pre-orders on sets of constrained atoms:

- *strong covering*: $I \sqsubseteq J$ iff for all $c|A \in I$ there exists $d|A \in J$ such that $th(\mathcal{A}) \models c \rightarrow d$,
- *finite covering*: $I \sqsubseteq_f J$ iff for all $c|A \in I$, there exists $\{d_1|A, ..., d_n|A\} \subseteq J$ such that $th(\mathcal{A}) \models c \rightarrow \bigvee_{i=1}^{n} d_i$,
- *infinite covering*: $I \sqsubseteq_\infty J$ iff for all $c|A \in I$, there exists a (possibly infinite) set $\{d_k|A\}_{k \in K} \subseteq J$ such that[2] $\mathcal{A} \models c \rightarrow \bigvee_{k \in K} d_k$.

Theorem 4 (Soundness of CSLD resolution) [13]. $\mathcal{O}(P) \subseteq \mathcal{L}(P)$.

Theorem 5 ($th(\mathcal{A})$-completeness) [18]. $\mathcal{L}(P) \sqsubseteq_f \mathcal{O}(P)$.

Theorem 6 ($\mathcal{A}$-completeness). $Alg(P) \sqsubseteq_\infty \mathcal{O}(P)$.

---

[2] Note that the infinite covering is defined via the truth in structure $\mathcal{A}$ of an infinite formula, whereas the finite and strong coverings are syntactic notions based on the logical consequences of $th(\mathcal{A})$.

It is worth noting that for the observation of answer constraints it is not equivalent to consider the logical consequences of $P \wedge th(\mathcal{A})$ or the truth in all $\mathcal{A}$-models of P. For the latter stronger algebraic semantics, the completeness result involves a possibly infinite set of c.a.c.

For example, with the logic program $P = \{p(0), \; p(s(X)) \leftarrow p(X)\}$ over the Herbrand universe $\mathcal{H}$ formed over function symbols 0 and s, the goal $\leftarrow p(X)$ admits an infinity of c.a.c. of the form $X = s^i(0)$ for $i \geq 0$. We have $P, \mathcal{H} \models \forall x p(x)$, and $\mathcal{H} \models \forall x \bigvee_{i \geq 0} x = s^i(0)$ indeed. However $P, CET \not\models \forall x p(x)$, we have $CET \not\models \forall x \bigvee_{i \geq 0} x = s^i(0)$, where CET is Clark's equational theory or any first-order theory of the Herbrand structure, as such a theory necessarily contains non-standard models in which $\bigvee_{i \geq 0} x = s^i(0)$ doesn't hold (otherwise the compactness theorem of first-order logic would be violated).

The departure of the algebraic semantics from the logical semantics becomes even more important with the study of finite failure.

3 Negative answers to definite goals

A further natural observable property of definite CLP program is finite failure, observed when all fair derivations of a goal are finite and not successful. A CSLD derivation is *fair* if it is finite or any atom in a goal of the derivation is selected within a finite number of steps. A goal G is *finitely failed* if any fair CSLD tree for G is finite and contains no successful derivations. Now the answer "no" is thus another possible outcome of an execution in addition to the computed answer constraints.

For this extra notion of observation, the logical semantics can no longer be based on the logical consequences of the clauses of the program as the set of all atoms instanciated in $\mathcal{A}$ (i.e. the $\mathcal{A}$-base) is a model of the program where everything is true. The solution proposed by Clark in 1978 is to consider instead the formula obtained from P by reading the definitions of the predicates with an equivalence symbol instead of implications.

The Clark's completion of a $CLP(\mathcal{A})$ program P is the conjunction of $th(\mathcal{A})$ with formulae
1) of the form

$$\forall X \; p(X) \leftrightarrow \bigvee_i \exists Y_i \; c_i \wedge \alpha_i$$

obtained for each predicate symbol p by collecting the clauses $\{p(X) \leftarrow c_i | \alpha_i\}$ in P, where $Y_i = FV(c_i | \alpha_i) \setminus X$,
2) or of the form $\forall X \; \neg p(X)$ if p doesn't appear in any head in P.
The Clark's completion of P is denoted by $P^*, th(\mathcal{A})$.

The finite failure rule is correct and complete w.r.t. the logical consequences of the program's completion without any restriction on the structure. It is instructive to see that the proof relies on the compactness theorem of first-order logic which holds for $P^*, th(\mathcal{A})$ but not necessarily in the $\mathcal{A}$-models of P^*.

Theorem 7 [13]. *A goal G is finitely failed if and only if $P^*, th(\mathcal{A}) \models \neg \exists(G)$.*

Proof. ⇒ By induction on the height of the CSLD derivation tree.

⇐ We show that if G is not finitely failed then $\{P^*, th(\mathcal{A}), \exists G\}$ is satisfiable. If G is not finitely failed, then either G admits a successful derivation, in which case $P^*, th(\mathcal{A}) \models \exists G$ by the soundness theorem, or G admits a fair infinite derivation

$$G = c_0|\alpha_0 \rightarrow c_1|\alpha_1 \rightarrow c_2|\alpha_2 \rightarrow \ldots$$

By the compactness theorem of first-order logic, $c_\omega = \bigcup c_i$ is $th(\mathcal{A})$-satisfiable. Let $\mathcal{B}$ be a model of $th(\mathcal{A})$ such that $\mathcal{B} \models \exists c_\omega$.

Let $I_0 = \{A\theta \mid A \in G_i \text{ for } i \geq 0 \text{ and } \mathcal{B} \models c_\omega \theta\}$ and let us consider the immediate consequence operator $T_P^{\mathcal{B}}$ of [13]. We have $I_0 \subseteq T_P^{\mathcal{B}}(I_0)$ (by fairness) hence as $T_P^{\mathcal{B}}$ is monotonic, by Knaster-Tarski's theorem, $T_P^{\mathcal{B}}$ admits a fixed point containing I_0, hence containing $G\theta$.

A fixed point of $T_P^{\mathcal{B}}$ is a $\mathcal{B}$-model of P^*, the previous fixed point is thus a $\mathcal{B}$-model of $P^*, \exists G$, therefore $P^*, th(\mathcal{A}), \exists G$ is satisfiable.

For example with the program $P = \{q(s(X)) \leftarrow q(X)\}$ over the Herbrand universe formed over function symbols 0 and s, the goal $\leftarrow q(0)$ is finitely failed and we have $P^*, CET \models \neg q(0)$. On the other hand the goal $\leftarrow q(X)$ admits an infinite fair derivation, we have $P^*, CET \not\models q(X)$ and $P^*, CET \not\models \neg q(X)$, despite the fact that $q(X)$ is false in all Herbrand models of P^*: $P^*, \mathcal{H} \models \neg q(X)$.

Therefore the logical consequences of $P^*, th(\mathcal{A})$ correctly capture the operational behavior of finite failure whereas the truth in all $\mathcal{A}$-models of P^* is not recursively enumerable and corresponds to an abstract notion of failure by ground derivations [14]. The situation is that from a knowledge representation point of view, the algebraic semantics is likely to reflect the intuition of the programmer who reasons in a fixed "domain of discourse" [13], but from a programming language point of view the algebraic semantics is not viable as it is highly undecidable. The logical semantics provides a declarative semantics which is faithful to the operational behavior of the program, and which constitutes a computable approximation of the "intended" algebraic semantics.

4   Goals with negation

The next step is to allow negation inside goals. The logical semantics can be extended accordingly with the following:

Definition 8. Let P be a definite $CLP(\mathcal{A})$ program. The logical semantics for positive and negative goals is defined by $\mathcal{L}_2(P) = <\mathcal{L}_2^+(P), \mathcal{L}_2^-(P)>$ where
$\mathcal{L}_2^+(P) = \{c|p(X) \mid P^*, th(\mathcal{A}) \models \forall(c \rightarrow p(X)) \wedge \exists c\}$
$\mathcal{L}_2^-(P) = \{c|p(X) \mid P^*, th(\mathcal{A}) \models \forall(c \rightarrow \neg p(X)) \wedge \exists c\}$

The operational semantics based on finite failure does not allow to compute an answer constraint for a negative goal containing variables, it is thus too weak w.r.t. the logical semantics. The principle of constructive negation proposed by

Chan [6] and Wallace provides a complete scheme. The main notion is the one of a frontier of a CSLD tree. A *frontier* of a CSLD tree is a finite set of nodes such that every derivation in the tree is either finitely failed or passes through exactly one frontier node. We can easily state the following:

Lemma 9. *Let P be a definite $CLP(\mathcal{A})$ program, G a goal, and $\{c_i|\alpha_i\}_{1\leq i\leq n}$ be a frontier in a CSLD tree for G. Then $P^*, th(\mathcal{A}) \models G \leftrightarrow (\exists Y_1 c_1 \wedge \alpha_1) \vee \dots \vee (\exists Y_n c_n \wedge \alpha_n)$.*

To resolve a goal $c|\neg A$, constructive negation amounts simply to develop a fair CSLD tree for $c|A$, take a frontier $\{c_i|\alpha_i\}_{1\leq i\leq n}$ in that tree, and return the answer constraint $c \wedge \bigwedge_{1\leq i\leq n} \neg \exists Y_i c_i$, whenever it is satisfiable, the deeper the frontier, the more general the answer (see figure 1).

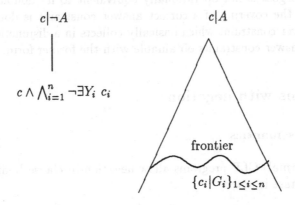

$$c|\neg A \qquad\qquad c|A$$

$$c \wedge \bigwedge_{i=1}^{n} \neg \exists Y_i\, c_i$$

frontier

$$\{c_i|G_i\}_{1\leq i\leq n}$$

Fig. 1. Constructive negation for definite CLP programs.

As constraints must be negated, we shall suppose from now on that the language of constraints is closed by negation, and thus that a constraint can be any Σ, V-formula (a weaker assumption based on the notion of admissible structure is studied in [24]). The satisfaction completeness condition is then equivalent to say that the theory of the structure is complete, and thus that all models of the theory are elementary equivalent. In this setting soundness and completeness of constructive negation w.r.t. the logical semantics are a simple corollary of the previous theorem for finite failure.

Theorem 10. *Let P be a $CLP(\mathcal{A})$ program, c be an $\mathcal{A}$-satisfiable constraint, and G a goal. Then $P^*, th(\mathcal{A}) \models c \rightarrow \neg G$ if and only if there exists a computed answer constraint d to the goal $\neg G$ such that $th(\mathcal{A}) \models c \rightarrow d$.*

Proof.

$\Leftarrow$ Let $\{c_i | \alpha_i\}_{i \in I}$ be a frontier in a CSLD tree for G such that $d = \bigwedge_{i \in I} \neg \exists Y_i \, c_i$ is satisfiable. We have $P^*, th(\mathcal{A}) \models G \leftrightarrow \bigvee_{i \in I} \exists Y_i \, c_i \wedge \alpha_i$,
so $P^*, th(\mathcal{A}) \models \neg G \leftrightarrow \bigwedge_{i \in I} \neg \exists Y_i \, c_i \vee \neg \alpha_i$,
hence $P^*, th(\mathcal{A}) \models \neg G \leftarrow d$.

$\Rightarrow$ We have $p^*, th(\mathcal{A}) \models \neg(c \wedge G)$, hence by theorem 7, the goal $c|G$ admits a finitely failed fair CSLD tree. Let $\{c_i | \alpha_i\}$ be the frontier corresponding to the lifting of that tree to the goal $true|G$.

For all $i \in I$, $c \wedge \exists Y_i c_i$ is $\mathcal{A}$-unsatisfiable, thus $c \wedge \bigvee_{i \in I} \exists Y_i c_i$ is $\mathcal{A}$-unsatisfiable. Let $d = \bigwedge_{i \in I} \neg \exists Y_i \, c_i$, we have $\mathcal{A} \models c \rightarrow d$, hence d is $\mathcal{A}$-satisfiable, therefore d is a computed answer constraint to the goal $\neg G$.

Note that for a negative goal a correct answer constraint is covered by a single computed answer constraint (strong completeness). Hence under the constructive negation rule a goal is not operationally equivalent to its double negation. In the later form the covering of a correct answer constraint is done by a single computed answer constraint which basically collects in a disjunction a finite set of computed answer constraints obtainable with the former form.

5 Programs with negation

5.1 Logical semantics

General (or normal) CLP programs allow negation in clause bodies. A *general (or normal) clause* is noted

$$A \leftarrow c|\alpha$$

where α is a finite sequence of literals (α^+ denotes the subsequence of atoms in α and $\square$ denotes the empty sequence). General logic programs have the power of expression of full first-order logic, as any definition of a predicate by a first order formula can be transformed into a normal CLP program [17], obtained basically by replacing a clause of the form $p(X) \leftarrow \alpha, \forall Y q(X, Y), \beta$ by $p(X) \leftarrow \neg q'(X)$ and $q'(X) \leftarrow \neg q(X, Y)$ where q' is a new predicate symbol.

Now the Clark's completion of a normal program can be inconsistent, e.g. with $P = \{p \rightarrow \neg p\}$, $P^* = \{p \leftrightarrow \neg p\}$, in which case the logical semantics demands that there exists a successful derivation for each goal, that is clearly not the intended semantics of logic programs. The solution proposed by Kunen [15] to make the program's completion consistent is to define the logical semantics within three valued logic [11]. The usual strong 3-valued interpretations of the connectives and quantifiers are assumed, except for the connective $a \leftrightarrow b$ used to form the Clark's completion, which is interpreted as t if a and b have the same truth value (f, t or u), and f otherwise (i.e. Lukasiewicz's 2-valued interpretation of $\leftrightarrow$). In the previous example taking p undefined we have $u \leftrightarrow \neg u$ true. In this way the Clark's completion of a normal program is always 3-valued consistent. The logical consequence relation in three-valued logic is denoted by $\models_3$.

The *logical semantics* of a normal CLP($\mathcal{A}$) program P w.r.t. answer constraints is thus defined by the following partial constrained interpretation[3]:
$\mathcal{L}_3(P) = < \mathcal{L}_3^+(P), \mathcal{L}_3^-(P) >$ where
$\mathcal{L}_3^+(P) = \{c|p(X) \in \mathcal{B} : P^*, th(\mathcal{A}) \models_3 c \rightarrow p(X)\}$,
$\mathcal{L}_3^-(P) = \{c|p(X) \in \mathcal{B} : P^*, th(\mathcal{A}) \models_3 c \rightarrow \neg p(X)\}$.

5.2 Operational semantics

A first way to adapt the principle of constructive negation to general logic programs, that is to use it not only for the top-level goal, but recursively at each resolution step with a negative literal, is to transform the entire frontier obtained for a negated atom into disjunctive normal form, and produce a resolvant with each complex goal in a disjunct. The constructive negation rule is then the following:

$$CN : \quad (c|\alpha, (\neg \exists Y \ \beta), \alpha') \ \rightarrow \ (c \wedge c_j|\alpha, \beta_j, \alpha')$$

for each $1 \leq j \leq n$ where $\bigvee_{1 \leq j < n} c_j \wedge \beta_j$ is a disjunctive normal form of $\bigwedge_{1 \leq k \leq m} \neg \exists Z_k(c \wedge d_k \wedge \alpha_k)$, where $\{c \wedge d_k|\alpha_k\}_{1 \leq k \leq m}$ is a frontier in a CSLDCN derivation tree for $c|\beta$, and $Z_k = (V(d_k|\alpha_k) \setminus V(c|\beta)) \cup Y$.

This is the way undertaken by Chan [6] for logic programs, and by Stuckey [24] for constraint logic programs. The effect is to introduce complex subgoals with explicit quantifiers and to compute the disjunctive normal form at each resolution step with a negative literal. This makes the scheme hardly amenable to a practical implementation for normal CLP programs in all generality. The compilative version proposed by Bruscoli et al. [5], named intensional negation, performs all disjunctive normal form transformations once and for all at compile time, but still all quantifiers need be explicit at run time and derivation rules need be defined for complex goals.

Another way undertaken independently in [7] and [8] is to use the principle of constructive negation as a concurrent pruning mechanism over standard CSLD

---

[3] It is worth noting that a complete notion of three-valued logic programming could also take into account the set

$$\mathcal{L}_3^u(P) = \{c|p(X) \in \mathcal{B} : P^*, th(\mathcal{A}) \models_3 c \rightarrow (p(X) = u)\}$$

of constrained atoms which are undefined in all three-valued models of the program's completion. This set is recursively enumerable. If it is not empty then the program's completion is clearly inconsistent. Of course the converse of that proposition doesn't hold. For instance the program

$$P = \{p \leftarrow \neg p, r, \ q \leftarrow \neg q, \neg r, \ r \leftarrow r\}$$

is inconsistent but $\mathcal{L}_3^u(P) = \emptyset$. To our knowledge, this generalized three-valued logic semantics has not been considered up to now, and there has been some confusion about the undefined truth value standing for goals which operationally loop forever. In fact the *absence* of a fixed truth valued for a goal should model operational loops, but a fixed undefined truth value for a goal could be distinguished and reported as a local contradiction in the program. A refinement of the operational semantics presented in the next section in order to detect such contradictions will be presented elsewhere.

trees. The idea to resolve a goal $c|\alpha, \neg A$ where $\neg A$ is the selected literal is to develop concurrently two CSLD-derivation trees, one Ψ for $c|\alpha, (\neg A)$ in which $\neg A$ is not selected, and one Ψ' for $c|A$.

Once a successful derivation is found in Ψ', say with answer constraint d, then Ψ is pruned by adding the constraint $\neg\exists Y d$ where $Y = V(d) \setminus V(c|A)$, to the nodes in Ψ where that constraint is satisfiable, and by removing the other nodes. This operation is called "pruning by success".

Once a successful derivation is found in Ψ, say with answer constraint e, we get a successful derivation for the main goal with answer constraint $f = e \wedge \bigwedge_{i=1}^{n} \neg\exists Y_i d_i$ where $Y_i = V(d_i) \setminus V(c|A)$, for each frontier $\{d_i|\alpha_i\}_{1 \le i \le n}$ in Ψ' such that f is satisfiable (the deeper the frontier is, the more general is the computed answer). This operation is called "success by pruning".

The main goal is finitely failed if Ψ gets finitely failed after pruning. Figure 2 illustrates the pruning mechanism.

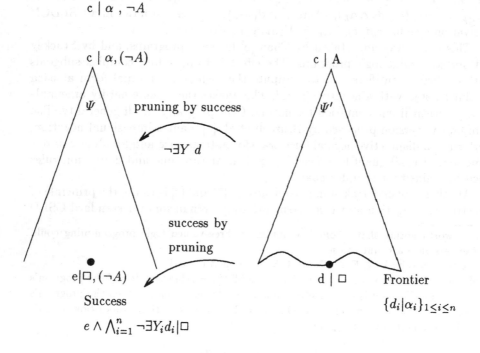

Fig. 2. Constructive negation by pruning.

The pruning by success rule is not redundant with the success by pruning rule. The former modifies the non successful nodes in a frontier of the first tree. This is necessary for finite failure or more generally for the completeness of the scheme if there are chains of dependencies through several negations.

Example 1. The nesting of negation can be illustrated by the following program:

```
p(0).
p(X):-p(X).
q(X):-not p(X).
```

with the goal:

```
? not q(X)
X=0
```

As the goal contains no positive literal the first derivation tree is a trivial success with constraint *true*. The second derivation tree for $q(X)$ contains one derivation to the goal $true|\neg p(X)$, thus a third derivation tree is developed for $p(X)$. As $X = 0$ is a success for $p(X)$, the pruning by success rule has for effect to prune the second with $X \neq 0$ (note that the success by pruning rule doesn't apply as any frontier in the third tree contains the goal $true|p(X)$ coming from the clause $p(X) \leftarrow p(X)$, and that goal cannot be negated). Hence by negating the frontier in the second tree after pruning we get a successful derivation for the main goal with answer constraint $X = 0$.

The practical advantage of constructive negation by pruning is that it relies on standard CSLD derivation trees for definite goals only. The only extra machinery to handle negation is a concurrent pruning mechanism over standard CSLD derivation trees, in particular there is no need for considering complex subgoals with explicit quantifiers.

In [8] constructive negation by pruning is formalized as a calculus over frontiers. The set of frontiers is the set $\mathcal{P}_f(\mathcal{G})$ of finite sets of goals. The main operation is the cross product of frontiers. Given two frontiers $F = \{c_i|\alpha_i\}_{1 \leq i \leq m}$, and $F' = \{d_j|\beta_j\}_{1 \leq j \leq n}$, the cross product of F and F' is the frontier:

$$F \times F' = \{(c_i \wedge d_j|\alpha_i, \beta_j) \mid 1 \leq i \leq m, 1 \leq j \leq n, \ \mathcal{A} \models \exists(c_i \wedge d_j)\}.$$

The negation of the projection of the constraint in a frontier F on a set of variables X is denoted by

$$\neg_X F = \bigwedge_{c|\alpha \in F, \ Y = V(c) \backslash X} \neg \exists Y\, c.$$

The operational semantics of general CLP programs is then defined by a relation $\vartriangleleft \in \mathcal{G} \times \mathcal{P}_f(\mathcal{G})$ which associates a frontier to a goal (big step semantics). Relation $\vartriangleleft$ is defined as the least relation satisfying the axioms and rules given in table 1.

The first rule (RES) is the usual resolution rule for positive literals (note that $c|p(x) \vartriangleleft \emptyset$ if $k = 0$). The second rule (FRT) expresses the formation of frontiers by cross products[4]. The third rule called "pruning" (PRN) is the new inference rule introduced for negative literals. It is worth noting that the usual negation as failure rule is the restriction of the pruning rule to the case $F = \emptyset$.

---

[4] Note that a more standard operational semantics where frontiers are not formed by cross products but by elementary CSLD resolution steps can be defined by replacing

TRIV: $c|\alpha \lhd \{c|\alpha\}$

RES: $$\frac{c \wedge c_1|\alpha_1 \lhd F_1 \quad \ldots \quad c \wedge c_k|\alpha_k \lhd F_k}{c|p(X) \lhd F_1 \cup \ldots \cup F_k}$$

where $\{(p(X) \leftarrow c_i|\alpha_i)\}_{1 \leq i \leq k}$ is the set of renamed clauses defining $p(X)$ in P such that $\mathcal{A} \models \exists(c \wedge c_i)$.

FRT: $$\frac{c|A \lhd F \qquad c|\alpha, \alpha' \lhd F'}{c|\alpha, A, \alpha' \lhd F \times F'}$$

PRN: $$\frac{c|A \lhd F \qquad c \wedge \neg_X S|\alpha, \alpha' \lhd F'}{c|\alpha, \neg A, \alpha' \lhd \{c|\neg A\} \times F' \cup F''}$$

where $X = V(c|A)$, S is a set of successful nodes in F and $F'' = \{(c \wedge \neg_X F|\alpha) : c|\alpha \in F', \alpha^+ = \emptyset\}$

Table 1. Definition of the goal-frontier relation for normal CLP languages.

Example 2. Going back to example 1, the goal $\neg q(x)$ has the following derivation:

$$x = 0|\Box \lhd \{x = 0|\Box\} \qquad\qquad true|p(X) \lhd \{true|p(X)\}$$

$$true|p(x) \lhd \{x = 0|\Box, \ true|p(x)\} \qquad\qquad x \neq 0|\Box \lhd \{x \neq 0|\Box\}$$

$$true|\neg p(x) \lhd \{x \neq 0|\Box, x \neq 0|\neg p(x)\}$$

$$true|q(x) \lhd \{x \neq 0|\Box, \ x \neq 0|\neg p(x)\} \quad x = 0|\Box \lhd \{x = 0|\Box\}$$

$$true|\neg q(x) \lhd \{x = 0|\Box, \ x = 0|\neg q(x)\}$$

Definition 11. The operational semantics of a general $CLP(\mathcal{A})$ program is the tuple: $\mathcal{O}(P) = <\mathcal{O}^+(P), \mathcal{O}^-(P)>$
$\mathcal{O}^+(P) = \{\exists Y c|p(X) \in \mathcal{B} : true|p(X) \lhd \{c|\Box\} \cup F, \ Y = V(c) \setminus X\}$
$\mathcal{O}^-(P) = \{c|p(X) \in \mathcal{B} : true|\neg p(X) \lhd \{c|\Box\} \cup F\}$

The next section presents completeness results for constructive negation by pruning through a fixed point semantics which is fully abstract for the observation of computed answer constraints

the RES and FRT rules by the following CSLD rule

$$CSLD : \frac{c \wedge c_1|\alpha, \alpha_1, \alpha' \lhd F_1 \quad \ldots \quad c \wedge c_k|\alpha, \alpha_k, \alpha' \lhd F_k}{c|\alpha, p(X), \alpha' \lhd F_1 \cup \ldots \cup F_k}$$

The only effect of this variant is to generate additional unnecessary redundant answer constraints. We refer to [8] for the details.

5.3 Fixed point semantics

Fitting [11] first introduced the idea that the formal semantics of normal logic programs should be defined in three-valued logic by partial interpretations. A partial interpretation I is a couple $< I^+, I^- >$ which determines truth and false things and leave undefined remaining atoms, and remaining formula by extension. Fitting's immediate consequence operator $\Phi_P^{\mathcal{A}}$ is defined for normal $CLP(\mathcal{A})$ programs by:

Definition 12. $\Phi_P^{\mathcal{A}}(I) = < \Phi_P^{\mathcal{A}+}(I), \Phi_P^{\mathcal{A}-}(I) >$ where

$\Phi_P^{\mathcal{A}+}(I) = \{ A\rho \mid \rho$ is a valuation s.t. for some clause $(A \leftarrow c|\alpha) \in P,$
$$A \models c\rho, \ I(\alpha\rho) = t \}$$

$\Phi_P^{\mathcal{A}-}(I) = \{ A\rho \mid \rho$ is a valuation s.t. for all clause $(A \leftarrow c|\alpha) \in P,$
either $A \models c\rho,$ or $I(\alpha\rho) = t \}.$

Non-ground versions of Fitting's operator based on pairs of sets of constrained atoms have appeared in [15], [24], [5], [3], [8], as they are more suitable to establish the links with the operational semantics. A partial constrained interpretation is a pair $I = < I^+, I^- >$ of constrained interpretations such that $[I^+]_{\mathcal{A}} \cap [I^-]_{\mathcal{A}} = \emptyset$. Partial constrained interpretations form a semi-lattice for pairwise set inclusion (not a lattice as the union of two partial interpretations may be inconsistent), it is denoted by $(\mathcal{I}, \subseteq_3)$. The covering preorders are also extended pairwise to partial constrained interpretations.

The operator used in [8] is a *finitary* non-ground version of Fitting's operator: each constrained atom in the image of a constrained interpretation depends on a finite number of constrained atoms, such an operator is thus continuous in the semi-lattice of constrained partial interpretation.

Definition 13. Let P be a $CLP(\mathcal{A})$ program. $T_P^{\mathcal{A}}$ is an operator over $2^{\mathcal{B}} \times 2^{\mathcal{B}}$ defined by $T_P^{\mathcal{A}}(I) = < T_P^{\mathcal{A}+}(I), T_P^{\mathcal{A}-}(I) >$ where:

$T_P^{\mathcal{A}+}(I) = \{ c|p(X) \in \mathcal{B}$: there exists a clause in P with local variables $Y,$
$p(X) \leftarrow d|A_1, ..., A_m, \neg A_{m+1}, ..., \neg A_n$
there exist $c_i|A_i \in I^+$ for $1 \leq i \leq m,$
$c_j|A_j \in I^-$ for $m+1 \leq j \leq n,$
such that $c = d \wedge \bigwedge_{i=1}^n c_i$ is $\mathcal{A}$-satisfiable$\}$

$T_P^{\mathcal{A}-}(I) = \{ c|p(X) \in \mathcal{B}$: for any clause defining p in P, with local variable $Y_k,$
$p(X) \leftarrow A_{k,1}, ..., A_{k,m_k}, \alpha_k,$ where $m_k \geq 0,$
there exist $\{e_{k,i}|A_{k,i}\}_{1 \leq i \leq m_k} \subseteq I^-, \ n_k \geq m_k$
$\{e_{k,j}|A_{k,j}\}_{m_k+1 \leq j \leq n_k} \subseteq I^+$ where $(\neg A_{k,j}) \in \alpha_k,$
such that $c_k = \forall Y_k (\neg d_k \vee \bigvee_{i=1}^{n_k} e_{k,i})$ is $\mathcal{A}$-satisfiable,
and $c = \bigwedge_k c_k$ is $\mathcal{A}$-satisfiable$\}$

Proposition 14. $T_P^{\mathcal{A}}$ *is a continuous operator in the semi-lattice* $(\mathcal{I}, \subseteq_3)$.

Definition 15. The fixed point semantics of a general CLP program is the set of constrained atoms
$$\mathcal{F}(P) = lfp(T_P^{\mathcal{A}}) = T_P^{\mathcal{A}} \uparrow \omega.$$

A somewhat surprising result from [8] is that this fixed point semantics is fully abstract for the observation of computed answer constraints with constructive negation by pruning.

Theorem 16 (Full abstraction)[8]. $\mathcal{O}(P) = \mathcal{F}(P)$.

Constructive negation by pruning is the first scheme to receive a fully abstract fixed point semantics w.r.t. computed answer constraints. This result means that the fixed point semantics fully characterizes the operational behavior of general CLP programs. It is thus possible to analyze and transform general CLP programs by reasoning at the fixed point semantics level of abstraction while preserving the equivalence based on the observation of computed answer constraints.

Completeness w.r.t. the logical semantics follows from the fact that the finite powers of T_P^A define the same ground partial interpretation as the finite powers of Φ_P^A. Hence by the result of Kunen [15] the fixed point semantics defines the same three-valued consequences as the Clark's completion of the program.

Lemma 17 [8]. $[\mathcal{F}(P)] = \Phi_P^A \uparrow \omega = [\mathcal{L}_3(P)]$.

Theorem 18 (Completeness of the operational semantics) [8]. $\mathcal{O}(P) \subseteq \mathcal{L}_3(P)$. $\mathcal{L}_3^+(P) \sqsubseteq_f \mathcal{O}^+(P)$ and $\mathcal{L}_3^-(P) \sqsubseteq \mathcal{O}^-(P)$.

Here again one can remark that putting double negations on positive goals in the program suffices to obtain a strong completeness result w.r.t. the logical semantics (i.e. $\mathcal{L}_3(P) \sqsubseteq \mathcal{O}(P)$ instead of $\mathcal{L}_3(P) \sqsubseteq_f \mathcal{O}(P)$).

6 Optimization higher-order predicates

For crucial practical reasons, most CLP systems with arithmetic constraints, such as CHIP, CLP(R) or Prolog III, include metalevel facilities for finding optimal solutions to a goal w.r.t. an objective function [26]. These constructs do not belong however to the formal scheme of constraint logic programming. In [9] and [21] it is shown that optimization higher-order predicates can be defined with a faithful logical semantics based on constructive negation. It is interesting to see that constructive negation by pruning specializes in this context into an efficient concurrent branch and bound like procedure. Furthermore, completeness w.r.t. logical semantics and full abstraction of the fixed point semantics continue to hold without any restriction on the degree of nesting of, and the degree of recursion through, optimization predicates in the program.

Definition 19. Let $(\mathcal{A}, \leq)$ be a total order. The *minimization* higher-order predicate

$$min(G(X), f(X))$$

where $G(X)$ is a goal and $f(X)$ is a term, is defined as an abbreviation for the formula:

$$G(X) \wedge \neg \exists Y (f(Y) < f(X) \wedge G(Y))$$

A μCLP program over $\mathcal{A}$ is a definite CLP program over $\mathcal{A}$ which may contain minimization predicates in clause bodies.

μCLP programs can be transformed into normal CLP programs by reading $min(G(X), f(X))$ as:

$$G(X), \neg gf(X)$$

where gf is a new predicate symbol, and by adding the following clause to the program:

$$gf(X) \leftarrow f(Y) < f(X)|G(Y).$$

It is easy to see that in this context negation of constraints and negation of frontiers amount to a simple form of term minimization:

Proposition 20. *Let $(\mathcal{A}, \leq)$ be a total order.*
Let $d(X, Y, Z) = c(X) \wedge f(X) < f(Y) \wedge d'(Y, Z)$, then $c(X) \wedge \neg \exists Y, Z\ d(X, Y, Z)$ is $\mathcal{A}$-equivalent to $c(X) \wedge f(X) \leq v$, if $v = min_{d(X,Y,Z)} f(Y)$ exists, false otherwise.

Corollary 21. *If $c(X) \wedge f(Y) < f(X)|G(Y) \triangleleft F$ then the $c(X) \wedge \neg_X F$ is $\mathcal{A}$-equivalent to $c(X) \wedge f(X) \leq v$ if $v = min_{d|\alpha \in F} min_d f(Y)$ exists, false otherwise.*

The pruning by success rule of the general scheme can thus be replaced by a restricted form of pruning with a term minimization constraint. The next corollary shows that the success by pruning rule can be replaced by a check for finite failure after pruning.

Corollary 22. *Let $c(X) \wedge f(Y) < f(X)|G(Y) \triangleleft F$, $c(X)|\alpha, G(X), \alpha' \triangleleft \{d|\Box\} \cup F'$. Then $d \wedge \neg_X F$ is $\mathcal{A}$-satisfiable iff $w = min_d f(X)$ exists and $(f(X) \leq w) \times F = \emptyset$.*

The procedural interpretation can thus be simplified accordingly by replacing frontier computations with a check for finite failure. To resolve a goal of the form $c|\alpha, min(G(X), f(X)), \alpha'$, two CSLD derivation trees are developed, one Ψ for $c|\alpha, G(X), \alpha'$, and one Ψ' for $c \wedge f(Y) < f(X)|G(Y)$.

Once a successful derivation is found in Ψ', say with answer constraint d, then Ψ is pruned by adding the constraint $f(X) \leq v$ if $v = min_d f(Y)$ exists, false otherwise.

Once a successful derivation is found in Ψ, say with answer constraint e, then Ψ and Ψ' are pruned by adding the constraint $f(X) \leq w$ if $w = min_e f(X)$ exists, false otherwise.

By definition a successful derivation for the minimization goal is a successful derivation in Ψ such that Ψ' is finitely failed after pruning. The minimization goal is finitely failed if Ψ is finitely failed after pruning. Figure 3 illustrates the pruning mechanism.

As these modifications preserve the equivalence with the general scheme in the context of optimization predicates the results of the previous section continue to hold.

Theorem 23. *[8] Let P be a $\mu CLP(\mathcal{A})$ program. The fixed point semantics $\mathcal{F}(P)$ is fully abstract w.r.t. computed answer constraints. The operational semantics is sound and complete w.r.t. the logical semantics $\mathcal{L}(P)$.*

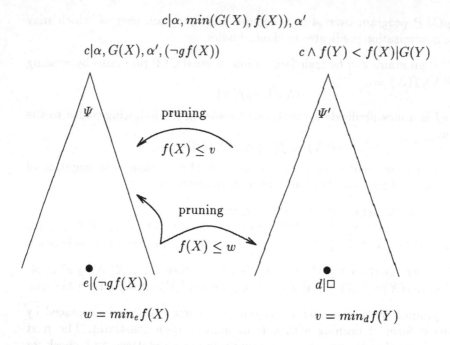

Fig. 3. Procedural interpretation of optimization predicates.

Example 3. An important particular case is when the only occurrence of the optimization predicate is in the head of the top-level goal. This is the case studied in [20]. This case is typical of scheduling applications for example where the top-level goal is

```
? min(schedule([X1,...,Xn], Xn))
```

and `schedule(L,X)` is defined by a definite CLP program over some numerical domain.

In that case both CSLD trees Ψ and Ψ' are identical up to variable renaming. The mutual pruning mechanism of the optimization scheme can thus be simplified into a single pruning in Ψ with constraint $f(X) \leq w$, as described in [20] or [26].

This is no longer true if the top-level goal contains a constraint or an atom outside the minimization predicate.

Example 4. Consider the $\mu CLP(R)$ program P

```
p(0)
p(X) :- X>1, p(X).
```

and the goal `X>1|min(p(X),X)`.

The first CSLD tree for `X>1|p(X)` is infinite. The second CSLD tree for `X>1,Y<X|p(Y)` contains a success with answer constraint $Y = 0$. The pruning

by success rule has for effect to prune the first tree with the constraint $X \leq 0$, therefore the first tree gets finitely failed and the answer to the minimization goal is no, in accordance to the logical semantics.

Note that the optimization procedures described in [26], [9] and [21] either incorrectly answer $X = 1$, or loop forever on this example. This shows the difficulty to define a complete scheme for optimization w.r.t. logical failures, and w.r.t. successes as well when minimization predicates are nested.

Completeness theorem 23 holds without any restriction on $\mu CLP(\mathcal{A})$ programs. Minimization predicates can thus be composed arbitrarily in a program, and, as an extreme case, one can also remark that recursion through optimization predicates is supported by the scheme.

The optimization predicates defined in [9] or [21] are however more general than those considered here as they allow to protect a set of variables in the goal subject to optimization. The effect is to localize the optimization to the remaining variables, and relativize the result to the set of *protected variables*.

Definition 24. The *local minimization* predicate

$$min(G(X, Y), [X], f(X, Y))$$

where $[X]$ is the set of protected variables is defined as an abbreviation for the formula

$$G(X, Y) \wedge \neg \exists Z(f(X, Z) < f(X, Y) \wedge G(X, Z)).$$

The local maximization predicate is defined similarly.

Example 5. For example local optimization predicates allow to express the min-max method of game theory simply with the following goal (for depth 2)

```
? max( min((move(X,Y),move(Y,Z)),[X,Y],val(Z)), [X], val(Z))
```

Note that protected variables are necessary in this example to conform to the intended semantics.

For local optimization predicates the previous operational scheme of optimization predicates is not correct as proposition 20 becomes irrelevant in presence of protected variables. This is not surprising and there is no hope to significantly improve a general scheme for negation in the context of local optimization predicates, as it is easy to see that any normal logic program can be encoded into a CLP program with local optimization predicates encoding negations [9].

7 Negation and optimization in CC languages

The class CC of concurrent constraint languages of Saraswat [23] adds to CLP languages a synchronization mechanism based on constraint entailment, called the *ask* operator. In this section we study the fundamental extension of CC languages with negation.

CC programs are usually presented with the following process algebra syntax to which we have added a negation operator, we call these programs *normal* CC programs:

$$
\begin{array}{lll}
\textit{Programs}\ \mathrm{P} ::= & \mathrm{D.A} & \text{(declarations and empty agent)} \\
\textit{Declarations}\ \mathrm{D} ::= & \epsilon & \text{(empty declaration)} \\
& |\ D.D & \text{(sequence of declarations)} \\
& |p(X) :: A & \text{(procedure declaration)} \\
\textit{Agents}\ \mathrm{A} ::= & c & \text{(tell)} \\
& |c \rightarrow A & \text{(ask)} \\
& |p(X) & \text{(procedure call)} \\
& |\exists X\ A & \text{(hiding)} \\
& |A \wedge A & \text{(conjunction)} \\
& |A \vee A & \text{(disjunction)} \\
& |\neg A & \text{(negation)}
\end{array}
$$

Provided the underlying structure $(\mathcal{A}, \leq)$ is a total order, normal CC programs allow to define an *optimization higher-order agent*

$$
min(A(X), f(X))
$$

as an abbreviation for the agent

$$
A(X) \wedge \neg \exists Y.(f(Y) < f(X) \wedge A(Y)).
$$

For the purpose of this article and to make clear the links with previous sections, we shall stick to the CLP syntax augmented with guarded literals to model the ask operator. A *guarded literal* will have the following syntax

$$
(c \rightarrow L)
$$

where c is a constraint and L a literal. A (normal) *CCLP program clause* is a clause

$$
A \leftarrow c|\alpha
$$

where A is a an atom, c is a (tell) constraint and α is a finite sequence of literals or guarded literals (α^+ will denote the subsequence of atoms in α, $\square$ will denote the empty sequence). A (normal) *concurrent constraint logic program* (CCLP) is a finite set of guarded clauses. A (normal) CCLP goal has the following syntax

$$
\leftarrow c|\alpha
$$

where c is a (tell) constraint and α is a conjunction of literals or guarded literals. Clearly CC declarations can rewritten as CCLP programs, CC agents as CCLP goals, and CC programs as CCLP programs with a query goal,

Example 6. Several Prolog implementations make it possible to execute a goal in coroutine. For example the system predefined predicate `freeze(X,A)` has for effect to delay the selection of atom A as long as X is a free variable (i.e. unless `nonvar(X)` becomes true). This is a typical use of the ask operator over the Herbrand domain $\mathcal{H}$. Predicate `freeze` can be defined by the $CCLP(\mathcal{H})$ program `freeze(X,A):-(nonvar(X) -> A)`.

Now the principle of constructive negation by pruning can be used to provide normal CCLP programs with an operational semantics. However the formation of frontiers by cross products for composite goals is not compatible with the guard mechanism based on the ask operator. Therefore we present the operational semantics of normal CCLP programs with a goal-frontier relation $\ll \in \mathcal{G} \times \mathcal{P}_f(\mathcal{G})$ defined with the CSLD rule in place of the RES and FRT rules, with a new rule for the ask, and with the PRN rule kept unchanged. Relation $\ll$ is defined as the least relation satisfying the axioms and rules given in table 2.

TRIV: $c|\alpha \ll \{c|\alpha\}$

CSLD: $$\frac{c \wedge c_1|\alpha, \alpha_1, \alpha' \ll F_1 \quad \ldots \quad c \wedge c_k|\alpha, \alpha_k, \alpha' \ll F_k}{c|\alpha, p(X), \alpha' \ll F_1 \cup \ldots \cup F_k}$$
where $\{(p(X) \leftarrow c_i|\alpha_i)\}_{1 \leq i \leq k}$ is the set of renamed clauses defining $p(X)$ in P such that $A \models \exists(c \wedge c_i)$.

ASK: $$\frac{c|\alpha, L, \alpha' \ll F \qquad A \models c \rightarrow d}{c|\alpha, (d \rightarrow L), \alpha' \ll F}$$

PRN: $$\frac{c|A \ll F \qquad c \wedge \neg_X S|\alpha, \alpha' \ll F'}{c|\alpha, \neg A, \alpha' \ll \{c|\neg A\} \times F' \cup F''}$$

where $X = V(c|A)$, S is a set of successful nodes in F and $F'' = \{(c \wedge \neg_X F|\alpha) : c|\alpha \in F', \alpha^+ = \emptyset\}$

Table 2. Definition of the goal-frontier relation for normal CCLP languages.

Note that the negation of frontiers ($\neg_X F$) is not affected by the presence of guarded literals. The guards are simply ignored just as in the standard semantics of CC [22] an agent $c \rightarrow A$ is blocked forever if the store entails $\neg c$[5].

Definition 25. Let P be a normal $CCLP(A)$ program. A *computed answer constraint* for a goal $c|\alpha$ is a constraint d such that $c|\alpha \ll \{c|\square\} \cup F$. A *computed answer suspension* for a goal $c|\alpha$ is a goal $G = d|(d_1 \rightarrow \mathcal{L}_1), \ldots, (d_n \rightarrow \mathcal{L}_n)$ composed of a constraint and guarded literals, such that $c|\alpha \ll \{G\} \cup F$.

---

[5] Clearly one can also argue that if the store entails $\neg c$ the ask agent $(c \rightarrow A)$ should fail [23]. This convention can be accommodated in our scheme simply by negating the ask constraints as well as the tell constraints in the negation of a frontier.

Note that the opposite convention is used in [25], i.e. $c \rightarrow A$ succeeds if the store entails $\neg c$. This choice corresponds to the interpretation of the arrow as an implication in classical logic. This should not be confused with the interpretation of the ask operator as a pure control mechanism. The classical implication operator $c \Rightarrow A$ is defined with two ask operators by $c \rightarrow A \wedge \neg c \rightarrow true$

Example 7. Consider the following CCLP program

```
p(0).
p(1).
q(X,Y):-p(X),(X#0 -> p(Y))
```

The goal ?q(X,Y) has one answer suspension and two answer constraints:

```
? q(X,Y)
X=1,Y=0;
X=1,Y=1;
X=0,(X#0 -> p(Y));
```

These answers are obtained with the following derivation:

$$\dfrac{x = 1, y = 0|\square \lll \{x = 1, y = 0|\square\} \qquad\qquad x = 1, y = 1|\square \lll \{x = 1, y = 1|\square\}}{\dfrac{x = 1|p(y) \lll \{x = 1, y = 0|\square, \ x = 1, y = 1|\square\}}{\dfrac{x = 1|(x \neq 0 \rightarrow p(y)) \lll \{x = 1, y = 0|\square, \ x = 1, y = 1|\square\}}{\dfrac{x = 0|\ (x \neq 0 \rightarrow p(y)) \lll \{x = 0|(x \neq 0 \rightarrow p(y))\} \qquad\qquad \prime\prime}{\dfrac{true|p(x), (x \neq 0 \rightarrow p(y) \lll \{x = 0|(x \neq 0 \rightarrow p(y)), \ x = 1, y = 0|\square, \ x = 1, y = 1|\square\}}{true|q(x,y) \lll \{x = 0|(x \neq 0 \rightarrow p(y)), \ x = 1, y = 0|\square, \ x = 1, y = 1|\square\}}}}}}$$

Example 8. If we place a negation on $p(x)$ in the definition of q in the previous example, then the program

```
p(0).
p(1).
q(X,Y):-not p(X),(X#0 -> p(Y))
```

produces two answer constraints and no answer suspension to the goal ?q(X,Y):

```
? q(X,Y)
X#0,X#1,Y=0;
X#0,X#1,Y=1;
```

The derivation is obtained basically with the following PRN derivation step:

$$\dfrac{p(x) \lll \{x = 0|\square, \ x = 1|\square\} \qquad \begin{array}{c} x \neq 0, x \neq 1|(x \neq 0 \rightarrow p(y)) \lll \\ \{x \neq 0, x \neq 1, y = 0|\square, \ x \neq 0, x \neq 1, y = 1|\square\} \end{array}}{\begin{array}{c}\neg p(x), (x \neq 0 \rightarrow p(y)) \lll \{x \neq 0, x \neq 1, y = 0|\square, \ x \neq 0, x \neq 1, y = 1|\square, \\ x \neq 0, x \neq 1, y = 0|\neg p(x), \ x \neq 0, x \neq 1, y = 1|\neg p(x)\}\end{array}}$$

If we look at the procedural interpretation, in order to resolve a goal $c|\alpha, \neg A, \alpha'$ where $\neg A$ is the selected literal, two CSLD resolution trees are developed following the CSLD and ASK rules, one Ψ for $c|\alpha, \alpha'$ and one Ψ' for $c|A$. Suspended goals in Ψ can be unblocked by the pruning by success rule, while suspensions in Ψ' limit the choice of frontiers. Suspended goals in Ψ' however are never unblocked once $\neg A$ has been selected, although the constraints of some nodes in Ψ may entail the guard. This is a limitation of our operational scheme due to the principle of developing a single auxiliary CSLD derivation tree for the resolution of a negative literal.

8 Conclusion

The principle of constructive negation by pruning provides normal CLP programs with a complete operational semantics w.r.t. Kunen's three-valued logic semantics. The practical advantage of constructive negation by pruning for constraint logic programming is that it relies on standard CSLD derivation trees for definite goals only. The only extra machinery to handle negation is a concurrent pruning mechanism over standard CSLD derivation trees, in particular there is no need for considering complex subgoals with explicit quantifiers.

Constructive negation by pruning provides also a fundament to branch and bound procedures and min-max methods lifted to a full first-order setting. We have indicated a class of optimization higher-order predicates for which the operational semantics of constructive negation by pruning simplifies into a concurrent branch and bound like procedure without frontier computation.

On the theoretical side, constructive negation by pruning possesses a fully abstract fixed point semantics w.r.t. computed answer constraints. The fixed point semantics is based on a simple finitary version of Fitting's operator. The full abstraction result shows that the operational behavior of the program is fully characterized by the fixed point semantics.

Finally we have shown that the principle of constructive negation by pruning could be used to extend the class CC of concurrent constraint languages with negation and optimization higher-order agents. The operational semantics of normal CLP programs has been generalized to deal with normal CC programs. This fundamental extension now raises many interesting questions both on the operational aspects of the interactions between ask and negation, and on the nature of a denotational semantics in the style of [23] for normal CC languages.

References

1. K. Apt, R. Bol, "Logic programming and negation: a survey", Journal of Logic Programming, 19-20, pp.9-71, 1994.
2. K. Apt, M. Gabrielli, "Declarative interpretations reconsidered", Proc. 11th ICLP'94, MIT Press, 1994.
3. A. Bossi, M. Fabris, M.C. Meo, "A bottom-up semantics for constructive negation", Proc of the 11th Int. Conf. on Logic Programming, pp.520-534, MIT Press, 1994.
4. A. Bossi, M. Gabbrielli, G. Levi, M. Martelli, "The s-semantics approach: theory and applications", Journal of Logic Programming, 19-20, pp.149-197, 1994.
5. P. Bruscoli, F. Levi, G. Levi, M.C. Meo, "Intensional negation", GULP'93, eight conference on logic programming, Italy. June 1993.

6. D. Chan, "Constructive negation based on the completed database", in: R.A. Kowalski and K.A. Bowen (eds), Proc. of the fifth International Conference on Logic Programming, MIT Press, Cambridge, MA, pp.11-125, 1988.

7. W. Drabent, "What is failure? An approach to constructive negation", to appear in Acta Informatica, 1994.

8. F. Fages, "Constructive negation by pruning", Technical report 94-14, Ecole Normale Supérieure, Paris. Sept. 1994. Submitted for publication.

9. F. Fages, "On the semantics of optimization predicates in CLP languages", 13th FSTTCS conference, Bombay, LNCS 761, Springer-Verlag, pp. 193-204, 1993.

10. F. Fages, J. Fowler, T. Sola, "Handling preferences in constraint logic programming with relational optimization", Proc of PLILP'94, Madrid, 1994.

11. M. Fitting, "A Kripke/Kleene semantics for logic programs", Journal of Logic Programming, 2(4), pp.295-312, 1985.

12. M. Gabbrielli, G. Levi, "Modeling answer constraint in constraint logic programs", ICLP'91, Paris, MIT Press, 1991.

13. J. Jaffar, J.L. Lassez, "Constraint Logic Programming", Proc. of POPL'87, Munich. 1987.

14. J. Jaffar, M.J. Maher, "Constraint logic programming: a survey", Journal of Logic Programming, 19-20, 1994.

15. K. Kunen, "Negation in logic programming", Journal of Logic Programming, 4(3), pp.289-308, 1987.

16. K. Kunen, "Signed data dependencies in logic programming", Journal of Logic Programming, 7(3), pp.231-245, 1989.

17. J.W. Lloyd, "Foundations of Logic Programming", Springer Verlag. 1987.

18. M.J. Maher, "Logic semantics for a class of committed-choice languages", Proc. 4th International Conference on Logic Programming, pp.858-876, MIT Press, 1987.

19. M.J. Maher, "A logic programming view of CLP", Proc. 10th International Conference on Logic Programming, pp.737-753, MIT Press, 1993.

20. M. Maher, P.J. Stuckey, "Expanding query power in constraint logic programming languages", Proc. NACLP'89, MIT Press, 1989.

21. K. Marriott, P.J. Stuckey, "Semantics of CLP programs with optimization", Technical report, Univ. of Melbourne, 1993.

22. V. Saraswat, "Concurrent constraint programming", Proc. POPL'90, San Francisco, pp.232-245, 1990.

23. V. Saraswat, "Concurrent constraint programming", MIT Press, 1993.

24. P. Stuckey, "Constructive negation for constraint logic programming", Proc. LICS'91, 1991.

25. P. Van Hentenryck, H. Simonis, M. Dincbas, "Constraint satisfaction using constraint logic programming", Artificial Intelligence 58, pp.11-159, 1992.

26. P. Van Hentenryck : "Constraint Satisfaction in Logic Programming", MIT Press 1989.

Constraint Handling Rules*

Thom Frühwirth

ECRC, Arabellastrasse 17, D-81925 Munich, Germany
email: thom@ecrc.de

Abstract. We are investigating the use of a class of logical formulas to define constraint theories and implement constraint solvers at the same time. The representation of constraint evaluation in a declarative formalism greatly facilitates the prototyping, extension, specialization and combination of constraint solvers. In our approach, constraint evaluation is specified using multi-headed guarded clauses called *constraint handling rules* (CHRs). CHRs define determinate conditional rewrite systems that express how conjunctions of constraints propagate and simplify.

In this paper we concentrate on CHRs as an extension for constraint logic programming languages. Into such languages, the CHRs can be tightly integrated. They can make use of any hard-wired solvers already built into the host language. Program clauses can be used to specify the non-deterministic behavior of constraints, i.e. to introduce search by constraints. In this way our approach merges the advantages of constraints (eager simplification by CHRs) and predicates (lazy choices by clauses).

1 Introduction

The advent of constraints in logic programming is one of the rare cases where both theoretical and practical aspects of a programming language have been improved. *Constraint logic programming* [JaLa87, VH89, VH91, F*92, JaMa94] combines the advantages of logic programming and constraint handling. In logic programming, problems are stated in a declarative way using rules to define relations (predicates). Problems are solved by the built-in logic programming engine (LPE) using chronological backtrack search. In constraint solving, efficient special-purpose algorithms are employed to solve sub-problems involving distinguished relations referred to as constraints.

Constraint logic programming (CLP) can be characterized by the interaction of a logic programming engine (LPE) with a constraint solver (CS). During program execution, the LPE incrementally sends constraints to the CS. The CS tries to solve the constraints. In the LPE the results from the CS cause *a priori* pruning of branches in the search tree spawned by the program. Unsatisfiability of the constraints means failure of the current branch, and thus reduces the number of possible branches, i.e. choices, to be explored via backtracking.

---

* Part of this work is supported by ESPRIT Project 5291 CHIC. This paper is a revised version of the technical report [Fru92].

A practical problem remains: Constraint solving is usually 'hard-wired' in a built-in constraint solver written in a low-level language. While efficient, this approach makes it hard to modify a CS or build a CS over a new domain, let alone reason about it. As the behavior of the CS can neither be inspected by the user nor explained by the computer, debugging of real life constraint logic programs is hard. It has been demanded for a long time that "constraint solvers must be completely changeable by users" (p. 276 in [CAL88]). The lack of declarativeness and flexibility becomes a major obstacle if one wants to

- build a new CS,
- extend the CS with new constraints,
- specialize the CS for a particular application,
- combine constraint solvers.

Our proposal to overcome this problem is a high-level language especially designed for writing constraint solvers, called *constraint handling rules* (CHRs) [Fru92, Fru93a, Fru93b, Fru94, B*94, FrHa95]. With CHRs, one can introduce *user-defined* constraints into a given high-level host language. In this extended abstract the host language is Prolog, a CLP language with equality over Herbrand terms as the only built-in constraint. We claim that using our logic based language allows for reasoning about, inspection and modification of a CS.

CHRs define *simplification* of and *propagation* over user-defined constraints. Simplification replaces constraints by simpler constraints while preserving logical equivalence, e.g.

X>Y,Y>X <=> false.

Propagation adds new constraints which are logically redundant but may cause further simplification, e.g.

X>Y,Y>Z ==> X>Z.

When repeatedly applied by a constraint handling engine (CHE) the constraints are incrementally solved as in a CS, e.g.

A>B,B>C,C>A results in false.

CHIP was the first CLP language to introduce constructs (demons, forward rules, conditionals) [VH89] for user-defined *constraint handling* (like constraint solving, simplification, propagation). These various constructs have been generalized into CHRs. CHRs are based on guarded rules, as can be found in concurrent logic programming languages [Sha89], in the Swedish branch of the Andorra family [HaJa90], Saraswats cc-framework of concurrent constraint programming [Sar93], and in the 'Guarded Rules' of [Smo91]. However all these languages (except CHIP) lack features essential to define non-trivial constraint handling, namely for handling conjunctions of constraints and defining constraint propagation. CHRs provide these two features using multi-headed rules and propagation rules.

In the next section, we introduce constraint handling rules by example. Then we give the syntax, semantics and describe an implementation of CHRs. In section 4, we give extensive examples of the use of CHRs for writing constraint solvers. Last but not least we discuss related work in more detail.

2   CHRs by Example

We define a user-defined constraint for less-than-or-equal, =<. In Prolog, the built-in *predicate* =< can only be evaluated if the arguments are known, while the user-defined *constraint* =< will also handle variable arguments.

```
% Constraint Declaration
(1a) constraints =</2.
(1b) label_with X=<Y if ground(X).
(1b) label_with X=<Y if ground(Y).

% Constraint Labeling
(2a) X=<Y :- leq(X,Y).
(2b) leq(0,Y).
(2c) leq(s(X),s(Y)) :- leq(X,Y).

% Constraint Handling
(3a) X=<Y <=> X=Y | true. % reflexivity
(3b) X=<Y,Y=<X <=> X=Y. % identity
(3c) X=<Y,Y=<Z ==> X=<Z. % transitivity
```

The CHRs of (3) specify how =< simplifies and propagates as a constraint. They implement reflexivity, identity and transitivity in a straightforward way. CHR (3a) states that X=<X is logically true. Hence, whenever we see the constraint X=<X we can simplify it to true. Similarly, CHR (3b) means that if we find X=<Y as well as X=<Y in the current constraint, we can replace it by the logically equivalent X=Y. CHRs (3a) and (3b) are called *simplification* CHRs. CHR (3a) detects satisfiability of a constraint, and CHR (3b) solves a conjunction of constraints returning an equality constraint. CHR (3c) states that the conjunction X=<Y,Y=<Z implies X=<Z. Operationally, we add logical consequences as a redundant constraint. This kind of CHR is called *propagation* CHR.

Redundancy produced by propagation CHRs is useful, as the following example shows. Given the query A=<B,C=<A,B=<C. The first two constraints cause CHR (3c) to fire and add C=<B to the constraint goal. This new constraint together with B=<C matches the head of CHR (3b). So the two constraints are replaced by B=C. The equality is applied to the rest of the constraint goal, A=<B,C=<A, resulting in A=<B,B=<A where B=C. CHR (3b) applies, resulting in A=B. The constraint goal contains no more inequalities, the simplification stops. The constraint solver we built has solved A=<B,C=<A,B=<C and produced the answer A=B,B=C:

```
:-    A=<B,C=<A,B=<C.
% C=<A,A=<B propagates C=<B by 3c.
% C=<B,B=<C simplifies to B=C by 3b.
% B=<A,A=<B simplifies to A=B by 3b.
      A=B,B=C.
```

Note that CHRs (3b) and (3c) have multiple head atoms, a feature that is essential in solving conjunctions of constraints. With single-headed CHRs alone, unsatisfiability of a conjunction of constraints (e.g. A<B,B<A) could never be detected and global constraint satisfaction (e.g. A=<B,C=<A,C=<B reduces to A=B,A=C) could not be achieved.

If no simplification and propagation is possible anymore, a constraint is chosen for automatic labeling. The labeling declaration (1b) and (1c) state that we may label using X=<Y if either X or Y are ground. Labeling is performed by using the CLP clauses of the constraint as labeling routine. In clause (2a), labeling using =< relies on a predicate leq which is defined by the two CLP clauses (2b) and (2c). For example, the query 4=<A,A=<3 propagates 4=<3 by CHR (3c). Then no more simplification is possible. 4=<3 is a constraint available for labeling. Executing its labeling routine produces a failure and so we know that 4=<A,A=<3 is unsatisfiable. A similar example is:

```
:-    s(s(0))=<A,A=<s(s(s(0))).
% s(s(0))=<A,A=<s(s(s(0))) propagates s(s(0))=<s(s(s(0))).
% Labeling using s(s(0))=<s(s(s(0))) succeeds.
% Labeling using s(s(0))=<A succeeds with A=s(s(X)).
% Labeling using A=<s(s(s(0))) succeeds with X=0.
      A=s(s(0)).
% On backtracking A=<s(s(s(0))) succeeds with X=s(0).
      A=s(s(s(0))).
% On backtracking A=<s(s(s(0))) fails.
      false.
```

When CHRs are integrated into a logic programming language, we can regard any predicate as a labeling routine of a constraint and add some CHRs for it. Seen this way, CHRs are lemmas that allow us to express the determinate information contained in a predicate. As a result, predicates and constraints are just alternate views. CHRs define "shortcuts" which allow us to arrive at an answer without backtracking and quicker than by executing the predicate. To see the power of such lemmas consider

```
append(X,[],L) <=> X=L,list(L).
```

A recursion on the list X in the usual definition of append is replaced by a simple unification X=L and a type check list(L).

3   Syntax, Semantics and Implementation

In this paper we assume that constraint handling rules extend a given constraint logic programming language. The syntax and semantics given here reflect this choice. It should be stressed, however, that the host language for CHRs need not be a CLP language. Indeed, work has been done at DFKI in the context of LISP [Her93]. This section follows [FrHa95].

3.1   Syntax

A CLP+CH program is a finite set of clauses from the CLP language and ¿from the language of CHRs. Clauses are built from atoms of the form $p(t_1, ...t_n)$ where p is a predicate symbol of arity n ($n \geq 0$) and $t_1, ...t_n$ is a n-tuple of terms. A term is a variable, e.g. X, or of the form $f(t_1, ...t_n)$ where f is a function symbol of arity n ($n \geq 0$) applied to a n-tuple of terms. Function symbols of arity 0 are also called constants. Predicate and function symbols start with lowercase letters while variables start with uppercase letters. Infix notation may be used for specific predicate symbols (e.g. $X = Y$) and functions symbols (e.g. $-X + Y$). There are two classes of distinguished atoms, built-in constraints and user-defined constraints. In most CLP languages there is a built-in constraint for syntactic equality over Herbrand terms, =, performing unification. The built-in constraint true, which is always satisfied, can be seen as an abbreviation for 1=1. false (short for 1=2) is the built-in constraint representing inconsistency.

A *CLP clause* is of the form

$$H :- B_1, ...B_n. \quad (n \geq 0)$$

where the head H is an atom but not a built-in constraint, the body $B_1, ...B_n$ is a conjunction of literals called *goals*. The empty body ($n = 0$) of a CLP clause may be denoted by the built-in constraint true. A *query* is a CLP clause without head.

There are two kinds of CHRs[2]. A *simplification* CHR is of the form

$$H_1, ...H_i \iff G_1, ...G_j \mid B_1, ...B_k.$$

A *propagation* CHR is of the form

$$H_1, ...H_i \implies G_1, ...G_j \mid B_1, ...B_k.$$

A *labeling declaration* for a user-defined constraint H is of the form

label_with H if $G_1, ...G_j$

where ($i > 0, j \geq 0, k \geq 0$) and the multi-head $H_1, ...H_i$ is a conjunction of user-defined constraints and the guard $G_1, ...G_j$ is a conjunction of literals which neither are, nor depend on, user-defined constraints.

---

[2] A third, hybrid kind as well as options and more declarations are described in [B*94].

3.2 Declarative Semantics

Declaratively, CLP programs are interpreted as formulas in first order logic. Extending a CLP language with CHRs preserves its declarative semantics. A CLP+CH *program* P is a conjunction of universally quantified clauses. A *predicate definition for* p is the set of all clauses in a program with the same predicate p in the head.

A CLP clause is an implication

$$H \leftarrow B_1 \wedge \ldots B_n.$$

Since we assume that a predicate definition defines a predicate completely, we strengthen the above using Clark's completion. Let $H_1 :\text{-}\ B_{11}, \ldots B_{n1}, \ldots, H_s$:- $B_{1s}, \ldots B_{ns}$, $(1 \leq s)$ be the clauses of the predicate definition for p. Then their logical reading is:

$$H \leftrightarrow (H = H_1 \wedge B_{11} \wedge \ldots B_{n1}) \vee \ldots \vee (H = H_s \wedge B_{1s} \wedge \ldots B_{ns})$$

H is of the form $p(X_1, \ldots, X_r)$ where $X_1, \ldots, X_r$ are different variables.

A simplification CHR is a logical equivalence provided the guard is true in the current context

$$(G_1 \wedge \ldots G_j) \rightarrow (H_1 \wedge \ldots H_i \leftrightarrow B_1 \wedge \ldots B_k).$$

A propagation CHR is an implication provided the guard is true

$$(G_1 \wedge \ldots G_j) \rightarrow (H_1 \wedge \ldots H_i \rightarrow B_1 \wedge \ldots B_k).$$

Procedurally, a CHR can fire if its guard allows it. A firing simplification CHR *replaces* the head constraint by the body, a firing propagation CHR *adds* the body to the head constraints.

3.3 Operational Semantics

The *operational semantics* of CLP+CH can be described by a transition system.

A *computation state* is a tuple

$$< Gs, C_U, C_B >,$$

where Gs is a set of goals, C_U and C_B are constraint stores for user-defined and built-in constraints respectively. A *constraint store* is a set of constraints. A set of atoms represents a conjunction of atoms.

The *initial state* consists of a query Gs and empty constraint stores,

$$< Gs, \{\}, \{\} >.$$

A *final state* is either *failed* (due to an inconsistent built-in constraint store represented by the unsatisfiable constraint `false`),

$$< Gs, C_U, \{\text{false}\} >,$$

or *successful* (no goals left to solve),

$$< \{\}, C_U, C_B >.$$

The union of the constraint stores in a successful final state is called *conditional answer* for the query Gs, written $answer(Gs)$.

The built-in constraint solver (CS) works on built-in constraints in C_B and Gs, the user-defined CS on user-defined constraints in C_U and Gs using CHRs, and the logic programming engine (LPE) on goals in Gs and C_U using CLP clauses. The following *computation steps* are possible to get from one computation state to the next.

Solve

$$< \{C\} \cup Gs, C_U, C_B > \longmapsto < Gs, C_U, C'_B >$$
if $(C \wedge C_B) \leftrightarrow C'_B$

The built-in CS updates the constraint store C_B if a new constraint C was found in Gs. To *update* the constraint store means to produce a new constraint store C'_B that is logically equivalent to the conjunction of the new constraint and the old constraint store.

We will write $H =_{set} H'$ to denote equality between the sets H and H', i.e. $H = \{A_1, \ldots, A_n\}$ and there is a permutation of H', $perm(H') = \{B_1, \ldots, B_n\}$, such that $A_i = B_i$ for all $1 \leq i \leq n$.

Introduce

$$< \{H\} \cup Gs, C_U, C_B > \longmapsto < Gs, \{H\} \cup C_U, C_B >$$
if H is a user-defined constraint

Simplify

$$< Gs, H' \cup C_U, C_B > \longmapsto < Gs \cup B, C_U, C_B >$$
if $(H \texttt{<=>} G \mid B) \in P$ and $C_B \to (H =_{set} H') \wedge answer(G)$

Propagate

$$< Gs, H' \cup C_U, C_B > \longmapsto < Gs \cup B, H' \cup C_U, C_B >$$
if $(H \texttt{==>} G \mid B) \in P$ and $C_B \to (H =_{set} H') \wedge answer(G)$

The constraint handling engine (CHE) applies CHRs to user-defined constraints in Gs and C_U whenever all user-defined constraints needed in the multi-head are present and the guard is satisfied. A guard G is *satisfied* if its local execution does not involve user-defined constraints and the result $answer(G)$ is entailed (implied) by the built-in constraint store C_B. Equality is entailed between two terms if they match. To *introduce* a user-defined constraint means to take it from the goal literals Gs and put it into the user-defined constraint store C_U. To *simplify* user-defined constraints H' means to replace them by B if H' matches the head H of a simplification CHR H `<=>` $G \mid B$ and the guard G is satisfied. To *propagate from* user-defined constraints H' means to add B to Gs if H' matches the head H of a propagation CHR H `==>` $G \mid B$ and G is satisfied.

Unfold

$$< \{H'\} \cup Gs, C_U, C_B > \longmapsto < Gs \cup B, C_U, \{H = H'\} \cup C_B >$$
if $(H \texttt{:-} B) \in P$.

The logic programming engine (LPE) unfolds goals in Gs. To *unfold* an atomic goal H' means to look for a clause $H: - B$ and to replace the H' by $(H = H')$ and B. As there are usually several clauses for a goal, unfolding is nondeterministic and thus a goal can be solved in different ways using different clauses. There can be CLP clauses for user-defined constraints. Thus they can be unfolded as well. This unfolding is called *(built-in) labeling*. Details can be found in [B*94].

Label
$$< Gs, \{H'\} \cup C_U, C_B > \longmapsto < Gs \cup B, C_U, \{H = H'\} \cup C_B >$$
if $(H \ :- \ B) \in P$ and (label_with H'' if $G) \in P$ and $C_B \to (H' = H'') \wedge$
$answer(G)$

Note that any constraint solver written with CHRs will be *determinate, incremental* and *concurrent*. By "determinate" we mean that the user-defined CS commits to every constraint simplification it makes. Otherwise we would not gain anything, as the CS would have to backtrack to undo choices like in a Prolog program. By "incremental" we mean that constraints can be added to the constraint store one at a time using the "introduce"-transition. Then CHRs may fire and simplify the user-defined constraint store. The rules can be applied concurrently, even using chaotic iteration (i.e. the same constraint can be simplified by different rules at the same time), because logically correct CHRs can only replace constraints by equivalent ones or add redundant constraints.

3.4 Implementation

The operational semantics are still far from the actual workings of an efficient implementation. At the moment, there exist two implementations, one prototype in LISP [Her93], and one fully developed compiler in a Prolog extension.

The compiler for CHRs together with a manual is available as a library of ECLiPSe [B*94], ECRC's advanced constraint logic programming platform, utilizing its delay-mechanism and built-in meta-predicates to create, inspect and manipulate delayed goals. All ECLiPSe documentation is available by anonymous ftp from ftp.ecrc.de, directory /pub/eclipse/doc. In such a sequential implementation, the transitions are tried in the textual order given before. To reflect the complexity of a program in the number of CHRs, at most two head constraints are allowed in a rule. A rule with more head constraints can be rewritten into several two-headed rules. This restriction also makes complexity for search of the head constraints of a CHR linear in the number of constraints on average (quadratic in the worst case) by using partitioning and indexing methods. Termination of a propagation CHR is achieved by never firing it a second time with the same pair of head constraints.

The CHRs library includes a debugger and a visual tracing toolkit as well as a full color demo using geometric constraints in a real-life application for wireless telecommunication. About 20 constraint solvers currently come with the release - for booleans, finite domains (similar to CHIP [VH89]), also over arbitrary ground terms, reals and pairs, incremental path consistency, temporal reasoning (quantitative and qualitative constraints over time points and intervals [Fru94]), for solving linear polynomials over the reals (similar to CLP(R) [J*92]) and rationals, for lists, sets, trees, terms and last but not least for terminological reasoning [FrHa95]. The average number of rules in a constraint solver is as low as 24. Typically it took only a few days to produce a reasonable prototype solver, since the usual formalisms to describe a constraint theory, i.e. inference rules, rewrite rules, sequents, first-order axioms, can be expressed as CHRs programs in a straightforward way. Thus one can directly express how constraints simplify and propagate without worrying about implementation details. Starting from this executable specification, the rules then can be refined and adapted to the specifics of the application.

On a wide range of solvers and examples, the run-time penalty for our declarative and high-level approach turned out to be a constant factor in comparison to dedicated built-in solvers (if available). Moreover, the slow-down is often within an order of magnitude. On some examples (e.g. those involving finite domains with the element-constraint), our approach is faster, since we can exactly define the amount of constraint simplification and propagation that is needed. This means that for performance and simplicity the solver can be kept as incomplete as the application allows it. Some solvers (e.g. disjunctive geometric constraints in the phone demo) would be very hard to recast in existing CLP languages.

4 Examples

4.1 Booleans

This example is taken from [F*92]. In the domain of boolean constraints, the behavior of an and-gate may be informally described by rules such as

- **If** one input is 0 **then** the output is 0,
- **If** the output is 1 **then** both inputs are 1.

We can define the and-gate with constraint handling rules as:

```
and(X,Y,Z) <=> X=0 | Z=0.
and(X,Y,Z) <=> Y=0 | Z=0.
and(X,Y,Z) <=> X=1 | Y=Z.
and(X,Y,Z) <=> Y=1 | X=Z.
and(X,Y,Z) <=> Z=1 | X=1,Y=1.
and(X,Y,Z1),and(X,Y,Z2) ==> Z1=Z2.
```

The first rule says that the constraint goal and(X,Y,Z), when it is known that the first input argument X is 0, can be reduced to asserting that the output Z must be 0. Hence the query and(X,Y,Z),X=0 will result in X=0, Z=0. The last rule says that if a goal contains both and(X,Y,Z1) and and(X,Y,Z2) then a consequence is that Z1 and Z2 must be the same.

Consider the following predicate from the well-known full-adder circuit:

```
add(I1,I2,I3,O1,O2):-
    xor(I1,I2,X1),
    and(I1,I2,A1),
    xor(X1,I3,O1),
    and(I3,X1,A2),
    or(A1,A2,O2).
```

The query add(I1,I2,0,O1,1) will produce I1=1,I2=1,O1=0. The computation proceeds as follows: Because I3=0, the output A2 of the and-gate with input I3 must be 0. As O2=1 and A2=0, the other input A1 of the or-gate must be 1. Because A1 is also the output of an and-gate, its inputs I1 and I2 must be both 1. Hence the output X1 of the first xor-gate must be 0, and therefore also the output O1 of the second xor-gate must be 0.

4.2 Maximum

We extend our solver for the inequality =< with a user-defined constraint over numbers, max(X,Y,Z), which holds if Z is the maximum of X and Y.

```
label_with max(X,Y,Z) if ground(X),ground(Y).
max(X,Y,Y):- X=<Y.
max(X,Y,X):- Y=<X.


max(X,X,Z) <=> X=Z.
max(X,Y,X) <=> Y=<X.
max(X,Y,Y) <=> X=<Y.
max(X,Y,Z),X=<Y <=> Y=Z,X=<Y.
max(X,Y,Z),Y=<X <=> X=Z,Y=<X.
max(X,Y,Z) ==> X=<Z,Y=<Z. % invariant and approximation
max(X,Y,Z1),max(X,Y,Z2) ==> Z1=Z2. % functional dependency
```

In the query max(A,B,C), max(A,C,D), the first constraint propagates A=<C, B=<C. The constraints A=<C, max(A,C,D) are simplified into C=D, A=<C. The new constraint goal is max(A,B,C), B=<C, C=D, A=<C. At this point, no more application of CHRs is possible. There is also no constraint that could be labeled. Therefore the conditional answer to our query max(A,B,C), max(A,C,D) is max(A,B,C), B=<C, C=D, A=<C.

Let $\leq$ be a built-in constraint, i.e. there is a built-in CS for inequalities (the user-defined constraint =< is no longer needed). Then we can replace the CHR

```
max(X,Y,Z),X=<Y <=> Y=Z,X=<Y
```

by

```
max(X,Y,Z) <=> X≤Y | Y=Z.
```

As a consequence, the first CHR becomes obsolete, as the built-in constraint X≤Y in the guard naturally covers the case when X=Y. Contrast this with the *user-defined* constraint =< in the head of the original CHR that clearly cannot match =. Now max can be defined by CHRs as follows.

```
max(X,Y,Z) <=> X≤Y | Y=Z.
max(X,Y,Z) <=> Y≤X | X=Z.
max(X,Y,X) <=> Y≤X.
max(X,Y,Y) <=> X≤Y.
max(X,Y,Z) ==> X≤Z,Y≤Z.
max(X,Y,Z1),max(X,Y,Z2) ==> Z1=Z2.
```

However, the CS for max is not complete, i.e. there are satisfiable or (worse) unsatisfiable constraint goals which are neither simplifiable nor available for labeling. For example, the query max(X,7,9) results in max(X,7,9),X≤9, but it is not reduced to X=9. In practice, a CS is often not complete for efficiency reasons [JaMa94]. If the application requires it, we can always add CHRs to cover the incomplete cases or modify the labeling declaration, while built-in constraint solvers cannot be as easily adopted. In our example, new CHRs of the form

```
max(X,Y,Z) <=> Y<Z | X=Z.
```

or an extended labeling declaration

```
label_with max(X,Y,Z) if ground(X),ground(Y).
label_with max(X,Y,Z) if ground(X),ground(Z).
label_with max(X,Y,Z) if ground(Y),ground(Z).
```

will help.

4.3 Temporal Time Point Constraints

In order to define a constraint solver for temporal constraints over time points we exploit the natural relationship of these constraints with ordering constraints in general. Therefore, we can start from the constraint solver for the less-than-or-equal constraint =<. We extend the inequality to the form X+N=<Y, where N is a given positive number, meaning that the distance in time of the two time points X and Y is at least N.

```
label_with XN =< Y if ground(XN),ground(Y).
XN=<Y :- XN ≤ Y.

X+N=<X <=> N=0.
X+N=<Y,X+M=<Y <=> NM is max(N,M) | X+NM=<Y.
X+N=<Y,Y+M=<X <=> N = 0, M = 0, X = Y.
```

```
X+N=<Y,Y+M=<Z ==> NM is N+M | X+NM=<Z.
```

In the labeling declaration the extension in syntax is reflected by requiring the first argument to be ground, such that X+N can be evaluated. The four CHRs are straightforward extensions of the ones for the simple inequality. Some auxiliary arithmetic computations with is are added to compute the distances for the resulting inequalities in the body. It is assumed that is delays if its right-hand side is not ground.

If we allow for negative N we can express maximal distances as well. The set of CHRs however will be non-terminating. There is no termination order, because there is no bound anymore on the minimal or maximal distances that could be computed. The termination problem is solved by introducing a new constraint =<* which stands for *derived* inequalities (resulting from simplification and propagation) as opposed to the initial ones written with =<.

```
label_with XN =< Y if ground(XN),ground(Y).
XN=<Y :- XN ≤ Y.

label_with XN =<* Y if ground(XN),ground(Y).
XN=<*Y :- XN ≤ Y.


X+N=<Y ==> X+N=<*Y.


X+N=<*X <=> N=<0.
X+N=<*Y,X+M=<*Y <=> NM is max(N,M) | X+NM=<*Y.
X+N=<*Y,Y+M=<*X <=> N=0,M=0 | X = Y.
X+N=<*Y,Y+M=< Z ==> NM is N+M | X+NM=<*Z.
```

The derived inequality constraint of course has the same labeling declaration and predicate specification as the original inequality. The original CHRs are turned into CHRs for the derived inequality. However, there is one exception, which is the crucial detail causing termination. In the last CHR performing transitive closure, one constraint must be not a derived but an original constraint. This also eliminates redundant inequalities that have been produced by the transitive closure before. To get the simplifications started, we have to give some initial derived constraints. This is done by the first CHR, which produces a derived inequality for each initial inequality.

In temporal reasoning applications, usually both minimal and maximal distance of two time points are given. Hence it is a good idea to merge the two constraints X+N=<Y,Y+M=<X (N positive and M negative) into a single constraint N=<Y-X=<(-M) (by abuse of the relational notation), where Y is the *starting point* and X is the *end point* of the interval Y-X. This is exactly the notation and meaning used in [DMP91].

```
label_with X =< Y =< Z if ground(X),ground(Y),ground(Y).
X =< Y =< Z:- X ≤ Y, Y ≤ Z.


label_with X =<* Y =<* Z if ground(X),ground(Y),ground(Y).
X =<* Y =<* Z:- X ≤ Y, Y ≤ Z.


A=<X-Y=<B ==> A=<*X-Y=<*B.


A=<*X-X=<*B <=> A=<0=<B.
A=<*X-Y=<*B <=> A=0,B=0 | X = Y.
A=<*X-Y=<*B,C=<*X-Y=<*D <=>
                     AC is max(A,C), BD is min(B,D) | AC=<*X-Y=<*BD.
A=<*X-Y=<*B,C=< Y-Z=< D ==> AC is A+C, BD is B+D | AC=<*X-Z=<*BD.
A=<*X-Y=<*B,C=< Z-Y=< D ==> AC is A-D, BD is B-C | AC=<*X-Z=<*BD.
```

Above, the CHRs have been extended correspondingly. The only interesting thing to note is that the last CHR about transitivity had to be split into two cases. The reason is that we rewrote X+N=<Y, Y+M=<X into N=<Y-X=<(-M) only, but not into M=<X-Y=<(-N), as the second formulation would have caused redundant computations for all CHRs except the one for transitivity.

The above CHRs will produce derived inequality constraints for every pair of time points (provided they are connected). Again this means redundant information and hence redundant computation, as we can compute all relations when knowing the distances from one given reference point to all other time points. We will specify the reference point X with a dummy constraint start(X). For this optimization only the first CHR has to be restricted from

```
A=<X-Y=<B ==> A=<*X-Y=<*B.
```

to

```
A=<X-Y=<B,start(X) ==> A=<*X-Y=<*B.
```

The resulting set of CHRs defines and implements a specialized constraint solver for temporal constraints on time points. Its behaviour has been tailored to temporal constraints starting from inequality constraints. Further optimizations are possible, for example using a dynamic shortest-path algorithm. If further speed-up is needed, once the prototype has been established and "tuned" as required, it can be reworked in a low-level language. For more on temporal reasoning with constraints, see [Fru94].

5 Reasoning

When seen as logical formulae, the logical *correctness* of CHRs with respect to a constraint theory can be established by using techniques from automated theorem proving. It is also useful to view CHRs as conditional rewrite systems. In this way we can establish that they are *canonical*, i.e. terminating and confluent by adopting well-known techniques such as termination proofs and unfailing completion. If we can prove a set of CHRs both canonical and correct we can be sure that the CHRs indeed implement a "well-behaved" constraint solver.

Briefly, *termination* [Der87] is proved by giving an ordering on atoms showing that the body of a rule is always smaller than the head of the rule. Such an ordering in addition introduces an intuitive notion of a "simpler" constraint, so that we also support the intuition that constraints get indeed simplified. When combining constraint solvers that share constraints, nonterminating simplification steps may arise even if each solver is terminating. E.g. one solver defines less-than in terms of greater-than and the other defines greater-than in terms of less-than.

The notion of *confluence* [Kir89] is important for combining constraint solvers as well as for concurrent applications of CHRs. Concurrent CHRs are not applied in a fixed order. As correct CHRs are logical consequences of the program, any result of a simplification or propagation step will have the same meaning, however it is not guaranteed anymore that the result is syntactically the same. In particular, a solver may be complete with one order of applications but incomplete with another one. Syntactically different constraint evaluations may also arise if combined solvers share constraints, depending on which solver comes first.

A set of CHRs is *confluent*, if each possible order of applications starting from any constraint goal leads to the same resulting constraint goal. A set of CHRs is *locally confluent* if any two constraint goals resulting from one application of a CHR to the initial constraint goal can be simplified into the same constraint goal. It is well-known from rewrite systems that local confluence and termination imply confluence. Furthermore, in a confluent set of CHRs, any constraint goal has a unique normal form, provided it exists. This means that the answer to a query will always be the most simple one[3].

6 Related Work

6.1 Constraint Logic Programming Languages

In the constraint logic programming CHIP [VH89], the general technique of *propagation* is employed over finite domains. The idea is to prune large search trees by enforcing local consistency of built-in and user-defined constraints. These techniques are orthogonal to our approach and thus can be integrated. *Demons* are essentially single-headed simplification CHRs without guards. However, labeling routines for a constraint are not possible. One version of CHIP also included

---

[3] It can, however, contain redundant constraints and introduce new variables.

forward rules [Gr89], which correspond to CHRs without guards. In practice, demons and forward rules have been proven useful in CHIP applications in the boolean domain for circuit design and verification. Their potential to define constraint solvers in general was not realised, maybe because of their limitations. [Gr89] also gives a detailed account of the semantics of forward rules and therefore CHRs without guards. In this sense, CHRs can be seen as an extension of the work on demons and forward rules in CHIP.

6.2 Combined and Extended Languages

In the following we relate our approach to other work on combining deterministic and nondeterministic computations into one logic programming language.

Amalgamating pure Prolog with single headed simplification CHRs results in a language of the family $cc(\downarrow, \rightarrow, \Rightarrow)$[4] of the cc framework proposed by Saraswat [Sar89, Sar93]. A close study of [Sar89] reveals that he proposes a special *Tell* operation called "inform" that could be used to simulate propagation CHRs. CHRs naturally fit the ask-and-tell interpretation of constraint logic programming introduced by Saraswat and applied by [VH91]. The constraint goal is viewed as constraint store for user-defined constraints. They are matched by the heads of CHRs and the guards ask if certain constraints hold in the built-in constraint store.

Guarded Rules [Smo91] correspond to single headed simplification CHRs. However, they are only used as "shortcuts" (lemmas) for predicates, not as definitions for user-written constraints. There are only built-in constraints. Interestingly, Smolka defines the built-in constraint system as a terminating and determinate reduction system. Hence it could be implemented by simplification CHRs.

The Andorra Model of D.H.D. Warren for parallel computation has inspired a rapid development of numerous languages and language schemes. The Andorra Kernel Language (AKL) [JaHa91] is a guarded language with built-in constraints based on an instance of the Kernel Andorra Prolog control framework. AKL combines don't care nondeterminism and don't know nondeterministism with the help of different guard operators. There are three kinds of guard operators, namely cut, commit and wait. In our approach, a logic programming language amalgamated with CHRs inherits the the commit operator of the CHRs as well as the guard operators of the host language (e.g. cut in the case of Prolog). Like most logic programming languages, AKL itself does not support two of the essential features for defining simplification of user-defined constraints: propagation rules and multiple head atoms.

---

[4] $\downarrow$ means *Ask* in addition *Tell* is supported, $\rightarrow$ is the commit operator for don't care nondeterminism used and $\Rightarrow$ is the commit operator for don't know nondeterminism able to describe pure Prolog.

6.3 Multiple Head Atoms

According to [Coh88] at the very beginning of the development of Prolog in the early 70's by Colmerauer and Kowalski, experiments were performed with clauses having multiple head atoms. More recently, clauses with multiple head atoms were proposed to model parallelism and distributed processing as well as objects, e.g. [AnPa90]. The similarity with CHRs is merely syntactical. Rules about distribution or objects cannot be regarded as specifying constraint handling. These rules are supposed to model the distribution and change of objects, while CHRs model equivalence and implication of constraints.

In committed choice languages, multiple head atoms have been considered only rarely. In his thesis, Saraswat remarks on multiple head atoms that "the notion seems to be very powerful" and that "extensive further investigations seems warranted" ([Sar89], p. 314). He motivates so-called *joint reductions* of multiple atoms as analogous to production rules of expert system languages like OPS5. The examples given suggest the use of joint reductions to model objects in a spirit similar to what is worked out in [AnPa90].

Multi-headed simplification CHRs are sufficient to simulate the parallel machine for multiset transformation proposed in [BCL88]. This machine is based on the chemical reaction metaphor as means to describe highly parallel computations for a wide spectrum of applications. Following [BCL88], we can implement the sieve of Eratosthenes to compute primes simply as:

```
primes(1) <=> true.
primes(N) <=> N>1 | M is N-1, prime(N),primes(M).
prime(I),prime(J) <=> 0 is J mod I | prime(I). % J is multiple of
I
```

The answer to the query primes(n) will be a conjunction of prime(p_i) where each p_i is a prime ($2 \leq p_i \leq n$).

7 Conclusions

Constraint handling rules (CHRs) are a language extension for writing user-defined constraints. Basically, CHRs are multi-headed guarded clauses. CHRs support rapid prototyping of built-in constraint solvers by providing executable specifications and implementations. They support specialization, modification and combination of constraint solvers.

By amalgamating a logic programming language with CHRs, a flexible, extensible constraint logic programming language results. It merges the advantages of constraints (simplification via CHRs) and predicates (choices via definite clauses). The result is a tight integration of the logic programming component and user-defined constraint solvers. In this way, a logical reconstruction for constraint solving in logic programming is achieved.

CHRs have been implemented as a library of ECLiPSe, ECRC's constraint logic programming platform and as a prototype in LISP at DFKI, Germany.

CHRs have been used to encode a wide range of constraint solvers, including new domains such as terminological and temporal reasoning. Although intended as a language for constraint simplification, CHRs could also serve as a powerful programming language on their own.

We believe that our approach has the potential to provide a comprehensive framework for constraints, because CHRs make it possible

- to add constraint solvers for any required domain of computation.
- to build and costumize constraint solvers for particular applications.
- to generate constraint solvers semi-automatically from constraint theories.
- to debug constraint systems.

Acknowledgements

Pascal Brisset implemented the CHRs library of ECLiPSe. Thanks to Alex, Jesper, Mark, Thierry and Volker, my colleagues at ECRC, who discussed these ideas with me. Thanks to Francesca Rossi and Gert Smolka as well as anonymous referees, who commented in detail on this paper in its various technical report versions.

References

[AnPa90] Andreoli J.-M. and Pareschi R., Linear Objects: Logical Processes with Built-In Inheritance, Seventh Intl Conf on Logic Programming MIT Press 1990, pp. 495-510.

[B*94] P. Brisset et al., ECLiPSe 3.4 Extensions User Manual, ECRC Munich, Germany, July 1994.

[BCL88] Banatre J.-P., Coutant A. and Le Metayer D., A Parallel Machine for Multiset Transformation and its Programming Style, Future Generation Computer Systems 4:133-144, 1988.

[CAL88] Aiba A. et al, Constraint Logic Programming Language CAL, Int Conf on Fifth Generation Computer Systems, 1988, Ohmsha Publishers, Tokyo, pp. 263-276.

[Coh88] J. Cohen, A View of the Origins and Development of Prolog, CACM 31(1):26-36, Jan. 1988.

[DMP91] R. Dechter, I. Meiri and J. Pearl, Temporal Constraint Networks, Journal of Artificial Intelligence 49:61-95, 1991.

[Der87] N. Dershowitz, Termination of Rewriting, Journal of Symbolic Computation, 3(1+2):69-116, 1987.

[Fru92] T. Frühwirth, *Constraint Simplification Rules*, Technical Report ECRC-92-18, ECRC Munich, Germany, July 1992 (revised version of Internal Report ECRC-LP-63, October 1991), available by anonymous ftp from ftp.ecrc.de, directory pub/ECRC_tech_reports/reports, file ECRC-92-18.ps.Z,

[F*92] T. Frühwirth, A. Herold, V. Küchenhoff, T. Le Provost, P. Lim, E. Monfroy and M. Wallace. *Constraint Logic Programming - An Informal Introduction*, Chapter in Logic Programming in Action, Springer LNCS 636, September 1992. Also Technical Report ECRC-93-05, ECRC Munich, Germany, February 1993.

[Fru93a] T. Frühwirth, *Entailment Simplification and Constraint Constructors for User-Defined Constraints*, Workshop on Constraint Logic Programming, Marseille, France, March 1993.

[Fru93b] T. Frühwirth, *User-Defined Constraint Handling*, Abstract, ICLP 93, Budapest, Hungary, MIT Press, June 1993.

[Fru94] T. Frühwirth, *Temporal Reasoning with Constraint Handling Rules*, Technical Report ECRC-94-05, ECRC Munich, Germany, February 1994 (first published as CORE-93-08, January 1993), available by anonymous ftp from ftp.ecrc.de, directory pub/ECRC_tech_reports/reports, file ECRC-94-05.ps.Z.

[FrHa95] T. Frühwirth and P. Hanschke, *Terminological Reasoning with Constraint Handling Rules*, Chapter in Principles and Practice of Constraint Programming (P. Van Hentenryck and V.J. Saraswat, Eds.), MIT Press, to appear. Revised version of Technical Report ECRC-94-06, ECRC Munich, Germany, February 1994, available by anonymous ftp from ftp.ecrc.de, directory pub/ECRC_tech_reports/reports, file ECRC-94-06.ps.Z.

[Gr89] T. Graf, Raisonnement sur les contraintes en programmation en logique, Ph.D. Thesis, Version of June 1989 Universite de Nice, France, September 1989 (in French).

[HaJa90] S. Haridi and S. Janson, Kernel Andorra Prolog and its Computation Model, Seventh International Conference on Logic Programming, MIT Press, 1990, pp. 31-46.

[Her93] Eine homogene Implementierungsebene fuer einen hybriden Wissensrepraesentationsformalismus, Master Thesis, in German, University of Kaiserslautern, Germany, April 1993.

[J*92] J. Jaffar et al., The CLP(R) Language and System, ACM Transactions on Programming Languages and Systems, Vol.14:3, July 1992, pp. 339-395.

[JaHa91] S. Janson and S. Haradi, Programming Paradigms of the Andorra Kernel Language, in Saraswat, Vijay and Ueda, Kazunori, editors, Logic Programming, Proceedings of the 1991 International Symposium, pp. 167–186. MIT Press, 1991.

[JaLa87] J. Jaffar and J.-L. Lassez, Constraint Logic Programming, ACM 14th POPL 87, Munich, Germany, January 1987, pp. 111-119.

[JaMa94] J. Jaffar and M. J. Maher, Constraint Logic Programming: A Survey, Journal of Logic Programming, 1994:19,20:503-581.

[Kir89] C. Kirchner and H. Kirchner, Rewriting: Theory and Applications, Working paper for a D.E.A. lecture at the University of Nancy I, France, 1989.

[Sar89] V. A. Saraswat, Concurrent Constraint Programming Languages, Ph.D. Dissertation, Carnegie Mellon Univ., Draft of Jan. 1989.

[Sar93] V. A. Saraswat, Concurrent Constraint Programming, MIT Press, Cambridge, 1993.

[Sha89] E. Shapiro, The Family of Concurrent Logic Programming Languages, ACM Computing Surveys, 21(3):413-510, September 1989.

[Smo91] G. Smolka, Residuation and Guarded Rules for Constraint Logic Programming, in F. Benhamou and A. Colmerauer, editors, Constraint Logic Programming: Selected Research, pages 405–419. MIT Press, 1993.

[VH89] P. Van Hentenryck, Constraint satisfaction in Logic Programming, MIT Press, Cambridge, 1989.

[VH91] P. van Hentenryck, Constraint Logic Programming, The Knowledge Engineering Review, Vol 6:3, 1991, pp 151-194.

Linear Constraint Solving in CLP-Languages*

Jean-Louis J. Imbert

Laboratoire d'Informatique de Clermont–Ferrand
Les Cezeaux, F–63177 Aubiere Cedex, France
Email: imbert@gia.univ-mrs.fr

Abstract. Linear constraint solving in Constraint Logic Programming languages rests on rewriting constraints under syntaxic forms. These syntaxic forms are generally called solved forms, since a satisfiable linear constraint system can be rewritten under one of these forms, and reciprocally, a linear constraint system of one of these forms is satisfiable. This paper aims to present three different solved forms two of which are used in the main CLP languages with linear constraints CHIP, CLP($\Re$) and Prolog III. The third form was proposed by JL. Imbert and P. Van Hentenryck in 1991 [8]. We discuss the advantages and disadvantages of each and present the results of some comparative tests.

Keywords: Solved Forms, Constraint Logic Programming.

1 Introduction

Constraint Logic Programming (CLP) is the combination of two programming paradigms: Logic Programming and Constraint Programming. The power of Logic Programming rests on its relational form, and on non-determinism and unification. Unification is an equational theory. The pioneers are A. Robinson [18] and R. Kowalski & D. Kuehner [11] for the automatic deduction, and A. Colmerauer & P. Roussel [1], and R. Kowalski [12, 13] for the specific part of Logic Programming. Constraint Programming makes it possible to formulate problems in a declarative way. Constraints express relations between objects. The pioneers are D. Waltz [24], A. Mackworth [17], J.L. Laurière [15, 16], G.L. Steele, G.J.Sussman [20, 21]. Constraint Logic Programming aims at generalizing Logic Programming in order to extend it to domains distinct from Herbrand universe, using more efficient computation mechanisms. Unification is replaced by Constraint Solving. ¿From this, we need to find Constraint Solvers which on the one hand are able to incrementally process constraints, on the other hand fit with backtracking techniques. The introduction of constraints into a Logic programming language was first realized with Prolog II (infinite trees and disequations ($\neq$) on trees) developed in Marseilles by Alain Colmerauer in 1982 [2]. However, Constraint logic Programming really takes wing in 1985. In 1986, J. Jaffar

---

* A short version of this paper appeared in [6].

JL. Lassez [9] proposed a general theoretical structure for this type of language. In this article, we are interested in linear constraints. The main languages ensuing from this approach and processing linear constraints on rationnal and/or float are CHIP [4] developed at E.C.R.C. (Munich, Germany) by M. Dincbas and his team, CLP($\Re$) [10]developed by JL. Lassez and his team (IBM, Yorktown Heights, NY, USA) and Prolog III [3]developed by A. Colmerauer and his team in Marseilles (France).

This paper presents and compares three solved forms for linear constraint systems. These forms fit the incremental objective very well, and fit the efficiency and backtracking objectives to different degrees. Each of them has some advantages and some drawbacks. A *solved form* is a syntactic form such that if a constraint or a constraint system is satisfiable, then it can be rewritten under this form, and reciprocally, a constraint or a constraint system under this form is satisfiable. A constraint system or a constraint is satisfiable if it has at least one solution. We are interested in constraints of the three following forms:

$$0 = a_n x_n + \ldots + a_1 x_1 + a_0 \text{ (equation)}$$
$$0 \leq a_n x_n + \ldots + a_1 x_1 + a_0 \text{ (inequation)}$$
$$0 \neq a_n x_n + \ldots + a_1 x_1 + a_0 \text{ (disequation)}$$

or equivalent forms. In practice, each inequation is replaced by an equation with a new variable s called *slack variable* as follows:

$$s = a_n x_n + \ldots + a_1 x_1 + a_0, \quad \text{et} \quad 0 \leq s$$

Generally, $0 \leq s$ is left understood. Since the slack variable s represents the inequation $0 \leq a_n x_n + \ldots + a_1 x_1 + a_0$, there are as many slack variables as there are inequations in the system. Now, we have only two types of constraints ($=$ and $\neq$), but we have two types of variables: *arbitrary variables* denoted by x_i which can take any value, and slack variables denoted by s_j which can take only non-negative values. Section 2 draws the main characteristics a constraint solver for CLP-languages have to satisfy. Section 3 presents the three solved forms for the equations: the Gauss-Jordan Solved Form (diagonal form) used in CHIP and CLP($\Re$), Gaussian Solved Form (triangular form) used in Prolog III, and *Classification Solved form* [8]. Section 4 tackles the problems of disequations. Finally, in Section 5, the results of some comparisons between these organisations are given along with general remarks on the advantages of each of them.

In the sequel, a variable is said *to be in* or *occurs in* a linear constraint if its coefficient is non-zero in this constraint. It is said to be k times in a linear constraint system when it exactly appears in k distinct constraints of this system. It is in a system if k is non-zero. We assume that each variable occurs at most once in each constraint. An equation is in *solved form* if it is written in one of the following two forms:

$$\begin{cases} x_j = \sum_{i \neq j} a_i x_i + \sum_k b_k s_k + a_0 \\ \\ s_j = \sum_{k \neq j} b_k s_k + a_0 \quad (0 \leq a_0). \end{cases}$$

The lefthand side (lhs) variable is said *defined*. Variables in the equation rhs member are called *parameters*. It is evident that a solution is obtained as soon as the parameter values are known. The solved form for a disequation is

$$0 \neq \sum_i a_i x_i + \sum_k b_k s_k + a_0$$

with $a_0 \neq 0$ when no variable is in the rhs member of the disequation.

2   General characteristics

Let us recall the operational semantics of CLP-languages: Let the following request

$$S_0 , \quad B_0, B_1, \ldots, B_n$$

where S_0 is a satisfiable constraint system, and $B_0, B_1, \ldots, B_n$ a list of predicates to be satisfied. Let

$$A \longrightarrow R , \quad A_0, \ldots, A_k$$

be a rule to be applied. The new request becomes

$$\underbrace{S_0, R, (B_0 = A)}_{S_1} , \quad A_0, \ldots, A_k, B_1, \ldots, B_n$$

where $S_0, R, (B_0 = A)$ [2] is the new satisfiable constraint system, and the sequence $A_0, \ldots, A_k, B_1, \ldots, B_n$ is the new predicate list. Successively applying rules, we obtain a sequence of requests

$$\vdots$$
$$S_2 , \quad B_1, \ldots, B_n$$
$$\vdots$$
$$S_p , \quad B_n$$
$$\vdots$$
$$S_{final}$$

each constraint system being satisfiable. When the predicate list becomes empty, we reach and output a solution which is the final system S_{final}. The backtracking occurs as soon as one of the three following cases is met:

---

[2] comma is for the juxtaposition of constraints.

- a solution is reached,
- no rule can be applied,
- the constraint system is unsatisfiable.

Moreover, the CLP model guarantees that, in the final constraint system S_{final}, each fixed variable x explicitly appears in the form

$$x = Constant.$$

An arbitrary or slack variable is *fixed* if in every solution of the system, it has the same value.

Example 1. The following system:

$$\begin{cases} x - y \geq 0 \\ y - x \geq 0 \\ x + 2y = 3 \\ x + z - t = 4 \end{cases}$$

will appear in the equivalent following form:

$$\begin{cases} x = 1 \\ y = 1 \\ z - t = 3 \end{cases}$$

We are interested in detecting fixed variables, firstly for arbitrary variables: on the one hand to simplify the constraint system, on the other hand, in systems which integrate non-linear delayed constraints to make their progressive linearisation possible, and secondly for slack variables: if the value is zero, to detect implicit equations and then the affine hull of the solution set, else, when the value is non-zero, the inequation associated with that slack variable is redundant.

Hence, the constraint solvers for CLP-languages have to satisfy the three following characteristics:

- Incrementality
- Backtracking
- Each fixed variable has to appear explicitly in the form $x = Constant$.

3 Equations

Consider a constraint system in a solved form and a new constraint. The objective of a Constraint Solver is to produce a new constraint system in the same solved form, equivalent to the conjunction of the old constraint system and the new constraint.

3.1 Gauss-Jordan Solved Form

An equation system is in *Gauss-Jordan Solved Form* denoted by GJSF, if its constraints are all in solved form and each defined variable appears only once in the whole system. In practice, the system is divided into two sub-systems E and S. E is the sub-system of equations with at least one arbitrary variable in each. In this case, the defined variable must be an arbitrary variable. S is the sub-system of other equations. Hence, there are only slack variables in S. The following system is in GJSF form.

$$\begin{cases} x_5 = x_3 + x_1 + 6 \\ x_4 = -8x_3 + 2s_4 - 1 \quad E \\ \underline{x_2 = -3x_1 + s_2 + 2} \\ s_3 = -s_4 + 5s_2 \\ s_1 = 2s_4 + s_2 + 1 \quad S \end{cases}$$

We will not speak about the S system. We assume that there exists a procedure named *simplex* which verifies that S is satisfiable, and when it is, outputs the system S in GJSF form and all the slack variables which are fixed. For more details on such a *simplex* procedure the reader is referred to [22]. The form GJSF is a solved form since assigning any acceptable values to parameter variables, we obtain a solution of the system. We will see below how to rewrite a satisfiable system under this form.

If we take a fixed ordering on the variables which occur in the system (for example: between variables of the same type, the greatest variable is the one with the greatest subscript. Arbitrary variables are greater than slack variables), and if, in each equation, the defined variable is the greatest one and the rhs is ordered, then two sets of equations defining the same affine space (solution set), have an identical solved form up to multiplying by a non-zero scalar for each equation [5]. This can be easily overcome with a normalization of coefficients of defined variables. This identical solved form is said the *canonical solved form* of the system. Generally, the E system is in this form. For the S system, this is not the case since the constant part of each equation must be positive when non-zero.

In practice, constraints are assumed to be inputed one after another. Let (E, S) [3] be a satisfiable system. We want to know if by adding in the new equation C, the new system is satisfiable. If it is, the new system must be in GJSF form. An algorithm adding a new equation in a system in GJSF form is given in Figure 1. This type of solved form is used in CLP-languages such as CHIP and CLP($\Re$).

---

[3] comma is for the juxtaposition of constraints.

Input: (E, S), an equation system in GJSF form. And C, an equation in solved form.

Output: A flag *Satisfiable* which indicates whether the system is or is not satisfiable. And if so, the new system in GJSF form.

begin

   0. Put the flag *Satisfiable* to *true*.

   1. In C, substitute for each variable defined in E its rhs member and simplify.

   2. If C is trivially satisfied, go to end.

      If C is trivially unsatisfied, put *Satisfiable* to *false* and go to end.

   3. If there is an arbitrary variable in C, rewrite C in solved form with an arbitrary variable as lhs member, then insert it into E and go to end.

   4. If there are only slack variables in C.

      Insert C into S using *simplex* procedure.

      If S is unsatisfiable, put *Satisfiable* to *false*,

      Else, replace in E each occurrence of a defined variable in S with its rhs member, and each occurrence of a fixed variable output by the *simplex* procedure with the value to which it is fixed.

end

Fig. 1. GJSF Algorithm to introduce a new equation

Example 2. Consider the initial system

$$(1)\ 0 = -x_5 + x_4 + x_3 + 3$$
$$(2)\ 0 = -x_5 + 2x_3 - x_1 + 1$$
$$(3)\ 0 = x_3 - x_1 - 3$$
$$(4)\ 2 \leq x_3$$

At the start E and S are empty. The equation (1) is introduced into E which becomes:

$$x_5 = x_4 + x_3 + 3.$$

In the equation (2), substitute out x_5, replacing it with $x_4 + x_3 + 3$. Then take x_4 as lhs member of the new constraint which becomes $x_4 = +x_3 - x_1 - 2$. Now to keep the system in GJSF form, we have to replace x_4 with $+x_3 - x_1 - 2$ in E, and introduce the new constraint into E. The system E is now:

$$\begin{cases} x_5 = 2x_3 - x_1 + 1 \\ x_4 = x_3 - x_1 - 2 \end{cases}$$

In equation (3) neither x_5 nor x_4 occur. It can be rewritten $x_3 = x_1 + 3$. Now replace x_3 with $x_1 + 3$ in E and introduce the new constraint into E:

$$\begin{cases} x_5 = x_1 + 7 \\ x_4 = 1 \\ x_3 = x_1 + 3 \end{cases}$$

Last, the inequation (4) rewritten $s_1 = x_3 - 2$ becomes $x_1 = s_1 - 1$ when $x_1 + 3$ is substituted in to x_3. Now, replace x_1 with $s_1 - 1$ in E and insert the new constraint into E. The final constraint system is:

$$\begin{cases} x_5 = s_1 + 6 \\ x_4 = 1 \\ x_3 = s_1 + 2 \\ x_1 = s_1 - 1 \end{cases}$$

One of the advantages of the GJSF form is that each fixed variable (arbitrary or slack[4]) is automatically detected. Among the drawbacks are the constant updating of constraints already processed in E. This makes the process heavy both in progress and in backtracking.

3.2 Gaussian Solved Form

To overcome the drawbacks of the previous solved form, a triangular form is chosen. As a result, some variables are now both defined in one constraint and parameters in others. The objective is to work as little as possible while backtracking. This solved form is called *Gaussian Solved Form* and is denoted GSF. It is based on a total ordering of the variables. In this ordering, each slack variable is less than each arbitrary variable. In some practical problems, we need a fictive variable to represent the constant part of equations. In these problems, this variable will be the least variable. In the sequel, to complete our variable ordering, if $\ll$ denotes the order relation, then we choose: $i \leq j$ implies $x_i \ll x_j$ and $s_i \ll s_j$. In an equation in GSF form, the defined variable is the greatest for the ordering $\ll$. It follows that when only slack variables appear in, $0 \leq a_0$ can be unsatisfied.

An equation system is in GSF form if each of its equations is in GSF form and each defined variable is defined only once in the whole system. In practice, not as in the GJSF form, the equation system is kept as a whole in E. However, to determine the satisfiability of the sub-system of equations in which only slack variables appear, it is necessary to duplicate this sub-system in another sub-system S, and to verify the satisfiability of S using the *simplex* procedure.

$$E = \begin{cases} x_5 = x_3 + x_1 + 6 \\ x_4 = -2x_2 + 2s_4 - 1 \qquad E_x \\ x_2 = -3x_1 + s_3 + 2 \\ \hline s_4 = s_3 - s_2 - 3 \qquad\qquad E_s \\ s_3 = 2s_2 + s_1 + 1 \end{cases}$$

$$S = \{$$

It is easy to show that the GSF form is a solved form when S is satisfiable. Figure 2 gives an algorithm which adds a new equation to a system in GSF form. The Prolog III language uses this type of organisation.

---

[4] these last ones by the *simplex* procedure

Input: An equation system E in GSF form. A system S in GJSF
        form equivalent to the sub-system of equations of E in
        which only slack variables appear. A new equation C in
        solved form.
Output: A flag named *Satisfiable* which indicates whether the
        system is satisfiable or not. And if so, the new system E
        in GSF form, and the new system S in GJSF form.
begin
  0. Put the flag *Satisfiable* to *true*.
  1. **while** the greatest variable of C is defined in E, replace it in C,
        then simplify and order C.
  2. If C is trivially satisfiable, go to end.
     If C is trivially unsatisfiable, put *false* in *Satisfiable* and go to end.
  3. Rewrite C in GSF form, then insert it in E.
  4. If only slack variables occur in,
        Duplicate C in C' and Insert C' in S using *simplex* procedure.
        If S is unsatisfiable, put *false* in *Satisfiable*,
        Else, for each fixed variable s found by the *simplex* procedure,
        insert the equation $0 = -s + c$ in E, only using steps 1 to 3.
        c is value to which s is fixed. (If s is already defined, the two
        constraints are exchanged)
end

Fig. 2. GSF Algorithm to introduce a new equation

Example 3. Consider the initial system of Example 2 augmented with a fifth
constraint:

$$(1)\ 0 = -x_5 + x_4 + x_3 + 3$$
$$(2)\ 0 = -x_5 + 2x_3 - x_1 + 1$$
$$(3)\ 0 = x_3 - x_1 - 3$$
$$(4)\ 2 \leq x_3$$
$$(5)\ 0 = -x_3 + x_2 - 1$$

At the start E is empty. In this example, S will not be used. The equation (1)
is added into) E:

$$x_5 = x_4 + x_3 + 3.$$

In equation (2), substitute $x_4 + x_3 + 3$ to x_5. The variable x_4 becomes defined:

$$\begin{cases} x_5 = x_4 + x_3 + 3 \\ x_4 = x_3 - x_1 - 2. \end{cases}$$

Equation (3) does not contain x_5 and x_4. It is rewritten $x_3 = x_1 + 3$ and added
into E which becomes:

$$\begin{cases} x_5 = x_4 + x_3 + 3 \\ x_4 = x_3 - x_1 - 2 \\ x_3 = x_1 + 3. \end{cases}$$

Inequation (4), rewritten $s_1 + 2 = x_3$, is transformed into $x_1 = s_1 - 1$ and inserted into E:

$$\begin{cases} x_5 = x_4 + x_3 + 3 \\ x_4 = x_3 - x_1 - 2 \\ x_3 = x_1 + 3 \\ x_1 = s_1 - 1 \end{cases}$$

Now, introduce the new constraint (5) $0 = -x_3 + x_2 - 1$. It is transformed into $0 = x_2 - x_1 - 4$. The variable x_1 is not replaced because it is not the greatest. Hence, the new system is

$$\begin{cases} x_5 = x_4 + x_3 + 3 \\ x_4 = x_3 - x_1 - 2 \\ x_3 = x_1 + 3 \\ x_2 = x_1 + 4 \\ x_1 = s_1 - 1 \end{cases}$$

Remark that, each time a new constraint is inserted into the system, no other constraint is modified. The uncontestable advantage of such an organisation in GSF is to minimize the work to be done while backtracking. We might think that a number of substitutions are avoided when the process is in progress, but sometimes this is misleading as shown in Example 4. Among the drawbacks are, firstly, that each fixed arbitrary variable is not detected, secondly, the same substitution can be done repeatedly, lastly it will be necessary to process some substitutions to output the final results. The first drawback can be overcome with a good ordering on variables, and with a demon to supervise some variables.

Example 4. Consider the initial system

$$(1)\ 0 = -x_5 + x_4 + x_3 - x_1 + 1$$
$$(2)\ 0 = +x_5 - 2x_4 + 2x_1$$
$$(3)\ 0 = +x_5 + x_4 - 4x_3 - 2x_1 - 2$$
$$(4)\ 0 = -x_5 + 2x_4 + x_3 - 2$$
$$(5)\ 0 = +x_5 + x_3 - x_2$$

The table of Figure 3 indicates the state of the system after the incremental introduction of constraints (1), (2), (3), (4) and (5). The first column indicates the number of the introduced constraint. Column Add gives the number of additions to be computed on the new constraint and column Updt gives the number of additions to be computed to update the GJSF system. Column Sum gives the sum of the additions computed so far. We see that for this particular example, the advantage had at the beginning with the GSF method disappears by the end. This example has no proof value, it just indicates that it is not clear that one method is better than another.

3.3 Classification

The *Classification Solved form* [8] denoted CSF aims at detecting all (arbitrary or slack) fixed variables, and to compute as few substitutions as possible. It

eq	GSF system		Ad	Sum	GJSF system		Ad	Updt	Sum
1	$x_5 = x_4 + x_3 - x_1 + 1$		0	0	$x_5 = x_4 + x_3 - x_1 + 1$		0	0	0
2	$x_5 = x_4 + x_3 - x_1 + 1$ $x_4 = x_3 + x_1 + 1$		4	4	$x_5 = 2x_3 + 2$ $x_4 = x_3 + x_1 + 1$		4	3	7
3	$x_5 = x_4 + x_3 - x_1 + 1$ $x_4 = x_3 + x_1 + 1$ $x_3 = -x_1 + 1$		7	11	$x_5 = -2x_1 + 4$ $x_4 = 2$ $x_3 = -x_1 + 1$		5	4	16
4	$x_5 = x_4 + x_3 - x_1 + 1$ $x_4 = x_3 + x_1 + 1$ $x_3 = -x_1 + 1$ $x_1 = 1$		9	20	$x_5 = 2$ $x_4 = 2$ $x_3 = 0$ $x_1 = 1$		5	2	23
5	$x_5 = x_4 + x_3 - x_1 + 1$ $x_4 = x_3 + x_1 + 1$ $x_3 = -x_1 + 1$ $x_2 = -3x_1 + 5$ $x_1 = 1$		9	29	$x_5 = 2$ $x_4 = 2$ $x_3 = 0$ $x_2 = 2$ $x_1 = 1$		2	0	25

Fig. 3. Example of drawback of the GSF method

divides the constraints into classes. As for the GJSF form, the equation system is composed of two sub-systems E and S. E is the sub-system of equations with at least one arbitrary variable in each. The defined variable must be an arbitrary variable. S is the sub-system of other equations in which appear only slack variables. The sub-system S is processed by the *simplex* procedure. In this solved form, E is divided into five classes $E_0, \ldots, E_4$ as defined in Figure 4. It is a solved form since, redefining the variable ordering, it is in GSF form. Figure 5 gives an algorithm which adds a new equation to a system in CSF form. The technique used is to maintain the constraints in the simplest form, without losing sight of the fact that we want to detect all the fixed variables. For example, let the equation be $x_j = a_i x_i + a_0$. Then, the variable x_j is fixed if and only if the variable x_i is fixed. The same reasoning holds for equations of the form $x_j = a_i s_i + a_0$. As a result, as soon as an equation can be put into one of these two forms, the substitution for the variables defined in E has not to be pushed beyond those defined in the classes E_0, E_1 and E_3 (substitutions from theses classes do not increase the number of variables in the new constraint). Then, if at least one of the variables defined in the new constraint is already defined in E, its definition being more complex than the new, it is temporarily removed. The new constraint is inserted in its class. Then the removed constraint is added to the new system as if it is a new constraint.

Example 5. Let $x_6 = x_4 - x_3 + 5x_2 + 2x_1 - 4$ be a constraint of E_2, and let $x_5 = 2x_6 + 1$ be the new constraint. While x_6 is not fixed, x_5 is not fixed, and reciprocally. It is unnecessary to substitute x_5 out of this new equation, we would obtain a more complicated system as shown below:

Class	Form of the equation	invariants
E_0	$x_j = a_0$	fixed variable
E_1	$x_j = a_i x_i + a_0$	E_1 must be in GSF or in GJSF. x_i can be defined in (E_2, E_4) but not in (E_0, E_3).
E_2	$x_j = \sum_{i \neq j} a_i x_i + \sum_k b_k s_k + a_0$ $rhs :$ at least one i and at least two variables	E_2 must be in GJSF. The x_i's cannot be defined in E. The s_k's can be defined in S.
E_3	$x_j = b_k s_k + a_0$	E_3 must be in GJSF. s_k can be defined in S.
E_4	$x_j = \sum_{k \neq j} b_k s_k + a_0$ at least two k	(E_4, S) must be in GJSF.

General invariant: the variables can be defined at most once in the whole system (E, S).

Fig. 4. Classification of the equations

$$
\left.
\begin{aligned}
x_5 &= 2x_6 + 1 \\
x_6 &= x_4 - x_3 + 5x_2 + 2x_1 - 4
\end{aligned}
\right\}
\begin{aligned}
E_1 \\
E_2
\end{aligned}
\; \text{CSF form}
$$

$$
\left.
\begin{aligned}
x_6 &= x_4 - x_3 + 5x_2 + 2x_1 - 4 \\
x_5 &= 2x_4 - 2x_3 + 10x_2 + 4x_1 - 7
\end{aligned}
\right\} \; \text{GSF and GJSF forms}
$$

For the constraints of the E_2 class, we do not have to substitute out slack variables since, while an arbitrary variable occurs in the right hand side member, it can take any value and the left hand side variable cannot be fixed.

Example 6. Let $x_6 = x_4 - x_3 + 5x_2 + 2x_1 - 4$ be a constraint of E_2, and let $x_6 = 2x_4 + 1$ be the new constraint. Remove $x_6 = x_4 - x_3 + 5x_2 + 2x_1 - 4$ from E_2, insert $x_6 = 2x_4 + 1$ in E_1, then input the removed constraint in the system gives the two following shorter constraints in the system:

$$
\left.
\begin{aligned}
x_6 &= 2x_4 + 1 \\
x_4 &= -x_3 + 5x_2 + 2x_1 - 5
\end{aligned}
\right\}
\begin{aligned}
E_1 \\
E_2
\end{aligned}
\; \text{CSF form}
$$

$$
\left.
\begin{aligned}
x_6 &= x_4 - x_3 + 5x_2 + 2x_1 - 4 \\
x_4 &= -x_3 + 5x_2 + 2x_1 - 5
\end{aligned}
\right\} \; \text{GSF form}
$$

$$
\left.
\begin{aligned}
x_6 &= -2x_3 + 10x_2 + 4x_1 - 9 \\
x_4 &= -x_3 + 5x_2 + 2x_1 - 5
\end{aligned}
\right\} \; \text{GJSF form}
$$

Input: (E, S), an equation system in CSF. C a new equation in solved form.
Output: A flag *Satisfiable* which indicates whether the system is
        satisfiable or not. And if so, the system increased by the
        new constraint, in CSF form.
begin
  0. Put the flag *Satisfiable* to *true*.
  1. Replace in C each variable defined in (E_0, E_1, E_3) by its
     rhs, and simplify.
  2. **While** it is possible and the constraint is not in a form of E_0,
        E_1 or E_3, replace in C each variable defined in E_2 and
        E_4 by its rhs, and simplify.
  3. If C is trivially satisfied, go to end.
     If C is trivially unsatisfied, put *false* in *Satisfiable* and go to end.
  4. If C can be put in one of the forms of E_0, E_1 or
     E_3, and if in C occurs a variable x_i defined in a
     constraint C' of E_2 or E_4,
     4.1.   Remove C' from E,
     4.2.   Rewrite C in solved form with x_i as lhs member,
     4.3.   Insert C in its class and update if necessary,
     4.4.   Insert C' in the system using CSF algo-
           rithm. Then, go to end.
  5. If an arbitrary variable still occurs in C, rewrite C in solved
     form with that variable as lhs member, then insert it into
     E and go to end.
  6. If only slack variables occur in C.
     Insert C in S using *simplex* procedure.
     If S is unsatisfiable, put *false* in *Satisfiable*,
     Else, replace in E_4 each slack variable defined in S by its
     rhs member, and replace in E each fixed variable given
     by the *simplex* procedure, by the value to which it is
     fixed. If necessary, change the constraints of classes.
end

Fig. 5. CSF Algorithm to introduce a new equation

For more details on this solved form, the reader is referred to [8].

4 Disequations

Let (F, D) be a linear constraint system, where F is the sub-system of the
equations and D the sub-system of the disequations. According to [14], such a
system is satisfiable if and only if, for each disequation d, the system $(F, \{d\})$
is satisfiable. Moreover, if F is satisfiable, the system $(F, \{d\})$ is unsatisfiable if
and only if by replacing in d every variable defined in F, by its rhs member, the
disequation $0 \neq 0$ is obtained.

Input: (E, S, D), a constraint system in GJSF, where (E, S) is
the set of equations, and D is the set of disequations. A
new disequation d in solved form.
Output: A flag named *Satisfiable* which indicates whether the
system is satisfiable or not. If it is, the system increased
by the new constraint in GJSF form.
begin
   0. Put the flag *Satisfiable* to *true*.
   1. Replace in d each defined variable of (E, S) by its rhs
      member, and simplify.
   2. If d is trivially satisfiable, go to end.
      If d is trivially unsatisfiable, put *false* in *Satisfiable*,
      Else insert d so modified in D.
end

Fig. 6. GJSF Algorithm to introduce a new disequation

4.1 Disequations and GJSF form

Let (E, S, D) be a linear constraint system, where (E, S) is an equation system, and D a disequation set. The system (E, S, D) is in GJSF form if the three following conditions are met: (E, S) is in GJSF form, each disequation of D is in solved form, and no variable defined in (E, S) occurs in D. In the GJSF form, the disequations are systematically updated, which implies a significant cost. Figure 6 gives an algorithm which adds a new disequation to a system in GJSF form. To take into account disequations when a new equation is added to the system, the algorithm of Figure 1 must be modified as follows: The system (E, S, D) is input in place of the system (E, S). The output system is of the same type of (E, S, D), and step 3 and 4 are modified as indicated in Figure 7.

Example 7. Let E be the following system:

$$E = \begin{cases} x_8 = x_3 + 2x_2 + 6 \\ x_7 = 1 \\ x_6 = x_3 - x_2 + 2 \\ x_4 = x_1 - 1 \end{cases}$$

Let $0 \neq x_8 + x_5 + x_4$ be the new disequation to be introduced. Eliminate the variables x_8 and x_4. This disequation becomes $0 \neq x_5 + x_3 + 2x_2 + x_1 + 5$, and is inserted into D.

$$D = \{\ldots, 0 \neq x_5 + x_3 + 2x_2 + x_1 + 5, \ldots\}$$

Now, let $0 = 2x_8 - x_3 - 1$ be a new equation to be introduced. Eliminate the variable x_8 from the equation, and rewrite it in solved form: $x_3 = -4x_2 - 11$.

3. If there is an arbitrary variable in C,
   3.1.   Rewrite C in solved form with an arbitrary variable as lhs member,
   3.2.   Replace in D the new defined variable of C, and simplify. If during the substitution, a disequation becomes trivially satisfied, remove it.
          If during the substitution, a disequation becomes trivially unsatisfied, put *false* in *Satisfiable*, and go to end.
   3.3.   Insert C into E, and go to end.
4. If there are only slack variables in C.
      Insert C into S using *simplex* procedure.
      If S is unsatisfiable, put *false* in *Satisfiable*,
      Else, replace in E and D each occurrence of a defined variable in S with its rhs member, and each occurrence of a fixed variable output by the *simplex* procedure with the value to which it is fixed. If during the substitution a disequation becomes trivially satisfiable, remove it, else if during the substitution a disequation becomes trivially unsatisfiable, put *false* in *Satisfiable*.

Fig. 7. Modifications in the GJSF equation Algorithm

The previous disequation then becomes $0 \neq x_5 - 2x_2 + x_1 - 6$, the system E is updated, and the equation $x_3 = -4x_2 - 11$ is inserted into E.

$$E = \begin{cases} x_8 = -2x_2 - 5 \\ x_7 = 1 \\ x_6 = -5x_2 - 9 \\ x_4 = x_1 - 1 \\ x_3 = -4x_2 - 11 \end{cases}$$

$$D = \{\ldots, 0 \neq x_5 - 2x_2 + x_1 - 6, \ldots\}$$

4.2 Disequations and GSF form

Let (E, D) be a linear constraint system, where E is an equation system, and D is a disequation set. The system (E, D) is in GSF form if the following three conditions are met: E is in GSF form, each disequation of D is in solved form and the greatest variable of each disequation is not defined in E. The objective is to do work only when necessary. Since when a variable is not defined it can take an infinite number of values giving a solution of E, there are an infinite number of solutions of a disequation having it as greatest variable. As a result, it suffices to put a device in place which makes it possible to supervise the moment when this variable becomes fixed. This device is called a daemon. Figure 8 gives an algorithm which introduces a new disequation d into (E, D). The algorithm of

Input: (E, D), a constraint system in GSF form, where E is the set of equations, and D the set of disequations. A new disequation d in solved form.

Output: A flag named *Satisfiable* which indicates whether the system is satisfiable or not. And if so, the system increased by the new constraint in GSF form.

begin

    0. Put the flag *Satisfiable* to *true*.

    1. **while** the greatest variable of d is defined in E, replace it, simplify and order d.

    2. If d is trivially satisfiable, go to end.

       If d is trivially unsatisfiable, put *false* in *Satisfiable*,

       Else insert d as modified in D.

end

Fig. 8. GSF Algorithm to introduce a new disequation

3.   3.1.   Rewrite C in GSF form, then insert it into E.

      3.2.   Replace in D the defined variable of C each time it is the greatest variable of a disequation of D, and simplify. For each modified disequation, continue to eliminate the greatest variable while it is defined in E.

          If during the substitution, a disequation becomes trivially satisfied, remove it.

          If during the substitution, a disequation becomes trivially unsatisfied, put *false* in *Satisfiable*, and go to end.

Fig. 9. Modifications of the GSF equation Algorithm

Figure 2 must be modified: the input systems are (E, D), and a system S in GJSF form equivalent to the sub-system of equations of E in which only slack variables appear. The output systems are of the same type, and step 3 is modified as indicated in Figure 9.

Example 8. Take again Example 7: Let $0 \neq x_8 + x_5 + x_4$ be the disequation to be introduced. Eliminate the variable x_8. This disequation becomes $0 \neq x_5 + x_4 + x_3 + 2x_2 + 6$, and is inserted into D, since x_5 is not defined in E.

$$E = \begin{cases} x_8 = x_3 + 2x_2 + 6 \\ x_7 = 1 \\ x_6 = x_3 - x_2 + 2 \\ x_4 = x_1 - 1 \end{cases}$$

$$D = \{\ldots, 0 \neq x_5 + x_4 + x_3 + 2x_2 + 6, \ldots\}$$

Now, let $0 = 2x_8 - x_3 - 1$ be the equation to be introduced. Eliminate the variable x_8 from this equation, and rewrite it: $x_3 = -4x_2 - 11$. Unlike the GJSF form, here, the previous disequation and the old equations in E are not modified, and the equation $x_3 = -4x_2 - 11$ is inserted into E.

$$E = \begin{cases} x_8 = x_3 + 2x_2 + 6 \\ x_7 = 1 \\ x_6 = x_3 - x_2 + 2 \\ x_4 = x_1 - 1 \\ x_3 = -4x_2 - 11 \end{cases}$$

$$D = \{\ldots, 0 \neq x_5 + x_4 + x_3 + 2x_2 + 6, \ldots\}$$

4.3 Disequations and CSF form

The CSF solved form aims at avoiding unnecessary substitutions. For example, let a constraint of D of the form $0 \neq a_i x_i + a_0$. While the variable x_i is not fixed, this constraint is satisfiable. Since this solved form detects all fixed variables, this type of disequation does not have to be modified while x_i is not fixed, even if x_i is defined. The same reasoning holds for constraints of the form $0 \neq a_i s_i + a_0$. For example, assume that we have the two following constraints in the system:

$$\begin{array}{ll} 0 \neq 2x_5 + 1 & D_1 \\ x_5 = x_4 - x_3 + 5x_2 + 2x_1 - 4 & E_2 \end{array}$$

If we had replaced x_5 by the rhs of the equation, we would have obtained the unnecessary following more complicated disequation.

$$0 \neq 2x_4 - 2x_3 + 10x_2 + 4x_1 - 7 \qquad D_2$$

Moreover, for constraints of the form $0 \neq \sum_i a_i x_i + \sum_k b_k s_k + a_0$ it is useless to substitute for slack variables while at least one arbitrary variable occurs in it. For any i, the variable x_i can take any value, and at least one makes $\sum_i a_i x_i + \sum_k b_k s_k + a_0$ non zero. For example, assume that we have the two following constraints in the system:

$$\begin{array}{ll} 0 \neq 2x_5 + s_3 - 1 & D_2 \\ s_3 = s_4 + 5s_2 + 2s_1 - 4 & S \end{array}$$

If we had replaced s_3 with the rhs of the equation, we would have done unnecessary work to obtain the following disequation.

$$0 \neq 2x_5 + s_4 + 5s_2 + 2s_1 - 5 \qquad D_2$$

With the same definitions and notations as Figure 4, the table of Figure 10 completes the classification for the disequations. The set D is divided into five classes $D_0, \ldots, D_4$ of which only the last four are kept. The algorithm of Figure 11 describes the operations to be realized in order to introduce a new disequation d into (E, S, D). When a new equation is inserted in one of the classes E_1 to E_4,

Class	Form of the disequation	invariants
D_0	$0 \neq a_0$	Trivial constraint
D_1	$0 \neq a_i x_i + a_0$	x_i must not be defined in E_0. It can be defined anywhere else.
D_2	$0 \neq \sum_i a_i x_i + \sum_k b_k s_k + a_0$ *at least one i and* *at least two variables*	The x_i's cannot be defined in E. The s_k's can be defined in S.
D_3	$0 \neq b_k s_k + a_0$	s_k can be defined in S, but cannot be fixed.
D_4	$0 \neq \sum_k b_k s_k + a_0$ *at least two k*	The s_k's cannot be defined in S.

Fig. 10. Classification of the disequations

only class D_2 is checked. If a constraint is inserted in E_0, then D_1 and D_2 are checked. When an equation changes class, there is no check except if it is in E_0. In this last case, only class D_1 is checked. Now, if a constraint is inserted in the system S, after its insertion using the *simplex* algorithm, class D_4 is updated, and each fixed variable is replaced in the whole system (E, D), by the value to which it is fixed. This can lead to new class changes. The modifications of Algorithm 5 implied by these considerations are evident and are found in the operations 4.4, 4.5, 5 and 6. For a precise example too long for this short paper, the reader is referred to [7]. Note that for this form there exist improvements using the *simplex* procedure, which are detailed in [8]. These improvements make it possible to divide in half the cost of updating in the disequations at the output of the *simplex* Algorithm.

5 Final Remarks

We have tested these solved forms [23, 19]. We have used three meta-interpreters similar to that presented in [7], one for each solved form. The *simplex* procedure used was the same for the three interpreters [22], and the ordering over variables, also the same: the defined variable, when we have this choice, is always the greatest one. We have not taken into account the improvements proposed in [8]: "Lazy dereferencing" and "Early detection of failure". The efficiency is measured by the number of additions processed in the substitutions, updatings included. The time to restore the system when backtracking has not been taken into account. In each case, the number of additions processed on the equations and the number of additions processed on the disequations have been counted separately. The tests have been carried out over eighteen small examples. We have brought

Input: (E, S, D), a constraint system in CSF, where (E, S) is a set of
  equations as defined in the CSF equation Algorithm, and D is
  the set of disequations. A disequation d in solved form.
Output: A flag named *Satisfiable* which indicates whether the system
  is satisfiable or not. And if so, the system increased by the
  new constraint, in CSF form.
begin
0. Put the flag *Satisfiable* to *true*.
1. Replace in d each defined variable of E_0 by its rhs member, and
  simplify.
2. **while** it is possible, and the disequation is not in a form of D_1 or
  D_3, replace in d each defined variable of (E_1, E_2, E_3, E_4)
  with its rhs member, and simplify.
3. If d is of the form of D_4, and while it is possible and the disequation is not of the form of D_3, replace in d each defined
  variable of S by its rhs member.
4. If d is trivially unsatisfiable, put *false* in *Satisfiable*,
  Else if not trivially satisfiable insert d so modified in its class.
fin

Fig. 11. CSF Algorithm to introduce a new disequation

the results together in the table of Figure 12. Even if the number of tests is not great, and the examples rather small, we can see that

- The CSF form often seems better than the GSF form. The scores are: for the disequations, 9 to 1, and for the equality contraints, 14 to 4.
- The GJSF form is more often less efficient than the CSF form. The scores are for the disequations, 0 to 7, and for the equality constraints, 1 to 7. In this last case (equalities), 10 out of 18 give next to the same total.
- In each method, if we look proportionally at the times (which are not in the table) to the number of additions, it can be noticed that when the number of backtracking increases, the GSF form becomes more efficient than the other methods.

It would be good to continue these tests with more numerous and bigger examples. These tests are not significant enough to draw general and definitive conclusions. However, they provide some interesting indications.

Of course, the GJSF form in CLP($\Re$) and CHIP, and the GSF form in Prolog III, are used with a certain number of fittings which we have not taken into account here. These fittings again improve the efficiency of these forms. In the same way, the CSF form which does not work in any well known programming language can be fitted efficiently. Our goal has been simply to make comparisons between the various solved forms, and to draw attention to the different qualities of each of them.

	GJSF			GSF			CSF		
	Equa	Diseq	Total	Equa	Diseq	Total	Equa	Diseq	Total
Badex	25743	22312	48055	5039	10040	15079	22640	5890	28530
Puzzle4	1354	0	1354	680	0	680	831	0	831
Puzzle8	254321	74899	329220	363790	323772	687562	254321	55973	310294
Fibonacci14	8063	0	8063	65056	0	65056	8063	0	8063
queens4	2262	531	2793	1043	631	1674	806	531	1337
queens8	156424	164659	321083	440646	336430	777076	156424	62728	219152
mortgage	391	0	391	196	0	196	269	0	269
sequence	32	2	34	34	2	36	25	2	27
sendmory	12460	12641	25102	25930	37550	63480	10466	10351	20817
magicsquare1	26572	9327	35899	26279	35679	61958	20392	2191	22583
magicsquare2	14817	0	14817	28982	0	28982	14817	0	14817
affectation	1974	0	1974	1737	0	1737	1452	0	1452
list	180	94	274	142	69	211	200	88	288
sort	6736	930	7666	38285	14010	52295	6736	930	7666
biker	270369	52	270421	844737	372	845109	268768	52	268820
number	24511	2158	26669	29134	1624	30758	16150	12	16162
combination	15874	0	15874	65276	0	65276	15874	0	15874
Hanoi	822	127	949	4734	769	5503	822	127	949

Fig. 12. Test results

Acknowledgements

I would like to thank Pamela Morton for her help with the English translation of this paper. This research was supported by the ACCLAIM Esprit Research Project (PE7195).

References

1. A. Colmerauer, H. Kanoui, R. Pasero and P. Roussel. "Un système de communication en français". *Rapport préliminaire de fin de contrat IRIA*, Groupe Intelligence Artificielle, Faculté des Sciences de Luminy, Université Aix-Marseille II, France, October 1972.
2. A. Colmerauer. "Equations and Inequations on Finite and Infinite Trees". In *Proceedings of the International Conference on Fifth Generation Computer Systems (FGCS-84)*, pages 85–99, Tokyo, Japan, November 1984. ICOT.
3. A. Colmerauer. "Opening the Prolog III Universe". In *BYTE*, August 1987, p177–182.
4. M. Dincbas, P. Van Hentenryck, H. Simonis, A. Aggoun, T. Graf and F. Berthier. "The Constraint Logic Programming Language CHIP". In *Proceedings of the International Conference on Fifth Generation Computer Systems*, Tokyo, Japan, December 1988.
5. S. Friedberg, A. Insel and L. Spence. "Linear Algebra". Prentice-Hall 1979.

6. JL. Imbert. "Solved Forms for Linear Constraints in CLP-languages" . In P. Jorrand and V. Sgurev, editors, *Proceedings of the Sixth International Conference on Artificial Intelligence: Methodology, Systems and Applications*, AIMSA'94, p 77-90. Sofia, Bulgaria. World Scientific. September 1994.

7. JL. Imbert, J. Cohen and MD. Weeger. "An Algorithm for Linear Constraint Solving: Its Incorporation in a Prolog Meta-Interpreter for CLP". In *Journal of Logic Programming. Special issue on Constraint Logic Programming*. Vol. 16, Nos 3 and 4, July-August 1993.

8. JL. Imbert and P. Van Hentenryck. "On the Handling of Disequations in CLP over Linear Rational Arithmetic". In F. Benhamou and A. Colmerauer, editors, *Constraint Logic Programming: Selected Research*, p 49-71, MIT Press, Cambridge, USA. Sept 1993.

9. J.Jaffar, JL. Lassez. "Constraint Logic Programming". Technical Report 86/73. Dept. of computer science. Monash University (June 1986).

10. J.Jaffar, S. Michaylov. "Methodology and Implementation of a CLP System". In *Proceedings of the Logic Programming Conference*. Melbourne, 1987. M.I.T. Press.

11. R.A. Kowalski and D. Kuehner. "Linear Resolution with Selection Function". Memo 78, University of Edinburgh, School of Artificial Intelligence, 1971.

12. R.A. Kowalski. "Predicate Logic as Programming Language". in *Proceedings of IFIP 1974*, North Holland Publishing Company, Amsterdam, pp. 569-574, 1974.

13. R.A. Kowalski and M. Van Emden. "The Semantic of Predicate Logic as Programming Language". in JACM 22, 1976, pp. 733-742.

14. JL. Lassez and K. McAloon. "Independance of Negative Constraints". In *TAP-SOFT 89, Advanced seminar on Foundations of innovative Software development*, Lecture Notes in Computer Science 351, springer Verlag 1989.

15. JL. Laurière. "Un langage et un problème pour énoncer et résoudre des problèmes combinatoires". Ph.D. Thesis, University Pierre et Marie Curie, Paris, May 1976.

16. JL. Laurière. "A Language and a Program for Stating and Solving Combinatorial Problems". In *Artificial Intelligence*, 10(1): p 29-127, 1978.

17. A.K. Mackworth. "Consistency in Networks of Relations". In *AI Jour* 8(1): p 99-118, 1977.

18. J.A. Robinson. "A Machine-Oriented Logic Based on the Resolution Principle". Journal of the ACM 12, 1, pp. 23-41, January 1965.

19. N. Singer. "Résolutions incrémentale de contraintes linéaires sur les nombres rationnels". mémoire de DEA, GIA, Faculté des sciences de Luminy, Marseille, 1993.

20. G.L. Steele. "The Definition and Implementation of a Computer programming Language based on Constraints". Ph.D. Thesis, MIT, USA. August 1980.

21. G.J. Sussman and G.L. Steele. "CONSTRAINTS. A language for Expressing Almost-Hierarchical Descriptions" In *AI Journal*, 14(1), 1980.

22. P. Van Hentenryck and T. Graf. Standard Forms for Rational Linear Arithmetics in Constraint Logic Programming. *Annals of Mathematics and Artificial Intelligence*, 1992.

23. JF. Verrier. "Résolutions numériques en programmation logique par contraintes". mémoire de DEA, GIA, Faculté des sciences de Luminy, Marseille, 1992.

24. D. Waltz. "Generating Semantic Descriptions from Drawings of Scenes with Shadows". Technical Report AI271, MIT, MA, USA. November 1972.

ON THE USE OF CONSTRAINTS IN AUTOMATED DEDUCTION

Hélène Kirchner

CRIN-CNRS & INRIA-Lorraine
BP 239
54506 Vandœuvre-lès-Nancy Cedex
E-mail: Helene.Kirchner@loria.fr

Abstract. This paper presents three approaches dealing with constraints in automated deduction. Each of them illustrates a different point. The expression of strategies using constraints is shown through the example of a completion process using ordered and basic strategies. The schematization of complex unification problems through constraints is illustrated by the example of an equational theorem prover with associativity and commutativity axioms. The incorporation of built-in theories in a deduction process is done for a narrowing process which solves queries in theories defined by rewrite rules with built-in constraints. Advantages of using constraints in automated deduction are emphasized and new challenging problems in this area are pointed out.

1 Motivations

Constraints have been introduced in automated deduction since about 1990, although one could find similar ideas in theory resolution [32] and in higher-order resolution [16]. The idea is to distinguish two levels of deduction and to use adequate and efficient tools at each level. When, for instance for syntactic reasons, these two levels do not interfere, this idea leads to an interesting modularization of provers. This is a case similar to the CLP framework which has been studied in the context of knowledge representation for instance by [7, 15]. But we are interested here in using formulas defined with the equality predicate (possibly among others) at both levels. This induces an additional difficulty and we focus here on this kind of problem.

A first motivation for introducing constraints in equational deduction processes arises when considering the problem of completion modulo a set of axioms A [2, 17]. A main drawback of this class of completion procedures is an inherent inefficiency, due to the computation of matchers and unifiers modulo A. A natural idea is to use constraints to record unification problems in the theory A and to avoid solving them immediately. Constraints are just checked for satisfiability, which is in general much simpler than finding a complete set of solutions or a solved form, especially in equational theories. Originally a completion procedure with associative commutative equational constraints has been proposed in [19] and a general framework for deduction with constraints developed in [20]. Ordering and equality constraints were proposed for several deduction processes in first-order logic with equality [4, 26, 27]. The same idea was used in implementations of ordered completion described in [24, 29], and completion modulo associativity, commutativity and identity [6, 18]. Completion with membership constraints is studied in [9]. More recent work involves irreducibility constraints [23] and deduction processes with AC-constraints [28, 33].

There are several advantages in using constraints in automated deduction. They provide a way to make explicit every symbolic computation step, especially unification, orientation and typing problems to check while applying an inference rule. Moreover they keep track of choices made along a derivation and this is a way to avoid a new choice inconsistent with previous ones. They help to modularize deduction and in particular to design better controls by delaying complex problem solving and pruning some parts of the search tree. Constraints also schematize (infinitely) many objects, especially substitutions or ground instances in our context, and thus give theorem provers more expressive power. This paper argues more deeply about these advantages. It relies on existing work by [27, 33, 22] whose results have been adapted or simplified for our purpose.

We first define precisely in Section 2 the notion of constraint we use here. Then we focus in this paper on three aspects:

- The expression of strategies using constraints, through the example of a completion process using ordered and basic strategies, in Section 3.
- The schematization of complex unification problems through constraints. We apply this idea to the example of an equational theorem prover with associativity and commutativity (AC) axioms, in Section 4.
- The incorporation of built-in theories in a deduction process. We describe a narrowing process to solve queries in theories defined by rewrite rules with built-in constraints, in Section 5.

A last section summarizes advantages of using constraints and new interesting problems and challenges set up by this framework.

2 Constraints

The reader may refer to [10] for the concepts of terms, substitution and rewrite systems. The notations used in this paper are consistent with [10]. In particular, given a first-order signature $\Sigma = (\mathcal{S}, \mathcal{F}, \mathcal{P})$ composed of a set of sort symbols $\mathcal{S}$, a set of function symbols $\mathcal{F}$ and a set of predicate symbols $\mathcal{P}$, $\mathcal{T}(\Sigma, \mathcal{X})$ denotes the set of terms built on Σ (i.e. involving function symbols $\mathcal{F}$) and variables $\mathcal{X}$ and $\mathcal{T}(\Sigma)$ is the set of ground terms, i.e. without variables. $Var(t)$ denotes the set of variables of a term t, $t_{|\omega}$ the subterm of t at position ω, $t(\omega)$ the symbol at position ω in t and $t[u]_\omega$ the term t that contains the subterm u at position ω. $Gpos(t)$ denotes the set of all non-variable positions ω in t and ϵ is the top position. We use letters $\sigma, \mu, \gamma, \phi, \ldots$ to denote substitutions and call *domain* of the substitution σ the finite set of variables $Dom(\sigma) = \{x | x \in \mathcal{X} \text{ and } \sigma(x) \neq x\}$, *range* of σ the set of terms $Ran(\sigma) = \cup_{x \in Dom(\sigma)} \sigma(x)$ and *variable range* of σ the set of variables $VRan(\sigma) = \cup_{x \in Dom(\sigma)} Var(\sigma(x))$. A substitution σ is *idempotent* if $\sigma \circ \sigma = \sigma$ and *ground* if $Ran(\sigma) \subseteq T(\Sigma)$. *SUBST* is the set of substitutions of $T(\Sigma, \mathcal{X})$. The restriction of an assignment or a substitution α to a set of variables X is denoted $\alpha_{|\mathcal{X}}$.

A first-order algebraic Σ-structure $\mathcal{K}$ is given by
- a carrier K which is a collection of non-empty sets $(K_s)_{s \in \mathcal{S}}$,
- for each function symbol in $\mathcal{F}$ with a rank $f : s_1, \ldots, s_n \mapsto s$, a function $f_\mathcal{K}$ from $K_{s_1} \times \ldots \times K_{s_n}$ to K_s,
- for each predicate symbol except $=$ in $\mathcal{P}$ with a rank $p : s_1, \ldots, s_n$, a relation $p_\mathcal{K}$ on $K_{s_1} \times \ldots \times K_{s_n}$. Whenever Σ contains the predicate symbol $=$, it will be interpreted as the equality relation in $\mathcal{K}$. $ASS_K^\mathcal{X}$ is the set of assignments α from the set of variables $\mathcal{X}$ to the Σ-structure $\mathcal{K}$, that extend to homomorphisms from $T(\Sigma, \mathcal{X})$ to $\mathcal{K}$.

A constraint is a first-order formula built on a signature $\Sigma = (\mathcal{S}, \mathcal{F}, \mathcal{P})$ where $\mathcal{S}$ is omitted when reduced to only one sort. This signature is used to build elementary constraints. For instance here $\mathcal{P} = \{=, \neq, >\}$ and elementary constraints are equations, disequations and inequations. Elementary constraints are then combined with usual first-order connectives and quantifiers. Constraints may be syntactically distinguished when needed by a question mark exponent on predicates.

The definition of symbolic constraint languages adopted in the context of theorem proving, is an instance of the definition given in [31, 20]. The main difference is that we restrict to one interpretation instead of considering a class of interpretations and do not allow negation.

Definition 1 Let $\Sigma = (\mathcal{S}, \mathcal{F}, \mathcal{P})$ be a signature and $\mathcal{X}$ a set of variables. A *constraint language* $L_\mathcal{K}[\Sigma, \mathcal{X}]$ (or $L_\mathcal{K}$ for short) is given by:

– A set of *constraints* $C[\Sigma, \mathcal{X}]$ defined as the smallest set such that
  • $\mathbb{T}, \mathbb{F} \in C[\Sigma, \mathcal{X}]$,
  • $p^?(t_1, \ldots, t_m) \in C[\Sigma, \mathcal{X}]$ if $p \in \mathcal{P}$ and $t_1, \ldots, t_m \in T(\Sigma, \mathcal{X})$,
  • $c \wedge c' \in C[\Sigma, \mathcal{X}]$ if $c, c' \in C[\Sigma, \mathcal{X}]$,
  • $(\exists x : c) \in C[\Sigma, \mathcal{X}]$ if $c \in C[\Sigma, \mathcal{X}]$.
  $Var(c)$ denotes the set of free variables of the constraint c.

– An interpretation $\mathcal{K}$, which is a Σ-structure, and a solution mapping that associates to each constraint the set of assignments $Sol_\mathcal{K}(c)$ defined as follows:
  • $Sol_\mathcal{K}(\mathbb{T}) = \{\alpha \in ASS_K^\mathcal{X}\}$
  • $Sol_\mathcal{K}(\mathbb{F}) = \emptyset$
  • $Sol_\mathcal{K}(p^?(t_1, \ldots, t_m)) = \{\alpha \in ASS_K^\mathcal{X} \mid (\alpha(t_1), \ldots, \alpha(t_m)) \in p_\mathcal{K}\}$
  • $Sol_\mathcal{K}(c \wedge c') = Sol_\mathcal{K}(c) \cap Sol_\mathcal{K}(c')$
  • $Sol_\mathcal{K}(\exists x : c) = \{\alpha \in ASS_K^\mathcal{X} \mid \exists \phi \in ASS_K^\mathcal{X}, \alpha_{|\mathcal{X}\setminus\{x\}} = \phi_{|\mathcal{X}\setminus\{x\}} \text{ and } \phi \in Sol_\mathcal{K}(c)\}$.

An assignment in $Sol_\mathcal{K}(c)$ is a *solution* of c in $L_\mathcal{K}$. A constraint c, as any first-order formula, is *valid* in $L_\mathcal{K}$, written $L_\mathcal{K} \models c$ or simply $\mathcal{K} \models c$, if any assignment is a solution of c in $L_\mathcal{K}$. Two constraints c and c' are *equivalent* (denoted by $c \equiv_\mathcal{K} c'$) if $Sol_\mathcal{K}(c) = Sol_\mathcal{K}(c')$.

In automated theorem proving, we are interested in interpretations $\mathcal{K}$ which are Σ-term algebras and in solution mappings that associate to each constraint c the set of its symbolic solutions.

Definition 2 A *symbolic solution* of a $L_\mathcal{K}[\Sigma, \mathcal{X}]$-constraint c is a substitution $\sigma \in SUBST$ such that $L_\mathcal{K} \models \sigma(c)$. The set of all symbolic solutions of c is denoted $SS_\mathcal{K}(c)$.

Each of the following sections will consider a different interpretation $\mathcal{K}$.

3 The expression of strategies using constraints

The kind of strategies we want to express are basic and ordered strategies. Basic strategies avoid applying inference rules in parts of the formulas which have been introduced by substitutions in previous steps. They can be handled via equational constraints. Ordered strategies select maximal terms or literals in formulas to apply inference steps. They assume an ordering given on terms and are dealt with through ordering constraints. We introduce first the constraint language needed here and the kind of formulas used by the provers, then the inference rules on these formulas.

3.1 Constraints and constrained formulas

Elementary constraints are equations $(t =^? t')$ and inequations $(t >^? t')$ with $t, t' \in \mathcal{T}(\Sigma, \mathcal{X})$. The constraint language contains conjunctions of elementary constraints and two additional symbols $\mathbb{T}$ and $\mathbb{F}$. The equality and ordering predicates are interpreted in the ground term algebra $\mathcal{K} = \mathcal{T}(\Sigma)$. The equality predicate is interpreted in $\mathcal{K}$ by syntactic equality and the ordering predicate by a simplification ordering $>$ [11], total on ground terms. Its multiset extension is denoted by $>^{mult}$. Symbolic solutions of constraints are substitutions on $\mathcal{T}(\Sigma, \mathcal{X})$, while solutions are ground substitutions.

A *constrained equality*, denoted $(l = r \parallel c)$, is given by two terms l and r in $\mathcal{T}(\Sigma, \mathcal{X})$ and a constraint c such that $Var(c) \subseteq Var(l) \cup Var(r)$. The constrained equality $(l = r \parallel c)$ schematizes on $\mathcal{T}(\Sigma, \mathcal{X})$ the set of equalities $\mathcal{S}(l = r \parallel c) = \{\sigma(l) = \sigma(r) \mid \sigma \in SS_\mathcal{K}(c)\}$. The constrained equality $(l = r \parallel c)$ also schematizes the set of its *ground instances* on $\mathcal{T}(\Sigma)$: $\mathcal{G}(l = r \parallel c) = \{\sigma(l) = \sigma(r) \mid \sigma \in Sol_\mathcal{K}(c)\}$. A set $E = \{(l = r \parallel c)\}$ of constrained equalities generates a congruence $=_E$ on terms defined as the congruence generated by $\mathcal{S}(E) = \{\mathcal{G}(l = r \parallel c) \mid (l = r \parallel c) \in E\}$. E is said to be *confluent on ground terms* if the corresponding set of ground rewrite rules $R_E = \{\sigma(l) \to \sigma(r) \mid (l = r \parallel c) \in E, (\sigma(l) = \sigma(r)) \in \mathcal{G}(l = r \parallel c), \sigma(l) > \sigma(r)\}$ is confluent on $\mathcal{T}(\Sigma)$.

3.2 Inference Rules

New constrained equalities are computed by superposition at non-variable positions.

Superposition

$$\frac{(l_1 = r_1 \parallel c_1) \qquad (l_2 = r_2 \parallel c_2)}{(l_2[r_1]_\omega = r_2 \parallel c_1 \wedge c_2 \wedge c_3)}$$

if $c_1 \wedge c_2 \wedge c_3$ is satisfiable

where $\omega \in Gpos(l_2)$ and c_3 is $(l_{2|\omega} =^? l_1) \wedge (l_1 >^? r_1) \wedge (l_2 >^? r_2)$

This inference rule is already sufficient to point out how constraints can improve inference systems.

- Here the constraint $(l_{2|\omega} =^? l_1)$ is crucial to implement the basic strategy, since considering this equation as a constraint prevents further inference steps to be applied elsewhere than in the part $l_2[r_1]_\omega$ in the deduced formula. Positions in $l_2[r_1]_\omega$ correspond to basic positions. The ordering constraint $(l_1 >^? r_1)$ expresses a part of an ordered strategy that states that inference steps are applied to bigger terms. We could also add an additional constraint to c_3, namely $(\{l_2, r_2\} >^? \{l_1, r_1\})$ to achieve another refinement of the ordered strategy.

- In this inference rule, constraints are inherited from premises and thus a trace is kept from previous choices, in particular in the ordering process.

- The decomposition between the equational part and the constraint part allows a clear separation of the constraint solving that may be delayed. However satisfiability has to be checked in order to avoid unnecessary inference steps.

The superposition rule generates new constraint formulas. In standard (i.e. without constraints) completion procedures, this rule is combined with simplification rules that eliminate redundant equalities or rewrite rules. However using simplification in conjunction with constrained superposition may lead to a loss of completeness, as in the next example.

Example 1 [26] Let $\mathcal{F} = \{f, g, a, b\}$ with $f > g > a > b$ and assume given the following equalities:

$$a = b \tag{1}$$

$$f(g(x)) = g(x) \tag{2}$$

$$f(g(a)) = b \tag{3}$$

Superposition of (2) and (3) leads to $(g(x) = b \parallel x =^? a)$. Using a naive notion of simplification, we could say that (3) is simplified into $(f(b) = b)$. Superposition yields again $(f(b) = g(x) \parallel x =^? a)$. But $(g(b) = b)$ has no convergent proof.

One possible solution is to use propagation [20]. This amounts to weakening the constraints by partially solving them and propagating the instantiations of variables in the equality. Formally:

Propagation

$$\frac{(g = d \parallel c)}{(\theta(g) = \theta(d) \parallel \theta(c'))}$$

if $c \equiv c' \wedge \hat{\theta}$,
where $\hat{\theta}$ is the equational form $(\bigwedge_{i=1}^{n}(x_i = t_i))$
of the substitution $\theta = (x_1 \mapsto t_1, \ldots, x_n \mapsto t_n)$.

Example 2 For instance in Example 1, **Propagation** generates $g(a) = b$. Then **Superposition** with $a = b$ yields $g(b) = b$.

Another possibility is to have an appropriate notion of redundancy [3]. Informally an equality is redundant if it can be proved from smaller ones. In the constraint context, all instances by solutions of constraints must be taken into account for redundancy definition.

Definition 3 Let $E_0, E_1, \ldots$ be a sequence of sets of constrained equalities, $E_\infty = \bigcup_{i \geq 0} \bigcap_{j \geq i} E_j$ and R_{E_∞} the corresponding set of ground rewrite rules. A constrained equality $(l = r \parallel c)$ is redundant in E_j if for any ground instance $(\sigma(l) = \sigma(r))$ with σ R_{E_∞}-irreducible solution of c, there exist R_{E_∞}-irreducible ground instances $e_1, \ldots e_n$ of constrained equalities in E_j such that $(\sigma(l) = \sigma(r))$ is an equational consequence of $R_{E_\infty} \cup \{e_1, \ldots, e_n\}$ and $\{(\sigma(l) = \sigma(r))\} >^{mult} \{e_1, \ldots, e_n\}$.

As a first example of redundant equalities, one can prove that, if a constrained equality of the form $(l = r \parallel \hat{\sigma})$ is R_{E_∞}-reducible in the range of σ, it is redundant. More work is needed to obtain satisfactory criteria for elimination of redundancies, but this problem is not addressed here. Further hints can be found in [4, 26, 27, 23, 21].

Definition 4 A *derivation* from a set of constrained equalities E_0 is a sequence $E_0, E_1, \ldots$ of sets of constrained equalities obtained by successive applications of superposition and eliminations of redundant constrained equalities. Formally:
$E_i = E_{i-1} \cup \{(l = r \parallel c)\}$ if $(l = r \parallel c)$ is deduced from E_{i-1} by superposition, or $E_i = E_{i-1} \setminus \{(l = r \parallel c)\}$ if $(l = r \parallel c)$ redundant in E_{i-1}.
A derivation denoted $E_0 \vdash E_1 \vdash \ldots$ is *fair* if each constrained equality $(l = r \parallel c)$ generated from E_∞ by superposition is redundant in $\bigcup_{i \geq 0} E_i$.

A set of equational axioms Γ can of course be considered as a set of constrained equalities with the trivial constraint $\mathbb{T}$. For such theories, the following result holds:

Theorem 1 *[27] Let $E_0 = \Gamma$ be a set of equational axioms without constraints. Then, every fair derivation from S produces a set E_∞ which is confluent on ground terms and generate the same congruence as Γ.*

Theorem 1 does not hold any more if equalities in Γ have constraints. Let us consider $\mathcal{F} = \{a, b, f, g\}$ and a simplification ordering $>$ induced by the precedence $f > g > a > b$. Let Γ be the set of two constrained equalities: $(g(a) = b \parallel \mathbb{T})$ and $(f(x) = a \parallel x =^? g(y))$. No inference rule applies, although the proof $a =_\Gamma f(g(a)) =_\Gamma f(b)$ contradicts confluence of R_Γ. The problem comes from the fact that there is a superposition in the constraint part which is not taken into account. A first idea is to look for cases where superposition into constraints is useless. Using a hierarchical approach in which constraints are restricted to a sub-signature is enough to recover completeness. This is done with so-called built-in constraints in [22] for instance. An alternative initially proposed in [20] is again to use propagation. Coming back to our example, the propagation applies straightforwardly and yields the (unconstrained) equality $(f(g(y)) = a)$. It generates with $(g(a) = b)$ the equality $(f(b) = a)$.

To close this section, let us give a simple example to illustrate the completion process.

Example 3 Let $\mathcal{F} = \{0, +\}$ and two initial equalities:

$$x + 0 = 0 + x$$
$$(x + y) + z = x + (y + z)$$

Let us consider as simplification ordering a lexicographic path ordering induced by the precedence $+ > 0$. Superposition of the first equality at position 1 in the second creates a new constrained equality

$$((0 + x) + z' = x' + (y' + z') \parallel c)$$

where $c = (x + 0 >^? 0 + x) \wedge ((x + y) + z >^? x + (y + z)) \wedge (x + 0 =^? x' + y')$. Another superposition at top gives:

$$(0 + x = x' + (y' + z') \parallel c)$$

where $c = (x + 0 >^? 0 + x) \wedge ((x' + y') + z' >^? x' + (y' + z')) \wedge (x + 0 =^? (x' + y') + z'))$.

After some simplification of constraints and propagation, we get

$$(0 + x) + z = x + (0 + z) \parallel x >^? 0$$
$$(0 + (x + y) = x + (y + 0) \parallel (x + y) >^? 0$$

The final system is

$$x + 0 = 0 + x \parallel x >^? 0$$
$$(x + y) + z = x + (y + z) \parallel \mathbb{T}$$
$$x + (0 + y) = 0 + (x + y) \parallel x >^? 0$$

4 The schematization of complex unification problems through constraints

The advantages of using deduction with constraints for avoiding the computation of AC-unifiers can be pointed out on the example of a superposition calculus for equational theories with associativity and commutativity axioms.[1] Unification in AC theories is a good example to illustrate the use of constraints, since solving equations in AC theories often leads to a huge set of most general solutions [13]. Again we first define the constraint language which is an extension of the one in the previous section and then give the inference rules with completeness results.

4.1 Constraints and constrained formulas

Assume now that the set of function symbols $\mathcal{F}$ includes a subset of AC function symbols $\mathcal{F}_{AC}$. Elementary constraints are again equations $(t =^? t')$ and inequations $(t >^? t')$ with $t, t' \in \mathcal{T}(\Sigma, \mathcal{X})$.

The constraint language always contains conjunctions of elementary constraints and the two additional symbols $\mathbb{T}$ and $\mathbb{F}$. But now the equality and ordering predicates are interpreted in the quotient term algebra $\mathcal{K} = \mathcal{T}(\Sigma)/=_{AC}$, where $=_{AC}$ denotes equality modulo AC. The equality predicate is interpreted in $\mathcal{K}$ by $=_{AC}$, and the ordering predicate by a simplification ordering $>_{AC}$. The ordering must be AC-compatible (i.e. $=_{AC} \circ >_{AC} \circ =_{AC} \subseteq >_{AC}$) and total on ground AC-congruence classes (i.e. for all ground terms s and t, either $s \xleftrightarrow{*}_{AC} t$, or $s >_{AC} t$ or $t >_{AC} s$). Such orderings have been described in [25, 30].

In order to incorporate in the constraints all the conditions checked for applying an inference rule, we also need additional constraints. First a constraint $Head(l_1, f)$ is satisfied by any instance of l_1 whose top symbol is f. Other constraints are multiset constraints, expressed with a function $\mathcal{H}terms$ defined as follows. For a term t with an AC-function symbol f at the top position, $\mathcal{H}terms(t, f)$ is the multiset of all subterms below f in the flattened form of t ; for instance, $\mathcal{H}terms(a * ((a * x) * g(b)), *)$ is $\{a, a, x, g(b)\}$. For other terms t without f at the top position, $\mathcal{H}terms(t, f) = \{t\}$. Multiset constraints are intersection or inclusion of multisets, written for instance $\mathcal{H}terms(t_1, f) \cap_{AC} \mathcal{H}terms(t, f) = \emptyset$ or $\mathcal{H}terms(t_1, f) \subseteq_{AC} \mathcal{H}terms(t, f)$. In a constraint such as $\{t_1, \ldots, t_n\} \cap_{AC} \{u_1, \ldots, u_m\} = \emptyset$ or as $\{t_1, \ldots, t_n\} \subseteq_{AC} \{u_1, \ldots, u_m\}$, the subscript AC indicates that the AC-equality is used for comparing terms. For example, if $* \in \mathcal{F}_{AC}$, $\{a * b, b, c\} \cap_{AC} \{b * a, c, d\} = \{a * b, c\}$. These additional constraints are satisfied if there exists a solution to equality and ordering constraints that does not contradict them.

Working in AC theories requires to introduce so-called extended rules in order to fulfill the condition of AC-coherence needed with AC-confluence to ensure a Church-Rosser property. Here also, in addition to constrained equalities, we have to build extended equalities. The *constrained AC-extended equality* of $(l = r \parallel c)$

---

[1] This section was the subject of a presentation at the CADE12 workshop on theory reasoning in automated deduction, co-authored with Laurent Vigneron.

such that $l(\epsilon) = f \in \mathcal{F}_{AC}$, is $(f(l, x) = f(r, x) \parallel c)$ where x does not belong to $\mathcal{V}ar(l) \cup \mathcal{V}ar(r) \cup \mathcal{V}ar(c)$. AC-extended equalities are never explicitly created, but their use is simulated through inference rules. So there is no need to define a special control on these rules.

4.2 Inference Rules

To prove an equational theorem $(t = t')$ in the theory defined by a set of equational axioms Γ, the theorem is negated and skolemized, and a contradiction is derived from $\Gamma \cup \neg(t = t')$. Such a contradiction is here an *empty constrained clause*, i.e. a clause with no literal (denoted $\square$) and a satisfiable set of constraints. (Actually this definition can be refined by requiring only that equality constraints are satisfiable.) An empty constrained clause can be deduced with the following inference rule:

Reflection

$$\frac{\neg(l = r) \parallel c_1}{\square \parallel c_1 \wedge (l =^? r)}$$

if $(c_1 \wedge (l =^? r))$ is satisfiable.

New constrained formulas are computed by applying the next rule Superposition at non-variable positions where either there is a non-AC function symbol, or there is an AC function symbol f but no f immediately above. More formally $Gpos^*(t)$ denotes the set of all non-variable positions ω in t such that either $t(\omega) \notin \mathcal{F}_{AC}$, or, if $\omega = \omega' \cdot i$, $t(\omega)$ and $t(\omega')$ are not the same AC function symbol.

Superposition

$$\frac{(l_1 = r_1) \parallel c_1 \qquad L_2 \parallel c_2}{L_2[x]_\omega \parallel c_1 \wedge c_2 \wedge c_3 \wedge c_3'}$$

if $(c_1 \wedge c_2 \wedge c_3 \wedge c_3')$ is satisfiable
where L_2 is $(l_2 = r_2)$ or $\neg(l_2 = r_2)$, $\omega \in Gpos^*(l_2)$, x is a new variable,
and c_3 is $(l_{2|_\omega} =^? l_1) \wedge (x =^? r_1) \wedge (l_1 >^? r_1) \wedge (l_2 >^? r_2)$,
and c_3' is $(\{l_2, r_2\} >^? \{l_1, r_1\})$ if L_2 is $(l_2 = r_2)$, or $\mathbb{T}$ if L_2 is $\neg(l_2 = r_2)$.

The next rule corresponds to a superposition of an AC-extended constrained equality into a positive or negative literal. It introduces the notion of *extension variable* for an AC function symbol to represent the context in contextual superposition steps. Such variables are created by the contextual superposition rule below and used only by this rule. To understand the constraint c_3' in this rule, one may first note that each term t in $\mathcal{H}terms(l_{2|_\omega}, f)$ is either a variable or a term whose top symbol is not f. So c_3' is satisfied only when variables of $\mathcal{H}terms(l_{2|_\omega}, f)$ (except extension variables) are instantiated by terms that do not unify with l_1, and when $l_1(\epsilon)$ is either f or a variable instantiated by a term whose top sympbol is f.

Contextual Superposition

$$\frac{(l_1 = r_1) \ \| \ c_1 \qquad L_2 \ \| \ c_2}{L_2[f(x, z_f)]_\omega \ \| \ c_1 \wedge c_2 \wedge c_3 \wedge c_3'}$$

if $(c_1 \wedge c_2 \wedge c_3 \wedge c_3')$ is satisfiable
where x is a new variable, z_f is a new extension variable for $f \in \mathcal{F}_{AC}$,
$\qquad L_2$ is $(l_2 = r_2)$ or $\neg(l_2 = r_2)$, $\omega \in Gpos^*(l_2)$,
and c_3 is $(l_2|_\omega =^? f(l_1, z_f)) \wedge (x =^? r_1) \wedge (l_1 >^? r_1) \wedge (l_2 >^? r_2)$,
and c_3' is $Head(l_1, f) \bigwedge_t \mathcal{H}terms(l_1, f) \not\subseteq_{AC} \mathcal{H}terms(t, f)$,
$\qquad\qquad$ for each term t in $\mathcal{H}terms(l_2|_\omega, f)$
$\qquad\qquad$ which is not an extension variable for f.

The last rule corresponds to a superposition between two AC-extended equalities. Constraints in the resulting clause express that the useful solutions are obtained when the left-hand sides l_1 and l_2 share a maximum of subterms (they have to share at least one subterm : the intersection between the $\mathcal{H}terms$ of l_1 and l_2 must not be empty ; they have to share a maximum of subterms : the intersection between the $\mathcal{H}terms$ of the contexts z_1 and z_2 has to be empty).

Extended Superposition

$$\frac{(l_1 = r_1) \ \| \ c_1 \qquad (l_2 = r_2) \ \| \ c_2}{(f(x_1, z_1) = f(x_2, z_2)) \ \| \ c_1 \wedge c_2 \wedge c_3}$$

if $(c_1 \wedge c_2 \wedge c_3)$ is satisfiable
where $f \in \mathcal{F}_{AC}$, x_1, x_2, z_1 and z_2 are new variables,
and c_3 is $(f(l_1, z_1) =^? f(l_2, z_2)) \wedge (x_1 =^? r_1) \wedge (x_2 =^? r_2)$
$\qquad \wedge (l_1 >^? r_1) \wedge (l_2 >^? r_2)$
$\qquad \wedge \mathcal{H}terms(l_1, f) \cap_{AC} \mathcal{H}terms(l_2, f) \neq \emptyset$
$\qquad \wedge \mathcal{H}terms(z_1, f) \cap_{AC} \mathcal{H}terms(z_2, f) = \emptyset$.

4.3 Elimination of redundancies

The definition of simplification rules compatible with the previous inference rules is proposed in [28, 33] for AC theories. For simplicity, we only consider here equality constraints. There are two main rules for elimination of redundancies :

- **Subsumption** : given a constrained literal $(L_1 \ \| \ c_1)$ (where L_1 may be $(l_1 = r_1)$ or $\neg(l_1 = r_1)$) and a solution σ_1 of c_1, $(L_1 \ \| \ \hat{\sigma_1})$ subsumes $(L_2 \ \| \ c_2)$ if, for each solution σ_2 of c_2, there is a substitution ρ such that $\{\rho(\sigma_1(l_1)), \rho(\sigma_1(r_1))\} =_{AC} \{\sigma_2(l_2), \sigma_2(r_2)\}$. The application of the subsumption rule consists in the deletion of $(L_2 \ \| \ c_2)$.

– **Simplification** : given a constrained equality $(l_1 = r_1 \parallel c_1)$ and a solution σ_1 of c_1, a constrained literal $(L_2 \parallel c_2)$ is simplified into $(L_3 \parallel c_3)$ at position ω with $(l_1 = r_1 \parallel \hat{\sigma_1})$ if, for each solution σ_2 of c_2, there is a match ρ such that $\rho(\sigma_1(l_1)) =_{AC} \sigma_2(L_{2|\omega})$, $\rho(\sigma_1(l_1)) >_{AC} \rho(\sigma_1(r_1))$ and $c_3 = \hat{\sigma_1} \wedge c_2 \wedge L_{2|\omega} =^? \sigma_1(l_1)$ is satisfiable. Then $L_3 = L_2[r_1]_\omega$. The application of the simplification rule consists in the replacement of $(L_2 \parallel c_2)$ by $(L_3 \parallel c_3)$. Simplification by a constrained extended equality is defined similarly.

However, to maintain refutational completeness, another sufficient condition has to be satisfied : if $(L_1 \parallel \hat{\sigma_1})$ is used to subsume or simplify $(L_2 \parallel c_2)$ with a substitution ρ, each term of the range of $\rho\sigma_1$ has to be included in a term of the range of each σ_2. When this condition is not satisfied, simplification steps can nevertheless be applied if $(L_1 \parallel \hat{\sigma_1})$ is transformed by propagation into a new constrained literal $(L_1\sigma_1' \parallel \hat{\sigma_1''})$, where $\sigma_1 = \sigma_1'\sigma_1''$ and the condition on ranges is satisfied for σ_1''. For more details, see [4], [33] and [21].

4.4 Completeness results

Let INF be the set of inference rules and simplification rules described in Sections 4.2 and 4.3. A set of clauses S is AC-unsatisfiable if it has no AC-consistent model, i.e. no model consistent with the AC axioms. A contradiction is witnessed by the empty constrained clause.

Theorem 2 (Completeness Theorem) *Let $S = \Gamma \cup \{\neg(t = t')\}$ be an AC-unsatisfiable set of clauses without constraints. Then, every fair derivation from S using INF generates an empty constrained clause.*

This result generalizes to the AC-case, the completeness result of basic superposition in [27, 4]. It is a restricted form to equalities of similar results on clauses obtained in [28] and in [33]. Let us illustrate Theorem 2 on an example of refutation.

Example 4 [33] Let $\mathcal{F}_{AC} = \{ * \}$ and assume the ordering to be an associative path ordering [5] based on the precedence $a > b > c > d$. Let us consider the initial set of equalities:

$$
\begin{aligned}
a * b &= c \quad\quad (1)\\
(a * a) * (b * b) &= d \quad\quad (2)\\
\neg (c * c &= d) \quad\quad (3)
\end{aligned}
$$

Contextual superposition from (1) and (2) produces

$$(x * z_* = d \parallel ((a * a) * (b * b) =^? (a * b) * z_*) \wedge (x =^? c)) \quad (4)$$

Ordering constraints $(a * b >^? c) \wedge ((a * a) * (b * b) >^? d)$ are satisfied, as well as additional constraints $Head((a * b), *) \wedge \{a, b\} \not\subseteq_{AC} \{a\} \wedge \{a, b\} \not\subseteq_{AC} \{a\} \wedge \{a, b\} \not\subseteq_{AC} \{b\} \wedge \{a, b\} \not\subseteq_{AC} \{b\}$, which are equivalent to $\mathbb{T}$ and simplified. The final constraint is equivalent to $(z_* =^? (a * b)) \wedge (x =^? c))$.

Contextual superposition from (1) and (4) generates

$$(y * z'_* = d \;\|\; (z_* =^? (a * b)) \wedge (x =^? c)) \wedge (x * z_* =^? (a * b) * z'_*) \wedge (y =^? c)) \quad (5)$$

Here again, ordering constraints $(a * b >^? c) \wedge (x * z'_* >^? d)$ are satisfied by the solution of equality constraints, as well as $Head((a * b), *)$ and multiset constraints $\{a, b\} \not\subseteq_{AC} \{x\}$, which are all simplified in the final constraint, equivalent to $(z_* =^? (a * b)) \wedge (x =^? c)) \wedge (z'_* =^? c) \wedge (y =^? c)$.
Superposition from (5) and (3) gives

$$\neg (d = d \;\|\; (c * c =^? y * z'_*) \wedge (z_* =^? a * b)$$
$$\wedge (x =^? c)) \wedge (z'_* =^? c) \wedge (y =^? c)) \quad (6)$$

Reflection derives a contradiction.

5 The incorporation of built-in theories in a deduction process

Theorems 1 and 2 hold for unconstrained theories. A natural question to ask now is: which syntactic restrictions could we put on the theories to allow some initial constraints? We define here a hierarchical construction of constraint solvers that partially answers this question. This is surely not the final point and especially the theories considered here are more restricted than those in [22]. Another point worth emphasizing and illustrated in this section, is that even in simple cases, we get combination problems when built-in theories are incorporated. We define first the three kinds of constraint languages we need, then give briefly the definition of constrained narrowing and its correctness and completeness result.

5.1 Constraints and constrained formulas

In this section, three different constraint languages will be considered:
(1) $L_{\mathcal{A}}$ denotes the built-in language, whose syntax is given by a signature Σ_0 and a set of variables $\mathcal{X}$. The interpretation is a Σ_0-structure $\mathcal{A}$. A built-in constraint solver is assumed given for $L_{\mathcal{A}}$.
(2) The combined language $L_{\mathcal{C}}$ is an enrichment of $L_{\mathcal{A}}$ based on a signature $\Sigma \supseteq \Sigma_0$ and variables $\mathcal{X}$. The interpretation is a Σ-algebra which is a consistent enrichment of $\mathcal{A}$. It is built as a quotient of the set of Σ-terms by a congruence generated by $Th(\mathcal{A})$, the set of all equalities valid in $\mathcal{A}$. Constraints in $L_{\mathcal{C}}$ are conjunctions of constraints built with the same predicates as in $L_{\mathcal{A}}$, terms in the whole enriched signature Σ and variables in $\mathcal{X}$. A constraint solver for $L_{\mathcal{C}}$ is built from the constraint solver in $L_{\mathcal{A}}$ and from a unification algorithm for additional free symbols by adapting combination techniques developed in [1] for unification algorithms.
(3) A constrained rule language $L_{R,\mathcal{C}}$ is based on the same signature $\Sigma \supseteq \Sigma_0$ and variables $\mathcal{X}$. Additional properties of symbols from $\Sigma \backslash \Sigma_0$ are defined using a set R of constrained rewrite rules. These rules are assumed to have constraints

expressed only in $L_{\mathcal{A}}$. This restriction allows building the interpretation as a Σ-algebra which is again a consistent enrichment of $\mathcal{A}$. Constraints in $L_{R,\mathcal{C}}$ are goals with constraints of the form $(p^?(t_1, \ldots, t_n) \parallel S)$ where $p \in \Sigma_0$, $t_1, \ldots, t_n$ are Σ-terms and S is a conjunction of $L_{\mathcal{C}}$-constraints. A constraint solver for $L_{R,\mathcal{C}}$ is based on constrained narrowing that reduces the constraint solving problem in $L_{R,\mathcal{C}}$ to rule application and constraint solving in $L_{\mathcal{C}}$.

Definition 5 Let $\mathcal{A}$ be a term-generated Σ_0-structure with $\Sigma_0 = (\mathcal{S}_0, \mathcal{F}_0, \mathcal{P}_0)$, and $L_{\mathcal{A}}[\Sigma_0, \mathcal{X}]$ ($L_{\mathcal{A}}$ for short) a constraint language. For simplicity we assume here that $\mathcal{A}$ is one-sorted. Let $\Sigma = (\mathcal{S}, \mathcal{F}, \mathcal{P})$ be an enrichment of Σ_0 such that $\mathcal{S} = \mathcal{S}_0 = \{s_*\}$, $\mathcal{F} \supseteq \mathcal{F}_0$ and $\mathcal{P} = \mathcal{P}_0$. A specification with built-in structure $\mathcal{A}$ is given by the 3-tuple $(\Sigma, E, L_{\mathcal{A}})$ where E is a set of constrained equalities $(l = r \parallel c)$ with $l, r \in \mathcal{T}(\Sigma, \mathcal{X})$ and $c \in L_{\mathcal{A}}$.

Note that the signatures Σ_0 and $\Sigma_1 = (\{s_*\}, \mathcal{F}_1 = \mathcal{F} \backslash \mathcal{F}_0, \{=\})$ have by construction disjoint function symbol sets but share the same sort and the equality predicate. This sort sharing introduces a combination problem and the need for some technical definitions.

A term t of $\mathcal{T}(\Sigma, \mathcal{X})$ is *i-pure* (for $i = 0, 1$) if t contains only function symbols from $\mathcal{F}_i$ and possibly variables of $\mathcal{X}$. An equation $(s =^? t)$ is *i-pure* if s and t are i-pure. An atomic constraint $p(t_1, \ldots, t_n)$ is *i-pure* (for $i = 0, 1$) if $p \in \mathcal{P}_i$ and $t_1, \ldots, t_n$ are i-pure. A term with its top symbol in $\mathcal{F}_i$ is called an *i-term*. Alien subterms of an i-term are j-(sub)terms $(i \neq j)$ such that each prefix symbol is in $\mathcal{F}_i$. The set of alien subterms of t is denoted $AST(t)$. The number of 1-levels in a term t, denoted by $nc_1(t)$ is inductively defined by: $nc_1(x) = 0$ if $x \in \mathcal{X}$, $nc_1(t) = 1 + \sum_{s \in AST(t)} nc_1(s)$ if $t(\epsilon) \in \mathcal{F}_1$ else $nc_1(t) = \sum_{s \in AST(t)} nc_1(s)$.

In order to define a new constraint language $L_{\mathcal{C}}$ as a combination of the built-in language and of equational constraints, we have to make precise the interpretation. We choose a Σ-term algebra built as the quotient algebra of $\mathcal{T}(\Sigma, \mathcal{X})$ by a congruence $\sim_{\mathcal{C}}$ generated by $Th(\mathcal{A})$. The problem is that we do not want to put any syntactic hypothesis, like regularity or non-collapsing, on axioms in $Th(\mathcal{A})$ since the built-in theory must be any theory. But in order to rewrite and perform narrowing modulo $Th(\mathcal{A})$ on $\mathcal{T}(\Sigma, \mathcal{X})$, we need to avoid cycles on equivalence classes. They could appear for instance by application of non-regular or collapse axioms in $Th(\mathcal{A})$ to a term of sort s_* but involving symbols from $\mathcal{F}_1$. The proposed solution is to apply $=_{Th(\mathcal{A})}$ on $\mathcal{T}(\Sigma, \mathcal{X})$, but only in such a way that the top symbol theory and the number of 1-levels are preserved for two equivalent terms. The relation $\sim_{\mathcal{C}}$ is defined by: $t \sim_{\mathcal{C}} t'$ if $t =_{Th(\mathcal{A})} t'$, $t(\epsilon), t'(\epsilon) \in \mathcal{F}_i \cup \mathcal{X}$ and $nc_1(t) = nc_1(t')$. It is worth emphasizing that with this definition no 1-term can be equivalent modulo $\sim_{\mathcal{C}}$ to a 0-term.

Example 5 If $\mathcal{A}$ is the structure of natural numbers, $Th(\mathcal{A})$ contains associativity and commutativity axioms for $+$, but also axioms $x * 0 = 0$ (non-regular) and $x + 0 = x$ (collapse). If $g \in \mathcal{F}_1$, we get $g(x, y) + g(y, z) \sim_{\mathcal{C}} g(y, z) + g(x, y)$, $g(x + y, z) \sim_{\mathcal{C}} g(y + x, z)$ but $g(x, y) + 0 \not\sim_{\mathcal{C}} g(x, y)$ and $g(x, y) * 0 \not\sim_{\mathcal{C}} 0$.

To interpret the predicates from $\mathcal{P}_0$ in the quotient algebra of $\mathcal{T}(\Sigma, \mathcal{X})$ by the congruence $\sim_{\mathcal{C}}$, we need to define an operation called abstraction. Abstraction is a top-down process that introduces new variables in places of alien subterms. It has to replace equivalent subterms by the same variable, which introduces some subtleties in its definition. For a precise definition, the reader may refer to [22]. Given a term t, its 0-abstraction is a term of $\mathcal{T}(\Sigma_0, \mathcal{X})$ denoted by t^{π_0}. For instance, in Example 5, $(g(x + y, z) * g(y + x, z))^{\pi_0}$ is the term $v * v$, where v is an abstraction variable.

The *combined language* denoted $L_{\mathcal{C}}$ is defined by the signature $\Sigma = \Sigma_0 \cup \Sigma_1$, the set of variables $\mathcal{X}$, and the Σ-structure $\mathcal{C} = \mathcal{T}(\Sigma, \mathcal{X})/ \sim_{\mathcal{C}}$. If $p \in \mathcal{P}_0$ then the interpretation of p in $\mathcal{C}$ is the relation $p_{\mathcal{C}}$ defined by $p_{\mathcal{C}}(t_1, \ldots, t_n)$ if $L_{\mathcal{A}} \models p(t_1^{\pi_0}, \ldots, t_n^{\pi_0})$. $L_{\mathcal{C}}$ is a conservative extension of $L_{\mathcal{A}}$, i.e. any 0-pure constraint is valid in $L_{\mathcal{A}}$ iff it is valid in $L_{\mathcal{C}}$.

Our goal now is to build a constraint solver for $L_{\mathcal{C}}$ from the built-in solver available for $L_{\mathcal{A}}$ and from a unification algorithm for the empty theory taking into account free symbols of $\mathcal{F}_1$. As before, we are interested in symbolic solutions that may generate the set of all solutions of a constraint. But a new difficulty appears. The congruence $\sim_{\mathcal{C}}$ is not preserved under substitutions in general, unless we restrict to substitutions that do not change the number of 1-levels, which is achieved when all terms in their range are 0-pure terms. The set of *built-in substitutions* is $SUBST_0 = \{\mu_0 \mid \mathcal{R}an(\mu_0) \subseteq \mathcal{T}(\Sigma_0, \mathcal{X})\}$. For a given constraint c, we restrict our attention to the set of solutions $SS_{\mathcal{C}}^*(c) = SS_{\mathcal{C}}(c) \cap SUBST_0$. They are obtained by solving constraints with respect to the equational theory $=_{Th(\mathcal{A})}$ in the whole signature Σ and restricting the set of solutions to built-in ones. Due to the additional free symbols of Σ_1, we get a combination problem between the constraint solver in $L_{\mathcal{A}}$ and the Σ_1-unification algorithm, which requires more than a blind use of each solver. The technique, similar to [1], is based on abstraction by variables, identification of variables, choice of a variable ordering called a linear restriction, solving pure constraints with linear restriction, and combining solutions obtained from both solvers. As a special case of a result proved in [22], we get that constraint solving in $L_{\mathcal{C}}$ is decidable (finitary) if constraint solving in $L_{\mathcal{A}}$ with linear restriction is decidable (finitary).

Definition 6 Let R be a *set of rewrite rules with built-in constraints*, i.e. of the form $(l \rightarrow r \parallel c)$ with l and r in $\mathcal{T}(\Sigma, \mathcal{X})$, $c \in L_{\mathcal{A}}$, $Var(r) \subseteq Var(l)$, $l(\epsilon) \notin \Sigma_0$. Let us define on $\mathcal{T}(\Sigma, \mathcal{X})$ the relation $t \rightarrow_{R,c} t'$ as follows: $t \rightarrow_{R,c} t'$ if $\exists (l \rightarrow r \parallel c) \in R$, $\exists \sigma$ s.t. $t_{|\omega} \sim_{\mathcal{C}} \sigma(l)$, $\sigma \in SS_{\mathcal{C}}^*(c)$ and $t' = t[\sigma(r)]_{\omega}$.

Let us now consider the quotient set $\mathcal{M} = \mathcal{T}(\Sigma, \mathcal{X})/ \sim_{R,c}$ where $\sim_{R,c} = (\sim_{\mathcal{C}} \cup \longleftrightarrow_{R,c})^*$ is the reflexive transitive closure of the union of $\sim_{\mathcal{C}}, \rightarrow_{R,c}$ and its symmetric relation $\leftarrow_{R,c}$. If the relation $\rightarrow_{R,c}$ is confluent modulo $\sim_{\mathcal{C}}$, $\mathcal{M}$ is a consistent enrichment of $\mathcal{A}$ [22]. The property of confluence modulo $\sim_{\mathcal{C}}$ can be checked by testing the convergence of critical pairs computed with the constraint solver in $L_{\mathcal{C}}$ [22]. From now on, we assume that R is convergent modulo $\sim_{\mathcal{C}}$ and denote a normal form of a term t by $t \downarrow_{R,c}$. Validity modulo $\sim_{R,c}$ then corresponds to validity modulo $\sim_{\mathcal{C}}$ after normalization w.r.t. $\rightarrow_{R,c}$. This allows interpreting predicates of $\mathcal{P}_0$ in $\mathcal{M}$. The constraint language $L_{R,c}$ associated to the specification $(\Sigma, R, L_{\mathcal{A}})$ is defined by the signature Σ, the set of variables $\mathcal{X}$ and the interpretation $\mathcal{M}$. If $p \in \mathcal{P}_0$ then the interpretation of p in $\mathcal{M}$ is the relation $p_\mathcal{M}$ defined by $p_\mathcal{M}(t_1, \ldots, t_n)$ if $L_\mathcal{C} \models p(t_1 \downarrow_{R,\mathcal{C}}, \ldots, t_n \downarrow_{R,\mathcal{C}})$.

5.2 Constrained narrowing

We now consider the constraint solving problem in the language $L_{R,\mathcal{C}}$. The idea is to define a process of constrained narrowing to enumerate solutions of goals expressed in this language. This provides an incremental way to build constraint solvers, since the method allows building a constraint solver in $L_{R,\mathcal{C}}$ from a constraint solver in $L_\mathcal{C}$. Similar definitions of constrained narrowing have been introduced in different contexts by [14, 8].

Constrained narrowing is defined on formulas called goals with constraints and of the form $(\exists X, p^?(t_1, \ldots, t_n) \parallel S)$ where X denotes a set of existentially quantified variables, $p^?(t_1, \ldots, t_n)$ is an atomic constraint such that $p \in \mathcal{P}_0$ to solve in $L_{R,\mathcal{C}}$, and S is a constraint to solve in $L_\mathcal{C}$. $Var(G)$ denotes the set of all variables occurring in a goal G.

Definition 7 The set of solutions modulo $\sim_{R,\mathcal{C}}$ of $G = (\exists X, p^?(t_1, \ldots, t_n) \parallel S)$ is $SOL_{R,\mathcal{C}}(G) = \{\sigma_{|Var(G) \backslash X} \mid \sigma \in SS_\mathcal{C}^*(S) \text{ and } L_{R,\mathcal{C}} \models p(\sigma(t_1), \ldots, \sigma(t_n))\}$. The set of solutions modulo $\sim_\mathcal{C}$ of a goal $G = (\exists X, p^?(t_1, \ldots, t_n) \parallel S)$ is defined by $SOL_\mathcal{C}(G) = \{\sigma_{|Var(G) \backslash X} \mid \sigma \in SS_\mathcal{C}^*(S \wedge p(t_1, \ldots, t_n))\}$.

Constraint narrowing can be formalized with the following two rules on goals with constraints.

Narrow

$$\frac{(\exists X, p^?(t_1, \ldots, t_m, \ldots, t_n) \parallel S)}{(\exists X \cup Var(l \to r \parallel c), p^?(t_1, \ldots, t_m[r]_\omega \ldots, t_n) \parallel S \wedge c \wedge (t_{m|\omega} =_\mathcal{C}^? l)}$$

if $(l \to r \parallel c) \in R$ and $S \wedge c \wedge (t_{m|\omega} =_\mathcal{C}^? l)$ is satisfiable in $L_\mathcal{C}$.

Block

$$\frac{(\exists X, p^?(t_1, \ldots, t_n) \parallel S)}{(\exists X, \mathbb{T} \parallel S \wedge p^?(t_1, \ldots, t_n))}$$

if $(S \wedge p^?(t_1, \ldots, t_n))$ is satisfiable in $L_\mathcal{C}$.

Theorem 3 Let $G_0 = (\exists \emptyset, p^?(t_1, \ldots, t_n) \parallel \mathbb{T})$ be a goal and μ_0 be a substitution defined and normalized for $\to_{R,\mathcal{C}}$ on $Var(G_0)$. If $\mu_0 \in SOL_{R,\mathcal{C}}(G_0)$ then there exists a narrowing derivation $G_0 = (\exists \emptyset, p^?(t_1, \ldots, t_n) \parallel \mathbb{T}) \rightsquigarrow G_1 \rightsquigarrow \ldots \rightsquigarrow G_k = (\exists X_k, p^?(u_1, \ldots, u_n) \parallel S_k)$ such that $\mu_0 \in SOL_\mathcal{C}(G_k)$.

So constraint solving in $L_{R,\mathcal{C}}$ is reduced to constraint solving in $L_\mathcal{C}$, itself obtained from constraint solving in $L_\mathcal{A}$.

Let us give an illustration of the narrowing process.

Example 6 Consider the constraint language L_B with the Σ_0-structure B of booleans with $\Sigma_0 = (\{Bool\}, \{\wedge, \vee : Bool, Bool \to Bool, {}^- : Bool \to Bool, 0, 1 :\to Bool\}, \{=, \neq, <\})$ and the set $\mathcal{X}$ of variables $\{x, y, z, v : Bool, \ldots\}$. Given the incomplete specification (Σ, R, L_B): $R = \{xor(x, x) \to 0, xor(x, 1) \to \bar{x}\}$, one want to solve the goal $G_0 = (\exists \emptyset, \ xor(xor(s, t), 0) \neq^? xor(1, v) \ \| \ \top)$ where s, t are 0-pure terms. By narrowing G_0, one gets

$$G_0 \rightsquigarrow G_1 = (\exists x, \ xor(0, 0) \neq^? xor(1, v) \ \| \ xor(s, t) =^? xor(x, x))$$

$$\rightsquigarrow G_2 = (\exists x, y, \ 0 \neq^? xor(1, v) \ \| \ xor(s, t) =^? xor(x, x)$$
$$\wedge xor(0, 0) =^? xor(y, y))$$

$$\rightsquigarrow G_3 = (\exists x, y, z, \ 0 \neq^? \bar{z} \ \| \ xor(s, t) =^? xor(x, x) \wedge xor(0, 0) =^? xor(y, y)$$
$$\wedge xor(1, v) =^? xor(z, 1)) \quad \text{such that}$$

$$SOL_C(G_3) = SS_C^*(\exists x, y, z, \ 0 \neq^? \bar{z} \wedge xor(s, t) =^? xor(x, x) \wedge xor(0, 0) =^? xor(y, y)$$
$$\wedge xor(1, v) =^? xor(z, 1))$$

$$= SS_C^*(\exists x, y, z, \ 0 \neq^? \bar{z} \wedge x =^? s =^? t \wedge y =^? 0 \wedge v =^? z =^? 1)$$

$$= SS_C^*(0 \neq^? \bar{v} \wedge s =^? t) = SS_B(0 \neq^? \bar{v} \wedge s =^? t)$$

6 Should we keep on using constraints?

It seems yet too early to definitely answer the question: should we keep on using constraints? Few implementations of theorem provers are available for now. Let us mention the Saturate system [28] and the DATAC system [33] which are two experimental theorem provers in first-order logic with equality. What can be stated for sure are some advantages illustrated by the specialized deduction processes presented in this paper.

- A large part of control in the deduction process is encoded through the constraints and their satisfiability condition. This is indeed the case for the ordered strategy through ordering constraints, and the basic strategy through equational constraints. The minimization of useful superpositions, through the additional constraints on multisets of terms, provides another example of this use of constraints.
- There is no more need to compute unifiers, thanks to unification constraints. In the AC-case, checking satisfiability is an exponential process, while computing all solutions is doubly exponential. Even better, in the case of an equation with only variables and one AC-symbol, checking satisfiability is polynomial w.r.t. the number of variables [12]. Moreover each inference step produces a single new literal, instead of as many literals as the number of most general AC-unifiers.
- Application of inference rules is separated from constraint solving which thus appears as a parameter of the deduction process. The constraint solver itself can be designed in a modular way and include built-in parts.
- Accumulation of constraints is a way to keep track of choices that are performed: for instance with ordering constraints, we keep track of each choice of orientation. So further deductions will be coherent.

144

- Our use of constraints is general enough to cover different calculi. Beyond the three examples given, another one could be given for a paramodulation based theorem prover [33]. Many more examples can be found in the cited literature.

The current limitations of using constraints in deduction processes are related to completeness and simplification. This also gives rise to new interesting problems.

- As we mix different kinds of constraints, a powerful constraint solver has to be designed to handle all of them. Combining solvers for each kind of constraints is complex in general and may be costly.
- An important property strongly desirable for the solver is incrementality. The problem is to optimize the constraint solving process for detecting inconsistencies, when a new set of constraints is added to a satisfiable set.
- The completeness requirement of deduction with constrained formulas leads one to consider restricted forms of initial formulas or constraints. Also including deletion of redundancies needs a special investigation effort for managing deduction rules and constraint solving in an efficient way.
- Applying simplification rules is more difficult. As solutions are not computed, a clause is simplifiable if all its instances are simplifiable. But this is not enough and for completeness, some additional conditions on solutions of unification constraints have to be fulfilled for applying simplifications. If we want to apply a similar deduction process to perform ordered completion of a set of equalities, simplification is essential and a special procedure has to be applied to eliminate redundant instances.

Acknowledgements: I sincerely thank Claude Kirchner, Christopher Lynch, Christophe Ringeissen and Laurent Vigneron for their contributions to the theoretical results presented here and for their comments on the manuscript. This work is partially supported by the Esprit Basic Research working group 6028, CCL.

References

1. Franz Baader and Klaus Schulz. Unification in the union of disjoint equational theories: Combining decision procedures. In *Proceedings 11th International Conference on Automated Deduction, Saratoga Springs (N.Y., USA)*, pages 50–65, 1992.
2. L. Bachmair and N. Dershowitz. Completion for rewriting modulo a congruence. *Theoretical Computer Science*, 67(2-3):173–202, October 1989.
3. L. Bachmair and H. Ganzinger. Rewrite-based equational theorem proving with selection and simplification. *Journal of Logic and Computation*, 4(3):1–31, 1994.
4. L. Bachmair, H. Ganzinger, C. Lynch, and W. Snyder. Basic paramodulation and superposition. In *Proceedings 11th International Conference on Automated Deduction, Saratoga Springs (N.Y., USA)*, pages 462–476, 1992.
5. L. Bachmair and D. A. Plaisted. Termination orderings for associative-commutative rewriting systems. *Journal of Symbolic Computation*, 1:329–349, 1985.

6. T. B. Baird, G. E. Peterson, and Ralph W. Wilkerson. Complete sets of reductions modulo associativity, commutativity and identity. In N. Dershowitz, editor, *Proceedings 3rd Conference on Rewriting Techniques and Applications, Chapel Hill (N.C., USA)*, volume 355 of *Lecture Notes in Computer Science*, pages 29–44. Springer-Verlag, April 1989.

7. H.-J. Bürckert. *A Resolution Principle for a Logic with Restricted Quantifiers*, volume 568 of *Lecture Notes in Artificial Intelligence*. Springer-Verlag, 1991.

8. Jacques Chabin. *Unification Générale par Surréduction Ordonnée Contrainte et Surréduction Dirigée*. Thèse de Doctorat d'Université, Université d'Orléans, January 1994.

9. H. Comon. Completion of rewrite systems with membership constraints. In W. Kuich, editor, *Proceedings of ICALP 92*, volume 623 of *Lecture Notes in Computer Science*. Springer-Verlag, 1992.

10. N. Dershowitz and J.-P. Jouannaud. *Handbook of Theoretical Computer Science*, volume B, chapter 6: Rewrite Systems, pages 244–320. Elsevier Science Publishers B. V. (North-Holland), 1990. Also as: Research report 478, LRI.

11. N. Dershowitz and J.-P. Jouannaud. Rewrite Systems. In J. van Leeuwen, editor, *Handbook of Theoretical Computer Science*, chapter 6, pages 244–320. Elsevier Science Publishers B. V. (North-Holland), 1990.

12. E. Domenjoud. *Outils pour la déduction automatique dans les théories associatives-commutatives*. Thèse de Doctorat d'Université, Université de Nancy 1, September 1991.

13. E. Domenjoud. A technical note on AC-unification. the number of minimal unifiers of the equation $\alpha x_1 + \cdots + \alpha x_p \doteq_{AC} \beta y_1 + \cdots + \beta y_q$. *Journal of Automated Reasoning*, 8:39–44, 1992. Also as research report CRIN 89-R-2.

14. M. Fernández. Narrowing based procedures for equational disunification. *Applicable Algebra in Engineering, Communication and Computation*, 3:1–26, 1992.

15. A. Frisch and Scherl R. A general framework for modal deduction. In J. A. Allen, R. Fikes, and E. Sandewall, editors, *Principles of Knowledge Representation and Reasoning: Proceedings of the Second International Conference*, San Mateo, CA, USA, 1991.

16. G. Huet. *Constrained Resolution: A Complete Method for Higher Order Logic*. PhD thesis, Case Western Reserve University, 1972.

17. J.-P. Jouannaud and Hélène Kirchner. Completion of a set of rules modulo a set of equations. *SIAM Journal of Computing*, 15(4):1155–1194, 1986. Preliminary version in Proceedings 11th ACM Symposium on Principles of Programming Languages, Salt Lake City (USA), 1984.

18. J.-P. Jouannaud and C. Marché. Completion modulo associativity, commutativity and identity (AC1). In A. Miola, editor, *Proceedings of DISCO'90*, volume 429 of *Lecture Notes in Computer Science*, pages 111–120. Springer-Verlag, April 1990.

19. Claude Kirchner and Hélène Kirchner. Constrained equational reasoning. In *Proceedings of the ACM-SIGSAM 1989 International Symposium on Symbolic and Algebraic Computation, Portland (Oregon)*, pages 382–389. ACM Press, July 1989. Report CRIN 89-R-220.

20. Claude Kirchner, Hélène Kirchner, and M. Rusinowitch. Deduction with symbolic constraints. *Revue d'Intelligence Artificielle*, 4(3):9–52, 1990. Special issue on Automatic Deduction.

21. H. Kirchner and P.-E. Moreau. Prototyping completion with constraints using computational systems. Technical report submitted, 1994.

22. H. Kirchner and C. Ringeissen. Constraint solving by narrowing in combined algebraic domains. In P. Van Hentenryck, editor, *Proc. 11th International Conference on Logic Programming*, pages 617–631. The MIT press, 1994.

23. C. Lynch and W. Snyder. Redundancy criteria for constrained completion. In C. Kirchner, editor, *Proceedings 5th Conference on Rewriting Techniques and Applications, Montreal (Canada)*, volume 690 of *Lecture Notes in Computer Science*, pages 2–16. Springer-Verlag, 1993.

24. U. Martin and T. Nipkow. Ordered rewriting and confluence. In M. E. Stickel, editor, *Proceedings 10th International Conference on Automated Deduction, Kaiserslautern (Germany)*, volume 449 of *Lecture Notes in Computer Science*, pages 366–380. Springer-Verlag, 1990.

25. P. Narendran and M. Rusinowitch. Any ground associative-commutative theory has a finite canonical system. In R. V. Book, editor, *Proceedings 4th Conference on Rewriting Techniques and Applications, Como (Italy)*. Springer-Verlag, 1991.

26. R. Nieuwenhuis and A. Rubio. Basic superposition is complete. In B. Krieg-Brückner, editor, *Proceedings of ESOP'92*, volume 582 of *Lecture Notes in Computer Science*, pages 371–389. Springer-Verlag, 1992.

27. R. Nieuwenhuis and A. Rubio. Theorem proving with ordering constrained clauses. In D. Kapur, editor, *Proceedings of CADE-11*, volume 607 of *Lecture Notes in Computer Science*, pages 477–491. Springer-Verlag, 1992.

28. R. Nieuwenhuis and A. Rubio. AC-superposition with constraints: no AC-unifiers needed. In A. Bundy, editor, *Proceedings 12th International Conference on Automated Deduction, Nancy (France)*, volume 814 of *Lecture Notes in Artificial Intelligence*, pages 545–559. Springer-Verlag, June 1994.

29. G. E. Peterson. Complete sets of reductions with constraints. In M. E. Stickel, editor, *Proceedings 10th International Conference on Automated Deduction, Kaiserslautern (Germany)*, volume 449 of *Lecture Notes in Computer Science*, pages 381–395. Springer-Verlag, 1990.

30. A. Rubio and R. Nieuwenhuis. A precedence-based total AC-compatible ordering. In C. Kirchner, editor, *Proceedings 5th Conference on Rewriting Techniques and Applications, Montreal (Canada)*, volume 690 of *Lecture Notes in Computer Science*, pages 374–388. Springer-Verlag, 1993.

31. G. Smolka. *Logic Programming over Polymorphically Order-Sorted Types*. PhD thesis, FB Informatik, Universität Kaiserslautern, Germany, 1989.

32. M. Stickel. Automated deduction by theory resolution. *Journal of Automated Reasoning*, 1(4):285–289, 1985.

33. L. Vigneron. Associative-Commutative Deduction with Constraints. In A. Bundy, editor, *Proceedings 12th International Conference on Automated Deduction, Nancy (France)*, volume 814 of *Lecture Notes in Artificial Intelligence*, pages 530–544. Springer-Verlag, June 1994.

Abstract Interpretation and Finite Domain Symbolic Constraints

Baudouin Le Charlier

Institut d'Informatique, University of Namur (F.U.N.D.P.)
rue Grandgagnage, 21, B-5000 Namur, Belgium
E-mail: ble@info.fundp.ac.be

Abstract. Abstract interpretation is a general methodology for building static analyses which are useful for program optimization and verification. Finite domain symbolic constraints constitute a restricted class of first order formulas which enjoy efficient representations. In this paper, it is shown how finite domain symbolic constraints can be used to implement a whole class of abstract domains applicable to any programming paradigm. Some interesting accuracy properties of these domains are discussed. The general approach is further developed in the context of logic programming and related to the well-known abstract domain *Prop* showing that combining finite domain symbolic constraints with bottom-up abstract interpretation provides analyses that are at the same time accurate, efficient and specializable. (Such analyses are called on-line, goal-independent or condensing.)

1 Introduction

Abstract interpretation is a general methodology for building static analyses of programs. It is currently a very active research area, especially for declarative paradigms (functional programming, logic programming, constraint logic programming, to name a few). This is, on the one hand, because declarative languages provide many opportunities for static analyses and, on the other hand, because such analyses are really needed to make declarative languages competitive with procedural languages. (See for instance [28, 43].)

The topic of this paper is to explain how certain kinds of constraints can be used to perform program analyses in the framework of abstract interpretation and to discuss the advantages and possible limitations of their use in that context.

In order to give a broad view of the subject, I first present some important aspects of abstract interpretation in general, independently of any particular programming paradigm. (Simple flow-chart programs will be used as examples.) This part of the paper does not assume previous knowledge of abstract interpretation and can be used as an introduction to this field. However the emphasis is not on the traditional mathematical framework, namely complete lattices and Galois insertions (for general presentations of these notions, see for instance [2, 21]). The emphasis is on pragmatic notions which act upon the accuracy and efficiency of the analyses: design of the abstract domain, granularity of the analysis, operational versus fixpoint approach. At the light of these notions, finite domain symbolic constraints are introduced as a particular choice of abstract domain, and the properties of such a domain are discussed.

The second major part of the paper specializes the results of the first part to the context of logic programming. First some peculiarities of abstract interpretation for logic programming are stressed: downwards closed abstract domains, top-down versus bottom-up frameworks, and the so-called goal-independent and condensing analyses. Then, I relate finite domain symbolic constraints to the well-known, and broadly studied, domain *Prop* [5, 16, 41, 48] and I show that finite domain symbolic constraints can be used to define a whole class of downwards closed abstract domains for which bottom-up abstract interpretation provides goal independent analyses which can be specialized optimally. These bottom-up analyses are equivalent to their top-down counterparts in the sense that specializing the result of the bottom-up analyses with respect to a given abstract input gives exactly the same result as the top-down analyses started for the same abstract input. It will be also shown that top-down analyses are "condensing" for those domains. That is : they can be run only once with the most general abstract input because results for other inputs can be optimally computed by specializing the general abstract output. These nice properties are due to the fact that logic programming is actually a (kind of) constraint logic programming, has equivalent bottom-up and top-down semantics and that its top-down semantics (SLD-resolution) is indeed condensing (for pure programs, assuming a complete search strategy).

The rest of the paper is organized as follows. Section 2 is a short overview of the benefits of abstract interpretation for program optimization and verification. Section 3 provides a general presentation of abstract interpretation and explains how finite domain symbolic constraints can be used in this framework. Section 4 specializes the previous material to the case of logic programming. I conclude with related works and acknowledgements of contributors to the material presented in this paper.

2 The Benefits of Abstract Interpretation

Static analysis and abstract interpretation in particular can be used either for program optimization or for program verification. We consider each aspect in turn and for both of them we consider different programming paradigms. The presentation is very brief. See the references for detailed information.

2.1 Optimization

Logic Programming There are many possible optimizations of logic programs. This is mainly due to the fact that logic programs are multi-directional : any argument of a logic procedure can be used as an input or as an ouput or can be only partially instantiated but this theoretical property is almost never used in actual programs. Abstract interpretation can be used to infer the form of the actual calls (the so-called input patterns). This information can be used by an optimizing compiler to generate specialized code.

Typical analyses are groundness analyses (is an argument surely ground at each possible call?), freeness analyses (is it surely free?), sharing analyses (do two terms share common free variables?), linearity analyses (does a term contain several occurrences of the same free variable?), type analyses, reference chain analyses, determinacy and functionality analyses.

Such analyses can be used, for instance, to specialize unification : instead of applying the general unification algorithm, a few instruction can be generated depending on the available information about groundness, freeness, reference chain length. In many situations the occur-check can be omitted thanks to the sharing and linearity information. Determinacy analyses allow to remove choice points and to detect true tail recursion. Automatic program parallelization uses groundness, freeness and sharing analyses.

For a more complete account of this area, the reader could refer to [30, 65].

Constraint Logic Programming Constraint specialization is a generalization of unification specialization. In many cases, the costly constraint solving mechanism can be replaced by the assignment of a single value. Groundness and freeness analyses are very important here. See [26] for details and a complete account of the possible optimizations.

Functional Programming Lazy functional languages require call by name or call by need to implement parameter passing. Transforming those costly mechanisms into call by value, whenever it is safe to evaluate the actual parameter, is a major optimization. Strictness analyses aim at inferring functions which are undefined when their argument is. For such strict functions, the above transformation may be applied.

Other analyses for functional languages include totality analysis [62] and various analyses allowing to save memory space. For more information, see [1, 43].

Object Oriented Programming Polymorphism in object oriented languages requires dynamic binding of the procedure names to their definitions. Type analyses allow to reduce the amount of needed polymorphism and hence to produce better code. See [3].

2.2 Verification

Logic Programming Prolog in an untyped language. Nevertheless, practical programs implicitly assume some typing of the arguments. Automatic type inference [4, 23, 24, 33] allows to check whether the actual values of arguments respect the types intended by the programmer. For more information about types in logic programming see also [25, 56, 60].

Termination of logic programs is a difficult topic. Abstract interpretation is based on computational induction and is therefore fundamentally unable to prove termination. However type analyses can be used to infer structural information from which proofs by structural induction can be derived. See [67].

Functional Programming Typed functional languages permit to detect most "silly programming mistakes" at compile time but sometimes reject useful programs because their type system is not powerful enough. Abstract interpretation can be the basis for more powerful typing methods (see [53]). Other verifications are possible, for instance the automatic detection of uncaught exceptions in ML programs [69].

Imperative Programming Static checking of array bounds and more generally automatic synthesis of invariants is a long time research topic (see [19, 20]). Powerful methods need to take into account the aliasing problem due to reference parameter passing [6]. For an account of a sophisticated implemented system, see [7].

Distributed Systems Abstract interpretation is particularly suitable for the verification of safety properties of parallel programs and distributed systems. Absence of deadlocks, reachability of some states are typical examples of such properties. There is an abundant literature on verification of distributed systems but relatively few papers use abstract interpretation. Examples of such works are [31, 32, 52].

3 Abstract Interpretation and Finite Domain Symbolic Constraints

The fundamental idea of abstract interpretation is quite simple but leads to many variations and formalizations. The idea is the following : in order to get general information about all possible executions of a program, instead of running the program over a set of particular data, we run it over a set of value descriptions encompassing infinitely many particular data. Such descriptions are called abstract values.

In this section, I describe how to implement this idea. Starting from the basic intuition, I formalize it, showing some problems to be solved (for instance, ensuring termination of the "abstract" execution). I discuss the nature of abstract domains and relate it to the granularity of the analysis. Then I introduce finite domain symbolic constraints as a possible abstract domain and I show that the coarsest analysis with such a domain is exactly as precise as the finest analysis with a "traditional" domain.

As finite domain symbolic constraints enjoy efficient representations, this result indicates that, for some classes of program analyses, abstract interpretation with finite domain symbolic constraints surely outperforms traditional methods, i.e. provides a better trade-off between accuracy and efficiency.

For completeness I close this section by a brief account of the fixpoint approach to abstract interpretation.

3.1 Abstract Interpretation : Operational Approach

As the basic idea of abstract interpretation is to "mimic" the actual "concrete" computation over an "abstract" domain of descriptions, it is natural to use the operational semantics of the language as the basis of the study. (Other approaches are possible but are ignored here. For an approach based on denotational semantics, see for instance [57].) Using the operational semantics is especially required for optimization since language implementation primarily relies on this kind of semantics. Moreover it should be convenient that the abstract semantics be in some sense "the same" as the standard one. I follow this approach as much as possible here. (See also [13].)

Then it is natural to express both semantics with transition rules. At the concrete level we assume a set Σ_c of "concrete" states. Similarly, at the abstract level, we have a set Σ_a of "abstract" states. The concrete semantics determines all possible concrete transitions which are of the form $\sigma_c \longmapsto \sigma_c'$ with $\sigma_c, \sigma_c' \in \Sigma_c$. Similarly, the abstract semantics determines transitions of the form $\sigma_a \longmapsto \sigma_a'$ with $\sigma_a, \sigma_a' \in \Sigma_a$. The correctness [1] of the abstract semantics relies on the definition of a so-called concretization function $Cc : \Sigma_a \longrightarrow \wp(\Sigma_c)$ which fixes, by definition, the meaning (or denotation) of each abstract state. The abstract semantics is correct if and only if, for each concrete transition $\sigma_c \longmapsto \sigma_c'$ and each abstract state σ_a such that $\sigma_c \in Cc(\sigma_a)$, there exists one abstract transition $\sigma_a \longmapsto \sigma_a'$ such that $\sigma_c' \in Cc(\sigma_a')$. Indeed, then it is clear that each concrete computation (i.e. sequence of concrete transitions) can be simulated by a corresponding abstract computation.

Non-determinism is easily introduced by means of transition rules : two different rules may possibly apply to the same state. This is important for abstract interpretation since the abstraction of a deterministic concrete semantics may be a non-deterministic abstract semantics. A typical example is given by the conditional statement **if** B **then** C_1 **else** C_2 . In general, an abstract state will neither imply B nor **not** B. Therefore two abstract transitions will be possible. This remark shows that it is better to put our study in the context of non-deterministic transition systems (of which deterministic system are considered a particular case).

Genericity It is important to define abstract semantics which are generic. This means that they do not rely on a specific abstract domain. On the contrary, abstract semantics should assume an unspecified abstract domains and a few abstract operations which are required to respect some correctness criteria.

3.2 Tabulation for Termination

Assuming that the concrete and abstract semantics are "homomorphic" (i.e. each concrete computation is simulated by a corresponding abstract computation), practical implementations of the concrete and abstract semantics are nevertheless of a different nature.

---

[1] also called consistency or safety.

Concrete Implementations Non-determinism of real programming languages can be implemented at least in two ways. The first way is "don't care" (one solution) determinism : whenever several transitions may apply, one chooses one of them and never reconsiders the other possibilities. The second way is "don't know" (all solutions) determinism : when several transitions apply, they are all considered, either by executing them in parallel or by means of a bactracking mechanism.

Abstract Interpretation Algorithms always use don't know determinism because the aim of abstract execution is to collect information about all possible concrete executions. Moreover termination is required even when some corresponding concrete execution does not terminate.

In fact, a naive abstract execution, which simply applies the transition rules according to don't know determinism, will often fail to terminate even when all the corresponding concrete executions terminate because different concrete states are represented by the same abstract state. So the image of a concrete computation with all different concrete states can be an abstract computation with some equal states. But, at the abstract level, transition rules will indefinitely apply to those equal states.

This problem can be solved thanks to a tabulation mechanism. All generated states are stored into a table. Whenever a state is generated by a transition, a look-up is performed to the table. If the state already belongs to the table, the current computation terminates. Otherwise the state is added into the table and the current computation continues. If the generated set of abstract states is finite, this tabulation method is sufficient to ensure termination while still computing all abstract states. Consequently many abstract interpretation frameworks assume that the abstract domain is finite. I will make this assumption in the rest of this paper because my main concern here is using finite domain symbolic constraints which constitute themselves finite domains. (For a discussion of the pros and cons of finite versus infinite abstract domains, see [34, 22].)

Finally it is worth noticing that some "concrete" programming languages have a built-in tabulation mechanism. Let us cite for instance OLDT-resolution based implementations of logic programs [63] and DyALog [68]. Such languages provide straightforward implementations of abstract interpretation algorithms : they only require the implementation of an abstract domain within their own data model.

3.3 Program Points and Granularity

The notion of program state can roughly be decomposed into two parts: a program point and a store. Program points can be differently defined depending on the kind of language to be analysed. In a machine language, they are machine addresses; in flow-chart programs, they are the arrows leading from a statement to another; in Prolog, they are textual points between two literals; ... No matter how they are technically defined, they are the "places" where the information has to be collected either for the optimizing compiler or for checking some correctness property. Therefore the "concrete" notion of program point will not be abstracted in general and an abstract state will consist of a (concrete) program point and of an (abstract) store. During the abstract computation, several states with the same program point but a different abstract store can be generated. Then, two design decisions are basically possible for the abstract interpretation algorithm.

Univariant Algorithms The first decision consists in "lumping" the two abstract stores together and continuing the computation with the "union" of the two. This choice is motivated by the fact that, in general, one generates a single code for each piece of program. Distinguishing several states for the same program point would imply generating different pieces of code. Univariant algorithms also require some additional properties of the abstract domain. Roughly speaking, some kind of upper bound operation must be defined. This implies in general a loss of accuracy (see paragraph 3.6).

Polyvariant Algorithms The second basic possibility is to keep all the generated abstract states. This choice does not require any additional property of the abstract domain but may lead to a huge amount of computation. Nevertheless, polyvariant algorithms are obviously more accurate than their univariant counterparts, they can be useful for languages where multiple specialization of procedures is meaningful (for instance Prolog), and it is theoretically possible to only "lump" the abstract stores at the end of the computation.

Discussion In fact, it is hopeless to try to decide a priori which of the two methods is the best since part of the complexity can be moved to the design of the abstract domain. But we will get an interesting result at paragraph 3.5 after adding some hypotheses about the abstract stores.

It is also worth noticing that many intermediate design choices are possible. In fact, they are often made implicitly because they are suggested by the syntax of the language. Some program points may be discarded because they are always reachable from some other ones (to save recording space). It is possible to classify program points and to use different granularities for different classes of program points. In Prolog for instance, one may distinguish two kinds of program points: procedure entry and procedure exit and for each kind of point one can independently decide to keep a single abstract store or several ones. (See paragraph 4.1 and reference [64] for further discussion.)

Sometimes it is even possible to design clever algorithms which dynamically adapt their granularity. This is called "dynamic partitioning" [7].

Specific Analyses A specific analysis is obtained by instantiating a generic abstract interpretation algorithm to a specific abstract domain (including some specific abstract operations). Now, let us move to abstract domains.

3.4 Abstract Domains

The literature on programming language semantics classically distinguishes between basic semantic domain of values and more elaborate domains of stores and environments. I follow the same classification here both at the concrete and abstract level.

Abstract Values

Flat Domains Let V_c be a concrete domain of values. The elements of V_c can be, for instance, integers, Booleans, strings, lists, terms. The simplest way to design an abstract domain is to define a partition $\{S_1, \ldots, S_n\}$ of V_c, an arbitrary set $V_a = \{v_a^1, \ldots, v_a^n\}$ and to define the concretization function $Cc : V_a \longrightarrow \wp(V_c)$, by

$$Cc(v_a^i) = S_i \quad (1 \leq i \leq n).$$

We call these domains flat domains since their elements are not comparable. They are only suitable for pure polyvariant analyses but they can be "completed" to derive domains suitable for univariant analyses.

Example 1 Sign Analysis. The classical domain for sign analysis is defined as

$V_c = \mathbf{Z}, \ V_a = \{\ominus, \odot, \oplus\},$
$Cc(\ominus) = \{i \mid i < 0\}, \ Cc(\odot) = \{0\}, \ Cc(\oplus) = \{i \mid i > 0\}.$

Example 2 Mode Analysis. A flat domain for mode analysis is obtained by choosing

$V_c = Term$ (the set of all Prolog terms), $V_a = \{g, v, ngv\},$
$Cc(g) = \{t \mid t \text{ is a ground term.}\}, \ Cc(v) = \{t \mid t \text{ is a variable.}\},$
$Cc(ngv) = \{t \mid t \text{ is not a ground term nor a variable.}\}.$

Completed Domains Flat domains are usually not suitable for a univariant analysis[2]. I call completed domain, a domain which is obtained from a flat domain by adding some elements in order that each pair of abstract values has an upper bound. The ordering is induced by the concretization relation. Note that it is not absolutely required to have a unique least upper bound, although this additional requirement is natural.

Once upper bounds have been added, one may remove some original elements because they can be approximated by one of the upper bounds. The idea is to keep only elements that bring "interesting" information. Hence there are many ways to complete a flat domain V_a.

The most complete is $\wp(V_a)$ with $Cc : \wp(V_a) \longrightarrow \wp(V_c)$ defined by

$$Cc(\{v_a^{i_1}, \ldots, v_a^{i_j}\}) = \bigcup_{k=1}^{j} Cc(v_a^{i_k}).$$

Such a completed domain is called a power set domain [9]. Obviously if n is the number of elements of V_a, $\wp(V_a)$ contains 2^n elements. Therefore power set domains can only be used for small values of n.

---

[2] But we will see at paragraph 3.5 that they are well suited for an univariant analysis with finite domain symbolic constraints.

An other systematic way to complete a flat domain is to only add one "top" element $\top$ with $Cc(\top) = V_c$. Notice that $\{\top\}$ is itself a completed (albeit not very interesting) domain.

Example 3 Sign Analysis. The power set domain for sign analysis is defined as

$V_c = \mathbf{Z}, V_a = \{\bot, \ominus, \odot, \oplus, \oslash, \varoslash, \oslash, \top\},$
$Cc(\bot) = \{\}, Cc(\ominus) = \{i \mid i < 0\}, Cc(\odot) = \{0\}, Cc(\oplus) = \{i \mid i > 0\},$
$Cc(\oslash) = \{i \mid i \leq 0\}, Cc(\varoslash) = \{i \mid i \neq 0\}, Cc(\oslash) = \{i \mid i \geq 0\},$
$Cc(\top) = \mathbf{Z}.$

Example 4 Mode Analysis. A classical domain for mode analysis [10, 54] is defined by

$V_c = Term, V_a = \{\mathbf{g}, \mathbf{v}, \mathbf{any}\},$
$Cc(\mathbf{g}) = \{t \mid t \text{ is a ground term.}\},$
$Cc(\mathbf{v}) = \{t \mid t \text{ is a variable.}\},$
$Cc(\mathbf{any}) = Term.$

Note that the original element ngv has been removed from this completed domain.

Example 5 Mode Analysis. The following domain was proposed in [25], studied in [54] and implemented in [27]. It is the power set domain of example 2.

$V_c = Term, V_a = \{\bot, \mathbf{g}, \mathbf{ngv}, \mathbf{v}, \mathbf{nv}, \mathbf{gv}, \mathbf{ng}, \mathbf{any}\},$
$Cc(\bot) = \{\},$
$Cc(\mathbf{g}) = \{t \mid t \text{ is a ground term.}\},$
$Cc(\mathbf{ngv}) = \{t \mid t \text{ is not a ground term nor a variable.}\},$
$Cc(\mathbf{v}) = \{t \mid t \text{ is a variable.}\},$
$Cc(\mathbf{nv}) = \{t \mid t \text{ is not a variable.}\},$
$Cc(\mathbf{gv}) = \{t \mid t \text{ is a ground term or a variable.}\},$
$Cc(\mathbf{ng}) = \{t \mid t \text{ is not a ground term.}\},$
$Cc(\mathbf{any}) = Term.$

Several other domains for mode analysis have been proposed. See [30] for a comprehensive account.

Other Domains of Abstract Values have been defined which are much more complex than the flat and completed domains above. Typical examples are the typegraph domain of [18, 33] for Prolog and the integer interval domain of [20]. I deliberately ignore such domains in this paper because they are not suited for the kind of constraint domains I want to illustrate in the next pages. It is nevertheless possible to combine constraint domains with other complex domains (of abstract values). As examples the reader may refer to [17] (the domain *Pat(Prop)*) and to [44] where set constraints are used to describe types.

Operations on Abstract Values

Operations on abstract values should mimic operations on concrete values in an obvious way. For instance, let $o_c : V_c \times V_c \longrightarrow V_c$.

o_c can be abstracted by any operation $o_a : V_a \times V_a \longrightarrow V_a$ such that for all $v_c^1, v_c^2 \in V_c$ and $v_a^1, v_a^2 \in V_a$:

$$v_c^i \in Cc(v_a^i) \ (i = 1, 2) \quad \Rightarrow \quad o_c(v_c^1, v_c^2) \in Cc(o_a(v_a^1, v_a^2)).$$

It is always possible to define such an operation o_a provided the abstract domain is a completed domain.

For flat domains (and polyvariant algorithms) it is possible to define $o_a : V_a \times V_a \longrightarrow \wp(V_a)$ such that for all $v_c^1, v_c^2 \in V_c$ and $v_a^1, v_a^2 \in V_a$:

$$v_c^i \in Cc(v_a^i) \ (i = 1, 2) \quad \Rightarrow \quad (\exists v_a \in o_a(v_a^1, v_a^2) : o_c(v_c^1, v_c^2) \in Cc(v_a)).$$

For completed domains it is not always possible to define the best possible (most accurate) o_a. This is however possible when each concrete value has a best abstract representation (i.e. an abstraction function $Abs : V_c \longrightarrow V_a$ is naturally defined) and a least upper bound operation exists in V_a. Such properties hold for power set domains, for instance.

Abstract Stores

Concrete states of computation usually consist of a program point, an environment (which maps identifiers on objects) and a store (which maps memory locations on values). In this presentation, I merge, for simplicity, the environment and the store and I assume that a store maps identifiers to values. (Therefore I ignore important aspects such as aliasing.) Let us note I the set of identifiers (or variables or variable names). A (concrete) store is thus a function $s_c : I \longrightarrow V_c$. A store can also be viewed as a tuple of values indexed by elements of I. In the following, I note $I \longrightarrow V$ the set of all functions from I to V. Since stores are viewed as tuples, such a set will be called a cartesian product (both when V is a concrete domain V_c or an abstract domain V_a).

Building an abstract domain for stores means : 1) building a set of *abstract stores* and 2) defining a concretization function from this set to $\wp(I \longrightarrow V_c)$. However, it is important to understand that a concrete notion does not need to be abstracted by a notion of exactly the same kind. Hence, abstract stores *may* but *need not* to be tuples of abstract values. We may call abstract tuple, any kind of object *provided that* we define a concretization function which maps those objects on sets of concrete tuples.

Two different ways to define an abstract domain for stores are described here under. The first one consists in choosing $I \longrightarrow V_a$ as the set of abstract stores. This domain is noted $CP(I, V_a)$ since its elements are tuples (CP stands for "Cartesian Product"). The second way consists in choosing $\wp(I \longrightarrow V_a)$ as the set of abstract stores. If the elements of I are viewed as variables, elements of $\wp(I \longrightarrow V_a)$ can be viewed as constraints over V_a with free variables in I. This domain is noted $CS(I, V_a)$ where CS stands for "ConStraint domain".

Cartesian Products In such a domain, abstract stores are functions $s_a : I \longrightarrow V_a$. The concretization function $Cc : (I \longrightarrow V_a) \longrightarrow \wp(I \longrightarrow V_c)$ is defined by:

$$Cc(s_a) \;=\; \{s_c \mid \forall x \in I : s_c(x) \in Cc(s_a(x))\}.$$

In this framework, operations on the abstract store are easy to define. Assume an update operation which yields a store $s_c[x/v_c]$, equal to s_c everywhere except that $s_c(x) = v_c$, it can clearly be abstracted by $s_a[x/v_a]$ where v_a abstracts v_c (i.e. $v_c \in Cc(v_a)$).

Constraint Domains Abstract stores are properties of concrete stores. So, they are elements of $\wp(I \longrightarrow V_c)$. This suggests to abstract $I \longrightarrow V_c$ by $\wp(I \longrightarrow V_a)$ (which is a finite set assuming that V_a is). Elements of $\wp(I \longrightarrow V_a)$ can be viewed as symbolic constraints over the finite domain V_a and can be represented by any first order formula built by means of quantifiers, logical connectives and literals of the form $x = v_a$ and $x \neq v_a$. Free variables are elements of I. This kind of constraints are exactly those which are expressible in the constraint language Toupie (see reference [61] in this book). They enjoy efficient representations in the form of decision diagrams (DD) (see [11, 61]). Each such formula f, interpreted over the domain V_a, defines a subset S_f of $I \longrightarrow V_a$ as follows[3]:

$$s \in S_f \;\iff\; f \text{ is true for the free variable assignment } s.$$

S_f is the semantic counterpart of (the syntactic object) f. In the following, I confuse the two kinds of objects since their correspondance is clearly established.

Elements of $\wp(I \longrightarrow V_a)$ can be used as abstract stores.
In the following, this domain is denoted $CS(I, V_a)$ and its concretization function $Cc : \wp(I \longrightarrow V_a) \longrightarrow \wp(I \longrightarrow V_c)$ is defined as follows:

$$Cc(s_a) \;=\; \{s_c \mid \exists s \in s_a : \forall x \in I : s_c(x) \in Cc(s(x))\}.$$

Note that s_a is now a set of functions instead of a single one. The update operation on the abstract store can be defined as

$$\{s[x/v_a] \mid s \in s_a\}.$$

Syntactically, using constraints (formulas) instead of sets, if a store is abstracted by the constraint f and if the next concrete store is obtained by updating x to the concrete value v_c which is abstracted by v_a, then this concrete store can be abstracted by the constraint

$$(\exists x : f) \wedge (x = v_a).$$

Similarly, any other "semantic" operation on the abstract store can be expressed as a formula "transformer".

The abstract domain $CS(I, V_a)$ is much bigger than $CP(I, V_a)$. Let us assume a flat domain V_a with n elements. Suppose that I contains m elements.

---

[3] See [61] for a more technical definition.

Then $CP(\mathbf{I}, V_a)$ has n^m elements while $CS(\mathbf{I}, V_a)$ has $2^{(n^m)}$. However, in the case of $CS(\mathbf{I}, V_a)$, V_a should be a flat domain because otherwise different elements of $CS(\mathbf{I}, V_a)$ would have the same concretization. For instance, both formulas $(x = \odot) \vee (x = \oplus)$ and $(x = \oslash)$ express that x has a non negative value (assuming the completed domain of example 3). On the contrary, in a cartesian product domain $CP(\mathbf{I}, V_a)$, V_a will be a completed domain in general. Now, assuming that V_a is flat, $CP(\mathbf{I}, \wp(V_a))$ is the most powerful cartesian product domain that we can build from V_a. It has "only" 2^{nm} elements and is therefore exponentially smaller than $CS(\mathbf{I}, V_a)$. So we could think that $CS(\mathbf{I}, V_a)$ is not usable in practice. However, constraint programming over symbolic finite domains has proved successful to solve many combinatorials problems mostly due to the use of decision diagrams [61]. So why should it not work for abstract interpretation? Well, recent experiments have shown that such domains can be used to design analyses which are not only very accurate but also efficient (see paragraph 4.4 and references [14, 17, 41, 50]).

3.5 Two General Results

Abstract interpretation with finite domain symbolic constraints is accurate for the following reasons.

1. Given a polyvariant abstract interpretation algorithm over $CP(\mathbf{I}, V_a)$, where V_a is a flat domain, it is possible to construct a univariant abstract interpretation algorithm over $CS(\mathbf{I}, V_a)$ which has exactly the same accuracy.

2. Given a flat domain V_a, the polyvariant abstract interpretation algorithm over $CP(\mathbf{I}, V_a)$ is at least as accurate as any other abstract interpretation algorithm over $CP(\mathbf{I}, V_a')$, working at any granularity, where V_a' is any completed domain constructed over V_a.

I do not prove those results formally here since it would require long technical developments, but the intuitive justifications are clear. First, the polyvariant abstract interpretation algorithm over $CP(\mathbf{I}, V_a)$ is as accurate as possible (assuming a given V_a) because it never "lumps" abstract values together. Second, the univariant algorithm over $CS(\mathbf{I}, V_a)$ is as accurate as the polyvariant algorithm over $CP(\mathbf{I}, V_a)$ because it is possible to design abstract operations on constraints which perform globally (at once) all individual operations (on the simple abstract stores) performed by the polyvariant algorithm.

Finally, the fact that constraints have efficient representations on which global operations can be performed efficiently (see [11, 61]) implies that the univariant algorithm on $CS(\mathbf{I}, V_a)$ can be made (much) more efficient than the polyvariant algorithm over $CP(\mathbf{I}, V_a)$: the combinatorial enumeration of abstract stores is avoided.

3.6 An Example

To illustrate this section, I provide a very simple example. Consider the simple flow-chart program of figure 1. Suppose we want to analyze the signs of the variables at each program point, assuming that the inputs verify the condition

$$(x > 0 \wedge y = 0) \vee (x = 0 \wedge y > 0).$$

Figure 2 depicts the (final) abstract stores which are computed by a univariant analysis of the program over $CP(I, V_a^3)$ where V_a^3 is the power set domain of example 3. Note that the input condition must be approximated by

$$\{x \mapsto \oslash, y \mapsto \oslash, z \mapsto \top\},$$

since the abstract domain is not able to capture the input condition exactly.

Figure 3 depicts the (final) abstract stores which are computed by a univariant analysis over $CS(I, V_a^1)$ where V_a^1 is the flat domain of example 1. To ease the reading of the abstract stores, I use some abbreviations such as, for example, writing $x > 0$ instead of $x = \oplus$ and $x \geq 0$ instead of $(x = \odot) \vee (x = \oplus)$.

```
1: input(x,y,z);
2: if x > y then  goto 5 else goto 3;
3: x := x + z;
4: goto 2;
5: output(x,y,z).
```

Fig. 1. A Simple Flow-chart program

PP	Abstract Stores
1	$\{x \mapsto \oslash, y \mapsto \oslash, z \mapsto \top\}$
2	$\{x \mapsto \top, y \mapsto \oslash, z \mapsto \top\}$
3	$\{x \mapsto \top, y \mapsto \oslash, z \mapsto \top\}$
4	$\{x \mapsto \top, y \mapsto \oslash, z \mapsto \top\}$
5	$\{x \mapsto \oplus, y \mapsto \oslash, z \mapsto \top\}$

Fig. 2. Univariant Analysis over $CP(I, V_a^3)$

It can be observed that the analysis which uses constraints is more accurate than the traditional one with a power set domain. The interested reader should perform these analyses in detail by hand. Then he should also try to perform the polyvariant analyses, first with $CP(I, V_a^1)$ and next with $CP(I, V_a^3)$ and $CS(I, V_a^1)$. He would observe that the former one entails a lot of calculations while the two later ones entail some redundancy.

PP	Abstract Stores
1	$(x > 0 \wedge y = 0) \vee (x = 0 \wedge y > 0)$
2	$(x > 0 \wedge y = 0) \vee (y > 0)$
3	$y > 0$
4	$y > 0$
5	$x > 0 \wedge y \geq 0$

Fig. 3. Univariant Analysis over $CS(\mathbf{I}, V_a{}^1)$

3.7 Fixpoint Approach

The concrete and abstract semantics which are used in the operational approach that I presented above can also be given a fixpoint presentation because transition rules can be seen as a relation transformation of which the intended transition relation is the least fixpoint.

This approach offers some advantages:

1. It is possible to design generic algorithms for fixpoint computation which include very sophisticated optimizations. (See [35, 40, 59, 66].) Such algorithms can then be instantiated to an abstract semantics leading to abstract interpretation algorithms. Sometimes the obtained algorithms will compute the fixpoint in a very different way than a naive "mimicking" algorithm. For instance, fixpoints can be computed top-down or bottom-up. A top-down algorithm receives an input value and only computes the part of the fixpoint which is relevant to the computation of the corresponding output. A bottom-up algorithm computes the fixpoint entirely, solving the simple cases first and going up to the more complex ones. Although the bottom-up algorithms seem to perform more work, there are cases where they are more efficient because their implementation cost is lower. (No look-up table is used.) See paragraph 4.3 for further discussion of this topic in the context of logic programming.

2. The choice of the granularity can be made at the abstract semantic level, independently of the algorithmic optimizations. (See [64].)

3. It is often convenient to design abstract semantics which are very far from the concrete operational one (see [39]). They can be expressed by fixpoint definitions but not as easily by transition rules. Moreover, abstract semantics for functional languages can be obtained from a standard fixpoint semantics which is not trivially equivalent to an operational semantics. (See also [37] for Prolog with Cut.)

4 Application (and Specialization) to Logic Programming

In this section, a basic knowledge of logic programming is assumed (see [46]). The material of section 3 is applied to logic programming and some specific aspects of logic programming which are important for abstract interpretation are discussed: top-down and bottom-up semantics and downwards closed abstract domains. Then it is shown that the famous abstract domain *Prop* is closed to (a particular case of) the constraint domains discussed in paragraph 3.4 but with a slightly different choice of the concretization function[4]. The pros and cons of each choice are discussed. It is also shown that the top-down abstract semantics are condensing for such domains and that the bottom-up abstract semantics, while being much more efficient to compute, contains all the information provided by the top-down frameworks. Experimental results are briefly discussed and related works are described.

4.1 Abstract Interpretation for Logic Programming

Frameworks

Logic programming has been given many (concrete) semantics which are all in some sense equivalent [5]. SLD-resolution is the basic (top-down) operational semantics for logic programming. The so-called T_P semantics is a (bottom-up) fixpoint semantics. Both semantics define the same set of (ground) success atoms (also called output patterns).

Top-down Frameworks Many abstract interpretation frameworks[6] based on SLD-resolution have been defined. Nilsson's framework [58] is a univariant framework which uses as program points all textual points in the program clauses. Most other frameworks distinguishes two kinds of program points: procedure entry and procedure exit. They use different granularities based on this classification. OLDT-based frameworks (e.g. [13, 44]) are polyvariant both for procedure entry and procedure exit. Mellish's early framework [51] is univariant both for procedure entry and procedure exit. Finally the frameworks of Bruynooghe [8, 55] and of Le Charlier and Van Hentenryck [27, 36, 42] are polyvariant for procedure entry and univariant for procedure exit.

Bottom-up Frameworks Other frameworks based on the T_P semantics or on generalizations of it (the S-semantics [29]) have been defined by Marriott and Sondergaard [47]. They are much simpler than top-down frameworks and hence more efficiently computable because they only compute (abstract) output patterns. (However the most relevant pieces of information for logic program optimization are input patterns.)

Such bottom-up frameworks are also called "goal independent".

---

[4] The generalization of *Prop* which is discussed in this section was first described in [14].

[5] Only pure Horn clause programs are considered.

[6] Only some are cited here.

Condensing Analyses A top-down analysis is said condensing [49] if the ouputs corresponding to the most general possible input can be specialized optimally for more specific inputs (without executing the analysis for those inputs).

The very possibility to have condensing analyses is specific to logic programs (and constraint programs). Indeed, SLD-resolution is condensing : assuming an initial goal of the form $p(x_1,\ldots,x_n)$ where the x_i are distinct variables and a complete search rule (e.g. breath-first search), it will produce a set of most general output patterns which can be specialized by unification to any specific input pattern $p(t_1,\ldots,t_n)$. A condensing analysis is thus an abstraction of SLD-resolution which preserves this property.

Downwards Closed Abstract Domains

In logic programming, concrete stores are called substitutions (noted θ in the following) and values (elements of V_a) are terms. Abstract domains can be defined as indicated in paragraph 3.4 but abstract operations are made complicated because some terms bound to different program variables (elements of **I**) may contain occurrences of the same free variable. Hence any instanciation of such a shared variable will modify several components of the store. For instance, executing the built-in $x = y$ will not only unify the terms bound to x and y but will also further instantiate all the terms which share a free variable with the terms bound to x and y. A major simplification arises if one restricts to abstract substitutions which are downwards closed. We say that an abstract substitution β is downwards closed if for all (concrete) substitutions θ and τ,

$$\theta \in Cc(\beta) \Rightarrow \theta\tau \in Cc(\beta).$$

In words, if β abstracts some concrete substitution, it abstracts any instance of it. Therefore, if β abstracts the current substitution before an execution of $x = y$, it will still abstract the substitution resulting from this execution. To get a more precise result, it is sufficient to "specialize" β to express that x and y are now bound to equal terms. Abstract unification reduces to "abstract equality".

4.2 Constraint Domains for Logic Programming

A Domain for Groundness Analysis

Using the ideas of section 3, we can define an abstract domain for groundness analysis by choosing

$V_c = Term$, $V_a = \{g, ng\}$,
$Cc(g) = \{t \mid t$ is a ground term.$\}$,
$Cc(ng) = \{t \mid t$ is a variable or a term containing a variable.$\}$.

Then $CS(\mathbf{I}, V_a)$, where **I** is the set of program variables "of interest" (the variables in a clause), is a constraint domain for groundness (and non groundness) analysis.

However, with the definition of the concretization function given in paragraph 3.4, this domain is not downwards closed. For instance, the abstract substitution $x = $ ng abstracts the set of substitutions θ such that $x\theta$ is (surely) not ground. If τ is a substitution which grounds all variables in $x\theta$, $\theta\tau$ is not abstracted by $x = $ ng which is therefore not downwards closed.

In order to get a downwards closed abstract domain, we can slightly change the definition of $CS(\mathbf{I}, V_a)$ as follows.

First, we modify the definition of the concretization function in such a way that all abstract substitutions are downwards closed (we use β instead of s_a and θ instead of s_c as usual in the literature on abstract interpretation of logic programming):

$$Cc(\beta) = \{\theta \mid \forall\tau\exists s \in \beta : \forall x \in \mathbf{I} : x\theta\tau \in Cc(s(x))\}.$$

With this definition $x = $ ng has now an empty concretization since for any substitution θ, there exists a substitution τ such that $x\theta\tau$ is ground.
So, $x\theta\tau \notin Cc(\text{ng})$. However, the empty set of concrete substitutions is better abstracted by the constraint **false**. This shows that the domain now contains redundant elements. The "noisy" elements can be removed by keeping only the abstract substitution **false** and the β such that $s \in \beta$ where s is the assignment which assigns g to all variables.

The abstract domain I just defined is equivalent to the domain *Prop* proposed in [48], theoretically studied in [16] and experimentally evaluated in [17, 41]. The only difference is that literals of the form $x = $ g and $x = $ ng are respectively replaced by the propositional formulas x and $\neg x$. Moreover, the semantic condition to eliminate "noisy" elements can then be replaced by the syntactic condition that an element of *Prop* does not contain any subformula of the form $\neg x$. It can be built using only the connectives $\wedge$, $\vee$ and $\Leftrightarrow$.

Our modification of domain $CS(\mathbf{I}, V_a)$ is more general than *Prop* since it applies to any flat domain V_a. This generic domain was first described in [14]. See this reference for further details and, in particular, a generic definition of abstract unification. In [14], other applications than groundness analysis are considered (type analysis). From now on, I will note $DW(\mathbf{I}, V_a)$ the domain $CS(\mathbf{I}, V_a)$ endowed with the "downwards" concretization function and from which "noisy" elements have been removed.

Abstract Unification in $DW(\mathbf{I}, \{\text{g}, \text{ng}\})$ The abstract execution of the built-in $x = y$ simply consists in "adding the constraint" $x = y$ to the current abstract substitution β. Now, consider the built-in $x = f(y_1, \ldots, y_n)$ where all program variables are distinct. Its abstract execution amounts to adding the constraint

$$x = g \Leftrightarrow (y_1 = g \wedge \ldots \wedge y_n = g)$$

to the current abstract substitution. This expresses not only that x is now ground if and only if $y_1, \ldots, y_n$ are all ground but the much stronger property that they are linked in this way forever. Since the domain is downwards closed, each instantiation of the current "concrete" substitution still enjoy the same property.

In other words, the property expresses that the terms bound to x, on the one hand, and to the y_i's, on the other hand, contains exactly the same set of free variables. So the constraint expresses in fact a (strong) dependency between x and the y_i's.

Expressivity and Abstract Union The domains $DW(\mathbf{I}, \{g, ng\})$ and $CS(\mathbf{I}, \{g, ng\})$ have strictly incomparable expressivity powers. $DW(\mathbf{I}, \{g, ng\})$ may express variable dependencies while $CS(\mathbf{I}, \{g, ng\})$ may not. Conversely $CS(\mathbf{I}, \{g, ng\})$ may express non groundness while $DW(\mathbf{I}, \{g, ng\})$ may not.

As a consequence, the abstract union operation (least upper bound) which is the disjunction of constraints in both domains is exact in $CS(\mathbf{I}, \{g, ng\})$ (i.e. $Cc(\beta_1 \vee \beta_2) = Cc(\beta_1) \cup Cc(\beta_2)$), but approximate in $DW(\mathbf{I}, \{g, ng\})$ (i.e. $Cc(\beta_1) \cup Cc(\beta_2) \subseteq Cc(\beta_1 \vee \beta_2)$).

For instance, consider the abstract substitutions

$$\beta_1 \equiv ((x = g) \Rightarrow (y = g)) \quad \text{and} \quad \beta_2 \equiv (x = g).$$

The substitution $\theta = \{x/z, y/g(z, u)\}$ is not abstracted by β_1 nor by β_2 in $DW(\mathbf{I}, \{g, ng\})$, but it is abstracted by $\beta_1 \vee \beta_2$ which is equivalent to **true**. So the abstract union looses information in $DW(\mathbf{I}, \{g, ng\})$. No information is lost in $CS(\mathbf{I}, \{g, ng\})$ since θ is abstracted by β_1 there.

4.3 Accuracy of the Analyses

The following results hold.

1. Since the abstract union is not exact in $DW(\mathbf{I}, \{g, ng\})$ univariant analyses are not as accurate as polyvariant analyses in general. Consider for instance the small logic program

   $p(x, y) :- x = f(z, y).$
   $p(x, y) :- x = a.$

   A polyvariant analysis with input **true** will produce the two outputs β_1 and β_2, above, while a univariant analysis will produce **true**. Hence the polyvariant analysis tells us that $p(z, g(z, u))$ is not a possible output pattern while the univariant analysis tells us nothing.

   This theoretical result is however of low practical value because if we interpret the analysis in $CS(\mathbf{I}, \{g, ng\})$ then we know that the univariant analysis is equivalent to the polyvariant one (see paragraph 3.5). This means that the disjunction of the constraints collected at each program point by the polyvariant analysis is equivalent to the single constraint collected at this point by the univariant analysis. So if we "lump" the information at the end, it will be the same in both analysis. Moreover the (definite) groundness information is exactly the same in both analysis. So, in practice polyvariant analyses are useless.

2. It can be shown that top-down analyses based on $DW(\mathbf{I}, V_a)$ are condensing. This is basically because replacing unifications by their abstract counterparts yields a constraint programming language which enjoys the same "condensing" properties as logic programs and constraint logic programs. This is true independently of the chosen granularity.

3. Bottom-up analyses based on $CS(\mathbf{I}, V_a)$ and $DW(\mathbf{I}, V_a)$ are easy to define and to prove correct (see [12, 14]). Using $CS(\mathbf{I}, V_a)$, the abstract semantics can be based on an extension of the T_P semantics to a non ground fixpoint semantics which uses syntactical equality instead of unification (see [15]). This semantics approximates the set of all output patterns. Using $DW(\mathbf{I}, V_a)$ the abstract semantics should be based on the S-semantics [29]. So we get a description of the most general output patterns. But since the domain is now downwards closed the results are in fact totally equivalent. These analyses are straightforwardly implemented in the Toupie language [14, 61] by translating the logic program to be analyzed into a Toupie program where unifications are replaced by their abstract counterparts. It can be shown that such an analysis gives exactly the same result as the univariant top-down analysis executed with the most general pattern (true) as input. As the later analysis is condensing, the results of the bottom-up analyses can be used to optimally compute abstract substitutions at each program point by means of a post-processing algorithm [38, 42]. This method is more efficient and flexible than methods based on the magic set transformations used by [12].

4.4 Experimental Results

The domain *Prop* was first evaluated for groundness analysis using binary decision diagrams and the polyvariant top-down algorithm *GAIA* in [41]. The analysis was shown more accurate than any previous groundness analysis and competitive in efficiency with those analysis. Bottom-up analyses with $CS(\mathbf{I}, V_a)$ were implemented in Toupie for various domains V_a. These experiments are reported in [14, 15]. They show that bottom-up analyses are significantly faster due to the simpler machinery (no input patterns, no tabulation). Other systems using other implementations techniques are described in [5, 12, 45]. Their conclusions are consistent with the previous works.

5 Conclusion

In this paper, I have shown how finite domain symbolic constraints can be used to build certain kinds of program analyses (based on a finite set of basic properties). Constraint domains are in general more accurate than other, more classical, abstract domains. The analyses should use univariant algorithms since no additional accuracy can be gained with polyvariant ones. In some cases, (for instance, logic programming) bottom-up algorithms are still more efficient.

Acknowledgements

The ideas presented in this paper would not have emerged without the collaboration of many researchers. Pascal Van Hentenryck has been continuously working with me on the topic of abstract interpretation of logic programs since 1990 and helped me to keep on doing research. Marc-Michel Corsini, Kaninda Musumbu and Antoine Rauzy invited me in Bordeaux in January 1993 to work on Toupie. Many of the ideas presented here were elaborated at that time. Thanks also to all my students in Namur who implemented so many abstract interpreters (most of them at Brown, under Pascal's supervision). Finally thanks to Andreas Podelski who invited me at the spring school and gave me the (exhausting) opportunity of writing this paper.

References

1. S. Abramsky and C. Hankin, editors. *Abstract Interpretation of Declarative Languages*. Ellis Horwood Limited, West Sussex, England, 1987.

2. S. Abramsky and C. Hankin. An introduction to abstract interpretation. In S. Abramsky and C. Hankin, editors, *Abstract Interpretation of Declarative Languages*, chapter 1, pages 9–31. Ellis Horwood Limited, 1987.

3. O. Agesen. Constraint-Based Type Inference and Parametric Polymorphism. In [43], pages 78–101, 1994.

4. A. Aiken and T.K. Lakshman. Directional Type Checking of Logic Programs. In [43], pages 43–60, 1994.

5. T. Armstrong, K. Marriott, P. Schachte, and H. Søndergaard. Boolean Functions for Dependency Analysis: Algebraic Properties and Efficient Representation. In [43], pages 266–280, 1994.

6. F. Bourdoncle. Interprocedural abstract interpretation of block structured languages with nested procedures, aliasing and recursivity. In P. Deransart and J. Małuszyński, editors, *Proceedings of the Programming Language Implementation and Logic Programming (PLILP'90)*, volume 456 of *Lectures Notes in Computer Science*, pages 307–323, Linköping, Sweden, August 1990. Springer-Verlag.

7. F. Bourdoncle. *Sémantique des Langages Impératifs d'Ordre Supérieur et Interprétation Abstraite*. PhD thesis, Paris, France, November 1992. In French.

8. M. Bruynooghe. A practical framework for the abstract interpretation of logic programs. *Journal of Logic Programming*, 10(2):91–124, February 1991.

9. M. Bruynooghe and D. Boulanger. Abstract Interpretation for (Constraint) Logic Programming. In B. Mayoh, E. Toügu, and J. Penjam, editors, *Constraint Programming*, Advanced Science Series, Computers and System Sciences. Springer Verlag, 1994.

10. M. Bruynooghe, G. Janssens, A. Callebaut, and B. Demoen. Abstract interpretation: Towards the global optimization of Prolog programs. In *Proceedings of the 1987 Symposium on Logic Programming*, pages 192–204, San Francisco, California, August 1987. Computer Society Press of the IEEE.

11. R. Bryant. Symbolic Boolean Manipulation with Ordered Binary Decision Diagrams. *ACM Computing Surveys*, 1992.

12. M. Codish and B. DeMoen. Analysing Logic Programs using "Prop"-ositional Logic Programs and a Magic Wand. In D. Miller, editor, *Proceedings of (ILPS'93)*, Vancouver, Canada, October 1993. MIT Press.

13. P. Codognet and G. Filé. Computations, abstractions and constraints in logic programs. In *Proceedings of the fourth International Conference on Programming languages (ICCL'92)*, Oakland, U.S.A., April 1992.

14. M.-M. Corsini, K. Musumbu, A. Rauzy, and B. Le Charlier. Efficient Bottom-up Abstract Interpretation of Logic Programs by means of Constraint Solving over Symbolic Finite Domains. In Penjam J. and M. Bruynooghe, editors, *Proceedings of the Fifth International Workshop on Programming Language Implementation and Logic Programming (PLILP'93)*, volume 714 of *Lecture Notes in Computer Science*, Tallin, August 1993. Springer-Verlag.

15. M.-M. Corsini, K. Musumbu, A. Rauzy, and B. Le Charlier. Efficient Bottom-up Abstract Interpretation of Logic Programs by means of Constraint Solving over Symbolic Finite Domains. Technical report, Institute of Computer Science, University of Namur, Belgium, (also LaBri, Bordeaux), March 1993.

16. A. Cortesi, G. Filè, and W. Winsborough. Prop revisited: Propositional formula as abstract domain for groundness analysis. In *Proceedings of the Sixth Annual IEEE Symposium on Logic in Computer Science (LICS'91)*, 1991.

17. A. Cortesi, B. Le Charlier, and P. Van Hentenryck. Groundness Analysis for Prolog: Implementation and Evaluation of the Domain *prop*. *Journal of Logic Programming*. to appear.

18. A. Cortesi, B. Le Charlier, and P. Van Hentenryck. Type analysis of prolog using type graphs. In *Proceedings of ACM SIGPLAN–SIGACT Symposium on Programming Language Design and Implementation (PLDI'94)*, Orlando, Florida, June 1994. (An extended version will appear in the Journal of Logic Programming.).

19. P. Cousot and R. Cousot. Static determination of dynamic properties of programs. In *Proceedings of the Second International Symposium on Programmings*, pages 106–130, Paris, April 1976. Dunod.

20. P. Cousot and R. Cousot. Abstract interpretation: A unified lattice model for static analysis of programs by construction or approximation of fixpoints. In *Conference Record of Fourth ACM Symposium on Programming Languages (POPL'77)*, pages 238–252, Los Angeles, California, January 1977.

21. P. Cousot and R. Cousot. Abstract interpretation and application to logic programs. *Journal of Logic Programming*, 13(2–3), 1992.

22. P. Cousot and R. Cousot. Comparison of the Galois connection and widening/narrowing approaches to abstract interpretation (invited paper). In M. Bruynooghe and M. Wirsing, editors, *Proceedings of the Fourth International Workshop on Programming Language Implementation and Logic Programming (PLILP'92)*, Lecture Notes in Computer Science, Leuven, August 1992. Springer-Verlag.

23. P. De Boeck and B. Le Charlier. Static type analysis of Prolog procedures for ensuring correctness. In *Proceedings of Programming Language Implementation and Logic Programming (PLILP'90)*, volume 456 of *Lecture Notes in Computer Science*, pages 222–237, Linköping, Sweden, August 1990. Springer-Velag.

24. P. De Boeck and B. Le Charlier. Mechanical Transformation of Logic Definitions augmented with Type Information into Prolog Procedures: Some Experiments. In *Proceedings of (LOPSTR'93)*. Springer Verlag, July 1993.

25. Y. Deville. *Logic Programming: Systematic Program Development*. MIT Press, 1990.

26. V. Dumortier. *Freeness and Related Analyses of Constraint Logic Programs using Abstract Interpretation*. PhD thesis, Department of Computer Science, Katholieke Universiteit Leuven, Belgium, November 1994.

27. V. Englebert, B. Le Charlier, D. Roland, and P. Van Hentenryck. Generic abstract interpretation algorithms for prolog: Two optimization techniques and their experimental evaluation. *Software Practice and Experience*, 23(4):419–459, April 1993.

28. Cousot et all (Eds.). *Static Analysis: Proceedings of the Third International Workshop on Static Analysis*. Number 724 in Lecture Notes in Computer Science. Springer-Verlag, September 1993.

29. M. Falaschi, G. Levi, M. Martelli, and C. Palamidessi. Declarative Modeling of the Operational Behaviour of Logic Languages. *Theoretical Computer Science*, 69(3):289–318, 1989.

30. Thomas W. Getzinger. The Costs and Benefits of Abstract Interpretation-driven Prolog Optimization. In [43], pages 1–25, 1994.

31. N. Halbwachs. About Synchronous Programming and Abstract Interpretation. In [43], pages 179–192, 1994.

32. N. Halbwachs. Verification of Linear Hybrid Systems by Means of Convex Approximations. In [43], pages 223–237, 1994.

33. G. Janssens and M. Bruynooghe. Deriving descriptions of possible values of program variables by means of abstract interpretation. *Journal of Logic Programming*, 13(4), 1992.

34. R.B. Kieburtz and M. Napierala. Abstract semantics. In S. Abramsky and C. Hankin, editors, *Abstract Interpretation of Declarative Languages*, chapter 7, pages 143–180. Ellis Horwood Limited, 1987.

35. B. Le Charlier, O. Degimbe, L. Michel, and P. Van Hentenryck. Optimization Techniques for General Purpose Fixpoint Algorithms: Practical Efficiency for the Abstract Interpretation of Prolog. In Cousot P. and all, editors, *Proc of the Third International Workshop on Static Analysis (WSA'93)*, number 724 in Lecture Notes in Computer Science, Padova, September 1993. Springer-Verlag.

36. B. Le Charlier, K. Musumbu, and P. Van Hentenryck. A generic abstract interpretation algorithm and its complexity analysis. In K. Furukawa, editor, *Proceedings of the Eighth International Conference on Logic Programming (ICLP'91)*, Paris, France, June 1991. MIT Press.

37. B. Le Charlier, S. Rossi, and P. Van Hentenryck. An Abstract Interpretation Framework Which Accurately Handles Prolog Search-Rule and the Cut. In M. Bruynooghe, editor, *Proceedings of the International Logic Programming Symposium (ILPS'94)*, Ithaca NY, USA, November 1994. MIT Press.

38. B. Le Charlier and P. Van Hentenryck. On the Design of Generic Abstract Interpretation Frameworks. In M. Billaud and all, editors, *Proceedings of the Workshop on Static Analysis (WSA'92)*, Bordeaux, France, September 1992. Bigre 81-82.

39. B. Le Charlier and P. Van Hentenryck. Reexecution in abstract interpretation of prolog. In K. Apt, editor, *Proceedings of the Join International Conference and Symposium on Logic Programming (JICSLP'92)*, Washington, U.S.A., November 1992. MIT Press.

40. B. Le Charlier and P. Van Hentenryck. A general top-down fixpoint algorithm (revised version). Technical Report 93-22, Institute of Computer Science, University of Namur, Belgium, (also Brown University), June 1993.

41. B. Le Charlier and P. Van Hentenryck. Groundness Analysis for Prolog: Implementation and Evaluation of the Domain *prop* (extended abstract). In *Proc. of*

the *1993 ACM Symposium on Partial Evaluation and Semantics-Based Program Manipulation* (PEPM'93), June 1993. (An extended version will appear in the Journal of Logic Programming.).

42. B. Le Charlier and P. Van Hentenryck. Experimental Evaluation of a Generic Abstract Interpretation Algorithm for Prolog. *ACM Transactions on Programming Languages and Systems (TOPLAS)*, January 1994.

43. B. Le Charlier (Ed.). *Static Analysis: Proceedings of the First International Static Analysis Symposium.* Number 864 in Lecture Notes in Computer Science. Springer-Verlag, September 1994.

44. C. Lecoutre. *Interprétation Abstraite en Programmation Logique avec Contraintes.* PhD thesis, Université de Lille, Lille, France, February 1994. In French.

45. P. Lefebvre, B. Le Charlier, and E. Villemonte de la Clergerie. Yet another efficient implementation of the domain Prop using a "Logical Push-Down Automaton"-based Logic Program Interpreter and a Constraint Solver Over Finite Domains. In *Proceedings of (Benelog'93)*, Antwerpen, September 1993.

46. J.W. Lloyd. *Foundations of Logic Programming.* Springer Series: Symbolic Computation–Artificial Intelligence. Springer-Verlag, second, extended edition, 1987.

47. K. Marriott and H. Søndergaard. Bottom-up abstract interpretation of logic programs. In R.A. Kowalski and K.A. Bowen, editors, *Proceeding of Fifth International Conference on Logic Programming (ICLP'88)*, pages 733–748, Seattle, Washington, August 1988. MIT Press.

48. K. Marriott and H. Søndergaard. Notes for a tutorial on abstract interpretation of logic programs. In *North American Conference on Logic Programming (NACLP'89)*, Cleveland, Ohio, 1989.

49. K. Marriott and H. Søndergaard. Precise and Efficient Groundness Analysis for Logic Programs. Technical Report 93/7, University of Melbourne, Australia, 1993.

50. L. Mauborgne. Abstract Interpretation using TDGs. In [43], pages 363–379, 1994.

51. C.S. Mellish. Abstract Interpretation of Prolog Programs. In S. Abramsky and C. Hankin, editors, *Abstract Interpretation of Declarative Languages*, chapter 8, pages 181–198. Ellis Horwood Limited, 1987.

52. N. Mercouroff. *Analyse Sémantique des Communications entre Processus de Programmes Parallèles.* PhD thesis, Ecole polytechnique, Paris, France, September 1990. In French.

53. B. Monsuez. Polymorphic Types and Widening Operators. In Cousot P. and all, editors, *Proc of the Third International Workshop on Static Analysis (WSA'93)*, number 724 in Lecture Notes in Computer Science, pages 267–281, Padova, September 1993. Springer-Verlag.

54. K. Musumbu. *Interprétation Abstraite de Programmes Prolog.* PhD thesis, Institute of Computer Science, University of Namur, Belgium, September 1990. In French.

55. K. Muthukumar and M. Hermenegildo. Compile-Time Derivation of Variable Dependency Using Abstract Interpretation. *Journal of Logic Programming*, 13(2-3):315–347, August 1992.

56. L. Naish. Specification = program + types. In K. Nori, editor, *Foundations of Software Technology and Theoretical Computer Science*, number 287 in LNCS. Springer-Verlag, 1987.

57. F. Nielson. Towards a denotational theory of abstract interpretation. In S. Abramsky and C. Hankin, editors, *Abstract Interpretation of Declarative Languages*, chapter 10, pages 219–245. Ellis Horwood Limited, 1987.

58. U. Nilsson. Systematic semantic approximations of logic programs. In P. Deransart and J. Małuszyński, editors, *Proceedings of the International Workshop on Programming Language Implementation and Logic Programming (PLILP'90)*, volume 456 of *Lecture Notes in Computer Science*, pages 293–306, Linköping, Sweden, August 1990. Springer-Verlag.

59. R.A. O'Keefe. Finite fixed-point problems. In J-L. Lassez, editor, *Proceedings of the Fourth International Conference on Logic Programming (ICLP'87)*, pages 729–743, Melbourne, Australia, May 1987. MIT Press.

60. F. Pfenning. *Types in Logic Programming*. Logic Programming Series. Addison Wesley, 1992.

61. A. Rauzy. Toupie : a constraint language for model checking. In *this volume*.

62. K. L. Solberg, H. R. Nielson, and F. Nielson. Strictness and Totality Analysis. In [43], pages 408–423, 1994.

63. T. Swift and D. S. Warren. An Abstract Machine for SLG Resolution : Definite Programs. In M. Bruynooghe, editor, *Proceedings of the International Logic Programming Symposium (ILPS'94)*, Ithaca NY, USA, November 1994. MIT Press.

64. P. Van Hentenryck, O. Degimbe, B. Le Charlier, and L. Michel. The impact of Granularity in Abstract Interpretation of Prolog. In Cousot P. and all, editors, *Proc of the Third International Workshop on Static Analysis (WSA'93)*, number 724 in Lecture Notes in Computer Science, Padova, September 1993. Springer-Verlag.

65. P. Van Roy. 1983–1993 : The Wonder Years of Sequential Prolog Implementation. *Journal of Logic Programming, Tenth Anniversary Issue*, 1994. to appear.

66. B. Vergauwen. Efficient FixPoint Computation. In [43], pages 314–328, 1994.

67. K. Verschaetse. *Termination Analysis of Logic Programs*. PhD thesis, Department of Computer Science, Katholieke Universiteit Leuven, Belgium, 1993.

68. E. Villemonte de la Clergerie. *Automates à Piles et Programmation Dynamique : DyALog, Application à la Programmation en Logique*. PhD thesis, Université Paris VII, Paris, France, June 1993. In French.

69. Kwangkeun Yi. Compile-time Detection of Uncaught Exceptions in Standard ML Programs. In [43], pages 238–254, 1994.

Concurrency
and
Concurrent Constraint Programming

Ugo Montanari and Francesca Rossi

Università di Pisa, Dipartimento di Informatica
Corso Italia 40, 56125 Pisa, Italy
E-mail: {ugo,rossi}@di.unipi.it

Abstract. The intent of this paper is to provide the basic ideas and the possible alternatives underlying the task of giving a semantics to a concurrent system/language, and to describe a particular approach which makes some specific choices in order to give a semantics to the class of CC languages. In particular, we will discuss how to handle the issues of concurrency and nondeterminism, and we will examine in detail the formalism of Petri nets, which, suitably extended, we will then use for CC languages. In our semantics for CC programs, the meaning of a program is in fact a net where the concurrency present in all computations, as well as the nondeterminism, can be naturally seen. We will also point out several extension of the basic semantics, that can be used for more complex classes of CC languages, like those with atomic tells, or with two kinds of nondeterminism.

1 Introduction

While an input-output semantics can be descriptive enough when used to model the computations of a sequential and deterministic language, this is not so any more when one is interested in languages which allow for both concurrency and nondeterminism. In fact, in such a case, a more detailed description of the interaction among the computation steps, which is able to recognize and discern among situations of *causal dependency*, *concurrency*, or *mutual exclusion*, is in general needed. This kind of information is in fact necessary for many important tasks (when applied to concurrent programs), like compile-time program optimization, program composition, debugging, and others.

In the literature there are many approaches to model concurrent languages. However, they all have to make a choice about at least two issues: how to model *concurrency*, and how to model *nondeterminism*. Both choices have basically two alternatives. The former one can be handled by following the *true-concurrency* approach, where concurrency is directly expressible, or the *interleaving* one, where instead it is reduced to nondeterminism. The latter one can instead be resolved by using either a *set-based structure*, which is not able to show the choice points, or a *branching structure* (like a tree) which instead is able to do that. Then there is also the issue of abstracting from some details and thus define some equivalence among programs which have the same abstract behaviour.

For our task, that of providing CC programs with a semantics that expresses the concurrency and nondeterminism present in them, we chose to use (an extension of) Petri nets, which is one of the best known true-concurrency models, and to adopt a branching structure. In this way, both the maximum level of available concurrency and the choice points of all the computations are directly visible in the structure.

A concurrent constraint (CC) program [Sar93, SR90, SRP91] consists of a set of agents interacting through a shared store, which is a set of constraints on some variables. The framework is parametric w.r.t. the kind of constraints handled. The concurrent agents do not communicate with each other, but only with the shared store, by either checking if it entails a given constraint (*ask* operation) or adding a new constraint to it (*tell* operation). Therefore computations proceed by monotonically accumulating information (that is, constraints) into the store.

The semantics of CC programs is usually given via the SOS-style operational semantics [SR90, SRP91, BP91], and thus following the interleaving approach. As noted above, our semantics follow instead the true-concurrency approach. This, together with a suitable non-monolithic model of the shared store and of its communication with the agents, allows one to express uniformly the behavior of the store and that of the agents, and, as a consequence, to derive a structure where it is possible and easy to see the maximal level of both concurrency and nondeterminism in a given program. Thus, for many aspects, we believe that our semantics can be more useful than an interleaving one, for example whenever one is interested in exploiting semantic information for compile-time optimizations which require knowledge about any one of these two concepts. In fact, an interleaving semantics is not able to express such knowledge correctly, mainly due to the fact that concurrency is not directly expressible but is instead reduced to nondeterminism. More precisely, the semantics based on input-output relations or sequences of agent operations that have been developed for CC programs [SR90, SRP91, BP91] are usually not able to provide enough knowledge about the amount of parallelism available in the program and the causality between agent interactions, and therefore identify too many programs. For example, they would identify two programs which perform the same operations, even though one exhibits parallelism and the other one is completely sequential. We believe instead that such programs should not be identified in any semantics which aims at being useful for the understanding, as well as the compile- and run-time optimization, of a given CC program.

Our semantics is based on an operational description of the behaviour of CC programs which is based on context-dependent rewrite rules, i.e. rules which have a left hand side, a right hand side, and a context. Each rule is applicable if both its left hand side and its context are present in the current state of the computation. A rule application removes the left hand side (but not the context) and adds the right hand side. In particular, the context is crucial in faithfully representing ask constraints, which are checked for presence but not affected by the computation. The evolution of each of the agents in a CC program, as well as the declarations of the program and its underlying constraint system, can all be expressed by sets of such rules. In this way each computation step (i.e. the application of one of such rules), represents either the evolution of an agent, or the expansion of a declaration, or the entailment of some new constraint token.

Such operational semantics is fundamentally different ¿from those presented elsewhere. First, there are no structural axioms that a computation state has to satisfy, apart from the usual axioms for multisets. Thus a state for us is a flat structure. Second, no inference rules are used in defining the possible state-to-state transitions, since the rewrite rules describe local changes that can be applied to any state. Third, agent evolutions and constraint generations are described uniformly and at the same level. This is crucial if one is interested in exploiting the maximal possible parallelism available at both the program level and the constraint system level. In fact, had we considered the constraint system as a black box, as is usually done in the other approaches, we would have lost parallelism both within the constraint system (because a monolithic description allows only one evolution at a time) and among the agents (since two agents which need different parts of the constraint store would have been, possibly unnecessarily, sequentialized).

The semantic structure is then built from the rules by starting from the initial agent and repeatedly applying a single inference rule. The result is a *contextual net* [MR], which is just an acyclic Petri net [Rei85] where the presence of context conditions, besides pre- and post-conditions, is allowed. Furthermore, such net is labelled, so that for each element we know the agent or constraint it corresponds to. This contextual net is able to represent all the computations of a given CC program (as defined by its operational semantics), and for each of such computations it provides a partial order expressing the dependency pattern among the events of the computation. More precisely, given such contextual net, it is possible to derive three relations among its objects (representing either agents or constraints or computation steps), describing respectively the *causal dependency*, the *mutual exclusion*, and the *concurrency* among them. By using contextual nets to give a semantics to CC programs, these relations are then interpreted as describing, respectively, the necessary sequentialization, the possible simultaneity, and the nondeterministic choices among steps of CC computations. As a result, all such computations are represented in a unique structure, where it is possible to see the maximal degree of both concurrency (via the concurrency relation) and nondeterminism (via the mutual exclusion relation) available both at the program level and at the underlying constraint system.

Note however that this structure has to be interepreted just as a semantic domain. That is, the net we obtain cannot directly be used to prove properties of CC programs. To do that, we need to apply to the net some proof method, like for example abstract interpretation [CC92].

In the following, we will first discuss the basic ideas and alternatives in giving a semantics to a concurrent language (Section 2), with particular enphasis to Petri nets. Then, we formally introduce the CC programming framework (Section 3) and we define its operational semantics (Section 4). In Section 5 we introduce contextual nets, and in Section 6 we present the semantics for CC based on such nets. Then, in Section 7 we informally describe several possible extensions of the semantics for the basic CC paradigm, and in Section 8 we give some hints at possible future directions for this line of research.

Most of the material contained in this paper appeared already elsewhere [MR93, Ros93, MR94, MRS94, BdlBH⁺94b, BdlBH⁺94a, RM94]. Indeed, here the aim is not to present a new result, but instead to present in a comprehensive and self-contained way all the main ideas and results that have appeared in the above cited papers, and to make explicit both the assumptions and the motivations of this line of work.

2 Semantics for Concurrent Languages

Here we review some of the basic ideas and models in the theory of concurrency that are relevant when giving a semantics to a concurrent system (or language). Among all the models, we consider in more detail Petri nets [Pet80, Rei85], since this is the model we choose to use for providing CC programs with a concurrent semantics.

2.1 Concurrency and Nondeterminism

In the literature there are many formalisms which have been proposed to model the behaviour of a concurrent system. But all of them can be said to fall within one of two approaches: the *interleaving* approach (see for example [Mil89, Hoa85, BK84, Hen88]) and the *true-concurrency* (or partial-order) approach (see [Rei85, NPW81, Pra86, DNM87, DNM90]).

Interleaving models describe concurrency among events by saying that they can occur in any order. Thus, a global state is assumed, and a state change can only consist of a single event happening at a certain time. Therefore a total order among concurrent events is forced. The main advantage of such models is its simplicity and mathematical elegance. However, they do not express concurrency very faithfully, since they reduce it to *nondeterminism*. In other words, interleaving models describe a concurrent system as a single processor system performing multitasking.

True-concurrency models, instead, describe concurrent computations by means of partial orders, and concurrency is represented by the absence of an ordering. They do not assume any global state, and thus the behaviour of a system is described in terms of the *causal dependencies* among events happening in (possibly) different parts of a *distributed state*.

Another way of describing the difference between an interlaving and a true-concurrency approach relies on the notion of an *observer* of the system. In the former approach, the observers are sequential, and thus one can only see a sequence of events. This means that the concurrent happening of two events can only be seen as their sequential happening in (possibly) opposite orders in two different computations. In the latter approach, instead, concurrency is considered as a primitive, and thus the observer is able to see the simultanous happening of two events.

True-concurrency models are more suited to handle and reason about some properties which explicitely refer to concurrency and causality, like deadlock, fairness, maximum amount of parallelism, and so on, while interleaving models present more difficulties in treating these same properties. However, due to their simpler mathematical techniques, interleaving models can also be very useful and easy to use, especially when the interest falls on other kinds of properties.

If one wants to describe all possible computations of a given concurrent system, then another issue, orthogonal to that of representing concurrency, arise: how to represent non-determinism. Also in this respect, there are basically two ways to give the semantics of a non-deterministic system: either we choose a *set-based* structure or a *branching* structure. The former approach consists of collecting all possible computations in a set, while the latter one collects the computations in a tree-like structure. The advantage of the latter approach is that it shows the points where nondeterministic choices have been taken during the computations. Examples of such an approach are *synchronization trees* [Mil80] and *causal trees* [DD89].

A third issue, which has to be resolved after a choice has been made about the first two, is that of abstracting from the chosen semantics structure some irrelevant detail. In other words, the idea is to define what one wants to observe of a system behaviour or program computation, and then to define as equivalent all computations which, if observed as defined, are exactly the same.

2.2 Petri nets

Petri nets [Pet80, Rei85] are the first and most representative model of the true-concurrency approach. In a Petri net, computation states are not monolithic, but they are defined in terms of more elementary items called *places*. Thus the states have a natural distributed shape. A place can be seen as a resource, and the presence of *token(s)* in a place can be interpreted as the avaliability of such resource. An event (or transition) is then an activity which consumes some resources and produces other resources. Some transitions can happen simultaneously if the resources they need are all available and their happening does not create any conflict among them (because of the multiple need of shared resources).

Petri nets, as most true-concurrency models, represent concurrency in terms of the *causal dependencies* between sets of places. Such dependency relation can be either cyclic or not. Petri nets with a (possibly) cyclic dependency relation are used to model systems (resp., programs), while nets with an acyclic dependency relation are used to model the system's behaviour (resp., the program's computations). In this latter case, concurrency is immediately derivable ¿from the causal dependency relation of the net: two transitions (or places) are concurrent whenever they are not related by the causal dependency relation.

In a Petri net it is very natural to describe in an explicit way also many other behaviours, besides concurrency, which are typical of concurrent systems, like *mutual exclusion, sequential composition,* and *nondeterminism.*

Once a distributed system is described through a Petri net, there are many ways to give a semantics to such net, depending on whether we choose a interleaving or true-concurrency approach, and whether we want to model nondeterminism via set-based or a braching structure (see previous section). In fact, although Petri nets are intrinsically true-concurrent, one can also forget about their expressivity in terms of concurrency and decide to describe their computations is an interleaving (thus sequential) way. Thus, by combining in all possible ways the alternatives to treat the two issues of concurrency and nondeterminism, one may choose among (at least) the following models:

- The set of all sequences of computation steps, where each step consist of the happening of just one event; these are called *firing sequences*, and are interleaving and set-based.
- The tree of all firing sequences, where the branching points denote the computation states where different alternatives were taken; this model is interleaving and branching.
- The set of all (acyclic and deterministic) unfoldings of the net; these are called *deterministic processes*, and are true-concurrent and set-based.
- One *non-deterministic process* (an acyclic unfolding with possibly nondeterminism), which is true-concurrent and branching.

The last model has also an alternative characterization via the so-called *event structures* [NPW81, Win86], which are just sets of events plus two relations among them, expressing *causality* (that is, when one event causes another one) and *conflict* (that is, when the happening of certain events excludes the happening of others due to the need of some shared resource).

Although Petri nets are very expressive, there are some circumstances that they fail to describe faithfully. In fact, in our opinion, they have two major drawbacks. First, the state is just a *set* (or a multiset) of tokens, while in general one may have to describe more complex state structures, like the very common situation where there are processes sharing some variables. For such a situations, a structure like a *graph* would be much more appropriate: processes are arcs and variables are nodes. Second, the only actions that a transition can take are the deletion and the production of some resource. In general, instead, one may also want to have the possibility of testing for the presence of some resource, without neither destroying it nor generating it. Thus a notion similar to a *context* would be desirable in many cases, like those where one wants to describe the whole variety of read/write operations.

For these reasons, one may think that *graph grammars*, which generalize Petri nets with both these features, are more desirable. This is true in general; however, there are cases where both Petri nets and something in between nets and grammars could be useful as well. For this reason, an extension of nets which provides the notion of context, called *contextual nets* [MR], has been defined and proven to be suitable for many situations.

For the semantics of contextual nets, the same considerations made previously about Petri nets still hold. Thus one may choose among the four possibilities of a true-concurrency/interleaving set-based/branching approach.

2.3 Our choices

In this paper, in order to provide a semantics to the programs written in the CC programming paradigm, we have chosen to use contextual nets, and we have decided to follow the true-concurrency model with a branching structure. Therefore, the computations of a CC program will be described by a non-deterministic contextual process, where it is possible to see both the concurrency present in all the computations and also the choice points.

Note however, that the program itself will not be represented by a net. That is, we use (acyclic) contextual nets to model the program's behaviour, not the program itself.

The reason why we chose a true-concurrency model lies in the observation that for concurrent languages an interleaving semantics is not expressive enough. In fact, while for sequential and deterministic systems and input/output semantics, or a semantics describing all possible sequences of computation steps, is often satisfactory, for concurrent languages and/or systems this is not sufficient, since in general one desires a more detailed description of the relationship among the computation steps, possibly including information about causality, concurrency, and the choice points.

No abstraction is here provided for our semantics. We believe that this is a subsequent issue, that can be tackled in several ways and defining very different observable equivalence according to what one is interested in observing of the computations of a CC program.

The operational semantics for CC programs is instead here modelled by following the interleaving set-based approach. In fact, for us the operational semantics of a CC program is a set of sequences of rule applications. This is a standard way of defining an operational semantics. However, other choices could be possible. For example, we could also choose to consider partial orders of sequences (thus an interleaving branching approach); this would allow us to make stronger statements about the relationship between the contextual net semantics and the operational semantics.

3 Concurrent Constraint Programming

In the CC paradigm, the underlying constraint system can be described [SRP91] as a *partial information system* (derived from the *information system* introduced in [Sco82]) of the form $\langle D, \vdash \rangle$ where D is a set of *tokens* (or primitive constraints) and $\vdash \subseteq \wp(D) \times D$ is the entailment relation which states which tokens are entailed by which sets of other tokens. The relation $\vdash$ has to satisfy the following axioms:

$u \vdash x$ if $x \in u$ (reflexivity), and
$u \vdash x$ if $v \vdash x$ and, for all $y \in v$, $u \vdash y$ (transitivity).

Note that there is no notion of consistency in a partial information system. This means that inconsistency has to be modelled through entailment. More precisely, the convention is that D contains a *false* element, so that an inconsistent set of tokens is that one which entails *false*.

Given D, $| D |$ is the set of all subsets of D closed under entailment. Then, a constraint in a constraint system $\langle D, \vdash \rangle$ is simply an element of $| D |$, that is, a set of tokens, closed under entailment. In the rest of the paper we will consider a constraint as simply a set of tokens.

Consider the class of programs P, the class of sequences of procedure declarations F, and the class of agents A. Let c range over constraints, and $\mathbf{x}$ denote a tuple of variables. The following grammar describes the CC language we consider:

$$P ::= F.A$$
$$F ::= p(\mathbf{x}) :: A \mid F.F$$
$$A ::= success \mid failure \mid tell(c) \rightarrow A \mid \sum_{i=1,\ldots,n} ask(c_i) \rightarrow A_i \mid A \parallel A \mid \exists \mathbf{x}.A \mid p(\mathbf{x})$$

Each procedure is defined once, thus nondeterminism is expressed via the $+$ combinator only (which is here denoted by $\sum$). We also assume that, in $p(\mathbf{x}) :: A$, $vars(A) \subseteq \mathbf{x}$, where $vars(A)$ is the set of all variables occurring free in agent A. In a program $P = F.A$, A is called initial agent, to be executed in the context of the set of declarations F.

Agent "$\sum_{i=1,\ldots,n} ask(c_i) \rightarrow A_i$" behaves as a set of guarded agents A_i, where the success of the guard $ask(c_i)$ coincides with the entailment of the constraint c_i by the current store. If instead c_i is inconsistent with the current store, then the guard fails. Lastly, if c_i is not entailed but it is consistent with the current store, then the guarded agent gets suspended. No particular order of selection of the guarded agents is assumed, and only one of the choices is taken. Assuming an *eventual* interpretation of the tell operation, agent "tell(c) $\rightarrow$ A" adds constraint c to the current store and then behaves like A; if the resulting store is inconsistent this will result in an uncontrolled behaviour of the system, since from now on all ask operations will succeed.

Given a program P, in the following we will refer to $Ag(P)$ as the set of all agents (and subagents) occurring in P, i.e. all the elements of type A occurring in a derivation of P according to the above grammar.

4 The Operational Semantics

Each state of a CC computation consists of a multiset of (active) agents and of (already generated) tokens. The reason why we consider a multiset instead of a set is that the same agent (and/or also the same token) may occur in a state with multiplicity higher than one (just think of the computations of $A \parallel A$), and we don't want to confuse between the several occurrences. Both agents and tokens will have associated the variables they involve.

Each computation step models either the evolution of a single agent, or the entailment of a new token through the $\vdash$ relation. Such a change in the state of the computation is performed via the application of a rewrite rule. There are as many rewrite rules as the number of agents and declarations in a program (which is finite), plus the number of pairs of the entailment relation (which can be infinite).

Definition 1 (computation state). Given a program $P = F.A$ with a constraint system $\langle D, \vdash \rangle$, a state is a multiset of elements of $Ag(P) \cup D$. $\square$

Definition 2 (rewrite rules). Have the form $r : L(r)(\mathbf{x}) \overset{c(r)(\mathbf{x})}{\rightsquigarrow} R(r)(\mathbf{xy})$ where $L(r)$ is an agent, $c(r)$ is a constraint, and $R(r)$ is a state. Also, $\mathbf{x}$ is the tuple of variables appearing in both $L(r) \cup c(r)$ and in $R(r)$, while $\mathbf{y}$ is the tuple of variables appearing free only in $R(r)$. $\square$

The intuitive meaning of a rule is that $L(r)^1$, which is called the left hand side of the rule, is rewritten into (or replaced by) $R(r)$, i.e. the right hand side, if $c(r)$ is present in the current state. $R(r)$ could contain some variables not appearing (free) in $L(r)$ nor in $c(r)$ (i.e. the tuple $\mathbf{y}$). As computations will be defined over *constants*, then the application of r would have to rename such variables $\mathbf{y}$ to constants which are different from all the others already in use. The items in $c(r)$ have to be interpreted as a context, since it is necessary for the application of the rule but it is not affected by such application. In the CC framework, such context is used to represent asked constraints.

The possibility of having a context-dependent formalism is very significant if we are interested in the causal dependencies among the objects involved in a computation. In fact, consider for example two rule applications with overlapping contexts but with disjoint left hand sides. Then, in a context-dependent formalism they can be applied independently. On the other hand, a context-independent formalism would simulate a context object by first cancelling it and then generating it again, and thus would not be able to express the simultaneous execution of the same rules, but only their sequential execution in any order. The CC framework is obviously context-dependent, since a constraint to be asked to the store is naturally interpreted as an object which is needed for the computation to evolve but which is not affected by such evolution. Therefore, the modelling of CC computations via a context-dependent formalism provides a more faithful description of this framework.

Definition 3 (from programs to rules). The rules corresponding to agents, declarations, and entailment pairs are given as follows:

$$(tell(c) \to A) \rightsquigarrow c, A$$
$$(\sum_{i=1,\ldots,n} ask(c_i) \to A_i) \overset{c_i}{\rightsquigarrow} A_i \quad \forall i = 1, \ldots, n$$
$$A_1 \parallel A_2 \rightsquigarrow A_1, A_2$$
$$p(\mathbf{x}) \rightsquigarrow A \text{ for all } p(\mathbf{x}) :: A$$
$$\exists \mathbf{x}.A \rightsquigarrow A$$

---

[1] Note that in a slight abuse of notation we consider $L(r)$ as a set, which will be either a singleton or the empty set.

$\overset{S}{\leadsto} t$ for all $S \vdash t$

Given a CC program $P = F.A$ and its underlying constraint system $\langle D, \vdash \rangle$, we will call $RR(P)$ the set of rewrite rules associated to P, which consists of the rules corresponding to all agents in $Ag(P)$, plus the rules representing the declarations in F, plus those rules representing the pairs of the entailment relation. $\square$

A rule r can be applied to a state S_1 if both the left hand side of r and its context can be found (via a suitable substitution) in S_1. The application of r removes its left and adds its right hand side to S_1.

Definition 4 (computation steps). Let a computation state $S_1(\mathbf{a})$ and a rule $r : L(r)(\mathbf{x}) \overset{c(r)(\mathbf{x})}{\leadsto} R(r)(\mathbf{xy})$, such that $(L(r) \cup c(r))[\mathbf{a/x}] \subseteq S_1(\mathbf{a})$. The application of r to S_1 is a computation step which yields a new computation state $S_2 = (S_1 \setminus L(r)[\mathbf{a/x}]) \cup R(r)[\mathbf{a/x}][\mathbf{b/y}]$, where the constants in $\mathbf{b}$ are fresh, i.e. they do not appear in S_1. We will write $S_1 \overset{r[\mathbf{a/x}][\mathbf{b/y}]}{\Longrightarrow} S_2$. $\square$

Thus, the correspondence beetween rules and agents or constraint entailments is the following. If the agent $(tell(c) \to A)$ is found in the current state, then such agent can be replaced by the agent A together with the constraint c. In other words, $(tell(c) \to A)$ is cancelled by the current state, while both c and A are added. Agent $A_1 \parallel A_2$ is instead replaced by the multiset containing the two agents A_1 and A_2. Note that if $A_1 = A_2 = A$ we would still have two distinct elements, since a state is a multiset of elements. Therefore, in that case we would denote by $2A$ the new computation state. Agent $\exists \mathbf{x}.A$ is replaced by agent A. This is the only rule where the right hand side has more variables than the left hand side. Agent $\sum_{i=1,\ldots,n} ask(c_i) \to A_i$ gives rise to as many rewrite rules as the number of possible nondeterministic choices. In each of such branches, say branch j, the whole agent is replaced by agent A_j only if c_j is present already in the store. Note that only this rule, which corresponds to an ask agent, needs a context. In fact, as noted before, asked constraints in CC programming are directly related to context objects in our context-dependent formalism. If instead c_j is inconsistent with the current store (thius is modelled by the fact that $\neg c_j$ is in the store), then the whole alternative j disappears. The other rules are needed for describing the environment in which agents evolve. Such environment is made up of the declarations in the given program and of the underlying constraint system. For declarations, the head of the clause (if declarations are seen as clauses in the logic programming sense) is replaced by its body. This is an unfolding rule which allows to pass from the agent $p(\mathbf{x})$ to the agent A, which will then evolve via the rules given above. For entailment pairs, the rules have an empty left hand side. In fact, the presence of the context S is enough to add the token t to the current store.

Example (computation step). Consider a computation state containing agent

$$A(a_1, a_2) = ask(t_1(a_1, a_2)) \to A'(a_2)$$

and tokens $t_1(a_1, a_2)$ and $t_2(a_2, a_3)$. Consider also the rewrite rule

$$(ask(t_1(x_1, x_2)) \rightarrow A'(x_2)) \overset{t_1(x_1, x_2)}{\leadsto} A'(x_2).$$

Then, since there exists a matching between the left hand side of the rule and (a subset of) the state (via the substitution $\{a_1/x_1, a_2/x_2\}$), the rule can be applied, yielding the new state containing agent $A'(a_2)$ and tokens $t_1(a_1, a_2)$ and $t_2(a_2, a_3)$. Note that token $t_1(a_1, a_2)$ has not been cancelled by the rewrite rule, since it was in its context part.□

Definition 5 (computations). Given a CC program $P = F.A$, a computation segment for P is any sequence of computation steps $S_1 \overset{r_1[a_1/x_1]}{\Longrightarrow} S_2 \overset{r_2[a_2/x_2]}{\Longrightarrow} S_3 \ldots$ such that $S_1 = \{A[a_0/x_0]\}$ and $r_i \in RR(P)$, i = 1,2, ... Two computation segments which are the same except that different fresh constants are employed in the various steps, are called α-equivalent. A computation is a computation segment CS such that for each computation segment CS', of which CS is a prefix, CS' adds to CS only steps applying rules for the entailment relation. □

Definition 6 (successful, suspended, and failing computations). A successful computation is a finite computation where the last state contains only a set of constraints, say S, and $S \nvdash false$. A suspended computation is a finite computation where the last state does not contain tell agents but contains ask agents, and its set of constraints S is such that $S \nvdash false$. A failing computation is a computation which is neither successful nor suspended. □

Notice that a computation has been defined as a sequence of computation steps which is maximal w.r.t. the evolution of the agents. This means that there could be some subsequent step due to the entailment relation, but no step due to the agents. The reason for this is that, after all the agents have evolved, there could be an infinite number of entailment steps, and still we do not want to consider such a computation failing just because of that. A consequence of this is that to recognize a successful computation we have to ask the constraint system for a consistency test even in an eventual environment. Thus, the difference between atomic and eventual tell is just *when* such a check is asked for.

In the following we will only consider either finite computations or infinite computations which are fair. Here fairness means, informally, that if a rule can continuously be applied from some point onwards, then it will eventually be applied. This implies that both goal selection (among several goals in the current state) and rule selection (among several rules applicable to a goal) are fair.

Definition 7 (operational semantics). Given a CC program $P = F.A$, its operational semantics, say $EO(P)$, is the set of all its computations.□

5 Contextual Nets

In the following, we assume the reader to be familiar with the classical notions of nets. For the formal definitions missing here we refer to [Rei85] and [MR].

In classical nets, as defined for example in [Rei85], each element of the set of conditions can be a pre-condition (if it belongs to the pre-set of an event) or a post-condition (if it belongs to the post-set of an event). In contextual nets a condition can also be a *context* for an event. Informally, a context is something which is necessary for the event to be enabled, but which is not affected by the firing of that event. Still, the usual three relations which are defined on classical nets, that is, dependency, mutual exclusion, and concurrency, can be defined for contextual nets as well, and similar properties hold.

The formal technique which we use to introduce contexts consists in adding a new relation, besides the usual flow relation, which we call the *context relation*. Such relations state which conditions are to be considered as a context for which event. Nets with such contexts will be called *contextual nets*.

Definition 8 (contextual nets). A contextual net is a quadruple $(B, E; F_1, F_2)$ where elements of B are called conditions and those of E events; $F_1 \subseteq (B \times E) \cup (E \times B)$ is called the flow relation; $F_2 \subseteq (B \times E)$ is called the context relation; and it holds that $B \cap E = \emptyset$ and $(F_1 \cup F_1^{-1}) \cap F_2 = \emptyset$. $\square$

Example (context-dependent nets). Contextual nets will be graphically represented in the same way as nets. Thus, conditions are circles, events are boxes, the flow relation is represented by directed arcs from circles to boxes or viceversa, and the context relation by undirected arcs. An example of a context-dependent net can be found in Figure 1, where there are five events $e_1, \ldots, e_5$ and nine conditions $b_1, \ldots, b_9$. In particular, event e_2 has b_2 and b_3 as preconditions, b_5 as postcondition, and b_7 as a context. Note, however, that b_7 is not a context for all events. In fact, it is a precondition for e_4 and a context for e_3, for which b_6 is a context as well, while b_4 is a precondition and b_8 is a postcondition. $\square$

Definition 9 (pre-set, post-set, and context). Given a contextual net $N = (B, E; F_1, F_2)$ and an element $x \in B \cup E$, the pre-set of x is the set ${}^\bullet x = \{y \mid yF_1x)\}$; the post-set of x is the set $x^\bullet = \{y \mid xF_1y)\}$; the context of x is defined if $x \in E$ and it is the set $\widehat{x} = \{y \mid yF_2x)\}$. $\square$

Here we are not interested in how a contextual net works, i.e. how and when events may be fired. We just need to know that an event can happen whenever its pre-set and context are present, and as a result the pre-set is consumed and the post-set is generated. For more formal definitions, we refer to [MR].

In our concurrent semantics the underlying notion is that of a contextual process, which is a contextual occurrence net together with a suitable mapping of the elements of the net to the syntactic objects of the program execution. Through the mapping, each condition of the contextual net represents an agent or a constraint, and each event represents a rule application.

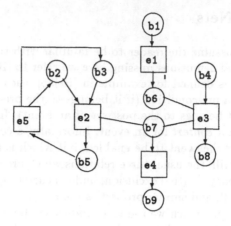

Fig. 1. A contextual net.

Informally, a contextual occurrence net is just an acyclic contextual net, where acyclicity refers to the dependency relation induced by F_1 and F_2. Such relation (seen as a set of pairs) contains all pairs in F_1, plus other pairs, derived by the combination of F_1 and F_2. In fact, if an element b is a postcondition of $e1$ and a context condition of $e2$, then $e2$ depends on $e1$ and this has to be reflected in the partial order. The same holds when b is a context condition of $e1$ and a precondition of $e2$. In fact, in this last case, in any computation where both e_1 and e_2 are present, e_1 must happen before e_2 (that is, b cannot be cancelled before being read).

Definition 10 (dependency). Consider a contextual net $N = (B, E; F_1, F_2)$. Then we define a corresponding structure $(B \cup E, \leq_N)$, where the dependency relation $\leq_N$ is the minimal relation which is reflexive, transitive, and which satisfies the following conditions: xF_1y implies $x \leq_N y$; e_1F_1b and bF_2e_2 implies $e_1 \leq_N e_2$; bF_2e_1 and bF_1e_2 implies $e_1 \leq_N e_2$. □

Therefore in the following we will say that x depends on y whenever $y \leq_N x$. However, a contextual net gives information not only about dependency of events and conditions, but also about concurrency and mutual exclusion (or conflict).

Definition 11 (mutual exclusion and concurrency). Consider a contextual net $N = (B, E; F_1, F_2)$ and the associated dependency relation $\leq_N$. Assume that $\leq_N$ is antisymmetric, and let $\leq \geq \in (B \cup E) \times (B \cup E)$ be defined as $\leq \geq = \{\langle x, y \rangle \mid x \leq_N y \text{ or } y \leq_N x\}$.

- The mutual exclusion relation $\#_N \subseteq ((B \cup E) \times (B \cup E))$ is defined as follows. First we define $x\#'y$ iff $x, y \in E$ and $\exists z \in B$ such that zF_1x and zF_1y. Then, $\#_N$ is the minimal relation which includes $\#'$ and which is symmetric and hereditary (i.e. if $x\#_Ny$ and $x \leq z$, then $z\#_Ny$).

– The concurrency relation co_N is just $((B \cup E) \times (B \cup E)) \setminus (\leq_{\geq} \cup \#_N)$. □

In words, the mutual exclusion is originated by the existence of conditions which cause more than one event, and then it is propagated downwards through the dependency relation. Instead, two items are concurrent if they are not dependent on each other nor mutually exclusive.

We now come to the notion of a contextual occurrence net, which is just a context-dependent net where the dependency relation is a partial order, there are no "forwards conflicts" (i.e., different events with a common postcondition), and $\#_N$ is irreflexive.

Definition 12 (contextual occurrence net). A contextual occurrence net is a contextual net N, where $N = (B, E; F_1, F_2)$ and: $\leq_N$ is antisymmetric; $b \in B$ implies $| \ {}^{\bullet}b \ | \leq 1$; $\#_N$ is irreflexive. □

A useful special case of a contextual occurrence net occurs when the mutual exclusion relation is empty. This means that, taken any two items in the net, they are either concurrent or dependent. Since no conflict is expressed in such nets, they represent a completely deterministic behaviour. For this reason they are called deterministic occurrence nets.

Definition 13 (deterministic contextual occurrence net). A deterministic contextual occurrence net is a quadruple $N = (B, E; F_1, F_2)$ such that N is a contextual occurrence net with $\#_N = \emptyset$. □

Example (contextual occurrence nets). Consider for example the deterministic contextual occurrence net in Figure 2 a). Then its dependency partial order can be seen in Figure 2 b).□

Given a (nondeterministic) contextual occurrence net, it is easy to derive the set of all its subnets which are deterministic. For this we use restrictions defined as $F_{|S} = \{x \in F | x \in S\}$ (set intersection).

Definition 14 (from contextual to deterministic contextual occ. nets). Let a contextual occurrence net $N = (B, E; F_1, F_2)$ and the associated relations $\leq_N$, $\#_N$, and co_N, a deterministic contextual occurrence net of N is a deterministic contextual occurrence net $N' = (B', E'; F_1', F_2')$ where $B' \subseteq B$ and $E' \subseteq E$ and

– $x \in (B' \cup E')$ and $y \in (B \cup E)$ s.t. $y \leq_N x$ implies that $y \in (B' \cup E')$;
– $F_1' = F_{1|(B' \times E') \cup (E' \times B')}$ and $F_2' = F_{2|(B' \times E')}$. □

The last condition states that the set $B' \cup E'$ is left-closed w.r.t. relation $\leq_N$. That is, the causes of the elements in $B' \cup E'$ are in $B' \cup E'$ as well. The intuition behind this condition is that deterministic nets which are not left-closed represent meaningless computations, since there are objects which are causally inconsistent.

We are now ready to define contextual processes, which, as anticipated above, will be used to give a concurrent semantics to CC programs. We recall that, informally, a contextual process is just a contextual occurrence net plus a suitable mapping from the items of the net (i.e. conditions and events) to the agents of the CC program and the rules representing it.

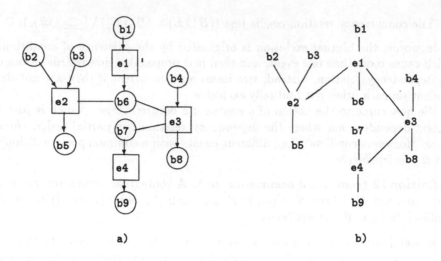

a)   b)

Fig. 2. A deterministic contextual occurrence net and the associated partial order.

Definition 15 (contextual process). Given a CC program P with initial agent
A, and the associated sets of rewrite rules $RR(P)$, agents $Ag(P)$, and tokens D,
consider the sets $RB = \{b\theta\}$ and $RE = \{r\theta\}$, with $b \in (Ag(P) \cup D)$, $r \in RR(P)$
and θ any substitution. Then a contextual process is a pair $\langle N, \pi \rangle$, where

- $N = (B, E; F_1, F_2)$ is a (nondeterministic) contextual occurrence net;
- $\pi : (B \cup E) \to (RB \cup RE)$ is a mapping where
  - $\forall b \in B$, $\pi(b) \in RB$ and $\forall e \in E$, $\pi(e) \in RE$;
  - $\forall x \in B$ such that $\not\exists y \in (B \cup E)$, $y \leq_N x$, $\pi(x) = A$;
  - let $\pi(e) = r\theta$, with $r = L \overset{c}{\leadsto} R$, then $\{\pi(x)|x \in {}^\bullet e\} = L\theta$,
    $\{\pi(x)|x \in \hat{e}\} = c\theta$, $\{\pi(x)|x \in e^\bullet\} = R\theta$. □

6   The True-Concurrency Semantics

The key idea in the semantics is to take the set of rewrite rules $RR(P)$ associated to a given CC program P and to incrementally construct a corresponding
contextual process. Such process is able to represent all possible computations
of the CC program P in a unique structure.

Definition 16 (from rewrite rules to a contextual process). Given a CC program P, the pair $CP(P) = \langle (B, E; F_1, F_2), \pi \rangle$ is constructed by means of the
following two inference rules:

- if $A(\mathbf{a})$ initial agent of P then $\langle A(\mathbf{a}), \emptyset, 1 \rangle \in B$;
- if $\exists r \in RR(P)$ such that $L(r) \cup c(r) = \{B_1(\mathbf{x}_1), \dots, B_n(\mathbf{x}_n)\}$, and
  - $\exists \{s_1, \dots, s_n\} \subseteq B$ such that $\forall i, j = 1, \dots, n$, s_i co_N s_j, and

- $\forall i = 1, \ldots, n$, $s_i = \langle e_i, B_i(\mathbf{a_j}), k_i \rangle$, and for some $\mathbf{a}$, $B_i(\mathbf{x}_i)[\mathbf{a}/\mathbf{x}] = B_i(\mathbf{a}_i)$

then

- $e = \langle r[\mathbf{a}/\mathbf{x}], \{s_1, \ldots, s_n\}, 1 \rangle \in E$,
- $s_i F_1 e$ for all $s_i = \langle e_i, B_i(\mathbf{a_j}), k_i \rangle$ such that for some $\mathbf{a}$, $B_i(\mathbf{x}_i)[\mathbf{a}/\mathbf{x}] = B_i(\mathbf{a}_i)$ and $B_i(\mathbf{x}_i) \in L(r)$
- $s_i F_2 e$ for all $s_i = \langle e_i, B_i(\mathbf{a_j}), k_i \rangle$ such that for some $\mathbf{a}$, $B_i(\mathbf{x}_i)[\mathbf{a}/\mathbf{x}] = B_i(\mathbf{a}_i)$ and $B_i(\mathbf{x}_i) \in c(r)$
- let h be the multiplicity of $B(\mathbf{x}, y_1, \ldots, y_m) \in R(r)$, then $\forall l = 1, \ldots, h$, $b_l = \langle B[\mathbf{a}/\mathbf{x}][\langle e, y_1 \rangle / y_1] \ldots [\langle e, y_m \rangle / y_m], e, l \rangle \in B$, and $e F_1 b_l$.

Moreover, for any item $x = \langle x_1, x_2, x_3 \rangle \in (B \cup E)$, $\pi(x) = x_1$. $\square$

Informally, we apply the rewrite rules, starting from the initial agent, in any possible way, so that different occurrences of the same rule are represented by different events of the net and generate different conditions. The technique used to achieve that consists of generating a new event representing the rule application and new conditions representing the right hand side of the rule, and by structuring each event or condition as a triple, where the first element contains the object being represented (either an agent, or a token, or a rule application), while the second element contains the whole history of the event or condition, and the third element is a number which allows us to distinguish different occurrences with the same history (we recall that a state is a multiset, while here we are generating a set of conditions). If there is only one of such occurrences, then the number will be 1, otherwise, the k-th occurrence will have number k. Note that, for the language we consider, k is always either 1 or 2, since there cannot be more than two occurrences with the same history. In fact, the only rule which may generate a multiset containing different occurrences of the same element is the one associated to the agent $A \parallel A$. However, our approach can also handle languages where an agent may fork into more than two agents. Note that we don't have to handle the problem of different rules generating different occurrences of the same agent, since the identity of such occurrences is automatically made distinct by the fact that they will have different histories. Moreover, the mapping π tells us either the rule or the object represented (with the applied substitution). In the following we will often omit the mapping π, since we know that π always maps a triple to its first element.

Each time the inference rule is applied, a rule in RR(P) is chosen whose left hand side and context are *matched* by some elements already present in the partially built process. Such elements have to be concurrent, otherwise it would mean that they cannot be together in a state. Then, a new element representing the rule application is added (as an event), as well as new elements representing the right hand side of the rule (as conditions).

Theorem 17 ($CP(P)$ is a contextual process). *Given a CC program P, its corresponding structure $CP(P)$ from Definition 16 is a contextual process.* $\square$

Theorem 18 (soundness and completeness of $CP(P)$ w.r.t. $EO(P)$). *Given a CC program P and its corresponding contextual process $CP(P) = \langle N, \pi \rangle$.*

– *For a given computation in $EO(P)$ there are (1) an α-equivalent computation* $S_1 \overset{r_1[\mathbf{a}_1/\mathbf{x}_1]}{\Longrightarrow} S_2 \overset{r_2[\mathbf{a}_2/\mathbf{x}_2]}{\Longrightarrow} S_3 \ldots$, *and (2) one linearization (restricted to events), say $e_1 e_2, \ldots$, of the partial order associated to a maximal deterministic contextual occurrence net of N, s.t. $\forall i = 1, 2, \ldots$, $\pi(e_i) = r_i[\mathbf{a}_i/\mathbf{x}_i]$*

– *For any linearization $e_1 e_2 \ldots$ of the partial order associated to a deterministic contextual occurrence net of N, there is a computation in $EO(P)$, say* $S_1 \overset{r_1[\mathbf{a}_1/\mathbf{x}_1]}{\Longrightarrow} S_2 \overset{r_2[\mathbf{a}_2/\mathbf{x}_2]}{\Longrightarrow} S_3 \ldots$, *such that, if $e_i = \langle e_{i1}, e_{i2}, e_{i3} \rangle$ and $\pi(e_i) = r$, then $r_i[\mathbf{a}_i/\mathbf{x}_i] = r$ for all $i = 1, \ldots$* □

Example (CC programs and contextual processes). Consider the CC program P consisting of the initial agent $IA = tell(c_1, c_2, c) \to A$, where
$A = (ask(c_1) \to A_1 + ask(c_2) \to success)$,
$A_1 = A_2 \parallel A_2$,
$A_2 = ask(c) \to success$,
and no declarations. The rules corresponding to such agent and all its subagents are:
$r_1 : A \rightsquigarrow c_1, c_2, c, A$
$r_2 : A \overset{c_1}{\rightsquigarrow} A_1$
$r_3 : A \overset{c_2}{\rightsquigarrow} success$
$r_4 : A_1 \rightsquigarrow 2A_2$
$r_5 : A_2 \overset{c}{\rightsquigarrow} success$.
For simplicity sake, we assume the entailment relation to be empty (or not relevant to the constraints involved in such program). Furthermore, the variables are not taken into consideration. This program has two alternative finite computations, depending on how agent A evolves. In one case, we have the parallel evolution of two occurrences of A_2 (even though they both ask for the same constraint c), and in the other case we have one computation step generating the success agent.

The process that is generated for this program is as follows (again, we will not explicitly write the mapping π, since each triple is mapped by π to its first element). First, condition $s_1 = \langle IA, \emptyset, 1 \rangle$ is generated for the initial agent IA. At this point, rule r_1 can be applied, and thus we generate event $e_1 = \langle r_1, \{s_1\}, 1 \rangle$ to represent the rule application, and conditions $s_2 = \langle A, e_1, 1 \rangle$, $s_3 = \langle c_1, e_1, 1 \rangle$, $s_4 = \langle c_2, e_1, 1 \rangle$, and $s_5 = \langle c, e_1, 1 \rangle$ to represent its right hand side. Moreover, we set $s_1 F_1 e_1$, and $e_1 F_1 s_i$ for $i = 2, \ldots, 5$.

Since there are conditions representing A, c_1, and c_2 (i.e., s_2, s_3, and s_4), rules r_2 and r_3 can now be applied, and thus we have events $e_2 = \langle r_2, \{s_2, s_3\}, 1 \rangle$ and $e_3 = \langle r_3, \{s_2, s_4\}, 1 \rangle$, as well as conditions $s_6 = \langle A_1, e_2, 1 \rangle$ and $s_7 = \langle success, e_3, 2 \rangle$. Moreover, we also have $s_2 F_1 e_2$, $s_3 F_2 e_2$, $e_2 F_1 s_6$, $s_2 F_1 e_3$, $s_4 F_2 e_3$, $e_3 F_1 s_7$.

Now there is a condition representing A_1, thus rule r_4 can be applied, and we have the event $e_4 = \langle r_4, \{s_6\}, 1 \rangle$, and the conditions $s_8 = \langle A_2, e_4, 1 \rangle$ and $s_9 = \langle A_2, e_4, 2 \rangle$. Moreover, $s_6 F_1 e_4$, $e_4 F_1 s_8$, and $e_4 F_1 s_9$.

Thus we obtained the contextual process $\langle N, \pi \rangle$, where $N = (B, E; F_1, F_2)$, and $B = \{s_1, \ldots, s_{11}\}$, $E = \{e_1 \ldots, e_6\}$, and F_1 and F_2 are as defined above. Figure 3 shows such a net N. In N, it is easy to see that e_2 causally depends on e_1, since they are related by a chain of F_1 pairs. Similarly, e_3 depends on e_1. However, e_3 and e_2 do not depend on each other, and they are not even concurrent. In fact, thet are mutually exclusive, since they have a common precondition. This means the the rules represented by e_2 and e_3, i.e., r_2 and r_3, cannot be applied in the same computation, but only in two alternative computations. Then, we have that e_4 depends on e_2 because of a chain of F_1 pairs. Also, e_5 depends on e_4. Finally, e_6 depends on e_4 as well. However, e_5 and e_6 are concurrent, since they do not depend on each other and they are not mutually exclusive. Note that e_5 and e_6 have a common context condition. However, this does not generate any dependency, as desired.□

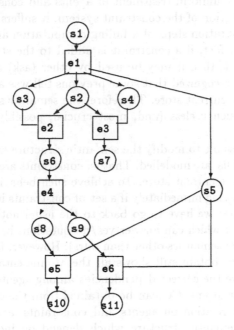

Fig. 3. The contextual occurrence net corresponding to a CC program.

7 Extensions

The true-concurrency semantics for CC languages that we have described in the previous section can be extended in several orthogonal directions, in order to achieve a complete and faithful model of a larger class of CC programs. Here we mention just two of such extensions, which involve the use of an *atomic* tell and the presence of two different kinds of nondeterminism. Other extension are however possible. In particular, we are studying the presence of *deep guards* in CC languages.

7.1 Atomic CC

There are two ways in which the tell operation of CC languages ca be interpreted: either *eventually*, which means that the constraint is added to the current store without any check, or *atomically*, which instead means that the constraint is added only if it is consistent with the current store. Of course these two operations behave very differently, and it is easy to see that the eventual tell is much easier to implement in a distributed environment but it is also much less powerful.

The concurrent semantics for CC programs that we have described in this paper follows the eventual interpretation. While this kind of tell operation allows for a completely uniform treatment of agents and constraints and thus a distributed representation of the constraint system, it suffers from the fact that possibly many computation steps of a failing computation are performed while not being needed. In fact, if a constraint is added to the store even though it is inconsistent with it, then it may be used by other (ask) agents, and maybe only much later it is recognized that some previous tell was adding a constraint inconsistent with the current store. Therefore, the semantic structure presented above contains all such useless (and, most crucial, possibly infinite) parts of computations.

However, it is possible to modify the semantic structure so that atomic tells, instead of eventual tells, are modelled. That is, constraints are added only if they are consistent with the current store. To achieve such behaviour, we must have the possibility of knowing immediately if a set of constraints is consistent or not. Thus it may seem that we have to go back to the usual notion of a constraint system as a black box which can answer yes/no questions in one step (which is what is used in all the semantics other than ours). However, this is not true: the semantic structure we obtain still shows all the atomic entailment steps, thus allowing one to derive the correct dependencies among agents.

The semantics for atomic CC can be obtained from the other one by defining an inconsistency relation on agents and constraints, and then cutting all those parts of the semantic structure which depend on inconsistently "told" constraints. The basic idea is to derive the inconsistency relation from the constraint system, where we assume that an inconsistent set of constraints always entails the token *false*. Then, the inconsistency relation is propagated through the contextual net via the dependency relation. If, as a result of that, some items are inconsistent with themselves, then it means that they could not appear in any computation without creating an inconsistent state of affairs. Therefore we just have to prune such items and everything that depends on them. Instead of pruning the semantic structure built for eventual CC, we can also define such semantics from scratch, by adopting a slightly more complicated inference rule.

Since this new semantics introduces an explicit representation for failure (i.e. the attempt to add a constraint which is inconsistent with the current store), we can say that it achieves a faithful model for capturing backtracking. This in turns means that such semantics, although originally intended for CC programs, can be used also for CLP programs, which employ atomic tells, no asks, and *don't know* nondeterminism. The idea in this case is to use the semantics to recognize the implicit possible parallelism in a CLP program [BdlBH+94b, BdlBH+94a].

7.2 Two Nondeterminisms

Classical CC programs, as defined above in this paper and also in the first part of [Sar93], employ a form of nondeterminism called *don't care* nondeterminism: among several choices, only one is taken and all the others are forgotten. Another possibility would instead be the so-called *don't know* nondeterminism, where all of the choices are taken, either one after the other one or all at the same time in an or-parallel fashion.

The presence of both types of nondeterminism in a CC language can be of great value. In fact, Prolog-style don't know nondeterminism allows for simple, perspicuous representations of search-spaces. Instead, don't care nondeterminism arises naturally in reactive distributed contexts, where the relative speeds of processors and relative communication delays across the network are unpredictable. Thus, the combination of the two is useful when one seeks to implement simple representations for search problems that are to be solved in a distributed, reactive context. Moreover, it also appears whenever, for any reason, one decides to make some of the choices backtrackable (that is, don't know nondeterministic, or collective), and others committed (that is, don't care nondeterministic).

The semantics for CC programs described in this paper can be adapted to model CC languages with both don't care and don't know nondeterminism [MRS94]. First, we have to represent each computation state as a collection of sets of agent and constraint occurrences (instead of just one set), where different sets in a collection represent situations which are reached by making different nondeterministic choices. The rewrite rules have, as usual, a left-hand side and a context, but now they must have (possibly) more than one right-hand side.

Then, to model also don't know nondeterminism, we have extend the contextual net formalism. We do that by splitting the concurrency relation into two: *and-concurrency* and *or-concurrency*, obtaining a new kind of net that we call an *and-or contextual net*. Such a refinement of the model is unavoidable if one wants to distinguish among four notions: don't care nondeterminism, don't know nondeterminism, concurrency and dependency.

8 Conclusions

We have discussed some of the basic issue to be considered when developing a semantics for a concurrent language, and we have presented a semantics for the CC paradigm which follows the true-concurrency approach and uses the formalism of contextual nets. We have then hinted at some extensions of the semantics described here to model larger classes of CC languages.

Among the promising future directions for this line of research there is the study of an abstraction of the semantics for CC programs. This can be done by defining a suitable notion of observables which however allows for a reasonably faithful modelling of the concurrency information.

Also, other extensions are possible. For example, we are studying the modelling of those CC languages which allow for *deep guards*, that is, guards which can also contain agents instead of only constraints.

Acknowledgments

This research has been partially supported by the BRA Esprit Project n. 7195 (ACCLAIM).

References

[BdlBH$^+$94a] F. Bueno, M. Jose Garcia de la Banda, M. Hermenegildo, U. Montanari, and F. Rossi. From eventual to atomic and locally atomic cc programs: A concurrent semantics. In *Proc. Int. Conference on Algebraic and Logic Programming (ALP94)*, 1994.

[BdlBH$^+$94b] F. Bueno, M. Jose Garcia de la Banda, M. Hermenegildo, F. Rossi, and U. Montanari. Towards true concurrency semantics based transformation between clp and cc. In *Proc. second Int. Workshop on Principles and Practice of Constraint Programming (PPCP94)*, 1994.

[BK84] J. Bergstra and W. Klop. Process algebra for sunchronous communication. *Information and Control*, 60, 1984.

[BP91] F.S. De Boer and C. Palamidessi. A fully abstract model for concurrent constraint programming. In *Proc. CAAP*. Springer-Verlag, 1991.

[CC92] P. Cousot and R. Cousot. Abstract interpretation and application to logic programming. *The Journal of Logic Programming*, 13 (2 and 3), 1992.

[DD89] P. Darondeau and P. Degano. Causal trees. In *Proc. ICALP*. Springer Verlag, LNCS 372, 1989.

[DNM87] P. Degano, R. De Nicola, and U. Montanari. Concurrent histories: A basis for observing distributed systems. *Journal of Computer and System Science*, 34, 1987.

[DNM90] P. Degano, R. De Nicola, and U. Montanari. A partial ordering semantics for CCS. *Theoretical Computer Science*, pages 223–262, 1990.

[Hen88] M. Hennessy. *Algebraic Theory of Processes*. MIT Press, 1988.

[Hoa85] C.A.R. Hoare. *Communicating Sequential Processes*. Prentice Hall, 1985.

[Mil80] R. Milner. *A Calculus of Communicating Systems*. Springer Verlag, LNCS 92, 1980.

[Mil89] R. Milner. *Communication and Concurrency*. Prentice Hall, 1989.

[MR] U. Montanari and F. Rossi. Contextual nets. *Acta Informatica*. To appear.

[MR93] U. Montanari and F. Rossi. Contextual occurrence nets and concurrent constraint programming. In *Proc. Dagstuhl Seminar on Graph Transformations in Computer Science*. Springer-Verlag, LNCS, 1993.

[MR94]   U. Montanari and F. Rossi. A concurrent semantics for concurrent con-
           straint programming via contextual nets. In *Proc. 1st Workshop on Prin-
           ciples and Practice of Constraint Programming (PPCP93)*. MIT Press,
           1994.

[MRS94]   U. Montanari, F. Rossi, and V. Saraswat. CC Programs with both In-
           and Non-Determinism: A Concurrent Semantics. In *Proc. second Inter-
           national Workshop on Principles and Practice of Constraint Program-
           ming (PPCP94)*. Springer-Verlag, LNCS, 1994.

[NPW81]   M. Nielsen, G. Plotkin, and G. Winskel. Petri Nets, Event Structures
           and Domains, part 1. *Theoretical Computer Science*, 1981. Vol.13.

[Pet80]   C.A. Petri. Concurrency. In *Net Theory and Applications*. Springer-
           Verlag, LNCS 84, 1980.

[Pra86]   V. Pratt. Modelling Concurrency with Partial Orders. *International
           Journal of Parallel Programming*, 1986. Vol.15.

[Rei85]   W. Reisig. *Petri Nets: An Introduction*. EATCS Monographs on Theo-
           retical Computer Science. Springer Verlag, 1985.

[RM94]   F. Rossi and U. Montanari. Concurrent semantics for concurrent con-
           straint programming. In J. Penjam B. Mayoh, E. Tyugu, editor, *Con-
           straint Programming*. NATO ASI Series, 1994.

[Ros93]   F. Rossi. *Constraints and Concurrency*. PhD thesis, University of Pisa,
           TD-14/93, 1993.

[Sar93]   V.A. Saraswat. *Concurrent Constraint Programming*. MIT Press, 1993.

[Sco82]   D. S. Scott. Domains for denotational semantics. In *Proc. ICALP*.
           Springer-Verlag, 1982.

[SR90]   V. A. Saraswat and M. Rinard. Concurrent constraint programming. In
           Proc. POPL. ACM, 1990.

[SRP91]   V. A. Saraswat, M. Rinard, and P. Panangaden. Semantic foundations
           of concurrent constraint programming. In *Proc. POPL*. ACM, 1991.

[Win86]   G. Winskel. Event structures. In *Petri nets: applications and relation-
           ships to other models of concurrency*. Springer-Verlag, LNCS 255, 1986.

Toupie : a Constraint Language
for Model Checking

Antoine Rauzy

LaBRI – CNRS URA 1304 – Université Bordeaux I
51, cours de la Libération, F-33405 Talence (France)
email: rauzy@labri.u-bordeaux.fr

Abstract. Constraint logic programming (CLP) has demonstrated its ability to handle difficult problems coming from operation research. We think that this approach is relevant to perform program analyses too. However, program analysis often requires solvers for second order constraints, i.e. mainly fixpoint equations, that are not available in CLP languages. In this paper, we present, the language Toupie that is designed to solve such constraints. Toupie uses an extension of Bryant's binary decision diagrams to encode relations which makes it possible to handle relations with huge numbers of elements.

1 Introduction

Constraint logic programming (CLP) has demonstrated its ability to handle problems coming from operation research. We think that basic ideas of this paradigm — simplicity of problem expressions, fast prototyping, flexibility, versatility of the tools — could be useful in other areas, especially for what concerns the analysis of systems of concurrent processes. However, program analysis requires often solvers for second order constraints, i.e. mainly fixpoint equations, that are not available in CLP languages.

We present here the language Toupie that handles such second order constraints. More precisely, Toupie implements an extension of the propositional μ-calculus to finite domain constraints. In addition to classical functionalities of finite domain constraint solvers, Toupie allows a full universal quantification and the definition of relations as least or greatest fixpoints of monotone functions. These definitions can be seen as a kind of quantification over relations.

The main implementation problem with second order constraints is to store efficiently tuples belonging to relations. Analyses of systems of concurrent processes — which is the main goal of Toupie — require to handle relations with huge numbers of elements because, even if each individual process can be described by means of a small finite state automaton, the whole system often goes through thousands and thousands of different states. This combinatorial explosion is due to the various possible interleaving of individual process actions. Toupie achieves this goal by encoding relations by means of decision diagrams, an extension to finite domains of Bryant's binary decision diagrams [Bry86].

The idea of using BDDs to encode large finite state automata is not new. Mac Millan & als on the one hand [BCM+90], Madre and Coudert on the other hand

[CBM89] have shown very impressive examples of its power. The contribution of Toupie is twofold : At a technical level, it integrates decision diagrams features and constraint solving. At a functional level, it integrates already mentioned basic ideas of the CLP paradigm into a model checking tool.

The remaining of this contribution is organized as follows : Syntax and semantics of Toupie are presented section 2. The use of Toupie for symbolic model checking is described section 3. Some technical implementation details are given section 4. Finally, we discuss the computational model of Toupie at section 5.

2 Syntax and Semantics of Toupie Programs

In order to present syntax and semantics of Toupie in an informal way, we deal, through this section, with the well-known two players Nim's game (the reader interested in a more formal presentation could see [Rau94b]).

Nim's game : The game starts with N lines numbered from 1 to N and containing $2 \times i - 1$ matches (where i is the number of the line). At each step, the player who has the turn takes as many matches as he wants in one of the line. Then the turn changes. The winner is the player who takes the last matches.

Variables, Constants, Domains, Composite Variables : A position in the Nim's game is characterized by the player who has the turn and the number of matches in each line. In Toupie, such a position is described by means of a composite variable that groups several individual variables. Before using a composite variable, one must declare its type. For the Nim's game with three lines of matches, the declaration is as follows.

```
let position = list (
    P  : {a,b},
    L1 : 0..1,
    L2 : 0..3,
    L3 : 0..5
    )
```

A variable of type **position** groups four individual variables : P (for Player) that takes its value in the set of symbolic constants {a,b} and L1, L2 and L3 (for Line 1, 2 and 3) that take there values in ranges of integers. {a,b}, 0..1, 0..3 and 0..5 are the domains of the variables P, L1, L2 and L3. Note that, as in Prolog, variable identifiers begin with upper case letters and symbolic constant identifiers begin with lower case letters.

Formulae, Predicates : Assume declared a variable Pos of type position. In order to constrain Pos to describe the initial state of the game, one uses a formula (a constraint) :

```
((Pos.P=a) & {Pos.L1=1, Pos.L2=3, Pos.L3=5})
```

The above formula is a conjunction — & stands for ∧ — of two atomic constraints : an equality and a system of linear inequations. The "field" F of a composite variable C is denoted by C.F. When a composite variable is manipulated per se its identifier is prefixed with a caret : ^C.

A move is described by means of binary predicate, i.e. a relation, whose first member (^S for Source) is the position before the move and the second member (^T for Target) is the position after the move :

```
move(^S:position,^T:position) += (
    (S.P#T.P)
  & (
        {S.L1>T.L1, S.L2=T.L2, S.L3=T.L3}
      | {S.L1=T.L1, S.L2>T.L2, S.L3=T.L3}
      | {S.L1=T.L1, S.L2=T.L2, S.L3>T.L3}
    )
)
```

The relation **move** is defined as a conjunction of the dysequality S.P#T.P meaning that the turn changes and the disjunction of three systems of linear inequations representing the different ways the player who has the turn can take matches in a line.

A Toupie program is a set of n-ary predicate definitions.

Quantifiers, Queries : Toupie is an interpreter. Once entered the definition of **position** and **move**, it is possible to ask queries. For instance, the positions where no move is playable are obtained by means of the following query.

```
lambda (^S:position) forall ^T:position ~move(^S,^T) ?
```

The form **lambda** is just a way to declare the type of the variable(s) of the query (here ^S is of type **position**). The quantifier **forall** has its intuitive meaning and ~ stands for ¬.

In response to the above query, one obtains :

```
{S.L1=0,S.L2=0,S.L3=0}
```

This encodes the two final positions (player **a** wins or player **b** wins). This example illustrates the fact that Toupie is a deterministic language. In response to a query it computes the decision diagram associated with this query and then goes through this data structure to display the tuples belonging to the relation. The result of a computation is thus an unique relation eventually containing several tuples. Decision diagrams perform some factoring of tuples which explains that only one tuple is displayed.

Fixpoints : All the positions are not reachable from the initial one (for instance, <a,0,3,5> is not). A position ^T is reachable either if it is the initial one or if there exists a reachable position ^S and a move from ^S to ^T. This characterization of reachable positions is recursive. It means that it is not possible to express it just with first order constraints. One needs a kind of quantification over relations. As a matter of fact, our characterization is typically a least fixpoint definition.

In Toupie, predicates are actually defined as least or greatest fixpoints of equations for the inclusion in the powerset $2^{\mathcal{D}}$ of the cartesian product $\mathcal{D} = D_1 \times \ldots \times D_n$ of the domains D_i's of their formal parameters. $2^{\mathcal{D}}$ equipped with the set inclusion forms a complete lattice. The Tarksi's theorem asserts that given a monotone function f from $2^{\mathcal{D}}$ to $2^{\mathcal{D}}$,

1. f is continuous.
2. The equation $R = f(R)$ $(R \in \mathcal{P}(\mathcal{D}))$ admits a least and a greatest solutions, denoted with $\mu R.f(R)$ and $\nu R.f(R)$, that are respectively equal to $\bigcap\{R|f(R) \subseteq R\}$ and $\bigcup\{R|f(R) \supseteq R\}$.
3. There exist two integers m and n such that $\mu R.f(R) = f^m(\emptyset)$ and $\nu R.f(R) = f^n(\mathcal{D})$ where $f^k(R)$ denotes the k-nth application of f to R.

It is easy to generalize this result to the case of systems of fixpoint equations. It provides the computation principle of Toupie predicates.

Syntactically, least and greatest fixpoint definitions are denoted by equations respectively in the form p += f and p -= f.

The predicate **move** is thus defined as a least fixpoint, but, since there is no recursive call in its equation, it could be defined as a greatest fixpoint as well.

The predicate encoding reachable positions is as follows.

```
reachable(^T:position) += (
    initial(^T)
  | exist ^S:position (reachable(^S) & move(^S,^T))
)
```

Winning Positions : A position is winning if there exists a move leading to a losing position and conversely a position is losing if any playable move leads to a winning position. This is simply what express the two following predicates.

```
winning(^S:position) +=
    exist ^T:position (move(^S,^T) & losing(^T))

losing(^S:state) +=
    forall ^T:position (move(^S,^T) => winning(^T))
```

The following table gives some running times necessary to compute reachable and winning positions on a SUN IPX Sparc Station with 48 megabytes of memory.

Number of lines	4	5	6	7	8
Number of reachable positions	763	7,674	92,153	1,290,232	20,643,831
Times reachable positions	0s21	0s43	0s75	1s25	1s93
Times winning positions	0s50	1s73	6s23	25s18	141s60

The reader should notice that it is not possible (at least simply) to analyze the Nim's game within usual $\text{CLP}(\mathcal{FD})$ languages because such an analysis requires fixpoint computations and universal quantifications.

Variable Ordering : Since the original paper by R. Bryant [Bry86], it is well known that the size of a decision diagram (binary or not) crucially depends on the indices chosen for the variables.

By default, in Toupie, the variables are indexed with a very simple heuristic, known for its rather good accuracy. It consists in traversing the formula considered as a syntactic tree with a depth-first left-most procedure and to number variables in the induced order.

Nevertheless, this heuristic can produce very poor performances. The user is allowed to define its own indices. A variable declaration in the form X@i indicates that the variable X has the index i. For composite variables, variable declarations with fixed defined indices are in the form ^X@i!j, meaning that the first field of X is numbered i, the second one i+j, the third one i+2j and so on.

3 Symbolic Model Checking within Toupie

In this section we study, by means of an example, how Toupie is used to perform system of concurrent process analyses.

The notion of *transition system* plays an important role for describing processes and systems of communicating processes. A simple way to represent processes widely used in many works on semantics and verification (*model checking*), is to consider that a process is a set of *states* and that an *action* or an *event* changes the current state of the process and can thus be represented as a transition between the two states. Transition systems are also used to describe systems of communicating processes: the states of the system are tuples of states of its components and the transitions are tuples of allowed transitions. The resulting automaton is called by Arnold and Nivat the synchronized product. This model is basically synchronous, even if it allows the description of non-synchronous phenomena.

The idea we use, first proposed by Mac Millan & al [BCM+90], is to encode transition systems in a symbolic way.

Milner's scheduler : In order to illustrate this section, we model in Toupie the well-known Milner's scheduler [Mil89], a standard benchmark for process algebra tools [Bou93, EFT93]. The methodology remains the same for other problems such as the verification of mutual exclusion algorithms (see [CGR93]).

The scheduler consists of one starter process and N processes which are scheduled. The communication is organized in a ring. The transition system describing each cycler is depicted figure 1.

Each cycler process C_i awaits the permit (rc) to start, performs the action a, and passes the turn (sc) to the next cycler either before or after some internal computation (tau). The starter just initializes the process.

The synchronized product of a starter and two cyclers is pictured Fig. 2.

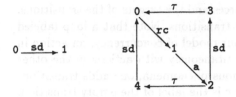

Fig. 1. The transition system encoding a cycler

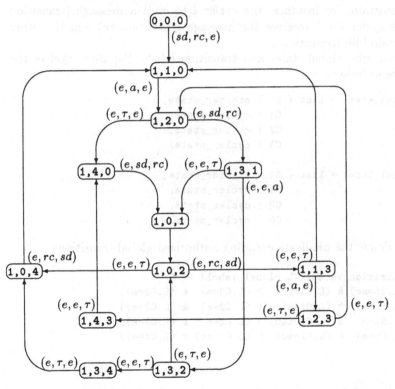

Fig. 2. The synchronized product of a starter and two cyclers

Coding of individual processes : A cycler is encoded in Toupie as follows:

```
let cycler_state = domain 0..4
let cycler_label = domain {e,tau,a,sc,rc}

cycler(S:cycler_state,L:cycler_label,T:cycler_state) += (
    ((L=e) & (S=T))
  | ((S=0) & (L=rc) & (T=1))  | ((S=1) & (L=a)   & (T=2))
  | ((S=2) & (L=sc) & (T=3))  | ((S=2) & (L=tau) & (T=4))
  | ((S=3) & (L=tau) & (T=0)) | ((S=4) & (L=sc)  & (T=0))
  )
```

The variables S and T stand for the sources and the targets of the transitions, the variable L stands for the labels of the transitions. Note that a loop labeled with e has been added on each state. In our model of concurrency, an action in some process is always executed only simultaneously with actions in the other processes. In order to represent asynchronous phenomena, one adds transitions of the form $s \xrightarrow{e} s$, where s is a state and e is the label of the empty transition.

Synchronization product : Now, we must synchronize the different processes, that is to constrain, for instance, the cycler i to emit a message (transition *sc*) when the cycler $i+1$ receives the message (transition *rc*) and the other processes remain idle (transition e).

We first describe global states and transition labels. For three cyclers the definitions are as follows.

```
let global_state = list ( St : starter_state,
                          C1 : cycler_state,
                          C2 : cycler_state,
                          C3 : cycler_state)

let global_label = list ( St : starter_state,
                          C1 : cycler_state,
                          C2 : cycler_state,
                          C3 : cycler_state)
```

Then, we define the predicate encoding authorized global transitions.

```
synchronization_vector(^L:global_label) += (
    ((L.St=sc) & (L.C1=rc)  & (L.C2=e)  & (L.C3=e))
 |  ((L.St=e)  & (L.C1=a)   & (L.C2=e)  & (L.C3=e))
 |  ((L.St=e)  & (L.C1=tau) & (L.C2=e)  & (L.C3=e))
 |  ((L.St=e)  & (L.C1=sc)  & (L.C2=rc) & (L.C3=e))
    ...
 )
```

Finally, edges of the synchronized product are defined as follows :

```
edge(^S01!3:global_state,^L02!3:global_label,^T03!3:global_state) += (
    starter(S.St,L.St,T.St) & cycler(S.C1,L.C1,T.C1)
  & cycler(S.C2,L.C2,T.C2)  & cycler(S.C3,L.C3,T.C3)
  & synchronization_vector(^L)
  )
```

Note the above definition fixes the variable indices. As remarked for instance in [EFT93] (for the Boolean case), the best order is the interleaved one, that is:

```
S.St < L.St < T.St < S.C1 < L.C1 < T.C1 < ... < S.CN < L.CN < T.CN
```

Reachable states : The set of the reachable states of the synchronized product is computed by means of the following predicate that is essentially the same than for the Nim's game.

```
reachable(^T@3!3:global_state) += (
    initial_state(^T)
  | exist ^S@1!3:global_state, ^L@2!3:global_label
    (reachable(^S) & edge(^S,^L,^T))
)
```

Verification of properties : The predicates **reachable** and **edge** allow the computation of properties of the system. For instance, we can verify that it is deadlock free. Let us recall that a dead-lock is a state wherein no transition is possible or only transitions leading to a deadlock state. The predicate to detect dead-locks is as follows.

```
dead_lock(^S@1!3:global_state) += (
    reachable(^S)
  & forall ^L@2!3:global_label, ^T@3!3:global_state
    ((reachable(^S) & edge(^S,^L,^T)) => dead_lock(^T))
)
```

Bisimulation A bisimulation is an equivalence relation between transition systems or different states of the same transition system (see the literature for a formal definition). The bisimulation generally considered on the Milner's scheduler is the observational equivalence that is to say that two states are equivalent if and only if there is a path labeled with τ-transition joining them. This bisimulation is computed in Toupie in two steps : First, compute the τ-closure of the synchronized product, that is the paths of the form $\tau^\star t\tau^\star$, where t is any transition (predicate **tau_path**). Second, compute the equivalence relation between states using the extended edges above.

The second step is performed with a greatest fixpoint predicate:

```
equivalent(^S@1!5:global_state,^T@2!5:global_state) -= (
    reachable(^S) & reachable(^T)
  & forall ^L@3!5:global_label (
        forall ^U@4!5:global_state
        (tau_path(^S,^L,^U)
          => exist ^V@5!5:global_state
              (tau_path(^T,^L,^V) & equivalent(^U,^V)))
      & forall ^V@5!5:global_state
        (tau_path(^T,^L,^V)
          => exist ^U@4!5:global_state
              (tau_path(^S,^L,^U) & equivalent(^U,^V)))

    )
)
```

The point is that the predicate **equivalent** mimics exactly the formal definition of the observational equivalence. Note also that if one wants to compute another bisimulation, it suffices to change the definition of the predicate **tau_path**.

In [CGR93], we show also how the fairness and the safety of a mutual exclusion algorithm can be studied in Toupie. All of these properties are expressed in Toupie in a very natural and declarative way.

Performances The table below indicates the running times for Toupie as well as those obtained by Bouali in the one hand [Bou93] and Enders & al in the other hand [EFT93] (the two last have been obtained on a SPARC 2 workstation, which is slightly faster than our own). These authors use BDDs based algorithms. The significant difference of performances in favor of Toupie comes, in our opinion, from the use of extended decision diagrams instead of binary ones. The interesting point is that very good performances can be obtained by using a general purpose constraint language instead of a specialized model checker.

processes	6	8	10	12	14	16	18	20
states	577	3073	15361	73729	$3 \cdot 10^6$	$1.2 \cdot 10^7$	$4.8 \cdot 10^7$	$1.8 \cdot 10^8$
transitions	2017	13825	84481	479233	$2 \cdot 10^7$	$8 \cdot 10^7$	$3.2 \cdot 10^8$	$1.28 \cdot 10^9$
reachable	0s70	1s30	2s03	3s36	4s41	5s76	7s36	9s36
Bouali	1s28	2s97	?	?	?	23s42	39s37	53s51
deadlock	0s10	0s13	0s18	0s21	0s26	0s30	0s38	0s38
bisimulation	4s08	6s70	9s95	14s23	18s01	23s20	28s40	34s76
Bouali	19s43	39s07	?	?	?	197s80	255s62	332s54
Enders & al	21s	40s	87s	145s	233s	348s	569s	850s

4 DDs versus BDDs

4.1 Decision Diagrams

Decision Diagrams used in Toupie to encode relations are an extension for finite domains of the Bryant's Binary Decision Diagrams [BRB90]. We do not present DDs here due to space limitations, the interested reader could see [Rau94b].

The main difference between the two representations is that a DD node is n-ary (and not binary), where n is the cardinality of the domain of the variable it is labeled with. Such a node encodes a *case* connective :

Definition 1. case connective
Let X be a variable, $\{k_1, \ldots, k_r\}$ be its domain, and $f_1, \ldots, f_r$ be formulae.

$$case(X, f_1, \ldots, f_r) = ((X = k_1) \wedge f_1) \vee \ldots \vee ((X = k_r) \wedge f_r)$$

The case connective keeps all good properties of the If-Then-Else (ITE) connective that labels the BDD nodes : It is orthogonal both with the connective ¬ — which makes a negation in constant time possible by putting a flag on negated edges, the leftmost outedge of a node being always positive to ensure the canonicity of the representation — and with the *ITE* connective — which makes possible to use exactly the same computation principle based on a unique connective (ITE) for DDs than for BDDs.

Example 1. a Decision Diagram
Let X and Y be two variables and 0..2 be their domain. The DD encoding the
constraint (X + Y <=1) is pictured Fig. 3(a) (complemented edges are marked
with a black dot).

(a)   (b)

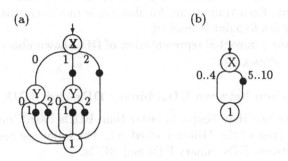

Fig. 3. The DD associated with $X + Y \leq 1, X, Y \in 0..2$ (a) and the compacted DD
associated with $X < 5, X \in 0..10$ (b)

4.2 Constraints Handling

The first step toward an efficient constraints handling is to remark that the DD
representation admits another canonical coding that can be more compact.

Compacted representation When dealing with variables having rather large domains (it could be the case especially for numerical variables) many consecutive
outedges of a node may point to the same son. In this case, one can compact the
representation by labeling outedges with ranges of constants rather than with
individual constant (such a DD is pictured Fig. 3(b)).

The "good" properties of DDs are preserved: negation in constant time,
canonicity. The representation is canonical if any two adjacent ranges that point
the same DD are merged. Logical operations can be accelerated by this coding since one can treat several values in one step when applying the recursive
computation principle :

$$ITE(case(X, 0..2 : F_1, 3..6 : F_2), case(X, 0..3 : G_1, 4..6 : G_2), 1)$$
$$=$$
$$case(X, 0..2 : ITE(F_1, G_1, 1), 3..3 : ITE(F_2, G_1, 1), 4..6 : ITE(F_2, G_2, 1))$$

Note, finally, that such a representation allows the coding of approximations
of relations between variables taking their values in dense domains : there is no
need for X to be a natural number in the DD pictured Fig. 3. It could be a real
variable as well.

Waltz Filtering In order to solve systems of linear equations, we use the classical implicit enumeration/propagation technique (see [Hen89]). Note that solving a system means here computing a DD that encodes all the solutions of the system.

The principle is thus to enumerate variables domains in the order of their indices, and to build the DD in a bottom-up way. The propagation we adopt – the Waltz's filtering – consists in maintaining, for each variable a minimum and maximum value. Each time a variable domain is modified, this modification is propagated until a fixpoint is reached.

Note that the compacted representation of DDs shown above is well adapted to this kind of propagation.

4.3   Comparison between DDs, binary DDs and BDDs

In section 3, we saw that Toupie is faster than BDDs based implementation to compute properties of the Milner's scheduler. The following results precise the comparison between DDs, binary DDs and BDDs.

Pigeon-Hole Since we do not have at our disposal a BDDs based μ-calculus interpreter, we compare these representations on a very classical artificial intelligence puzzle : the Pigeon-Hole problem. The problem is to put M pigeons in N holes in such way that there is at most one pigeon per hole.

The following tables give running times obtained with :

1. Toupie using N-ary DDs, the outedges being labeled with constants.
2. Toupie using N-ary DDs, the outedges being labeled with ranges.
3. Toupie using binary DDs. In order to encode that a variable takes its value in a domains of size N, one uses $\lceil log_2(N) \rceil$ Boolean variables. These variables being ordered consecutively.
4. Same as 3, but with an interleaved order on variables.
5. Toupie using binary DDs. In order to encode that a variable takes its value in a domains of size N, one uses N Boolean variables. These variables being ordered consecutively.
6. Same as 3, using the BDD package Aulne [Rau94a]. Aulne is implemented following the Bryant's paper [BRB90] which makes it a good comparison tool.
7. The constraint logic language CHIP [Hen89] using finite domain constraints[1].

We first consider instances with N pigeons and N holes ($N!$ solutions).

N	5	6	7	8	9	10	11	12	13	14	15
1	0s05	0s10	0s18	0s43	1s03	2s56	6s56	16s91	46s00	127s35	336s00
2	0s08	0s11	0s26	0s65	1s63	4s21	10s65	27s16	69s45	174s58	449s15
3	0s11	0s23	0s53	1s53	6s51	29s40	114s28	?	?	?	?
4	0s11	0s20	1s13	2s16	38s58	265s83	?	?	?	?	?
5	0s25	0s91	5s16	41s25	325s98	?	?	?	?	?	?
6	0s05	0s11	0s25	0s63	2s18	5s80	15s11	39s28	102s33	279s03	?
7					82s96	848s80	?	?	?		

---

[1] Daniel Diaz communicated us these times, we would like to thanks him here

Now, instances with $N + 1$ pigeons and N holes (no solution).

N	5	6	7	8	9	10	11	12	13	14
1	0s06	0s11	0s25	0s51	1s21	2s98	7s56	20s25	50s58	138s50
2	0s08	0s16	0s35	0s80	1s98	4s96	12s33	32s15	78s93	197s60
3	0s11	0s21	0s50	1s51	6s56	29s40	111s55	?	?	?
4	0s15	0s28	1s33	2s70	39s98	?	?	?	?	?
5	0s28	1s28	7s95	61s86	467s56	?	?	?	?	?
6	0s06	0s25	0s31	0s75	2s61	6s76	17s38	44s00	115s46	?
7					92s80	?	?	?	?	?

As one can see on the tables above, DDs are slightly more efficient than BDDs one the Pigeon-Hole problem. We must precise here that the Aulne package is far more optimized than Toupie. It appears clearly when comparing binary DDs with BDDs. The next version of Toupie should be better from this point of view.

The compacted representation has no interest on this example. However, it is not too bad too.

The logarithmic coding of finite domains is more efficient than the linear one. Notice that is not true for methods such as the Davis and Putnam's procedure.

Finally, DDs give better results than enumerative methods on this problem as shown by the comparison with CHIP running times.

4.4 Advantages of the Compacted Representation

The compacted representation could be far more efficient than the standard one. The following example, coming from data base literature, gives an illustration.

Cousins The problem is to compute the relation "cousin" in a complete binary tree of height H (two vertices are cousins if they are at the same deep in the tree).

```
set domain 1..31
set addressing compacted

father(P,F) += ((F=2*P) | (F=2*P+1))

cousin(C1@3,C2@4) += (
    exist P@1 (father(P,C1) & father(P,C2))
  | exist P1@1, P2@2 (father(P1,C1) & father(P2,C2) & cousin(P1,P2))
  )
```

The following table gives the running times following the same numbering than previously.

H	5	6	7	8	9	10
1	0s65	4s10	28s58	219s06	?	?
2	0s10	0s35	1s28	5s38	27s86	173s26
3	0s20	0s53	1s91	9s86	105s31	?

5 Comparison with the μ-calculus

This section is devoted to a comparison between the computational model of Toupie and the μ-calculus from which it is derived.

One must first point out that there exist several different presentations of the μ-calculus in the literature. This formalism allows the expression of state properties of automata. The differences between the presentations stand mainly in the type of the considered automata. The key point being to know whether transitions are labeled or not. Authors working with labeled transitions add to the formalism connectives allowing to characterize transition labels and coming typically from the Henessy & Milner's logic [HM85].

Toupie is closer to the Park's original presentation [Par70] (used for instance in the already cited paper [BCM+90]). We prefer this version because it is as expressive as the former but does not impose interpretations in terms of automata and thus is far more versatile. This version is as follows.

We assume we are given a finite signature $\mathcal{S}$. Each symbol of $\mathcal{S}$ is either an *individual variable* or a *predicate variable* with some positive arity. There are two syntactic categories: *formulae* and *relational terms*. Formulae have the following form:

- The Boolean constants **True** and **False**.
- $[X_1 = X_2]$, where X_1 and X_2 are individual variables in $\mathcal{S}$
- $\neg f$, $f \vee g$, $\exists X[f]$, where f and g are formulae and X is an individual variable in $\mathcal{S}$.
- $\Gamma(X_1, X_2, \ldots, X_n)$, where Γ is an n-ary relational term and $X_1, X_2, \ldots, X_n$ are individual variables in $\mathcal{S}$ not free in Γ.

The syntax for the n-ary relational terms is given below:

- p, where p is an n-ary predicate variable in $\mathcal{S}$.
- $\lambda X_1, X_2, \ldots, X_n[f]$, where f is a formula and $X_1, X_2, \ldots, X_n$ are distinct individual variables in $\mathcal{S}$.
- $\mu p[\Gamma]$, where p is an n-ary predicate variable in $\mathcal{S}$ and Γ is an n-ary relational term that is formally monotone in p.

$\forall$, $\wedge$, $\Longrightarrow$ ...are treated as abbreviations in the usual manner. The term $\nu p[\Gamma]$ is introduced as an abbreviation for $\neg\mu p[\neg\Gamma\langle p \leftarrow \neg p\rangle]$, where $\Gamma\langle p \leftarrow \neg p\rangle$ denotes the relation term formed from Γ by substituting $\neg p$ for p.

The semantics is the attended one, that is essentially the same than the Toupie semantics presented 2.

Toupie is different from this theoretical formalism for the following reasons.
- Atoms of the propositional μ-calculus are in the form $[X = Y]$, where X and Y are individual variables. If individual variables are interpreted in a finite domain, there is no substantial difference with Toupie. In general, the authors consider only individual variables belonging to $\{0, 1\}$. The extension to finite domain variables improves the efficiency, especially when dealing with arithmetical constraints (of course, it does not provide any improvement for what concerns expressiveness). Infinite interpretation domains would raise some effectiveness problems ...

– The μ-calculus does not allow to name relations and thus it does not consider systems of fixpoint equations. However, this extension is easy and useful.

– The μ-calculus allow nested fixpoint definitions as Toupie does not. This restriction is not so important than it firstly seems.

In the literature, nested fixpoint definitions are used mainly to express infinite path properties. This is achieved by means of a $\nu\mu$ term, i.e. a greatest fixpoint of a least fixpoint.

However, a hierarchy of fixpoint definitions suffices to obtain this kind of characterization. This comes from a difficult result by Arnold and Niwiński about the relationship between sets of infinite binary trees characterizable by means of hierarchical fixpoint definitions and those weakly definable in monadic second order logic [AN92]. Moreover, we don't know natural properties requiring more than two nested fixpoints.

Example 2. [Infinite paths]

Let us consider the automaton pictured Fig.4, and let us characterize states that are source of paths going infinitely often through odd states.

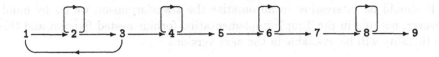

Fig. 4. An automaton

In the classical μ-calculus, this could be achieved by means of following term (we use Toupie notation).

```
let vertex = domain 1..9

g(S:vertex,T:vertex) += /* description of the automaton */

odd(S:vertex) += exist N:0..4 {S=2*N+1}

tau(U:vertex) -=
   let aux(V:vertex) += (    /* local definition */
         exist W:vertex (g(V,W) & aux(W))
       | exist W:vertex (g(V,W) & odd(W) & tau(W))
       )
   in  aux(U)                /* body of the definition */
```

The idea of this definition is to compute the set of predecessors of even states, then to intersect this set with the set of even states, then to restart the computation of predecessors from this last set and so on. The remaining states are those belonging to a loop going through at least an even state.

The same result can be obtained for instance by computing the transitive closure of the automaton, then the subset `inloop` of even states that are both successors and predecessors of an even state, and finally predecessors of `inloop` states.

```
path(S:vertex,T:vertex) += (
    g(S,T)
    | exist U:vertex (g(S,U) & path(U,T))
    )
inloop(V:vertex) += (
    odd(V)
    & exist W:vertex (odd(W) & path(V,W) & path(W,V))
    )
tau(V:vertex) += (
    inloop(V)
    | exist W:vertex (g(V,W) & tau(W))
    )
```

The reader could easily verify that this computation gives the same result than the previous one. However, this surely not the best way to proceed because the computation of the transitive closure could be costly.

It should be interesting to automatize the transformation we do by hand. However, nothing in the Toupie implementation forbids nested fixpoint and this functionality will be available in the next versions [2].

6 Conclusion

Experiments with Toupie [CGR93, CCMR93, BR94] show that μ-calculus over finite domains has a great expressive power and that this expressiveness is coupled with a good practical efficiency thanks to the use of Decision Diagrams.

Nevertheless, Toupie can be improved is several ways : DD management, introduction of arithmetic builtins, heuristics for variable indexing, ...

A very interesting way to extend Toupie is to handle constraints over dense domains (real or rational). The union of two relations being approximated, as proposed by Halbwachs [Hal93], by computing the convex hull of the union of each relation.

References

[AN92]   A. Arnold and D. Niwiński. Fixed point characterization of weak monadic second order logic definable sets of trees. In M. Nivat and A. Podelski, editors, *Tree Automata and Languages.* Elsevier Science Publishers, 1992.

[BCM+90] J.R. Burch, E.M. Clarke, K.L. McMillan, D.L. Dill, and L.J. Hwang. Symbolic Model Checking: 10^{20} States and Beyond. *IEEE transactions on computers*, 1990.

---

[2] The version 0.26 of Toupie actually incorporates such a possibility

[Bou93]   A. Bouali. *Etudes et mises en œuvre d'outils de vérification basée sur la bisimulation*. PhD thesis, Université Paris VII, 03 1993. in french.

[BR94]   S. Brlek and A. Rauzy. Synchronization of Constrained Transition Systems. In *Proceedings of the First International Symposium on Parallel Symbolic Computation (PASCO'94)*, Linz, Ostreich, 1994. World Scientific Publishing.

[BRB90]   K. Brace, R. Rudell, and R. Bryant. Efficient Implementation of a BDD Package. In *Proceedings of the 27th ACM/IEEE Design Automation Conference*. IEEE 0738, 1990.

[Bry86]   R. Bryant. Graph Based Algorithms for Boolean Fonction Manipulation. *IEEE Transactions on Computers*, 35:677–691, 8 1986.

[CBM89]   O. Coudert, C. Berthet, and J-C. Madre. Verification of Synchronous Sequential Machines Based on Symbolic Execution. In J. Sifakis, editor, *Automatic Verification Methods for Finite State Systems*, volume 407. LNCS, 1989.

[CCMR93]   M-M. Corsini, B. Le Charlier, K. Musumbu, and A. Rauzy. Efficient Abstract Interpretation of Prolog Programs by means of Constraint Solving over Finite Domains (extended abstract). In *Proceedings of the 5th Int. Symposium on Programming Language Implementation and Logic Programming, PLILP'93*, Estonie, 1993.

[CGR93]   M-M. Corsini, A. Griffault, and A. Rauzy. Yet another Application for Toupie: Verification of Mutual Exclusion Algorithms. In *proceedings of Logic Programming and Automated Reasonning, LPAR'93*, volume 698. LNAI, 1993.

[EFT93]   R. Enders, T. Filkorn, and D. Taubner. Generating BDDs for Symbolic Model Checking in CCS. *Journal of Distributed Computing*, 6:155–164, 6 1993.

[Hal93]   N. Halbwachs. Delay Analysis in Synchronous Programs. In *in Proceedings of the 5th international conference on Computer Aided Verification CAV'93*, volume 697 of *LNCS*. Springer Verlag, June 1993.

[Hen89]   P. Van Hentenryck. *Constraint Satisfaction in Logic Programming*. Logic Programming Series. MIT Press, 1989.

[HM85]   M. Henessy and R. Milner. Algebraic laws for non-determinism and concurrency. *J. Assoc. Comput. Mach.*, 32:137–161, 1985.

[Mil89]   R. Milner. *Communication and Concurrency*. Prentice Hall, New York, 1989.

[Par70]   D. Park. Fixpoint Induction and Proofs of Program Properties. *Machine Intelligence*, 5, 1970.

[Rau94a]   A. Rauzy. Aulne Version 0.2 : User's Guide. Technical Report ??, LaBRI – URA CNRS 1304 – Université Bordeaux I, 1994.

[Rau94b]   A. Rauzy. Toupie Version 0.25 : User's Manual. Technical Report 959-94, LaBRI – URA CNRS 1304 – Université Bordeaux I, 1994.

Imagining CLP($\Lambda, \equiv_{\alpha\beta}$)

Olivier Ridoux

IRISA, Campus Universitaire de Beaulieu, 35042 RENNES Cedex, FRANCE
ridoux@irisa.fr

Abstract. We study under which conditions the domain of λ-terms (Λ) and the equality theory of the λ-calculus ($\equiv_{\alpha\beta}$) form the basis of a usable constraint logic programming language (CLP). The conditions are that the equality theory must contain axiom η, and the formula language must depart from Horn clauses and accept universal quantifications and implications in goals. In short, CLP($\Lambda, \equiv_{\alpha\beta}$) must be close to λProlog.

1 Introduction

Logic programming is a programming paradigm in which programs are logical formulas, and executing them amounts to search for a proof. The most famous practical incarnation of logic programming is Prolog, which is based on Horn formulas [30].

The formalism of Horn programs is computationally complete [1, 48], but one has often tried to augment it to gain more flexibility and expressivity. One of these attempts is the paradigm of constraint logic programming [11, 27, 10, 49]. It amounts to replacing unification of first-order terms, considered as a procedure for solving equations on first-order terms, by other procedures for solving a wider range of problems (equations but also inequations and disequations, etc) on a wider range of domains: booleans, finite domains, integers, rationals, reals, etc. An important point is that the constraint handler searchs for satisfiability of the constraints, but not necessarily for solutions. This extension preserves the model-theoretic results of Prolog. It adds flexibility because, computation on some domains must be done in a directional way in Prolog, though it can be done fully relationally when considered a constraint, For instance in Prolog, *13 is X+12*, where variable X is not bound at execution time, is a mistake, though its equational counterpart, *13 = X+12*, makes perfect sense, and is solved by substituting 1 to X. The extension also add efficiency because searching for satisfiability instead of searching for solutions saves non-determinism.

The general scheme for constraint logic programming is noted CLP, instances of which can be formed by passing domains and theories to the scheme. In this work, we study CLP($\Lambda, \equiv_{\alpha\beta}$) which is an instance of CLP where the domain is of λ-terms (Λ) and the theory is $\alpha\beta$-equivalence ($\equiv_{\alpha\beta}$).

The study of the general scheme has focused on what properties the domains and theories must satisfy for some model-theoretic results to hold. Much less is said on the *usability* of the solutions of the constraints. By usability we mean the ability to be used by the program itself that generated the constraints in order to analyse the result, take further decisions, build new constraint etc. Usability is in fact a meta-programming capability. Little is said of usability probably for two reasons:

1. it is just natural for numerical or finite domains, for which operations exist in any reasonable instance of Prolog,

2. most examples in the literature, and many reported applications, obey a query-answer scheme in which a CLP program builds a constraints system for solving some problem, pass it to the solver, and reports the solutions to some operator.

Incorporating λ-terms in Prolog stimulates the study of the notion of usability because the condition above are no longer true:

1. it is not just natural since Prolog offers no operation to access λ-terms,
2. and the motivation for incorporating λ-terms is to represent programs or formulas which we want to manipulate in Prolog and not only display to the operator.

We motivate adding λ-terms in Prolog in section 2. Then, we give a proof-theoretic account of Horn clause programming in section 3. We study the consequences of adding λ-terms and $\alpha\beta$-equivalence in Prolog in section 4. Finally, we conclude in section 5. We assume everywhere a basic knowledge of Prolog.

2 Motivations

We give a brief account of the syntax of λ-terms and of the theory of λ-calculus. Then we explain to what purpose λ-terms can be used in Logic Programming.

2.1 The λ-Terms

λ-Terms are generated by the following grammar:

$$\Lambda \quad ::= \quad \mathcal{C} \mid \mathcal{V}$$
$$\Lambda \quad ::= \quad \lambda\mathcal{V} \, (\, \Lambda \,) \tag{i}$$
$$\Lambda \quad ::= \quad (\, \Lambda \, \Lambda \,) \tag{ii}$$

where the $\mathcal{C}$ and $\mathcal{V}$ are respectively identifiers of constants and identifiers of variables. Rule (i) generates *abstractions*, and rule (ii) generates *applications*. An abstraction can be interpreted as a function, and an application can be interpreted as the result of applying some function to some actual parameter. For instance, the identity function is written $\lambda x(x)$. We assume application associates to the left, which makes some brackets useless: for instance, *(append A B C)* denotes the same term as *(((append A) B) C)* does. Similarly we drop nested brackets or brackets in nested abstractions: for instance, $\lambda x \lambda y(x\ y)$ denotes the same term as $\lambda x(\lambda y((x\ y)))$ does.

Abstraction leads to the notions of *heading*, *head*, and *body*. In term $\lambda a \lambda b \lambda c(b\ a\ c)$, the heading is $\lambda a \lambda b \lambda c$, the head is b, and the body is *(b a c)*. One says a term *binds* the variables of its heading.

One distinguishes between *free* and *bound* occurrences of variables. In the term $(x\ y\ \lambda z \lambda x(x\ y\ z))$, y has only free occurrences, the only occurrence of z is bound, and x has a free occurrence (the first) and a bound one (the second). In the underlined subterm, z and y have only free occurrences, and the only occurrence of x is bound. More generally, an occurrence of some variable is bound in a given term if it is a subterm of an abstraction that binds the variable and is a subterm of the given term. An occurrence of some variable is free if it is not bound. One calls *free variables* of a given term the variables that have a free occurrence in it, *bound variables* those that have a bound occurrence in the term. One writes $\mathcal{F}V(t)$ the *free variables* of t, and $\mathcal{B}V(t)$ the *bound variables*. A term without any free variable is called *closed* or a *combinator*. One writes $[x \leftarrow y]$ the operation of replacing all free occurrences of x by y, and $E[x \leftarrow y]$ the application of this operation to term E.

2.2 A Taste of λ-Calculus

The domain of λ-terms is endowed with an equivalence relation which is defined as the smallest congruence based on the following axioms:

α — $\lambda x(E) \equiv_\alpha \lambda y(E[x \leftarrow y])$, if y has no occurrence in E.
   This axiom formalizes the renaming of bound variables. For instance, $\lambda x(f\ x) \equiv_\alpha \lambda y(f\ y)$, but $\lambda x(g\ x\ y) \not\equiv_\alpha \lambda y(g\ y\ y)$.
β — $(\lambda x(E)\ F) \equiv_\beta E[x \leftarrow F]$, if $\mathcal{F}V(F) \cap \mathcal{B}V(E) = \emptyset$.
   This axiom formalizes the evaluation of an application by substituting an actual parameter, F, to a formal parameter, x. For instance, $(\lambda x(f\ x)\ 12) \equiv_\beta (f\ 12)$, but $(\lambda x \lambda y(x)\ y) \not\equiv_\beta \lambda y(y)$ because $y \in \mathcal{F}V(y) \cap \mathcal{B}V(\lambda x \lambda y(x))$. However, $(\lambda x \lambda y(x)\ y) \equiv_\alpha (\lambda x \lambda w(x)\ y) \equiv_\beta \lambda w(y)$. In fact, it is always possible to apply axiom β to a term like $(\lambda x(E)\ F)$ if one uses axiom α for renaming the bound variables of E.
η — $\lambda x(E\ x) \equiv_\eta E$, if $x \notin \mathcal{F}V(E)$.
   This axiom formalizes the principle of *functional extensionality*: "Different functions yield different results". According to this principle, we have $[\forall x(E\ x){=}(F\ x)] \Rightarrow E{=}F$, which is not provable using axioms α and β alone. For instance, $\lambda x(f\ x) \equiv_\eta f$, but $\lambda x((g\ x)\ x) \not\equiv_\eta (g\ x)$. Note that axiom α can never help applying axiom η.

Axioms α and β are always present in the λ-calculus, but axiom η is optional: it gives nothing as far as the computational properties of the λ-calculus are concerned. However, we will see it is crucial for the equality theory.

   Application $(\lambda x(E)\ F)$ is called a β-redex. Abstraction $\lambda x(E\ x)$ where variable x is not free in E is called an η-redex. A λ-term with no β-redex (resp. η-redex) is called β-normal (resp. η-normal). The axioms may be oriented to form *rewriting rules*. To apply β-equivalence for suppressing a β-redex is to β-reduce a term. To apply η-equivalence for suppressing a η-redex is to η-reduce a term.

   A given term may be applied different reduction rules simply because it contains several redexes. One may wonder whether the reduction order is significant or not. In fact, it is not. This system of reduction rules (with or without η-reduction) enjoys the Church-Rosser property: *"For every two β-equivalent terms A and B, there is a term N to which A and B reduce in some number of steps"*. Hence, every term has at most one normal form. If every term has a normal form, and any arbitrary strategy finds it, we say the calculus enjoys the *strong normalisation property*.

   Some terms have no normal form: e.g. term $\Omega = (\lambda x(x\ x)\ \lambda x(x\ x))$ is not in β-normal form, but it only β-reduces to itself. Some terms with a normal form have non-terminating sequences of reductions: e.g. term $(\lambda x \lambda y(x)\ \lambda x(x)\ \Omega)$ β-reduces to $\lambda x(x)$ (a normal form) by its first redex, and it β-reduces to itself by the redex in Ω. Repeating the second reduction produces a non-terminating sequence of reductions.

2.3 λ-Terms and Logic Programming

The motivation to manipulate λ-terms in logic programming is simple: they are the most natural representation for structures that feature either scoping, compositionality, or some form of genericity [32].

Scoping, compositionality and genericity are not exclusive. Among the structures that feature scoping, we see logical and mathematical formulas (logical quantifications: $\forall u, \ldots$; sums and products: $\sum_{x \in X} x$, $\int_0^1 f(x).dx, \ldots$; derivations: $d/dx, \ldots$), and computer programs (parameterisation: $f(x)$ int $x;$ { $\ldots$ } $, \ldots$; blocks: { int $x;$ $\ldots$ } $, \ldots$). Among those that feature compositionality, we see expressions of compositional semantics (denotational: $T_g[\![B_1, B_2]\!] = \lambda \kappa (T_g[\![B_1]\!] \ (T_g[\![B_2]\!] \ \kappa))$ [8], $\ldots$; Montague semantics for natural language [12]). Finally, logical quantifications in automated demonstration feature a form of genericity: one instantiates them using substitutions for building proofs.

The following table pictures some possible representations using λ-terms.

$\forall u.P(u)$	*forall $\lambda u(P\ u)$*
$\int_0^1 f(x).dx$	*integral 0 1 $\lambda x(f\ x)$*
df/dx	*derivative $\lambda x(f\ x)$*
$f(x)$ int $x;$ { $\ldots$ }	*function f int $\lambda x(\ldots)$*
{ int $x;$ $\ldots$ }	*block int $\lambda x(\ldots)$*
$T_g[\![B_1, B_2]\!] = \lambda \kappa (T_g[\![B_1]\!] \ (T_g[\![B_2]\!] \ \kappa))$	*t_g (B1 and B2) $\lambda k(D1\ (D2\ k))$:-*
	t_g B1 D1, t_g B2 D2

Scoping introduces the notion of *scoped variable* or *parameter*. The key operation for composing structures is the *substitution* of a term to a parameter; it must be sound with respect to scoping. Axiom β models such a substitution. This is why λ-terms are well suited for representing these structures: abstraction serves as a generic quantification. All these structures can be represented with first-order terms, but the correct handling of substitution with respect to scoping needs a lot of attention. The most frequent solution is to represent the parameters (the *object-level variables*) with Prolog variables (the *metavariables*). There are numerous examples of this solution in text-books. They can be found in chapters dedicated to the manipulation of programs and formulas.

We take as an example the following clause from program 16.2 (page 259) in *The Art of Prolog* by Sterling and Shapiro [47][1].

> *translate((A,B), (A1,B1), Xs\Ys) :-*
> *translate(A, A1, Xs\Xs1) , translate(B, B1, Xs1\Ys) .*

This clause is part of a program for translating grammar rules into Prolog. Every clause of predicate *translate* has the same structure. The first parameter is a component of some grammar rule, the second is the corresponding component in the target Prolog clause, and the last one is a pair of variables that must occur in the target Prolog clause. So, these two variables are object-level variables. The problem

---

[1] This is an almost verbatim copy of the clause. The only modification is for avoiding a clash with notations used in this article. In the original text, ':-' is noted ←.

is that it is no longer possible to give a declarative reading to this clause because the object-level variables are represented directly with metavariables. The declarative reading of Prolog does not spell out the actual rôle of *Xs*, *Xs1* and *Ys*. They are variables of the target clause, and it makes no sense to consider instances of them as the declarative semantics of Prolog does. It works in Prolog because the interpreter always computes the most general solutions. So, it is the operational semantics that gives the meaning of this clause, instead of the declarative semantics.

In the same book, clause *derivative(X,X,s(0))* (program 3.29, page 63) is part of a program that computes the derivative with respect to X of a function. One of its logical consequences is *derivative(12,12,s(0))*, which is absurd. Clause *polynomial(X,X)* (program 3.28, page 62) is a part of the definition of what a polynomial in X is. It has also absurd logical consequences like *polynomial(12,12)*.

In Prolog, substitution of object-level variables is easy at the price of declarativity. Then, it forces the programmer to check the correctness of object-level terms manipulations with respect to the operational semantics.

Instead of the above clauses, we would like to write the following ones[2]:

> *derivative($\lambda x(x)$, s(0)) .*
> *polynomial($\lambda x(x)$) .*
> *translate((A,B), $\lambda xs\lambda ys$(exists $\lambda xs1$(A1 xs xs1, B1 xs1 ys))) :-*
> *   translate(A, A1) , translate(B, B1) .*
> *exists G :- (G _) .*

λ-Terms permits a coherent and declarative handling of scopes and substitutions.

3 Sequent Proof Theory for Horn Clauses

We present a language of clauses and goals that encompasses the language of Horn clauses. It is a convenient basis for the extensions described in the sequel. Indeed, it stresses a fundamental asymmetry in the language of Horn Clauses that the extensions will eliminate.

Clauses and goals are generated by the following grammar:

$$\mathcal{D} \quad ::= \mathcal{A} \mid \mathcal{A} \Rightarrow \mathcal{D} \mid \forall \mathcal{V}_t \, \mathcal{D} \mid \mathcal{D} \land \mathcal{D} \qquad \text{(iii)}$$
$$\mathcal{G} \quad ::= \mathcal{A} \qquad \text{(iv)}$$

Rules (iii) and (iv) generate *clauses* and *goals*, respectively.

The semantics of the connectives is given by the following deduction rules of the intuitionistic sequent calculus[3].

$$\frac{P, D[x \leftarrow t] \vdash G}{P, \forall x D \vdash G} \qquad \forall_{\mathcal{D}} \qquad \qquad t \text{ is an arbitrary term.}$$

---

[2] It is not only the matter of these clauses, the predicates they belong to must be rewritten entirely along the same scheme.

[3] A sequent $P \vdash G$ reads "goal G is a consequence of program P". A rule $\frac{Sequent^*}{Sequent}$ reads "conclusion *Sequent* is true if all premises *Sequent** are true".

$$\frac{P, D_1, D_2 \vdash G}{P, D_1 \wedge D_2 \vdash G} \qquad \wedge_{\mathcal{D}}$$

$$\frac{P, D \vdash G \qquad P \vdash A}{P, A \Rightarrow D \vdash G} \qquad \Rightarrow_{\mathcal{D}}$$

All these rules are left introduction rules; their connective of interest is in the left part of the conclusion sequent.

To show that this language encompasses Horn formulas, we observe that the right introduction rules of more connectives can be defined by second-order clauses[4]:

$$((\; G_1 \wedge_{\mathcal{G}} \; G_2 \;) \Leftarrow_{\mathcal{D}} G_1) \Leftarrow_{\mathcal{D}} G_2$$
$$(\; (G_1 \vee_{\mathcal{G}} \; G_2 \;) \Leftarrow_{\mathcal{D}} G_1 \;) \wedge_{\mathcal{D}} (\; (G_1 \vee_{\mathcal{G}} \; G_2 \;) \Leftarrow_{\mathcal{D}} G_2 \;)$$

Thus, we can include conjunctions and disjunctions in goals. Using them allows us to restrict the use of implication for building clauses. Furthermore, we adopt the convention that all conjunctions in clauses are pushed to the top of the $\mathcal{D}$-formulas, and that all universal quantifications are pushed right underneath (clausal form). So, we see that Horn formulas can serve as a concrete syntax for our language.

Because of the clausal form, conjunctions and universal quantifications in clauses need no more be noted explicitly because they can be reconstructed if required. So, the concrete syntax is as follows:

$$
\begin{array}{llll}
\mathcal{P} & ::= \mathcal{D} & | \; \mathcal{D} \cdot \mathcal{P} & \text{(v)} \\
\mathcal{D} & ::= A & | \; A :- \mathcal{G} & \text{(vi)} \\
\mathcal{G} & ::= A & | \; \mathcal{G}, \mathcal{G} \; | \; \mathcal{G}; \mathcal{G} & \text{(vii)}
\end{array}
$$

Rules (v), (vi) and (vii) generates *programs*, *clauses*, and *goals*, respectively. A program is a sequence of input units, all terminated by a full-stop, '.'. Input units are clauses, and every variable that is free in an input unit is considered as universally quantified at the clause level. We call these variables *logical variables* or *unknowns*.

In rule (vi), terminal ':-' is the concrete writings for connective $\Leftarrow_{\mathcal{D}}$. Connective $\forall_{\mathcal{D}}$ has no concrete notation because it is implicit. In rule (vii), terminals ',' and ';' are the concrete writings for connectives $\wedge_{\mathcal{G}}$ and $\vee_{\mathcal{G}}$.

4 Adding λ-Terms and $\alpha\beta$-Equivalence

To add λ-terms to Prolog is still a fuzzy objective; one must decide the circumstances. A first observation is that there is no use for adding λ-terms without $\alpha\beta$-equivalence. Indeed, it is $\alpha\beta$-equivalence that allows us to substitute terms to variables with respect to scoping. So, system $CLP(\Lambda,=)$ where '=' denotes Prolog's equality, or even $CLP(\Lambda,\equiv_\alpha)$ without β-equivalence, are useless.

4.1 Typing

In order to add λ-terms and $\alpha\beta$-equivalence to Prolog, one must also add the handling of axioms α and β to unification. One wants also to be sure that there is always

---

[4] Occurrences of connective X in syntactic units of type $\mathcal{Y}$ ($\mathcal{D}$ or $\mathcal{G}$) are noted $X_{\mathcal{Y}}$.

a normal form to λ-terms, and that it can be found by any reduction strategy: the strong normalization property.

The domain of simply typed λ-terms has a (almost) well-behaved unification problem, and it is strongly normalizable. The unification problem for simply typed λ-terms modulo axioms α and β is semi-decidable and infinitary[5]. For instance, the unification problem $\lambda z(N \, \lambda x(x) \, z) = \lambda z(z)$ has an infinite number of solutions in N: $\theta_0 = [N \leftarrow \lambda s \lambda z(z)]$, $\theta_1 = [N \leftarrow \lambda s \lambda z(s \, z)]$, $\theta_2 = [N \leftarrow \lambda s \lambda z(s \, (s \, z))]$, $\theta_i = [N \leftarrow \lambda s \lambda z(s^i \, z)]$, etc. Term $\lambda s \lambda z(s^i \, z)$ is the Church encoding of integer i.

In practice, one uses the semi-algorithm proposed by Huet [25]. The unification problem for simply typed terms is roughly the same whether axiom η is assumed or not. In fact Huet's semi-algorithm searchs for pre-unifiers: i.e. substitutions that make the problem trivially solvable, but that are not necessarilly solutions.

Other, more sophisticated, typed domains exist that have also the strong normalization property and a practical unification problem [17, 16, 44, 43, 42].

Simple Types The new term language is the language of the simply typed λ-terms.

Simple types are generated by the following grammar:

$$
\begin{aligned}
T \quad &::= \mathcal{U} \quad | \quad (\, \mathcal{K}_i \, T^i \,) \\
T \quad &::= (\, T \, \text{->} \, T)
\end{aligned}
\tag{viii}
$$

where the $\mathcal{U}$ and $\mathcal{K}_i$ are identifiers of type variables and type constructors with arity i, respectively. Rule (viii) generates function types. A type $(A\text{->}B)$ can be interpreted as the type of functions whose domain is A and co-domain is B. We assume $\mathcal{K}_0$ contains at least the constant 'o' for propositional types. We also assume the arrow, ->, associates to the right. This makes many brackets useless: for instance, $o\text{->}o\text{->}o$ denotes the same type as $(o\text{->}(o\text{->}o))$ does.

We assume type constructors are declared using a directive *kind*: for instance,

kind o type .	$\% \, o \in \mathcal{K}_0$
kind list type -> type .	$\% \, list \in \mathcal{K}_1$

The declaration of *list* shows it is a type constructor that must be applied to some type to actually produce a type.

Typed Terms Simply typed λ-terms are generated by the following grammar:

$$
\begin{aligned}
\Lambda_t \quad &::= \mathcal{C}_t \quad | \quad \mathcal{V}_t & t \in T \\
\Lambda_{t'\text{->}t} &::= \lambda \mathcal{V}_{t'} \, (\, \Lambda_t \,) & t, t' \in T \\
\Lambda_t \quad &::= (\, \Lambda_{t'\text{->}t} \, \Lambda_{t'} \,) & t, t' \in T
\end{aligned}
$$

where the $\mathcal{C}_t$ and $\mathcal{V}_t$ are respectively identifiers of constants and identifiers of variables whose type is t. Attributes in terminal and non-terminal symbols are used to constrain types and to ensure the well-typing of generated terms.

Every term of the simply typed λ-calculus has a β-normal form. Because of the Church-Rosser property, it is unique. Moreover, it can be computed using any arbitrary strategy. Hence, the calculus has the strong normalisation property.

We assume the types of constants are declared using a directive *type*: for instance,

---

[5] There can be infinitely many most general unifiers.

type $[]$ (list T) . $\% \, \forall T \, ([] \in C_{(list\ T)})$
type '.' T -> (list T) -> (list T) . $\% \, \forall T \, ('.' \in C_{T->(list\ T)->(list\ T)})$
type append (list T) -> (list T) -> (list T) -> o .
                    $\% \, \forall T \, (append \in C_{(list\ T)->(list\ T)->(list\ T)->o})$

The type of $[]$ shows it is a non-functional constant. The type of '.' shows it is a function that takes two arguments. These two constants allows us to build *homogeneous* polymorphic lists: polymorphic lists all elements of which have the same type. Finally, the result type of *append*, '*o*', shows it is a predicate constant.

Typed Programs Having chosen a type discipline for the terms does not say everything on the type discipline of programs.

The first point is that we adopt the *prescriptive typing* point of view: the typing discipline defines a *well-typing* predicate, and not well-typed programs (*ill-typed* programs) are simply not considered as programs.

The usual principles of polymorphic typing are transposed to CLP(Λ, $\equiv_{\alpha\beta}$):

- *type* declarations act as a *let* in ML [39], it introduces a type scheme for some constant symbol,
- quantifications (including abstraction) act as an abstraction in ML,
- every occurrence of a constant symbol has a type that is an instance of the type scheme of that constant,
- and every occurrence of a variable has the same type.

The second point is that we adopt the *definitional genericity* principle: *"Every occurrence of a predicate constant in the head of a clause must have a type that is a renaming of its type scheme"*. In other words, the types at these occurrences cannot be just any instance of the type scheme; only renamings are allowed.

This principle is assumed in the work by Mycroft and O'Keefe [40], but not discussed. It appears under the name *head condition* in works by Hanus, and Hill and Lloyd [21, 22]. It also appears under the name *definitional genericity* in Lakshman and Reddy's work [29]. Hanus have shown it is a necessary condition for a *semantic soundness* theorem stating roughly that *"Well-typed programs cannot go wrong"*.

An example illustrates the effect of definitional genericity. Assuming the curried syntax for terms, the CLP(Λ, $\equiv_{\alpha\beta}$) writing for predicate *append* is as follows:

append $[] \, X \, X$.
append $[E\,|\,X] \, Y \, [E\,|\,Z]$:- append $X \, Y \, Z$.

This program is well-typed with respect to the type schemes given in section 4.1. However, the same program plus the clause

append $[0,1,2,3,4]$ $[5,6,7,8,9]$ $[0,1,2,3,4,5,6,7,8,9]$.

is ill-typed because it violates the head-condition. The occurrence of *append* in the above clause has a type, *(list int)->(list int)->(list int)->o*, that is a strict instance of the type scheme, not just a renaming.

We note CLP($\Lambda_{\rightarrow}$, $\equiv_{\alpha\beta}$) the instance of CLP in which the domain is of simply typed terms ($\Lambda_{\rightarrow}$), the equality theory is $\alpha\beta$-equivalence ($\equiv_{\alpha\beta}$), the programs are typed prescriptively, and the definitional genericity principle is adopted.

4.2 Adding $\alpha\beta$-Equivalence

We have seen that some terms of $\mathrm{CLP}(\Lambda_\to, \equiv_{\alpha\beta})$ (i.e. those with an arrow type) can be interpreted as functions. We have also seen that proofs in $\mathrm{CLP}(\Lambda_\to, \equiv_{\alpha\beta})$ are done modulo $\alpha\beta$-equivalence. So, it looks like if one can program in a functional style in $\mathrm{CLP}(\Lambda_\to, \equiv_{\alpha\beta})$, and that unification is able to discriminate applications from abstractions and to analyse their components. We will show that these are two misconceptions about the capabilities of λ-terms in $\mathrm{CLP}(\Lambda_\to, \equiv_{\alpha\beta})$.

Programming in a functional style in $\mathrm{CLP}(\Lambda_\to, \equiv_{\alpha\beta})$ One must recall that $\mathrm{CLP}(\Lambda_\to, \equiv_{\alpha\beta})$ terms are essentially simply typed λ-terms. As such, they have a computing power that is too weak for really serving as a programming language.

ML programs are also essentially made of simply typed λ-terms, but the language also offers a construction (i.e. *letrec*) that is interpreted by a fix-point combinator. That is what gives its computing power to ML.

What gives $\mathrm{CLP}(\Lambda_\to, \equiv_{\alpha\beta})$ its computer power (which is the same as for any reasonable programming language) is the structure of its clauses, but not its λ-terms. In other words, β-reduction in $\mathrm{CLP}(\Lambda_\to, \equiv_{\alpha\beta})$ is not really used for evaluating functions. It is mainly used for instantiating term schemes represented by λ-terms.

However, λ-terms allow us to functionally encode operations that are sufficiently simple. Since variables are allowed in types, but the quantifications of these variables are always prenex, the domain of $\mathrm{CLP}(\Lambda_\to, \equiv_{\alpha\beta})$ terms is essentially equivalent to ML^- (ML minus *letrec*). This domain allows us to program extended polynomial functions only [24]. For instance, one may encode concatenation as a λ-term, via a suitable encoding of lists as functional lists [9].

Discriminating applications from abstractions in $\mathrm{CLP}(\Lambda_\to, \equiv_{\alpha\beta})$ A λ-term can be a constant, a variable, an abstraction, or an application. We will show that it is impossible to discriminate abstractions from applications, and to access their components without using a specific programming discipline.

In $\mathrm{CLP}(\Lambda_\to, \equiv_{\alpha\beta})$ as in Prolog, the only means for discriminating terms and for accessing their subterms is unification. Hence, a naïve solution to recognize that a term is an application and to access its components is to unify it with the term $(T_1\ T_2)$ in order to bind its components to variables T_1 et T_2. In fact, it is much too naïve because term $(T_1\ T_2)$ is unifiable modulo $\alpha\beta$-equivalence with *any* term. For instance, terms 12, $(A\ B)$ and $\lambda x(x)$ are all unifiable with $(T_1\ T_2)$. All three problems have an infinite number of solutions, among which

- problem $12{=}(T_1\ T_2)$ has solution $[T_1{\leftarrow}\lambda x(12),\ T_2{\leftarrow}13]$,
- problem $(A\ B){=}(T_1\ T_2)$ has solution $[T_1{\leftarrow}\lambda x(x\ B),\ T_2{\leftarrow}A]$,
- and problem $\lambda x(x){=}(T_1\ T_2)$ has solution $[T_1{\leftarrow}\lambda x(x),\ T_2{\leftarrow}\lambda x(x)]$.

In the case of term $(A\ B)$, the solution that allows us to actually access A and B is lost among the infinitely many others without any means for distinguishing it. Hence, the property of being unifiable with an application does not discriminate applications from other terms, and unification does not allow us to access to the components of applications.

Similarly, a too naïve solution to recognize that a term is an abstraction and to access its component (the body) is to unify it with term $\lambda v(T)$ in order to bind the body of the abstraction to variable T. This does not work because term $\lambda v(T)$, which does indeed only unify with abstractions, does not unify with every abstraction. The problem is that the substitution theory that underlies higher-order unification forbids capturing λ-variables outside the abstraction that bind them; binding values of logical variables and parameters of goals must be closed terms.

However, by unifying an abstraction (say $\lambda x(x)$) with $\lambda v(T)$, and expecting that it will bind its body (here x) to T, we are precisely trying to capture a variable. In fact, the body of some abstraction can be substituted to variable T only if the body does not contain any free occurrence of the bound variable. The term $\lambda v(T)$ describes precisely those abstractions that represent constant functions. Hence, to be unifiable with $\lambda v(T)$ does distinguish only very particular abstractions.

One may compare these difficulties with well-known Prolog difficulties. The language of Prolog terms allows for variables in terms, but there is no means in pure Prolog for checking that a term is a variable. In fact, the semantics of Prolog actually uses a saturation of the term domain, the Herbrand universe, in which there is no room for variable terms. Similarly, the semantics of $\mathrm{CLP}(\Lambda_\to, \equiv_{\alpha\beta})$ uses $\alpha\beta$-equivalence, which leaves no room for the application/abstraction discrimination.

The problem has two sides: to discriminate applications from abstractions, and to access their components. The solution for the first side is to label with a constructor the applications and abstractions we want to recognize. For instance, the representation of ML terms in $\mathrm{CLP}(\Lambda_\to, \equiv_{\alpha\beta})$ can use the two following constructors:

kind mlt type .
type app (mlt->mlt) -> mlt -> mlt .
                                  % Application: write (app F X) instead of (F X)
type fun (mlt->mlt) -> mlt .
                              % Abstraction: write (fun $\lambda x(x+1)$) instead of $\lambda x(x+1)$

Using this technique, one can easily discriminate abstractions from applications. One can also access the components of some discriminated application. The problem of accessing the body of an abstraction is solved in the next section.

For the purpose of further examples, we declare kinds and types of constants for representing formulas of the first-order predicate calculus and terms of the simply typed λ-calculus. We need two types for representing the formulas of the first-order predicate calculus: a type for truth values, and a type for individuals. They are *object-level* truth values and individuals. They are represented by $\mathrm{CLP}(\Lambda_\to, \equiv_{\alpha\beta})$ λ-terms, but they must not be mistaken with $\mathrm{CLP}(\Lambda_\to, \equiv_{\alpha\beta})$ formulas or terms.

kind (formula, individual) type .

One also needs connectives for object-level formulas.

type (and, or, impl) formula -> formula -> formula .
type not formula -> formula .
type (forall, exists) (individual->formula) -> formula .
type (p, ...) individual -> individual -> formula .
type (q, ...) formula .

So, formula $\forall x(p(x,x) \Rightarrow q)$ is encoded by *(forall $\lambda x(impl\ (p\ x\ x)\ q))$*. The only constructors that are original with respect to Prolog are *forall* and *exists*. They have an argument that is an abstraction. Its rôle is to formalize the scope of object-level quantifications and to handle the fact that quantified variables are substitutable.

One also needs two types for representing the terms of the simply typed λ-calculus: a type for λ-terms and another for simple types. As for the representation of object-level formulas of the predicate calculus, they must not be mistaken for the metalevel λ-terms and types.

    kind (l_term, simple_type) type .

One needs constructors for representing object-level applications and abstractions, the arrow of object-level simple types, and constant object-level types and terms.

    type app l_term -> l_term -> l_term .
    type abs (l_term->l_term) -> l_term .
    type arrow simple_type -> simple_type -> simple_type .
    type (one, two, three, ...) l_term .
    type (integer, real, ...) simple_type .

The only constructor that is original with respect to Prolog is *abs*. Its argument is an abstraction of $\mathrm{CLP}(\Lambda_\rightarrow, \equiv_{\alpha\beta})$ whose rôle is to formalize the scope of the object-level abstraction and the fact that the bound variable is substitutable.

It is important to understand that the $\mathrm{CLP}(\Lambda_\rightarrow, \equiv_{\alpha\beta})$ abstraction in the representation does not model all the semantics of the object-level abstraction. For instance, *(app (abs E) F)* $\not\equiv_{\alpha\beta}$ *(E F)*. If such relation holds at the object level it must be described in $\mathrm{CLP}(\Lambda_\rightarrow, \equiv_{\alpha\beta})$ by a suitable predicate:

    type beta_conv l_term -> l_term -> o .
    beta_conv (app (abs E) F) (E F) .

In this clause, the metalevel β-reduction of *(E F)* performs the actual substitution of term F to the variable bound by *(abs E)*.

4.3 Axiom η

We have added simply typed λ-terms and $\alpha\beta$-equivalence to Prolog. Does this result in a usable logic programming language? The answer is no.

We have shown in section 4.2 that unification (even higher-order) alone does not allow us do discriminate abstractions from applications or to access their components. Having added simply typed λ-terms and $\alpha\beta$-equivalence to Prolog, we are able to build and compare them, but we cannot analyse them. In other words, we cannot perform an inductive traversal of the terms we are able to build.

The difficulty with abstractions comes from the fact that it is not possible to capture free λ-variables in bindings of logical variables.

The intuition of the solution is that to access the body of an abstraction A, the only means is to apply A to a term t and use term $A'=(A\ t)$. Knowing A' and t, one must be able to compute A by solving $A'=(X\ t)$ for an unknown X. So, the equality theory of the λ-terms and the term t must be such that given two distinct terms A and B, the terms $(A\ t)$ and $(B\ t)$ are also distinct. We call this condition the *conservation condition*. It ensures that accessing the body of an abstraction is a reversible operation.

To apply an abstraction to a term in order to access its body does not allow us to discriminate between η-equivalent terms (e.g. E and $\lambda x(E\ x)$). Indeed, $(\lambda x(E\ x)\ t) \equiv_{\alpha\beta} (E\ t)$ even if $\lambda x(E\ x) \not\equiv_{\alpha\beta} E$. Hence, the conservation condition implies η-equivalence.

So, $\mathrm{CLP}(\Lambda_{\to}, \equiv_{\alpha\beta})$ is not yet a usable logic programming system. We note $\mathrm{CLP}(\Lambda_{\to}, \equiv_{\alpha\beta\eta})$ the instance of CLP in which the domain is of simply typed terms ($\Lambda_{\to}$), and the equality theory is $\alpha\beta\eta$-equivalence ($\equiv_{\alpha\beta\eta}$).

4.4 Universal Quantification in Goals : $\forall_{\mathcal{G}}$

Discussion We have seen that we plan to analyse an abstraction A by applying it to some term t and analysing the result $A'=(A\ t)$.

If one wants to be able to compute A by solving $A'=(X\ t)$ for an unknown X, it must be that t is recognizable among the subterms of A'. As a counter-example, if $A=\lambda x(x+12)$ and $t=12$, we get $A'=(12+12)$. The equation $(12+12)=(X\ 12)$ has four solutions among which there is no formal reason to prefer one: $[X\leftarrow\lambda x(x+x)]$, $[X\leftarrow\lambda x(x+12)]$, $[X\leftarrow\lambda x(12+x)]$, and $[X\leftarrow\lambda x(12+12)]$. The four solutions correspond to four A's that are not $\alpha\beta\eta$-equivalent but still yield the same term $(A\ t)$ for $t=12$. The underlined solution is the one we informally prefer. We need some formal means to select this one.

One could object that it was really gross to choose $t=12$ when A already has 12 as a subterm. This objection does not hold for two reasons. First, because a term A can have unknown subterms, it is not always possible to check that a candidate t does not occur in A. Second, even when the term A is fully determined (ground), to choose a t that does not occur in it does not completely solve the problem. For instance, if $A=\lambda x(x+12)$ and $t=13$, we get $A'=(13+12)$. Equation $(13+12)=(X\ 13)$ has two solutions among which there is still no formal means for selecting one: $[X\leftarrow\lambda x(x+12)]$ and $[X\leftarrow\lambda x(13+12)]$. Again, two non-$\alpha\beta$-equivalent A's yield the same $(A\ t)$ for $t=13$. In fact, for any equation $(A\ t)=(X\ t)$ in X, and if t is an ordinary term, there are always at least solutions $[X\leftarrow\lambda x(A\ t)]$ and $[X\leftarrow A]$.

Something must prevent term t from occurring in A and in X. This will bar all the solutions that are not underlined. In other words, it will provides the formal means we want for preferring the underlined solutions. Universal quantification in goals, $\forall_{\mathcal{G}}$, is such a logical means for producing a recognizable term t. Its deduction rule is as follows:

$$\frac{P \vdash G[x \leftarrow c]}{P \vdash \forall x\ G} \quad \forall_{\mathcal{G}} \qquad\qquad c \text{ occurs free neither in } P \text{ nor in } G.$$

In order to be coherent with the distinction made between $\mathcal{G}$-formulas and $\mathcal{D}$-formulas one must restrict the universally quantified formulas to be $\mathcal{G}$-formulas. This restriction is compatible with our motivation for adding implication in goal.

The operational semantics of this new connective is as follows. To prove a goal $(\forall_{\mathcal{G}}\ v\ G)$, prove goal $G[v\leftarrow c]$, where c is a new constant which has the type of v, taking care that c does not occur in the binding values of older logical variables.

If t is universally quantified in the scope of the quantifications of A and X, then the only solution of equation $(A\ t)=(X\ t)$ is $[X{\leftarrow}A]$. The goal to prove has the following form: $\exists A\exists X\forall_G\, t(A\ t)=(X\ t)$. Because of η-equivalence, this goal is equivalent to $\exists A\exists X(A=X)$, which has the trivial solution $[X{\leftarrow}A]$ [6].

This shows a fundamental correspondence between abstraction and universal quantification. They cannot be considered independently. Informally speaking, abstraction is an essentially universal quantification operating at the term level. Abstraction is a storable/manipulable form of universal quantification, and universal quantification is the way for interpreting abstraction.

Application We apply the technique of using $\forall_G$ to the task of relating a first-order predicate calculus formula to its negative normal form.

A first-order predicate calculus formula is in negative normal form if the negation connective is only applied to atomic formulas. For instance, $(\neg A)\vee(\neg B)$ is in negative normal form, but $\neg(A\wedge B)$ is not. It is always possible to make a first-order predicate calculus formula into the negative normal form using De Morgan's identities.

We first declare the type of the relation.

  type nnf formula -> formula -> o .

Now we define relation *nnf* by structural induction on type *formula*. The cases for all the connectors are elementary and could be described in Prolog.

    nnf (and F1 F2) (and G1 G2) :- nnf F1 G1 , nnf F2 G2 .
    nnf (or F1 F2) (or G1 G2) :- nnf F1 G1 , nnf F2 G2 .
    nnf (not (and F1 F2)) (or G1 G2) :- nnf (not F1) G1 , nnf (not F2) G2 .
    nnf (not (or F1 F2)) (and G1 G2) :- nnf (not F1) G1 , nnf (not F2) G2 .
    nnf (p A B) (p A B) .
    nnf (not (p A B)) (not (p A B)) .   % nnf$_1$
    ...

The cases for quantifications is more interesting. One must continue the induction in the quantified formula. Then a universal quantification in goal is required. It introduces a universal constant of type *individual*, which is not the induction type. Then, augmenting the inductive definition for this new constant is not required.

    nnf (forall F) (forall G) :- ∀_G i(nnf (F i) (G i)) .
    nnf (exists F) (exists G) :- ∀_G i(nnf (F i) (G i)) .   % nnf$_2$
    nnf (not (forall F)) (exists G) :- ∀_G i(nnf (not (F i)) (G i)) .
    nnf (not (exists F)) (forall G) :- ∀_G i(nnf (not (F i)) (G i)) .   % nnf$_3$

A few observations are in order.

– The metalevel universal quantification has nothing to do with the semantics of object-level formulas. It has only to do with their structure. The two object-level quantifications, *exists* and *forall*, presumably respectively existential and universal, are both interpreted by a universal quantification.

---

[6] Other most general solutions exist, but they are renaming of this one.

– When we use predicate *nnf* for normalizing a formula, the universal quantification works both in analysing and in synthesising abstractions. Abstraction F is analysed and its body passed as a parameter to the recursive call to *nnf*. The second argument is unified with a term *(exists G)* or *(forall G)* where G is an unknown. The application of G to i is also passed as a parameter to the recursive call to *nnf*. The unknown G being quantified out of the scope of the i, it cannot have any occurrence of i in its binding values. Hence, it is bound to an abstraction that becomes more and more precise as long as formula F is traversed.

We present the processing of an actual proof for illustrating the last observation.

1. The question.
   (nnf (exists λx(not (exists λy(p x y)))) X)
2. Resolution with clause nnf_2 of *nnf* (page 13): *[X←(exists G)]*.
   $\forall_G$ *i(nnf (not (exists λy(p i y))) (G i))*
3. Rule $\forall_G$.
   (nnf (not (exists λy(p c y))) (G c))
4. Resolution with clause nnf_3 of *nnf*: *[G←λx(forall (H x)), G'←(H c)]* is the most general solution to *(G c)=(forall G')* [25].
   $\forall_G$ *i(nnf (not (p c i)) (H c i))*
5. Rule $\forall_G$.
   (nnf (not (p c c')) (H c c'))
6. Resolution with clause nnf_1 of *nnf*: *[H←λxλy(not (p x y))]*.
   Success
7. The solution is *[X←(exists λx(forall λy(not (p x y))))]*.

4.5   Implication in Goals : $\Rightarrow_G$

We have seen that the universal quantification allows us to interpret abstractions. We also have seen in section 4.4 that the deduction system interprets universal quantifications by substituting a *new* constant to the universal variable. The constant is simply added to the current signature.

Discussion This new constant is a new problem: how can the programmer take it into account? It is trivial that, because the constant is new, no predicate definition can take it into account. Predicates that are supposed to be defined for every constructor of a data-structure are no longer completely defined when a new constant is introduced.

   We illustrate this on an example. Suppose we want to define a predicate for computing de Bruijn's representation of λ-terms [15]. The purpose of de Bruijn's representation is avoid names clash problems, which are usually solved by α-conversion, by simply eliminating names. The idea is to replace every occurrence of names by a number that count how many abstractions separate this occurrence of the name from the abstraction that binds it. The following diagram briefly illustrates de Bruijn's representation using the textual notation for λ-terms and their graph notation.

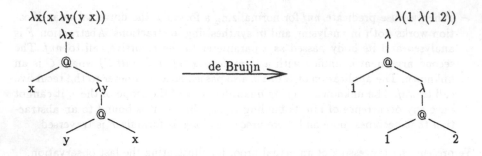

Object-level λ-terms are supposed to be represented with constants *app* and *abs* (see page 11). De Bruijn's trees can be represented by the following constants:

kind db_tree type .
type app_db db_tree -> db_tree -> db_tree .
type abs_db db_tree -> db_tree .
type var_db int -> db_tree .

The definition of the relation begins as follows:

de_bruijn l_term -> db_tree -> int -> o .

de_bruijn (app T1 T2) (app_db D1 D2) N :-
   de_bruijn T1 D1 N , de_bruijn T2 D2 N .
de_bruijn (abs T) (abs_db D) N :- ∀$_G$ x(de_bruijn (T x) D (succ N)) .

The procedure will eventually reach x at some leaf of the term. At this point, one would like to use the following clause:

de_bruijn x (var_db Ix) Nx :- plus $\underline{N}$ Ix Nx .

Variable N is underlined to stress its special status. It is supposed to be the same as the N in the instance of the last clause of the program where x is introduced. This contradict the usual convention that the scope of variables is limited to the clause it occurs in. Variables Ix and Nx are perfectly normal. They are local to the clause. Variable Nx gets its value when the head is unified with a calling goal, and variable Ix gets its value when proving the body.

 Furthermore, there should be one such clause for every x created during the execution of predicate *de_bruijn*. This is impossible to achieve using standard Prolog tools because one does not know in advance what the x's will be.

 We need some means for augmenting a predicate definition during the life of a new constant: i.e. during a subproof. This means must tolerate clause definitions with free variables. Implication in goals, $\Rightarrow_G$, is such a means because it allows us to augment the program for the life-time of a subproof.

 The introduction rule for implication in goals is as follows:

$$\frac{P, D \vdash G}{P \vdash D \Rightarrow G} \qquad \Rightarrow_G$$

In order to be coherent with the distinction made between $\mathcal{G}$-formulas and $\mathcal{D}$-formulas one must restrict the premises of implications in goal to be $\mathcal{D}$-formulas, and the conclusions to be $\mathcal{G}$-formulas. This restriction is compatible with our motivation for adding implication in goal.

The operational semantics of implication in goal is as follows. To prove a goal $D \Rightarrow_\mathcal{G} G$, add clause D to the program and prove G. Clause D is kept in the program during the proof of G. It is suppressed from it as soon as the proof of G is over.

Using implication in goals, the clauses for *abs* and for x are as follows:

$$de\_bruijn \ (abs \ T) \ (abs\_db \ D) \ N :-$$
$$\forall_\mathcal{G} \ x \ (\qquad \forall_\mathcal{D} \ Nx (\forall_\mathcal{D} \ Ix ($$
$$de\_bruijn \ x \ (var\_db \ Ix) \ Nx :- \ plus \ N \ Ix \ Nx \ ))$$
$$\Rightarrow_\mathcal{G} \quad de\_bruijn \ (T \ x) \ D \ (succ \ N) \ ) \ .$$

The $\forall_\mathcal{D}$'s in the assumed clause make variables Nx and Ix local to the clause, as it is initially intended. They correspond to the quantifications that are usually implicit. In this case, the nesting of clauses forces us to make them explicit for avoiding confusion of scopes. Variable N is intentionally left free in the assumed clause.

Application We use as an application the problem of relating a λ-term to its type.

The well-typing relation is defined by structural induction on object-level terms. The type of the well-typing relation is as follows:

$$type \ typing \ l\_term \ \text{->} \ simple\_type \ \text{->} \ o \ .$$

Then it is defined by induction on the constructors of type l_term. The case for applications is elementary and could be written in Prolog.

$$typing \ (app \ T1 \ T2) \ B :- \ typing \ T1 \ (arrow \ A \ B) \ , \ typing \ T2 \ A \ .$$

The case for abstractions is more interesting. The induction through object-level abstractions uses a universal quantification because object-level abstractions are represented by $CLP(\Lambda_\rightarrow, \equiv_{\alpha\beta\eta})$ abstractions. This universal quantification introduces a universal constant of type l_term, which is the type on which the induction operates. So, one must augment the inductive definition for the life-time of the universal constant using an implication.

$$typing \ (abs \ E) \ (arrow \ A \ B) :- \forall_\mathcal{G} \ x (\ typing \ x \ A \Rightarrow_\mathcal{G} \ typing \ (E \ x) \ B \ ) \ .$$

The added clause is *(typing x A)*. It contains a free logical variable A. This forces all the occurrences of constant x to have the same type. If the added clause had been $\forall_\mathcal{D} \ T(typing \ x \ T)$, every occurrence would have had its own type.

The above sequence of reasoning provides only the structure of the $CLP(\Lambda_\rightarrow, \equiv_{\alpha\beta\eta})$ program. To work out the full details needs to know the logic of the defined relation. In this case, the logic is given by the deduction rules of the theory of simple types [2, 24]. For the abstraction, the rule is called *arrow introduction*:

$$\frac{\Gamma, x : \alpha \ \vdash \ E : \beta}{\Gamma \ \vdash \ \lambda x.E : \alpha \rightarrow \beta} \ \rightarrow_I$$

One may wonder why an implication was required for relations *typing* and *de_bruijn*, but not for relation *nnf*. The answer is in the notion of inductive type. These relations are defined by an induction on the constructors of the λ-terms representation of one of their parameters. If the type of this parameter is *inductive* then it is easy to deduce an induction function on the constructors [5].

One says the type of a data structure is inductive if its constructors admit arguments of that same type only in positive occurrences [46]. We recall that following the *Curry–Howard isomorphism* [13, 23] the arrow of simple types is analogous to implication in propositional intuitionistic calculus. As does implication, arrow introduces a notion of positive and negative occurrences as follows:

$$pos(A\text{->}B) \stackrel{\text{def}}{=} neg(A) \cup pos(B)$$
$$neg(A\text{->}B) \stackrel{\text{def}}{=} pos(A) \cup neg(B)$$
$$pos(T) \stackrel{\text{def}}{=} \{T\} \qquad\qquad \text{\% if } T \text{ is not an arrow type}$$
$$neg(T) \stackrel{\text{def}}{=} \emptyset \qquad\qquad \text{\% if } T \text{ is not an arrow type}$$

For instance, $pos((a\text{->}b)\text{->}(c\text{->}d))=\{a,d\}$ and $neg((a\text{->}b)\text{->}(c\text{->}d))=\{b,c\}$.

What causes the differences between the relations is that type *l_term* is not inductive, whereas type *formula* is inductive. When the type is inductive, implication is not required because there cannot be new constants of that type; when it is not inductive, implication is required for handling the new constants of that type.

Let us show that type *l_term* is not inductive. Constant *abs* is a constructor of *l_term*, and its type is *(l_term->l_term)->l_term*. Because *l_term* has a negative occurrence in the type of the only argument of *abs* ($neg(l\_term\text{->}l\_term)=\{l\_term\}$) it is not inductive.

Let us show that type *formula* is inductive. Its constructors are either like *and*, or like *forall*. Every argument of *and* has type *formula*. The only argument of *forall* has type *individual->formula*. Because *formula* does not occur negatively in them ($neg(formula)=\emptyset$ and $neg(individual\text{->}formula)=\{individual\}$) it is inductive.

If the object-level theory in the negative normal form example had been a higher-order logic in which variables of type *formula* can be quantified, then type *formula* would not have been inductive, and it would have been required to augment the inductive definition using implication.

4.6 Summing-up

This section can be summed-up as follows: for adding λ-terms and αβ-equivalence to Prolog, one needs to type terms in a discipline that makes the unification problem well-defined. For defining relations by structural induction on abstractions, and still satisfy the conservation condition, one must also add η-equivalence and universal quantification in goals. To be able to maintain the completeness of the inductive definitions in presence of universal variables (new constants) of a non-inductive type, one needs to add implication in goals. All this forms the core of λProlog [36, 38, 37]. Formulas generated as presented above are called *hereditary Harrop formulas*.

We have already observed that the right introduction rules of ∧, ∨ can be defined by second order Horn clauses. The introduction rule for ∃ can also be defined by a second order Horn clause using higher-order terms. Its definition is as follows:

$(\exists_{\mathcal{G}}\ G\ ) \Leftarrow_{\mathcal{D}} (G\ X)$

Thus, all the connectives that belong to $\mathcal{G}$-formulas, but not to $\mathcal{D}$-formulas (i.e. $\exists$ and $\vee$), are definable in the language of $\mathcal{D}$-formulas. So, they can be suppressed from the $\mathcal{G}$-formulas, making the two classes of formulas identical. The result is that the logic of λProlog (or of CLP($\Lambda_{\rightarrow}$, $\equiv_{\alpha\beta\eta}$)) is the logic of the formulas freely constructed with connectives $\forall$, $\wedge$, and $\Rightarrow$.

The semantics of λProlog is usually given in proof-theoretic terms [38, 37], as opposed to the model-theoretic semantics used for Prolog [30]. The main result is that a class of goal-directed proofs, called *uniform proofs*, is complete with respect to intuitionistic provability for hereditary Harrop formulas. In other words, every hereditary Harrop formula that is a theorem in intuitionistic logic has a uniform proof. In still other words, restricting proofs to be uniform eliminates proofs, but does not eliminate any theorem among hereditary Harrop formulas.

The word "scope" sums-up the new constructs of λProlog:

- abstraction limits the scope of variables in terms,
- quantifications limit the scope of variables in formulas,
- and the deduction rules for universal quantification and implication limit the scope of constants and clauses, respectively, in the proof process.

Predicates *nnf* (pp. 13), *de_bruijn* (pp. 14), and *typing* (pp. 16) show that programming in λProlog often amounts to make the three scoping levels interact.

5 Conclusion

5.1 The Structure of λProlog (Alias CLP($\Lambda_{\rightarrow}$, $\equiv_{\alpha\beta\eta}$))

The following picture illustrates the relationships that give a structure to the features of λProlog. Arrows read "requires".

We consider λ-terms and $\alpha\beta$-equivalence as the principal components of λProlog; those that draw every other component. Adding these components to Prolog is motivated by the need for a more declarative handling of notions such as scoping and substitution. Then come types for making unification well-defined and tractable, and universal quantification in goals for handling induction through abstractions. Then η-equivalence in the equality theory is required for making the interpretation of abstraction by universal quantification correct and reversible. Finally, for inductive definitions to remain complete with respect to types when universal quantification introduces new constants, implication is needed for completing the induction.

Among the preliminary designs for $CLP(\Lambda_\rightarrow, \equiv_{\alpha\beta\eta})$ we have presented, we see that $CLP(\Lambda, \equiv_{\alpha\beta})$ and $CLP(\Lambda_\rightarrow, \equiv_{\alpha\beta})$ are useless because they feature components that are high in the diagram without featuring the components that are below them (i.e. that come as a consequence).

The symmetry between abstraction and universal quantification in goals makes us consider the first as an essentially universal quantification. This is an important point for programming. This duality is often the cause of a conjoint use of abstraction and universal quantification in goals. It may be pictured as follows:

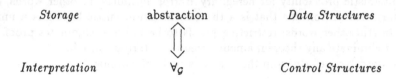

Abstraction is a *reified* form of universal quantification, the latter being a *reflection* of the former. For analysing/consuming/reflecting an abstraction, one must apply it to a universal variable whose scope is included in the scope of the variable that is bound to the abstraction. For synthesising/producing/reifying an abstraction, it is required to build a term that represents its body in which a unique universal variable represents every occurrence of the variable bound by the abstraction, and compute the function that yields that term when it is applied to the same universal variable (e.g. the proof of *(nnf (exists λx(not (exists $\lambda y(p\ x\ y)))) X)$, page 14).

Finally, note that the analogy between λProlog and a CLP language still works at the implementation level. Implementing the unification algorithm raises issues on delaying under-specified problems that are familiar to CLP implementers [31].

5.2 The Structure of a Restriction of λProlog

All the steps leading from $CLP(\Lambda, \equiv_{\alpha\beta})$ to λProlog offer no alternative, except for the way of making the λ-calculus strongly normalizable and the corresponding unification problem tractable.

Miller proposes a fragment of λProlog, L_λ, that restricts more strongly the term domain than simple types do. In this fragment, the unification problem is decidable and unitary [34]. The term domain of L_λ is the greatest subset of λ-terms for which β_0-equivalence (defined below) is equal to β-equivalence.

$\beta_0 \ — \ (\lambda x(E)\ x) \equiv_{\beta_0} E.$

This axiom formalizes a weak form of β-equivalence for the case the actual parameter is a variable. β_0-Reduction amounts to variable renaming.

The subdomain of the λ-terms for which β_0 is complete with respect to β is described by a restriction of the rule for building applications. The only allowed applications with a variable head are those whose head is applied to distinct essentially universal variables. A similar restriction applies to all systems of Barendregt's cube [3, 2] to make their unification problems unitary and decidable [45].

Despite its algorithmic interest, the L_λ fragment is not widely used because lots of useful definitions do not belong to L_λ. For instance, the definition of $\exists_G$ (p. 18) does not belong to L_λ because of term *(G X)*. Relation *mapfun* is not in L_λ either.

```
type mapfun (A->B) -> (list A) -> (list B) -> o .
mapfun F [] [] .
mapfun F [E|L] [(F E)|FL] :- mapfun F L FL .    % (F E) is not in Lλ
```

However, the L_λ fragment can be used as a heuristic criterion to avoid using the general but costly unification procedure [7, 6].

One may wonder if the L_λ fragment is restricted enough for modifying the overall structure of the language. In fact, L_λ has exactly the same structure as λProlog. Unification in L_λ still does not allow us to analyse every data-structure. The restriction is such that even application $(T_1\ T_2)$ cannot be formed in L_λ. So, one still needs universal quantification, η-equivalence, and implication.

5.3 λProlog's Status

We finish with a few words on the applications and availability of λProlog.

Possible applications are chiefly those that motivated the λ-terms: manipulation of formulas, computation of denotation, etc (see section 2). Among actual applications, we find automatic theorem proving [4, 19], analysis of natural and formal languages [41, 14, 26], and the manipulation of functional programs [20]. Notice also that the structure of λProlog encompasses such constructions as modules [35] and abstract data types [33] without any extra-logical addition.

Two implementations of λProlog can be used: one, called eLP, is an interpreter written in Lisp [18], the other, called Prolog/Mali, is a compiler written in λProlog which generates C programs [6]. A third implementation is in progress [28].

Acknowledgements I wish to thank Catherine Belleannée and Pascal Brisset for the fruitful discussions we add on the matter presented in this paper.

References

1. H. Andreka and I. Nemeti. *The Generalised Completeness of Horn Predicate-Logic as a Programming Language*. DAI Research Report 21, University of Edinburgh, 1976.
2. H. Barendregt. Introduction to generalized type systems. *J. Functional Programming*, 1(2):125–154, 1991.
3. H. Barendregt and K. Hemerik. Types in lambda calculi and programming languages. In N. Jones, editor, *European Symp. on Programming, LNCS 432*, pages 1–35, Springer-Verlag, 1990.
4. C. Belleannée. *Vers un démonstrateur de théorèmes adaptatif*. Thèse, Université de Rennes I, 1991.

5. C. Böhm and A. Berarducci. Automatic synthesis of typed λ-programs on term algebras. *Theoretical Computer Science*, 39:135–154, 1985.

6. P. Brisset and O. Ridoux. The architecture of an implementation of λProlog: Prolog/Mali. In *Workshop on λProlog*, Philadelphia, PA, USA, 1992. ftp: //ftp.irisa.fr/local/lande.

7. P. Brisset and O. Ridoux. *The Compilation of λProlog and its execution with MALI*. Technical Report 687, IRISA, 1992. ftp: //ftp.irisa.fr/local/lande.

8. P. Brisset and O. Ridoux. Continuations in λProlog. In D.S. Warren, editor, *10th Int. Conf. Logic Programming*, pages 27–43, MIT Press, 1993.

9. P. Brisset and O. Ridoux. Naïve reverse can be linear. In K. Furukawa, editor, *8th Int. Conf. Logic Programming*, pages 857–870, MIT Press, 1991.

10. J. Cohen. Constraint logic programming languages. *CACM*, 33(7):52–68, 1990.

11. A. Colmerauer. An introduction to Prolog III. *CACM*, 33(7), 1990.

12. S. Coupet-Grimal. Représentation sémantique dans le traitement des langues naturelles en Prolog. In *Journées Francophones sur la Programmation en Logique*, pages 69–91, Teknea, Nîmes, France, 1993.

13. H.B. Curry and R. Feys. *Combinatory Logic, Volume I*. North-Holland, Amsterdam, 1968.

14. M. Dalrymple, S.M. Shieber, and F.C.N. Pereira. Ellipsis and higher-order unification. In *Linguistics and Philosophy*, pages 399–452, 1991.

15. N.G. de Bruijn. Lambda calculus notation with nameless dummies, a tool for automatic formula manipulation, with application to the Church-Rosser theorem. *Indagationes Mathematicae*, 34:381–392, 1972.

16. C.M. Elliott. *Extensions and Applications of Higher-Order Unification*. Research Report CMU-CS-90-134, School of Computer Science, Carnegie Mellon University, 1990.

17. C.M. Elliott. Higher-order unification with dependent function types. In N. Derschowitz, editor, *3rd Int. Conf. Rewriting Techniques and Applications, LNCS 355*, pages 121–136, Springer-Verlag, 1989.

18. C.M. Elliott and F. Pfenning. A semi-functional implementation of a higher-order logic programming language. In P. Lee, editor, *Topics in Advanced Language Implementation*, pages 289–325, MIT Press, 1991.

19. A. Felty. Implementing tactics and tacticals in a higher-order logic programming language. *J. Automated Reasoning*, 11(1):43–81, 1993.

20. J. Hannan and D. Miller. From operational semantics to abstract machines. *Mathematical Structures in Computer Science*, 4(2):415–459, 1992.

21. M. Hanus. Horn clause programs with polymorphic types: semantics and resolution. *Theoretical Computer Science*, 89:63–106, 1991.

22. P.M. Hill and J.W. LLoyd. *The Gödel Report*. Technical Report TR-91-02, University of Bristol, 1991.

23. W.A. Howard. The formulae-as-types notion of construction. In J.P. Seldin and J.R. Hindley, editors, *To H.B. Curry: Essays on Combinatory Logic, Lambda Calculus and Formalism*, pages 479–490, Academic Press, London, 1980.

24. G. Huet. *Introduction au λ-calcul typé*. INRIA, Collection Didactique, 1991.

25. G. Huet. A unification algorithm for typed λ-calculus. *Theoretical Computer Science*, 1:27–57, 1975.

26. S. Le Huitouze, P. Louvet, and O. Ridoux. Logic grammars and λProlog. In D.S. Warren, editor, *10th Int. Conf. Logic Programming*, pages 64–79, MIT Press, 1993.

27. Joxan Jaffar and Jean-Louis Lassez. Constraint logic programming. In *14th ACM Symp. Principles of Programming Languages*, pages 111–119, ACM, Munich, Germany, 1987.

28. B. Jayaraman and G. Nadathur. Implementation techniques for scoping constructs in logic programming. In K. Furukawa, editor, *8th Int. Conf. Logic Programming*, pages 871–886, MIT Press, 1991.

29. T.K. Lakshman and U.S. Reddy. Typed Prolog: a semantic reconstruction of the Mycroft-O'Keefe type system. In *Int. Logic Programming Symp.*, pages 202–217, 1991.

30. J.W. Lloyd. *Foundations of Logic Programming. Symbolic computation — Artificial Intelligence*, Springer-Verlag, Berlin, FRG, 1987.

31. S. Michaylov and F. Pfenning. An empirical study of the runtime behavior of higher-order logic programs. In *Workshop on λProlog*, 1992. Preliminary version.

32. D.A. Miller. Abstract syntax and logic programming. In A. Voronkov, editor, *2nd Russian Conf. Logic Programming, LNCS 592*, Springer-Verlag, 1991.

33. D.A. Miller. Lexical scoping as universal quantification. In G. Levi and M. Martelli, editors, *6th Int. Conf. Logic Programming*, pages 268–283, MIT Press, 1989.

34. D.A. Miller. A logic programming language with lambda-abstraction, function variables, and simple unification. *J. Logic and Computation*, 1(4):497–536, 1991.

35. D.A. Miller. A proposal for modules in λProlog. In R. Dyckhoff, editor, *Int. Workshop Extensions of Logic Programming, LNAI 798*, pages 206–221, Springer-Verlag, 1993.

36. D.A. Miller and G. Nadathur. Higher-order logic programming. In E. Shapiro, editor, *3rd Int. Conf. Logic Programming, LNCS 225*, pages 448–462, Springer-Verlag, 1986.

37. D.A. Miller, G. Nadathur, F. Pfenning, and A. Scedrov. Uniform proofs as a foundation for logic programming. *Annals of Pure and Applied Logic*, 51:125–157, 1991.

38. D.A. Miller, G. Nadathur, and A. Scedrov. Hereditary Harrop formulas and uniform proof systems. In D. Gries, editor, *2nd Symp. Logic in Computer Science*, pages 98–105, Ithaca, New York, USA, 1987.

39. R. Milner. A theory of type polymorphism in programming. *J. Computer and System Sciences*, 17:348–375, 1978.

40. A. Mycroft and R.A. O'Keefe. A polymorphic type system for Prolog. *Artificial Intelligence*, 23:295–307, 1984.

41. R. Pareschi and D.A. Miller. Extending definite clause grammars with scoping constructs. In D.H.D. Warren and P. Szeredi, editors, *7th Int. Conf. Logic Programming*, pages 373–389, MIT Press, 1990.

42. F. Pfenning. Dependent types in logic programming. In F. Pfenning, editor, *Types in Logic Programming*, pages 285–311, MIT Press, 1992.

43. F. Pfenning. Logic programming in the LF logical framework. In G. Huet and G. Plotkin, editors, *Logical Frameworks*, pages 149–181, Cambridge University Press, 1991.

44. F. Pfenning. Partial polymorphic type inference and higher-order unification. In *ACM Conf. LISP and Functional Programming*, pages 153–163, ACM Press, 1988.

45. F. Pfenning. Unification and anti-unification in the calculus of constructions. In *Symp. Logic in Computer Science*, pages 74–85, 1991.

46. B. Pierce, S. Dietzen, and S. Michaylov. *Programming in Higher-Order Typed Lambda-Calculi*. Research Report CMU-CS-89-111, School of Computer Science, Carnegie Mellon University, 1989.

47. L. Sterling and E. Shapiro. *The Art of Prolog*. MIT Press, 1986.

48. S-Å. Tärnlund. Horn clause computability. *BIT*, 17:215–226, 1977.

49. P. Van Hentenryck. *Constraint Satisfaction in Logic Programming*. MIT Press, Cambridge, MA, 1989.

An Architecture for Cooperating Constraint Solvers on Reals

Michel RUEHER

I3S, UNSA / CNRS, Route des Colles, B.P. 145,
06903 Sophia Antipolis Cedex, FRANCE
e-mail: mr@essi.fr

Abstract. In this paper we introduce a cooperative scheme for solving systems of constraints over the reals. First, we informally show how an appropriate combination of *symbolic and numeric solvers* makes it possible to solve problems that none of these solvers can tackle alone. Then, we specify a cooperative architecture which allows *to use concurrently heterogeneous solvers* when handling constraints over the reals. This architecture is based upon agents that communicate via *asynchronous message passing*. Agent are synchronized when a failure or a success occurs. Disjunctive constraints are handled by backtracking. Operational semantics and terminating conditions of such systems are discussed. Message processing is detailed for both the general case where several non-deterministic solvers are involved in the cooperation, and for more specialized architectures.

1 Introduction

1.1 Motivation

Numerous industrial problems can be modeled by a set of constraints defined over the reals (e.g., financial applications, thermal flow problems, electro-mechanical engineering problems). However, these constraints are usually non-linear and often non-polynomial. They can neither be handled by existing *CLP* languages [Col90, JMSY92, JM94] which require the constraints to be linear, nor can they be solved by the existing computer algebra systems [Buc85, GCL91, CGG+91] which cannot solve systems of non-polynomial equations and inequalities[1]. Moreover, these problems cannot be solved by the techniques used in CSPs [Wal72, Mac77, Tsa93] which operate on discrete domains only. Numeric solving techniques, such as *interval propagation* [LvE92, HSS+92, Lho93] allow one to narrow the domains of the variables for any system of constraints over the reals. Unfortunately, in the general case they are unable to compute the range of values of

---

[1] The Collins' method [Col75] used by RISC-CLP [Hon92, Hon93] makes it possible to solve polynomial systems of equations and inequalities. However, the high complexity of the proposed algorithms confines their usefulness to very small (albeit interesting) problems.

the variables and they cannot detect whether a system of constraints is inconsistent or not[2]. However, a careful examination of the particular applications often shows that an appropriate combination of symbolic and numerical techniques allows one to compute the solutions expected by the end user.

In particular, even trivial problems cannot be solved in a straightforward way by systems based on the above mentioned techniques, while a combination of these different solvers can solve them easily. For instance, let $S1$ be the following system of constraints:

$$x^2 - y^2 = 0 \qquad (1)$$
$$x + y < 25 \qquad (2)$$
$$x + y > 0 \qquad (3)$$
$$-100 \leq x \leq 100 \qquad (4)$$

Neither a solver based on the simplex algorithm, nor a solver based on the Groebner basis algorithm[3] can solve the whole system. Interval propagation techniques —like the 3-Bconsistency algorithm [Lho93]— can only narrow y to $[-100, 100]$. Nevertheless, a solver based on the Groebner basis algorithm can simplify (1) and generate the following disjunctive constraints:

$$x = y \qquad (5)$$
$$x = -y \qquad (6)$$

The simplex algorithm trivially detects the inconsistency of $\{2, 3, 4, 6\}$ and it can compute from $\{2, 3, 4, 5\}$ the upper and lower bounds of x and y, i.e., it will determine that x and y are inside the interval $[0, \frac{25}{2}]$.

1.2 Aims of the paper and related work

The purpose of this paper is to provide a support for the automatic sequencing of different constraint solvers. Thus, we propose here an approach to *solve systems of constraints over real numbers* based on a *cooperation* between solvers. To allow such a cooperation, the system of constraints is split into different subsets of constraints according to the capabilities of the available solvers. Each solver manages its own constraint store[4] and has its own solving strategies. The architecture of our system is based upon the concept of *agents* [Hew77, Agh86] that

---

[2] The interval calculus is usually unable to narrow the intervals to the range of values of the variables, especially when one variable occurs more than once in a constraint [Moo66].

[3] Of course, such very simple problems can often be tackled with a Groebner basis algorithm after some recasting. For instance, inequalities can be substituted by equations with a slack variable and complex solutions can be removed. However, when the system of constraints holds strict inequalities or non-polynomial equations such a recasting of the problem can no longer be performed automatically.

[4] On should note that the same constraint may be dispatched to different solvers. Local stores do therefore not represent a distributed store as in Janus [SKL90].

communicate via *asynchronous message passing*. Messages propagate failures as well as new derived constraints.

The underlying model we propose here is inspired from works on *Concurrent Constraint Logic Programming languages (cc)* which are based on communication and synchronization by *Ask* and *Tell* messages (e.g., [Sar93, SRP91, dBKPR93, MRS94]). The originality of our approach lays in our objective to mix *heterogeneous solvers* to tackle systems of constraints over the reals whereas previously mentioned works aim at giving a general framework for processing constraints concurrently with homogeneous solvers. Thus, the most important differences with the *cc framework* are:

- Checking up the consistency of any system of constraints over the reals is an undecidable problem. Therefore, no global store can be maintained and entailment can only be defined at the level of each solver and for restrictive forms of constraints.
- Nondeterminism is handled by backtracking and *synchronization* of all solvers is done after each successful or failing resolution, while in most *cc* systems the agents are duplicated. Of course, when a choice point occurs one could also consider processing the various alternatives concurrently. From an operational point of view, this solution is nevertheless unrealistic due to the resources that the solvers require and the huge amount of disjunctive constraints that may appear in numerous cases.

Nelson and Oppen [NO79] first proposed a method for combining decision procedures for several theories into a single decision procedure. In their system, each satisfiability procedure deduces and propagates to the other satisfiability procedures all equalities between variables entailed by the conjunction it is considering. The equalities propagation procedure is based upon an algorithm which *sequentially* applies the different solvers and which handles successively the choices points (i.e., the disjunctions).

Cooperative problem solving has also been investigated in the field of artificial intelligence. For instance, in [DLC89] the authors study how a *loosely coupled network* of problem solvers can work together to solve problems that are beyond their individual capabilities. In their approach, cooperative nodes can use local expertise, resources, and information to individually solve different sub-parts of an overall problem. However, their focus is on very general issues (e.g., cognitive modeling of negotiation) and no formalization of the resolution process is proposed.

Colmerauer [Col92] has proposed a "naive and incomplete algorithm" for solving systems of non-linear constraints. The initial system of constraints S is split into two subsystems, a linear one and a non-linear one which only contains constraints of the form $z = x \times y$, where x and y are variables. The algorithm repeatedly applies the following actions:

1. Solving the linear part of S,

2. Considering the equations $x = constant$ that are entailed by the linear part of S and replacing each variable x by $constant$ in the right hand sides of non-linear equations.

This algorithm is implemented in PrologIII by using delay mechanisms. In the same spirit, a more elaborated coupling of a quadratic and a linear solver has recently been implemented in QUAD-CLP(R) [PB94].

Quite recently, Hoon Hong [Hon94] has proposed a scheme for the design of a cooperative constraint solver. He suggests repeatedly applying each sub-solver until no change occurs. His paper is devoted to the study of confluence of such algorithms but does not explicitly address the problem of communication between the sub-solvers.

In a forthcoming paper, Beringer and De Backer [BB94] propose a tight coupling between two deterministic solvers: a domain reduction solver and a real linear solver. The domain reduction solver signals each bound it has inferred for variables which are also included in some real linear constraints, while the linear solver sends to the domain reduction solver the values of shared variables as soon as they are fixed. To implement efficiently the cooperation the authors have designed a specific domain reduction algorithm and a "'revised" simplex algorithm. Since their goal is the design of a new language (i.e., ICE), the emphasis is rather on the integration of the algorithms than on the cooperation between distinct solvers.

1.3 Layout of the paper

Section 2 introduces a general scheme for (heterogeneous) cooperating solvers on reals. Agents and messages are formally defined. The operational semantics and terminating conditions are studied in section 3. Section 4 is devoted to the definition of the messages handling process. Particular attention will be paid to backtracking and synchronization issues. Optimizations and properties of specialized cooperative systems are discussed in section 5.

2   A general scheme for cooperation between solvers on reals

2.1   Overall Architecture

In our system, a solver is encapsulated in an agent, i.e., a process endowed with some solving capabilities and its own data ("local store"). An interface module —in charge of the communication— is associated with each agent. Interface

modules go beyond simple data transcoding and store management: they analyze the messages and they can schedule[5] the work of the solver according to
some heuristics.

The resolution process starts by a decomposition of the initial system of constraints and by sending subsets of constraints to the solvers (according to their
capabilities). Each agent tells the other ones about its relevant results (e.g., instantiations or simplifications). Of course, results sent back by a solver should
neither be equivalent to the constraints it has just received, nor be deductible
from the previous value of its local store. Thus, the form of the propagated
constraints will depend on the entailment capabilities of the solvers. A terminal
state is a state where each solver has processed all its messages. The termination
of the resolution can be guaranteed if the resolution process of each solver halts,
and if the propagated constraints do not contain any new variables.

Agents do not communicate directly one with each other. Instead they only
communicate —by means of messages— with a specific agent called the *monitor*
which supervises the resolution. The monitor is in charge of the decomposition
of the initial system of constraints and of the detection of a terminal state. It
also collects the messages sent by the *solver* agents and forwards constraints
only to the agents able to process them. This way of processing the messages
has been chosen instead of a "broadcasting" mode *to simplify the processing of
disjunctive constraints*. Indeed, the resolution of non-linear constraints is always
likely to generate disjunctive constraints which lead to the definition of choice
points. When a solver retrieves disjunctive constraints, the monitor agent asks
the *solver* agents to generate choice points. Conceptually, making a choice point
corresponds to a copying of the current value of the local store. The successive
values of the local store are stacked[6] up at the level of each solver. The different disjuncts of such constraints will be sequentially processed. One should note
that the management of the disjunctive constraints at the monitor level entails
that the messages sent to the solvers can only carry conjunctions of elementary
constraints.

The result of a successful resolution corresponds to the conjunction of the
constraints held in all the local stores. The degree of consistency of this result
is, in the best case, the strongest consistency degree guaranteed by the solvers
that work on the whole set of constraints. For instance, if the resolution of a
constraints system involves a solver based on the simplex algorithm and a solver

---

[5] Discussion on interface modules capabilities is out of the scope of this paper. However, we assume that works done at the level of the interface modules preserve the
semantics of the cooperating solvers system. For instance, selection of the message
to be processed according to the "first fail" heuristic requires a property of commutativity on the "composition" of all available messages.

[6] On the operational level, one can avoid copying the whole context by using more
efficient mechanisms when the solvers have backtracking capabilities.

based on interval propagation, and if the resolution succeeds, one can only conclude that *if the initial system has solutions, the values of the non-instantiated variables are inside of the computed intervals.* Of course, in the worst case, nothing can be said about the degree of consistency of the result. This corresponds to the situation where no solver works on the whole set of constraints.

When a failure occurs, all the solvers should backtrack and restore the appropriate local store and messages. However, as the messages are processed concurrently, all solvers have not necessarily generated the same choice points when a failure occurs. Thus, a systematic backtrack to the last choice point would lead to a non-coherent configuration and message interleaving problems. To avoid such problems, backtracking will be based on labeling of messages and local stores, while the restoration of already processed messages will be achieved at the level of the monitor.

The overall architecture and the main functions of the different components are sketched in figure 1. As shown, we assume that there is an additional agent — named *user*— which communicates with the end user. This agent is in charge of sending the initial set of constraints to the monitor and it displays the results according to information provided both by the monitor and the local stores of the solvers.

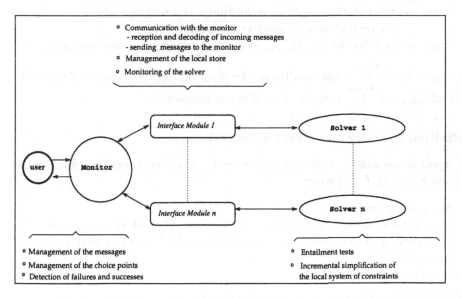

Fig. 1. Overall architecture

2.2 Agents and Messages

We now specify more formally the interactions between the solvers and the monitor. In the following we assume that Γ, the set of the available solvers,[7] is restricted to:

- $\mathcal{A_L}$, the set of the solvers that are able to handle linear equalities and inequalities,
- $\mathcal{A_P}$, the set of the solvers that are able to handle polynomial equalities,
- $\mathcal{A_{NP}}$, the set of the solvers that are able to handle systems of non-polynomial equalities and inequalities.

We use tuples to represent successive states and messages queues. A tuple made of the elements $L_1, ..., L_n$ is noted $< L_1, ..., L_n >$. The empty tuple is noted by $<>$ while $L1 \cdot < e > \cdot L_2$ denotes the concatenation of the tuple L_1 with the tuple made of one element e and the tuple L_2. We use the notation $e \in L$ to mean that e is an element of the tuple L.

We also use the following notations, possibly subscripted:

- a, b, c denote real constant numbers,
- x, y, z denote real variables, '_' denotes the anonymous variables which are assumed to be existentially quantified,
- c denotes an "elementary" constraint over the reals (i.e, an equation, a disequation or an inequality over the reals)
- $C = \bigwedge_{j=1}^{n} c_j$ represents a conjunction of elementary constraints; we sometimes use the notation $c \in C$ to mean that c is a conjunct of C,
- $D = \bigvee_{i=1}^{n} C_i$ represents a disjunctive constraint,
- S_{olver} is any solver agent, M_{onitor} is the monitor agent, A denotes any agent.

We denote by $S \overset{solver}{\vdash} c$ the entailment of c from the current value S of the local store of S_{olver}. $S \overset{solver}{\vdash} \perp$ means that S is not consistent.

Definition 1 (solver and monitor agents)

An *agent* is associated with each solver in Γ. A solver *agent* is defined by a relation $S_{olver}(\Pi, F, M)$ where:

- S_{olver} is the name of the agent,
- Π is a stack containing the values of the local store which are required for backtracking. The current value (noted S_π in the following) corresponds to the top of Π,
- F is the state flag of the agent:

---

[7] The proposed architecture has been defined for solving constraints over real numbers. The decomposition of Γ done here lays on the usual classification in this field. In a more general context, one could define subsets of Γ as solver classes based on the domains and on the forms of the constraints.

- $F = success$ if the last constraint C processed by the agent was consistent with respect to the current value of its local store,

  i.e, $\neg(S_\pi \wedge C \overset{solver}{\vdash} \bot)$

- $F = fail$ if the last constraint C processed by the agent was not consistent with respect to the current value of its local store,

  i.e, $S_\pi \wedge C \overset{solver}{\vdash} \bot$

- M is the queue of messages that S_{olver} has to process.

The monitor is a specific agent defined by the relation $M_{onitor}(F, M, L_D)$ where M has the same meanings as above, and where L_D is a queue of disjunctive constraints to be handled. F is a state flag whose value is $success$ if the value of the state flag of all the solver agents is $success$; otherwise $F = fail$.

The configuration or *current state* Σ_A of an agent A is defined by the following information:

- the state flag,
- the values of the local store,
- the queue of messages to be processed.

We note respectively $S_\pi(A)$, $flag(A)$ and $Mess(A)$ the current value of the local store, the flag and the queue of messages of an agent A.

Definition 2 (message)

A **message** can have one of the following forms:

- $\texttt{Tell}(M_{onitor} \rightarrow S_{olver}, C)$,
- $\texttt{Tell}(S_{olver} \rightarrow M_{onitor}, D)$,
- $\texttt{M\_Choice}(M_{onitor} \rightarrow S_{olver})$,
- $\texttt{Restore}(M_{onitor} \rightarrow S_{olver})$,
- $\texttt{Fail}(S_{olver} \rightarrow M_{onitor})$,

A **Tell** message is sent by the monitor agent to the solvers in order to transmit them the constraints they have to process. A **Tell** message is sent by a solver to monitor in order to forward the result of the resolution[8]. A **M_Choice** message is sent by the monitor agent to the solvers in order to notify them to create a choice point. A **Restore** message is sent by the monitor agent to the solvers to ask them to backtrack and to restore the appropriate local store (according to the state labeling). A **Fail** message is sent to the monitor agent by a solver if the latter has detected an inconsistency while trying to add a constraint to its local store.

---

[8] For generalization's sake, one considers this result as a disjunction of constraints even though in numerous cases the result will be a conjunction of constraints.

3 Operational Semantics

In our cooperative architecture, each state of the computation consists of the set of all current states associated with the different agents. Each computation step will model the evolution of an agent. Such an evolution will be performed by applying a transition rule (i.e, the processing of a message by the agent).

Definition 3 (transition rule)

For the agent A, the processing of the messages corresponds to a sequence of *inference steps* defined by a transition rule r of the form:

$$r : \Sigma_A^i \overset{r(A)}{\rightarrow} \Sigma_A^{i+1}, \mathcal{M}$$

where:

- Σ_A^i is the current state of agent A before transition r,
- Σ_A^{i+1} is the state of agent A after transition r,
- $\mathcal{M}$ is the queue, possibly empty, of the messages sent by A after commitment of the transition r.

Definition 4 (computational state)

A computational state consists of the set of current states of all agents. For instance, the initial computational state is defined by:

$\{\forall A_l \in \mathcal{A_L} \,.\, A_l(<>, success, <>), \; \forall A_p \in \mathcal{A_P} \,.\, A_p(<>, success, <>),$
$\quad\quad \forall A_{np} \in \mathcal{A_{NP}} \,.\, A_{np}(<>, success, <>), \; M_{onitor}(success, <>, <>)\}$

Definition 5 (computational step)

Let $\Sigma^1 = \{\Sigma_{A_i}^1 | A_i \in \mathcal{A_L} \cup \mathcal{A_P} \cup \mathcal{A_{NP}} \cup \{M_{onitor}\}\}$ be a computational state, and r a transition rule which enables the evolution of agent A_j. Then, the application of r to Σ^1 is a computational step which yields a new computational state $\Sigma^2 = \Sigma^1 \backslash \{\Sigma_{A_j}^1\} \cup \{\Sigma_{A_j}^2\}$.

Definition 6 (successful computational state, failing computational state)

A successful computational state is a state Σ where the monitor and each solver are in a successful state and where their queues of messages are void, i.e.,

$$\forall \Sigma_A \in \Sigma.(flag(A) = success) \wedge (Mess(A) =<>)$$

The result of the computation corresponds to the *conjunction* of the constraints in the current local stores of all the solvers.

A failing state is a state where at least one solver is in a failing state, i.e.,

$$\exists \Sigma_A \in \Sigma.(flag(A) = fail)$$

Definition 7 (terminal computational state)

A terminal computational state is a state Σ where no more transition rules can be applied, i.e., a successful or failing state where no more backtracking can be performed. Thus, a terminal state is characterized by one of the following conditions:

- Every solver agent has processed successfully its messages and the monitor's stack of disjunctive constraints is empty, i.e.,
$$(\forall \Sigma_A \in \Sigma.(flag(A) = success) \wedge (Mess(A) =<>))$$
$$\wedge M_{onitor}(success, <>, <>) \in \Sigma,$$
- The monitor is in a definitive failure state, i.e.,
$$\exists \Sigma_A \in \Sigma.\Sigma_A = M_{onitor}(fail, <>, <>).$$

To warrant termination of the resolution process, the following conditions are required:

1. The constraints sent back by a solver S_{olver} should neither be equivalent to a subset of the ones that it has just received, nor be deductible from the previous value of its local store. Thus, we define the new inferred constraints (when a state transition occurs) as a disjunction of constraints of S'_π which do not occur in C and which cannot be entailed by S_π.
$\Delta(S'_\pi, S_\pi) \setminus C = D$ such that:
$$\forall C_i \in D . C_i = \bigwedge c_j \mid ((S'_\pi \overset{solver}{\vdash} c_j) \wedge \neg(S_\pi \overset{solver}{\vdash} c_j) \wedge (c_j \notin C))$$
where S_π is the top of $\Pi_{S_{olver}}$ and S'_π is its new value after the processing of C by S_{olver},
2. The constraints sent back by a solver should not contain any new variables:
$$var(\Delta(S'_\pi, S_\pi) \setminus C) \subseteq \{var(S_\pi) \wedge var(C)\}$$
where $var(S_\pi)$ (resp. $var(C)$) is the set of variables of S_π (resp. C).

Thus, the form of the constraints that can be forwarded by a solver will depend on the entailment tests it can perform. For instance, if the entailment capabilities are limited to the detection of fixed values, upper bounds and lower bounds of a variable, one has to restrict the forwarded deductions to new instantiations of variables and narrowings of the domains of non ground variables. In this case one might define:

$$\Delta(S'_\pi, S_\pi) \setminus C = restrict(S'_\pi - S_\pi) \cup ground(S'_\pi - S_\pi)$$

where:

- $restrict(S'_\pi - S_\pi)$ is the set of constraints in the store S'_π restraining the domain of free variables in the store S_π:
$restrict(S'_\pi - S_\pi) = \{(a < x) \mid new\_bound(x, a, S'_\pi, S_\pi\}$
$$\cup \{(b > x)\} \mid new\_bound(x, b, S'_\pi, S_\pi\}$$
where $new\_bound(x, c, S'_\pi, S_\pi\}$ is a predicate which is true iff the lower bound (resp. upper bound) c of x in S'_π is greater (resp. smaller) than the lower bound (resp. upper bound) of x in S_π.

− $ground(S'_\pi - S_\pi)$ the set of variables that are fixed in S'_π but free in S_π:

$$ground(S'_\pi - S_\pi) = \{(x = a) \mid (S'_\pi \overset{solver}{\vdash} (x = a)) \wedge x \in var(S_\pi)\}$$

Proof of termination

To prove that the resolution of a cooperating solvers system always terminates two additional conditions must hold:

1. The resolution process must be guaranteed to halt for each solver,
2. Numeric solvers have to work on a finite set of numbers[9].

The above conditions and the restriction of forwarded constraints to relations defined on the initial set of variables guarantee that the set of messages is finite. The definition of $\Delta(S'_\pi, S_\pi) \setminus C$ —based upon local entailment tests— ensures that a solver will not forward twice the same message, and hence, that no cycle will occur in the resolution process.

Definition 8 (class of problems)

The class of problems which can be tackled by a cooperating solvers system subsumes the classes of problems that can be individually tackled by the different solvers involved in the cooperation. Indeed, the first transition applied to a solver yields exactly the same result as the one this solver would produce when handling the relevant subset of the initial set of constraints. As the different agents can work concurrently, computing these first solutions with a cooperating solvers system will not entail any significant overhead.

As long as no failure occurs, each computational step enforces the constraints system of one of the local store by including some propagated constraints. As all these constraints are deduced by one of the solvers from a subset of the initial set of constraints, these "tell operations" are sound. Thus, the class of problems which can be tackled by a cooperating solvers system can informally be defined by the constraints systems which can be transformed —by repeatedly applying the transition rules— into a constraints system which is either in a solved form[10] or which contains a sub-system whose inconsistency can be detected at least by one of the solvers of Γ.

More formally, let $\mathcal{R} = \{\Sigma^1, \Sigma^2, ..., \Sigma^n\}$ be the successive computational states yield by a cooperating solvers system when processing a system of constraints D, then the following properties hold :

− If Σ^n is a failing computational state and no Σ^i in $\mathcal{R}$ corresponds to a successful computational state, then D is inconsistent, i.e., if a definitive failure occurs before any solution is exhibited, then $D \vdash \bot$,

---

[9] This condition just requires that numeric solvers work on an approximation of real numbers by "machine interval", e.g., fixed length floating point numbers equipped with safe rounding operations [BMV94].

[10] A solved form is a simplified form (canonical form or expected end user form).

 – If Σ^n is a successful computational state, then the solution $S = \bigwedge_{A_i \in \Gamma} S_\pi(A_i)$
 is an approximation which is at least as accurate than the ones provided by
 the different solvers involved in the cooperation.

4   Processing of the messages

The way messages have to be processed[11] depends both on the form of the constraints forwarded by the solvers and on the number of non-deterministic solvers
(solvers which may generate disjunctive constraints) involved in the cooperation.
In a first step we consider that any disjunction of constraints satisfying the termination conditions (see definition 7) can be sent by the solvers to the monitor,
and that several non-deterministic solvers may be involved in the cooperation.
In this section, message processing by the solvers is assumed to be sequential,
i.e., the messages queues of the solvers are handled according to the FIFO rule.
The next section describes some optimization which can be achieved if the
Restore messages are processed first (i.e., the messages queues are handled according to priority rules). We also show which simplifications can be performed
if one accepts some restrictions either on information propagation or on the
solvers' capabilities.

When several non-deterministic solvers are involved in the cooperation, a
complete exploration of the search tree will require to restore both previous
states of the solvers and some already processed messages. While the management of the local stores can easily be realized at the level of each solver, the
restoration of already processed messages would be tricky to achieve locally.
Thus, we propose to store at the level of the monitor all messages dispatched to
the solvers. When a failure occurs, some messages dispatched since the set up
of the corresponding choice point have just to be reinserted in the queue of the
messages M of the monitor.

In the following we assume that messages, values of a local store Π, and
disjunctions in the queue L_D of the monitor can be identified unambiguously
through their labels. We also assume that labels hold all relevant path information required for defining matching operation between labels. We note respectively $label(S_\pi)$, $label(m)$ and $label(D)$ the labels of local store value S_π, message
m and disjunction D.

---

[11] Problems concerning the protocol for exchanging information are not addressed here.
We assume that the communication between agents is based on a reliable communication language (e.g. KQML [FMM94, LF94]) which guarantees that messages to
a single destination arrive in the order they were sent, and that messages delivery
is reliable. Communication between the monitor and the solvers is assumed to be
instantaneous (i.e., transmission of messages takes no time).

4.1 Initialization

Let $D = \bigvee_{i=1}^{m} C_i$ be the initial set of constraints. The resolution process starts by sending to the monitor the message $\text{Tell}(I_{nit} \rightarrow M_{onitor}, D)$.

The monitor agent builds a partition of the constraint C_1 into $part(C_1) = (C_{li}, C_{le}, C_{pe}, C_{np})$ where:

1. $C_1 \Leftrightarrow C_{li} \wedge C_{le} \wedge C_{pe} \wedge C_{np}$
2. elements of C_{li} are linear inequalities,
3. elements of C_{le} are linear equalities,
4. elements of C_{pe} are polynomial equalities whose total degree is greater than one,
5. elements of C_{np} are non-polynomial equalities, (e.g., constraints defined with functions like log, sin, cos, etc...). A non-linear inequality is converted to a non-linear equality and a linear inequality thanks to a slack variable.

The different subsets of the decomposition of C_1 are sent to the solvers that are able to handle them. Then, the monitor agent pushes in its stack L_D the remaining constraints of the disjunction. Thus, the initialization can be defined by the following transition:

$$Monitor(success, <>, <>)$$
$$Init \downarrow$$
$$Monitor(success, <>, L_D), \mathcal{M}$$

where:
$$L_D = < \text{Tell}(I_{nit} \rightarrow M_{onitor}, \bigvee_{j=2}^{m} C_j >$$
$$\mathcal{M} = \{\text{Tell}(M_{onitor} \rightarrow A, C_{li} \wedge C_{le}) \mid A \in \mathcal{A_L}\}$$
$$\cup \{\text{Tell}(M_{onitor} \rightarrow A, C_{le} \wedge C_{pe}) \mid A \in \mathcal{A_P}\}$$
$$\cup \{\text{Tell}(M_{onitor} \rightarrow A, C_1) \mid A \in \mathcal{A_{NP}}\}$$

4.2 Processing of the Tell messages by the *solvers* agents

When the head of the messages queue M of a solver A consists in a message $\text{Tell}(M_{onitor} \rightarrow A, C)$, the constraint C is handled[12] in the following way:

- if C can be deduced from S_π, then C is ignored,
- if there exists c_i in C such that c_i can be disproved from S_π, then S_π is set to $\perp$ and a Fail message is sent to the monitor,
- if the constraint C can neither be deduced nor disproved from S_π by A, then its non-redundant conjuncts c_i are added to the local store and $\Delta(S'_\pi, S_\pi) \backslash C$ is sent to the monitor.

More formally, processing of a Tell message enables the evolution of solver agent A in the following way:

---

[12] Keep in mind that Tell messages sent back by the monitor to solver agents do not contain disjunctive constraints.

$$A(< S_\pi > \cdot \Pi, success, < \texttt{Tell}(M_{onitor} \to A, C) > \cdot M)$$
$$Tell_{solver} \downarrow$$
$$A(< S'_\pi > \cdot \Pi, F, M), \, \mathcal{M}$$

where the values of S'_π, F and $\mathcal{M}$ depend on C:

1. $(\forall c_i \in C.S_\pi \overset{A}{\vdash} c_i)$
   $\Rightarrow (S'_\pi = S_\pi) \wedge (F = success) \wedge (\mathcal{M} = \emptyset)$

2. $(S \wedge C \overset{A}{\vdash} \bot)$
   $\Rightarrow ((S'_\pi = \bot) \wedge (F = fail) \wedge$
   $(\mathcal{M} = \{Fail(A \to M_{onitor})\})$

3. $(\exists c_i \in C.\neg(S \overset{A}{\vdash} c_i) \wedge \neg(S \wedge C \overset{A}{\vdash} \bot)$
   $\Rightarrow (S'_\pi = S_\pi \wedge C) \wedge (F = success) \wedge$
   $(\mathcal{M} = \{\texttt{Tell}(A \to M_{onitor}, \Delta(S'_\pi, S_\pi) \setminus C)\})$

4.3 Processing of the M_Choice and the Restore messages by the *solver* agents

Processing a M_Choice message requires simply that the solver duplicate its current value of the local store. More formally:

$$A(< S > \cdot \Pi, success, < \texttt{M\_Choice}(M_{onitor} \to A) > \cdot M)$$
$$M\_Choice \downarrow$$
$$A(< S, S > \cdot \Pi, success, M)$$

Processing a Restore message corresponds to the reverse operation: the appropriate state of the local store has just to be restored. More formally, a Restore message enables the evolution of A in the following way:

$$A(\Pi_1 \cdot < S_\pi > \cdot \Pi_2, success, < \texttt{Restore}(M_{onitor} \to A) > \cdot M)$$
$$Restore \downarrow$$
$$A(< S_\pi > \cdot \Pi_2, success, <>)$$

where the label of the Restore message matches[13] the one of S_π.

---

[13] Label l_0 is said to match label l_1 iff :

1. l_0 is a predecessor of l_1, i.e., l_1 has been generated after l_0 in the same branch of the actual search tree built by the cooperating resolution system, and thus, the path associated with l_0 is included in the one of l_1,
2. label l_0 is the closest —still available— predecessor of label l_1, i.e., there exists no message or state —in the current queue— with label l' such that l_0 is a predecessor of l' and that l' is a predecessor of l_1.

4.4 Processing of `Tell` messages by the monitor

The monitor processes `Tell` messages in the order of arrival as long as its messages queue M does not hold any `Fail` message. Except this latter condition, processing of `Tell` messages is similar to the processing of the initial message described in section 4.1. For each conjunction C of a constraint carried by a `Tell` message, the monitor builds a partition of C and the different subsets of the decomposition of C are sent to the solvers able to handle them. In case of disjunctive constraints, the monitor asks them to create a choice point before handling the first conjunction and pushes the remaining constraints of the disjunction in L_D.

More formally,

$$Monitor(success, < \texttt{Tell}(S_{olver} \rightarrow M_{onitor}, D) > \cdot M, L_D)$$
$$\texttt{Tell}_{monitor} \downarrow \quad \text{if } \texttt{Fail} \notin M$$
$$Monitor(success, M, L'_D), \mathcal{M}$$

where $\mathcal{M}$ and L'_D depend on D:

1. $D = C \Rightarrow L'_D = L_D \land \mathcal{M} = \mathcal{M'}$
2. $(D = \bigvee_{i=1}^{n} C_i) \land (n > 1) \Rightarrow$
   $$L'_D = < \texttt{Tell}(S_{olver} \rightarrow M_{onitor}, \bigvee_{i=2}^{n} C_i > \cdot L_D$$
   $$\mathcal{M} = \{\texttt{M\_Choice}(M_{onitor} \rightarrow A) \,|A \in \Gamma\} \uplus \mathcal{M'} \quad [14]$$

with $\mathcal{M'} = \{\texttt{Tell}(M_{onitor} \rightarrow A, C_{li} \land C_{le}) \,|\, A \in \mathcal{A_L}\}$
$\cup \{\texttt{Tell}(M_{onitor} \rightarrow A, C_{le} \land C_{pe}) \,|\, A \in \mathcal{A_P}\}$
$\cup \{\texttt{Tell}(M_{onitor} \rightarrow A, C) \,|\, A \in \mathcal{A_{NP}}\}$

4.5 Processing of `Fail` messages by the monitor

When the monitor is in a successful computational state and its messages queue M is holding a `Fail` message, this one is immediately taken into account. If the queue L_D does not hold any disjunction whose label matches the one of the `Fail` message, a definitive failure occurs. Otherwise, a `Restore` message is dispatched to all solvers and the monitor's flag is set to $fail$. More formally, processing of a `Fail` message enables the evolution of monitor in the following way:

$$Monitor(success, M, L_D)$$
$$Fail \downarrow \quad \text{if } \texttt{Fail} \in M$$
$$Monitor(fail, M', L'_D), \mathcal{M}$$

where the values of M', L'_D and $\mathcal{M}$ depend on the value of M and L_D:

1. If there is no message M_D in L_D such that $label(M_D)$ matches $label(\texttt{Fail})$, then a definitive failure occurs, and thus, M', $\mathcal{M}$ and L'_D are set to $<>$.

---

[14] Notation $\uplus$ is used instead of $\cup$ because the relative order between the two subsets of messages is important.

2. If $L_D = L_{D_1} \cdot < M_D > \cdot L_{D_2}$ such that $M_D = \texttt{Tell}(S_{olver} \to M_{onitor}, \bigvee_{i=n}^{m} C_i)$ and the label of M_D matches the one of the $\texttt{Fail}$ message, then $L'_D = L_{D_2}$, $\mathcal{M} = \{\texttt{Restore}(M_{onitor} \to A) \mid A \in \Gamma\}$ and M' holds:

- the messages of M which have not been generated with information resulting from the dispatching of message C_{n-1},
- the messages dispatched by the monitor since the set up of the choice point corresponding to M_D and which have not been generated with information resulting from the dispatching of message C_{n-1}.
- the message $\texttt{Tell}(S_{olver} \to M_{onitor}, \bigvee_{i=n}^{m} C_i)$.

The ordering of all these messages is done according to increasing labels.

As long as the monitor flag is set to $fail$ all messages except $\texttt{Fail}$ messages will be ignored. A $\texttt{Fail}$ message which occurs when the monitor is in a failing state will only be taken into account if its label is a predecessor of the one of the previous processed $\texttt{Fail}$ message. In the latter case, the same processing as in a successful state of the monitor will be performed.

4.6 Backtracking and synchronization of the solvers

In case of success, if the queue of remaining disjunctive constraints is not empty, the monitor dispatches a $\texttt{Restore}$ message[15] to the solvers, moves the first message from L_D to M and sets its flag to $Fail$. More formally, backtracking is defined by the following rule:

$$Monitor(success, <>, < \texttt{Tell}(S_{olver} \to M_{onitor}, D > \cdot L_D)$$
$$Back \downarrow$$
$$Monitor(fail, < \texttt{Tell}(S_{olver} \to M_{onitor}, D >, L_D), \mathcal{M}$$

where $\mathcal{M} = \{\texttt{Restore}(M_{onitor} \to A) \mid A \in \Gamma\}$

Thus, when a failure or a success occurs, the $\texttt{Restore}$ messages dispatched by the monitor will both guarantee the restoration of an appropriate local state and entail a *synchronization* of all solvers agents. This synchronization results from the fact that as long as the monitor flag is set to $fail$ only $\texttt{Fail}$ messages will be considered. The monitor will switch to a success state as soon as all solvers have processed the $\texttt{Restore}$ message successfully.

More formally, synchronization is defined by the following rule:

$$Monitor(fail, M, L_D)$$
$$Sync \downarrow \quad \text{if for all } A \text{ in } \Gamma, A(\_, success, <>) \text{ holds}$$
$$Monitor(success, M, L_D)$$

---

[15] The label of this $\texttt{Restore}$ message has to match the one of the first disjunction in L_D.

5   Optimizations and properties of specialized cooperative systems

The first part of this section is devoted to optimizations concerning processing of messages. In the second part, we show which simplifications can be done if one accepts restrictions on information propagation or on the capabilities of the solvers. First, we assume that the only information propagated by the solver concerns the detection of inconsistencies. In a second step, we consider that any disjunction of constraints satisfying the termination conditions can be sent by the solvers to the monitor, but that Γ is holding at most one non-deterministic solver.

5.1   Optimization of messages processing

A cooperating solvers system will be significantly more efficient if **Restore** messages are processed as soon as possible. As a matter of fact, if a solver has detected an inconsistency each solver should restore an appropriate state immediately. However, before processing an incoming **Restore** message, an agent has to check whether all anterior[16] **M_Choice** and **Tell** messages have been processed. If M contains such messages, they have to be processed first (all other messages will be removed from M). Otherwise, the **Restore** message will be processed in immediately.

Processing of disjunctive constraints could also be improved by generating some choice points earlier. Currently, when solver A infers a new disjunction, this disjunction is kept in its local store as long as A has not processed the corresponding **M_Choice** message from monitor. Thus, the integration of new constraints might generate numerous disjunctions. If the first choice point were set up by the solvers as soon as they have inferred a new disjunction, the number of disjunctions could drastically be reduced. However, this would lead to a less uniform and more tricky communication protocol.

5.2   Restriction of communication to failures propagation

Without loss of generality, we will assume that the initial set of constraints does not hold any disjunction. Indeed, processing an initial set of constraints with disjunctions just corresponds to the processing of the different disjuncts (i.e., successive calls of the monitor). Thus, there is no backtracking and one has not to worry about messages or states restoration. Cooperation between different solvers will just help to detect the inconsistencies that one of the solvers can identify on a subsystem of the initial system of constraints. The result of a successful computation correspond to the simplified sub-systems which are holding in the local states of the solvers.

---

[16] According to path information held in the corresponding labels.

5.3 Architecture with at most one non-deterministic solver

When only one non-deterministic solver is involved in the cooperation, no message interleaving problems may arise. Thus, already processed messages have not to be restored and it is therefore useless to store them at the level of the monitor. On failure or success, the exploration of alternative branches in the search tree just requires systematic backtrack to the appropriate choice point.

6 Conclusion

Inter-operability is certainly a key issue for progress in constraint solving. The architecture for a cooperating constraint solvers system we have defined in this paper is based on an asynchronous communication between heterogeneous solvers. Thus, it enables to *put together both symbolic and numerical solvers* for tackling systems of constraints that none of them could solve alone. Solutions provided by cooperating solvers systems are always at least as accurate than the one which could individually be computed by the different solvers. Moreover, as the latter solutions are computed in the first step of the cooperative resolution, there is no significant overhead for obtaining them.

A prototype for a cooperative system including two deterministic solvers and one non-deterministic solver has been developed [MR94]. This prototype —which makes use of various well known solvers (e.g., PrologIII [Col90, Rue93], MapleV [CGG+91])— enables to concurrently use a solver of linear equations and inequalities, a solver of polynomial equalities, and a solver based on interval propagation.

Further work concerns the introduction of redundant constraints in order to improve efficiency of such cooperative systems. For instance, when a conjunction of elementary constraints is split into several sub-systems, shared information could be augmented by defining some "redundant" linear equations: for each non-linear equation, a linear form can be defined by introducing new intermediate variables. Such redundant information could help detecting inconsistencies earlier. In the same way, redundant polynomial equations could also be generated from non-polynomial equations.

Thanks: Philippe Marti has implemented the prototype and we have had many constructive discussions. Thanks to Patrice Boizumault, Olivier Lhomme, Christine Solnon and Dan Vlasie for their careful reading of the different versions of the paper and for their helpful comments.

References

[Agh86]   Gul Agha. *Actors:A model of Concurrent Computation in distributed Systems*. MIT Press, 1986.

[BB94]   Henri Beringer and Bruno De Backer. Combinatorial problem solving in
           constraint logic programming with cooperative solvers. In C. Beierle and
           L. Plumer, editors, *Logic Programming: formal methods and practical ap-
           plications.* Elsevier Science Publisher B.V., 1994. to appear.

[BMV94]   Frédéric Benhamou, David McAllester, and Pascal Van Hentenryck.
           Clp(intervals) revisited. Technical Report CS-94-18, Department of Com-
           puter Science, Brown University, April 1994.

[Buc85]   Bruno Buchberger. Gröbner bases: An algorithmic method in polynomial
           ideal theory. In N. K. Bose, editor, *Multidimensional Systems Theory*,
           pages 184–232. Reidel Publishing Co., 1985.

[CGG+91]   B.W. Char, K.O. Geddes, G.H. Gonnet, M.B. Monagan B.L. Leong, and
           S.M. Watt al. *Maple V Language Reference Manual.* Springer-Verlag, New
           York, ISBN 0-387-97622-1, 1991.

[Col75]   G.E. Collins. Quantifier elimination for the elementary theory of real closed
           fields by cylindrical algebraic decomposition. *LNCS*, pages 134–183., 1975.

[Col90]   Alain Colmerauer. An introduction to PROLOG-III. *Communications of
           the ACM*, 33(7):69–90, July 1990.

[Col92]   Alain Colmerauer. Résolution naive de contraintes non linéaires. Technical
           report, Groupe Intelligence Artificielle, Université Aix – Marseille II, March
           1992.

[dBKPR93] F. de Boer, J. Kok, C. Palamidessi, and J. Rutten. Non-monotonic con-
           current constraint programming. In *Proc. of International Logic Program-
           ming Symposium*, pages 315–334, 1993.

[DLC89]   E.H. Durfee, V.R. Lesser, and D.D. Corkill. Cooperative distributed prob-
           lem solving. In E.A. Feigenbaum A. Barr, P.R. Cohen, editor, *The Hand-
           book of Artificial Intelligence*, volume IV, pages 83–147. Addison-Wesley
           Pub. Co., Reading, MA, 1989.

[FMM94]   T. Finin, D. McKay, and R. McEntire. KQML - A Language and Protocol
           for Knowledge and Information Exchange. Technical Report CS-94-02,
           Computer Science Department, University of Maryland, UMBC, Baltimore
           MD 21228, 1994.

[GCL91]   K. O. Geddes, S. R. Czapor, and G. Labah. *Algorithms for computer al-
           gebra.* Kluwer Academic Publishers, 1991.

[Hew77]   Carl Hewitt. Viewing control structures aspatterns of message passing.
           Artificial Inteligence, 8, 1977.

[Hon92]   Hoon Hong. Non-linear constraints solving over reals numbers in constraint
           logic programming (introducing RISC-CLP. Technical Report 92-08, Re-
           search Institute for Symbolic Computation, Johannes Kepler University,
           Linz, Austria, 1992.

[Hon93]   Hoon Hong. Risc-clp(real): Logic programming with non-linear constraints
           over the reals. In F. Benhamou and A. Colmerauer, editors, *Constraint
           Logic Programming: Selected Research.* MIT Press, 1993.

[Hon94]   Hoon Hong. Confluence of cooperative constraint solver. Technical report,
           Research Institute for Symbolic Computation, Johannes Kepler University,
           Linz, Austria, 1994.

[HSS+92]   W. S. Havens, S. Sidebottom, G. Sidebottom, J. Jones, and R. Ovans.
           Echidna: A constraint logic programming shell. In *Proc. Pacific Rim In-
           ternational Conference on Aritificial Intelligence*, Seuol, Korea, 1992.

[JM94]   Joxan Jaffar and Michael J. Maher. Constraint logic programming: A sur-
           vey. *Journal of Logic Programming*, 1994.

[JMSY92]   Joxan Jaffar, Spiro Michaylov, Peter J. Stuckey, and Roland H. C. Yap. The CLP($\mathcal{R}$) language and system. *ACM Transactions on Programming Languages and Systems (TOPLAS)*, 14(3):339–395, July 1992.

[LF94]   Y. Labrou and T. Finin. A semantic approach for KQML – a general purpose communication language for software agents. In *Proc of CIKM'94*, 1994. to appear.

[Lho93]   Olivier Lhomme. Consistency techniques for numeric CSPs. In *Proc. IJ-CAI93, Chambery, (France)*, pages 232–238, August 1993.

[LvE92]   J. H. M. Lee and M. H. van Emden. Adapting CLP($\mathcal{R}$) to floating-point arithmetic. In *Fifth Generation Computer Systems*, pages 996–1003, Tokyo, Japan, 1992. (also appears as report LP-18 (DCS-183-IR) Univ. of Victoria).

[Mac77]   A. Mackworth. Consistency in networks of relations. *Artificial Intelligence*, 8(1):99–118, 1977.

[Moo66]   R.E. Moore. *Interval Analysis*. Prentice Hall, 1966.

[MR94]   Philippe Marti and Michel Rueher. A cooperative scheme for solving constraints over the reals. In Hoon Hong, editor, *Proc. of PASCO94: First Parallel Symbolic Computation Symposium*, volume 5 of *Lecture Notes in Computing*, pages 284–293. World Scientific, 1994.

[MRS94]   U. Montanari, F. Rossi, and V. Saraswat. CC programs with both in- and non-determinism: A concurrent semantics. In Alan Borning, editor, *Proc. of PPCP'94: Second Workshop on Principles and Practice of Constraint Programming*, 1994.

[NO79]   Greg Nelson and Derek C. Oppen. Simplification by cooperating decision procedures. *ACM Transactions on Programming Languages and Systems (TOPLAS)*, 1(2):245–257, October 1979.

[PB94]   G. Pesant and M. Boyer. QUAD-CLP(R): Adding the power of quadratic constraints. In Alan Borning, editor, *PPCP'94: Second Workshop on Principles and Practice of Constraint Programming*, Seattle, May 1994.

[Rue93]   Michel Rueher. A first exploration of prologIII's capabilities. *Software–Practice and Experience*, 23:177–200, 1993.

[Sar93]   Vijay Anand Saraswat. *Concurrent Constraint Programming*. MIT Press, 1993.

[SKL90]   Vijay A. Saraswat, Kenneth M. Kahn, and Jacob Levy. Janus: A step towards distributed constraint programming. In *Proceedings North American Conference on Logic Programming*, 1990.

[SRP91]   V.A. Saraswat, M. Rinard, and P. Panangaden. Semantic foundation of concurrent constraint programming. In *Proceedings of the 18th ACM Symposium on Principles of Programming Language*, pages 333–352, 1991.

[Tsa93]   E. Tsang. *Foundations of Constraint Satisfaction*. Academic Press, 1993.

[Wal72]   D.L. Waltz. Generating semantic descriptions from drawings of scenes with shadows. Tech. rept. ai-tr-271, IT, Cambridge, MA, 1972.

The Definition of Kernel Oz

Gert Smolka*

Programming Systems Lab
German Research Center for Artificial Intelligence (DFKI)
Stuhlsatzenhausweg 3, 66123 Saarbrücken, Germany
email: smolka@dfki.uni-sb.de

Abstract. Oz is a concurrent language providing for functional, object-oriented, and constraint programming. This paper defines Kernel Oz, a semantically complete sublanguage of Oz. It was an important design requirement that Oz be definable by reduction to a lean kernel language. The definition of Kernel Oz introduces three essential abstractions: the Oz universe, the Oz calculus, and the actor model. The Oz universe is a first-order structure defining the values and constraints Oz computes with. The Oz calculus models computation in Oz as rewriting of a class of expressions modulo a structural congruence. The actor model is the informal computation model underlying Oz. It introduces notions like computation spaces, actors, blackboards, and threads.

1 Introduction

Oz is a concurrent language providing for functional, object-oriented, and constraint programming. It is defined by reduction to a lean sublanguage, called Kernel Oz, which is defined in this paper. The fact that we can elegantly define the semantic essence of Kernel Oz in less than ten pages indicates that such a multi-paradigm language is feasible. Further evidence is provided by the existence of a complete and efficient implementation.

The research behind Oz is driven by practical and theoretical considerations.

On the practical side, we see the need for a concurrent high-level language. Clearly, such a language should subsume higher-order functional programming, and organize state and concurrent functionality by means of objects. For tasks that involve search, the problem solving capabilities known from constraint logic programming would be advantageous.

On the theoretical side, we would like to advance towards a unified computation model subsuming and explaining seemingly incompatible programming paradigms. Concurrency and constrained-based problem solving are particularly challenging. Important considerations in the development of a unified programming model are its simplicity and generality as a mathematical construction,

---

* Supported by the Bundesminister für Forschung und Technologie (contract ITW 9105), the Esprit Basic Research Project ACCLAIM (contract EP 7195), and the Esprit Working Group CCL (contract EP 6028).

its usefulness as a basis for designing practical programming languages, and the existence of simple and efficient implementation models.

Programming languages can be classified by the computation model they are based on. Imperative programming, functional programming, logic programming, and concurrent logic programming are established classes based on different computation models. Oz does not fit in any of these classes. Rather, it is based on a new computation model incorporating ideas from functional programming, logic programming, and concurrent computation (the π-calculus, in particular). Here are some principles realized in Kernel Oz:

- Expressions are composed concurrently, with references made by lexically scoped logic variables.
- All values are defined as the elements of a first-order structure, called the Oz universe.
- Values are described by constraints, which are logic formulas over the Oz universe, and are combined automatically by means of constraint simplification and propagation.
- Reference to fresh names is possible, where names are special values of the Oz universe.
- Procedural abstraction is provided with full generality, where abstractions are referred to by names.
- State is provided through cells, which are primitive concurrent agents holding a reference.
- Speculative constraint computation is delegated to local computation spaces.
- Search is provided by a combinator spawning a local computation space and returning nondeterministic alternatives as procedural abstractions.

A guiding principle in the design of Oz was the requirement that Oz be definable by reduction to a kernel language as lean as possible. This led us to look for minimal primitives for expressing computational concepts such as functions, objects, and search. The search for a coherent collection of such primitives has been an exciting journey through a jungle of complexity to a glade of simplicity.

Structure of the Definition

The formal definition of a real programming language is a complex task. To be useful it must be simple. To be simple, it must introduce different abstractions, identifying different concerns that can be treated independently. For powerful abstractions to exist, the language design must be based on these abstractions. Thus designing a programming language subsumes creating the abstractions explaining the language.

The definition of Kernel Oz introduces three essential abstractions: the Oz universe, the Oz calculus, and the actor model.

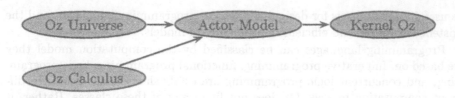

The Oz universe defines values and constraints. It is a structure of first-order predicate logic whose elements are the values and whose formulas are the constraints Oz computes with. The values of Oz are closed under tuple and record construction and include numbers, atoms and names. The fact that Oz provides for full higher-order programming but has first-order values only is a radical departure from the established models of functional computation.

The actor model[2] is the informal computation model underlying Oz. It introduces notions like computation spaces, actors, blackboards, and threads. Computations can be described by a class of elaborable expressions.

The Oz Calculus formalizes the actor model, with the exception of the reduction strategy and input and output. It models concurrent computation as rewriting of a class of expressions modulo a structural congruence. This set-up, which is also employed in more recent presentations of the π-calculus [8, 7], proves particularly useful for Oz since constraint propagation and simplification can be accommodated elegantly by means of the structural congruence.

Kernel Oz itself consists of a class of expressions whose semantics is defined by a translation into the elaborable expressions of the actor model. Kernel Oz restricts the expressivity of constraints so that an efficient implementation becomes possible.

How to read the Definition

This report gives a complete and concise definition of Kernel Oz. Supplementary literature is needed to understand the language design and programming in Oz. The reader is expected to have an intuitive understanding of Oz, as conveyed by [14]. More thorough introductions to programming in Oz are [5, 9]. The document [4] defines Oz by reduction to Kernel Oz.

On first reading, we recommend to ignore the constraint programming aspects of Oz (disjunctions, solvers, finite domains). The study of the Oz calculus should be prepared by reading [13], which introduces a simplified calculus not covering constraints and search. Other aspects of the calculus, in particular deep guards and the relationship to logic programming, are discussed in [12]. The search combinator is introduced in [10, 11].

Acknowledgements

The following persons have contributed directly to the design and/or implementation of Oz: Martin Henz, Michael Mehl, Martin Müller, Tobias Müller, Joachim

---

[2] The actor model for Oz is quite different from Hewitt's actor model of computation [6]. However, both models have in common that they are inherently concurrent (Hewitt speaks of ultra concurrency).

Niehren, Konstantin Popow, Ralf Scheidhauer, Christian Schulte, Gert Smolka, Ralf Treinen, Jörg Würtz.

2 The Oz Universe

The Oz universe is a mathematical model of the data structures Oz computes with. It is defined as a structure of first-order predicate logic with equality. All variables in Oz range over the elements of the Oz universe. The elements of the Oz universe are called **values**, and the first-order formulas over its signature are called **constraints**.

2.1 Values

Values are classified as shown in Figure 1. A value is either a primitive or a compound value. A **primitive value** is either a literal or a number. A **literal** is either an atom or a name. A **number** is either an integer or a float. A **compound value** is either a proper tuple or a proper record.

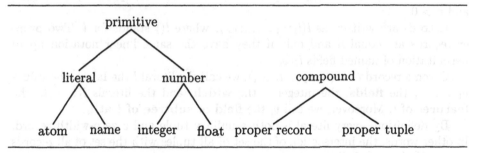

Fig. 1. Classification of values.

It remains to define the basic classes of atoms, names, integers, floats, proper records, and proper tuples, which are pairwise disjoint. Every value is in one and only one basic class.

Atoms are finite sequences of positive integers between 1 and 255. For convenience, atoms are usually written as strings, exploiting a mapping specified in [4] (e.g., 'fred', 'Atom', '', or '$#@\'78'). For alphanumeric atoms starting with a lower case letter we usually omit the quotes; for instance, we may write **fred** for 'fred'. Atoms are totally ordered by the lexical order induced by the canonical order on integers.

Names are primitive values without any structure. There are infinitely many names. There is no order on names.

The **integers** are the integers you know from school. They are ordered as usual.

The **floats** are the finitely many floating point numbers defined by the implementation. They are totally ordered.

A **tuple** is either a literal or a proper tuple. A **proper tuple** is an ordered tree

where l is a literal, $v_1, \ldots, v_n$ are values, and $n > 0$. Tuples are written as $l(v_1 \ldots v_n)$, where $l()$ stands for l. Two tuples are equal if and only if they have the same linear notation.

Given a tuple $t = l(v_1 \ldots v_n)$, we call the literal l the **label**, the values $v_1, \ldots, v_n$ the **components**, the integer n the **width**, and the integers $1, \ldots, n$ the **features** of t. Moreover, we call v_i the **component** or **subtree of t at i**.

A **record** is either a literal or a proper record. A **proper record** is an unordered tree

where l is a literal, $l_1, \ldots, l_n$ are pairwise distinct literals, $v_1, \ldots, v_n$ are values, and $n > 0$.

Records are written as $l(l_1\!:\!v_1 \ldots l_n\!:\!v_n)$, where $l()$ stands for l. Two proper records are equal if and only if they have the same linear notation up to permutation of named fields $l_i\!:\!v_i$.

Given a record $t = l(l_1\!:\!v_1 \ldots l_n\!:\!v_n)$, we call the literal l the **label**, the values $v_1, \ldots, v_n$ the **fields**, the integer n the **width**, and the literals $l_1, \ldots, l_n$ the **features** of t. Moreover, we call v_i the **field** or **subtree of t at l_i**.

By definition, every literal is both a nullary tuple and a zero-width record. In other words, the intersection of the set of all tuples with the set of all records is exactly the set of all literals.

The Oz universe is closed under tuple and record construction. It also contains all infinite trees that can be obtained from primitive values by tuple and record construction. Consequently, the equation

$$x = l(l_1\!:\!x\ l_2\!:\!v)$$

has exactly one solution for x given l, l_1, l_2, v. The straightforward mathematical details of the underlying construction can be found in [15].

An important operation on records is adjunction. The **adjunction** of two records s and t is the record $s * t$ defined as follows: the label of $s * t$ is the label of t; the features of $s * t$ are the features of s together with the features of t; and v is the subtree of $s * t$ at l if and only if either v is the subtree of t at l, or if l is not a feature of t and v is the subtree of s at l. Thus record adjunction amounts to record concatenation, where for common features the right argument takes priority. For instance,

$$l(a\!:\!1\ \ b\!:\!2\ \ c\!:\!3)\ *\ k(b\!:\!7\ \ d\!:\!4) = k(a\!:\!1\ \ b\!:\!7\ \ c\!:\!3\ \ d\!:\!4).$$

Lists are special tuples defined inductively as follows: the atom nil is a list (called the **empty list**); and if v is a value and w is a list, then the tuple '|'(v w) is a list (where v is called the **head** and w is called the **tail**). For instance,

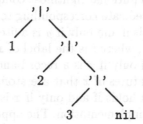

is the list containing the integers 1, 2, 3 in ascending order.

2.2 Constraints

The **signature of the Oz universe** consists of all primitive values and of finitely many predicates called **constraint predicates**. Every primitive value is a constant denoting itself. Note that the signature of the Oz universe contains no proper function symbol. The first-order formulas over the signature of the Oz universe are called **constraints**. The variables occurring in constraints are taken from a fixed infinite set.

The constraint predicates of the Oz universe are defined as follows:

- isAtom(x), isName(x), isLiteral(x), isInt(x), isFloat(x), isNumber(x), isRecord(x), and isTuple(x) are defined as one would expect from their names.
- intPlus(x,y,z) and intTimes(x,y,z) are the predicates corresponding to integer addition and multiplication. For instance, the formulas intMult(3,6,18), ¬intMult(3.0,6,18), and ¬intMult(3.0,6,18.0) are all true in the Oz universe.
- floatPlus(x,y,z), floatMinus(x,y,z), floatTimes(x,y,z), floatDiv(x,y,z), floatPow(x,y,z), floatAbs(x,y), floatCeil(x,y), floatFloor(x,y), floatExp(x,y), floatLog(x,y), floatSqrt(x,y), floatSin(x,y), floatASin(x,y), floatCos(x,y), floatACos(x,y), floatTan(x,y), and floatATan(x,y) are the predicates corresponding to the respective functions on the floats (defined by the implementation).
- floatToInt(x,y) and intToFloat(x,y) are the predicates corresponding to the respective conversion functions (defined by the implementation).
- atomString(x,y) holds if and only if y is the list of integers corresponding to the atom x. Note that atomString(x,y) is functional from left to right and from right to left.
- intLE(x,y), floatLE(x,y), and atomLE(x,y) are the predicates corresponding to the respective total orders on integers, floats, and atoms.
- label(x,y) holds if and only if x is a tuple or record whose label is y.
- width(x,y) holds if and only if x is a tuple or record whose width is y.

- **subtree**(x, y, z) holds if and only if x is a tuple or record, y is a feature of x, and z is the subtree of x at y.
- **extendTuple**(x, y, z) holds if and only if x and z are tuples and z is obtained from x by adding y as additional rightmost component.
- **adjoin**(x, y, z) is the predicate corresponding to record adjunction.
- **adjoinAt**(x, y, z, u) holds if and only if y is a literal and x and u are records such that $x * l(y : z) = u$, where l is the label of x.
- **arity**(x, y) holds if and only if x is a record and y is the list of the atomic features of x (i.e., all features of x that are atoms) in ascending order.
- **finiteDomainBound(x)** holds if and only if x is the upper bound for finite domains defined by the implementation. The upper bound must be an integer larger or equal than 255.

An important property of the Oz universe is the fact that validity of sentences is preserved under permutation of names; that is, given two first-order sentences S, T over the signature of the Oz universe such that T is obtained from S by a bijective renaming of names, S is valid in the Oz universe if and only if T is valid in the Oz universe. To obtain this property, no order on names is defined, and consequently the arity of a record does not contain those features that are names.

We write $\top$ for the trivial constraint true, and $\bot$ for the trivial constraint false. We say that

- a constraint ϕ **entails** a constraint ψ if the implication $\phi \to \psi$ is valid in the Oz universe
- a constraint ϕ is **equivalent** to a constraint ψ if the equivalence $\phi \leftrightarrow \psi$ is valid in the Oz universe
- a constraint ϕ is **satisfiable** if it does not entail $\bot$.

For convenience, we write

$$x \doteq l(l_1 : y_1, \ \ldots, \ l_n : y_n)$$

for the constraint

$$\mathtt{label}(x, l) \wedge \mathtt{width}(x, n) \wedge \mathtt{subtree}(x, l_1, y_1) \wedge \ldots \wedge \mathtt{subtree}(x, l_n, y_n).$$

and

$$x \doteq l(y_1, \ \ldots, \ y_n)$$

for the constraint

$$\mathtt{label}(x, l) \wedge \mathtt{width}(x, n) \wedge \mathtt{subtree}(x, 1, y_1) \wedge \ldots \wedge \mathtt{subtree}(x, n, y_n).$$

Moreover, we write

$$x \doteq y_1 | \ldots | y_k | \mathtt{nil}$$

for the constraint constraining x to the list $y_1, \ldots, y_k$.

Since the Oz universe has integers with addition and multiplication, satisfiability of constraints is undecidable, even for conjunctions of atomic integer constraints (Hilbert's Tenth Problem). Furthermore, satisfiability of constraints involving no other predicate but the subtree predicate is undecidable [16].

Kernel Oz restricts the use of constraints such that satisfiability and entailment of the occurring constraints is efficiently decidable.

More about the logic and algorithmic properties of record and tuple constraints can be found in [15, 3, 1, 2].

3 The Actor Model

The actor model is the informal computation model underlying Oz. It can be seen as a computational metaphor for the Oz calculus, the formal computation model underlying Oz. The two models formulate complementary views of computation in Oz supporting different intuitions. The actor model takes an operational perspective introducing notions like computation spaces, actors, and blackboards.

An important aspect of an inherently concurrent computation model like the one underlying Oz is the reduction strategy determining the partial order according to which possible reduction steps are to be performed. The reduction strategy has semantical significance as it comes to fairness, and practical significance as it comes to efficient implementation. Finding the right reduction strategy has been one of the more difficult issues in designing Oz.

By its nature, an informal model must rely on the intuition of the reader and cannot compete with the rigor of a formal model. Thus the Oz calculus is taken as the defining model, except for the reduction strategy and input and output, which are only formulated in the actor model. The formally inclined reader may prefer to study the Oz calculus first.

3.1 Computation Spaces, Blackboards, and Actors

Computation in Oz takes place in a computation space called the **top level**. A **computation space** consists of a finite number of **actors** connected to a **blackboard**. Computation proceeds by reduction of actors. When an actor reduces, it may create new actors and write information on the blackboard. As long as an actor does not reduce, it does not have an outside effect. Actors are short-lived: once they reduce they disappear.

A **blackboard** is a store containing a constraint and a partial function **binding** names to abstractions and variables. Names, variables, and constraints are defined by the Oz universe, and abstractions will be defined later. The blackboard stores its constraint only up to logical equivalence in the Oz universe. A blackboard is called **empty** if it binds no name and if its constraint is ⊤.

A blackboard **entails** a constraint ψ if the constraint of the blackboard entails ψ. A blackboard **binds a variable** x to a variable or constant $s \neq x$ if the constraint $x \doteq s$ is entailed by the constraint of the blackboard.

As computation proceeds, the information stored by the constraint of a blackboard increases monotonically. More precisely, if a blackboard evolves from a state B to a state B', then:

- If B entails a constraint ϕ, then B' entails ϕ.
- If B binds a name a to an abstraction $\overline{y}/E$, then B' binds a to $\overline{y}/E$.
- If B binds a name a to an once-only abstraction $\overline{y}/\!\!/E$, then B' binds a to either $\overline{y}/\!\!/E$ or $\overline{y}/\bot$.
- If B binds a name a to a variable, then B' binds a to a (possibly different) variable.

Abstractions will be defined shortly.

Some actors spawn **local computation spaces**, thus creating a tree of computation spaces taking the top level as root (see Figure 2). As computation proceeds, new local computation spaces are created and existing local spaces are discarded or merged with their parent space.

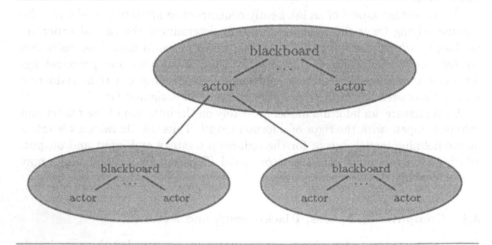

Fig. 2. A tree of computation spaces.

We say that a computation space S' is **subordinated** to a computation space S if $S' = S$ or if S' is subordinated to a local computation space of an actor of S. We say that a blackboard B is **subordinated** to a computation space S if B is the blackboard of a space subordinated to S. We say that a blackboard B' is **subordinated** to a blackboard B if B' is subordinated to the computation space of B. We say that X is **superordinated** to Y if Y is subordinated to X.

Every computation space is equipped with a possibly empty set of **local variables** and **local names**. As computation proceeds, computation spaces may acquire fresh local variables and names. A variable or name can be local to at most one computation space. If a variable or name is local to a space, the space is called its **home space**. Every occurring name must have a home space. Moreover, every variable having occurrences that are not statically bound (defined below) must have a home space. Variables and names with a home space can only occur in spaces subordinated to their home space.

The hierarchy of computation spaces rooted in the top level satisfies the following invariants:

- The constraints of subordinated blackboards entail the constraints of super-ordinated blackboards (slogan: local spaces know the constraints of global spaces).
- Names can only be bound by the blackboard of their home space, and there is at most one binding for a name.

An important operation on a blackboard is the **imposition of a constraint**. A constraint ψ is **imposed** on a blackboard storing a constraint ϕ by making the blackboard store the constraint $\psi \wedge \phi$, where imposing ψ includes imposing ψ on all subordinated blackboards (thus the invariants are maintained).

We say that a computation space **fails** if a constraint is imposed such that the constraint of the blackboard becomes unsatisfiable. If a computation space fails, all its subordinated spaces fail. When a computation space fails, the actors of the space are discarded and computation in the space is aborted. While failure of a local space is a regular event, failure of the top level is considered a run-time error.

While some actors can reduce immediately once they have been created, others have to wait until the blackboard contains sufficient information. Once an actor becomes reducible, it remains reducible, except if its computation space fails or is discarded. An actor has an outside effect only once it reduces.

We assume that actors are reduced one after the other, an important assumption known as **interleaving semantics**. While we anticipate that an implementation reduces actors in parallel, we insist that the effect of such a parallel computation must always be achievable by a sequence of single actor reductions. Interleaving semantics separates concurrency from parallelism such that parallelism has no semantic significance and is only visible at the implementation level.

An Oz computation takes places concurrently with other computations, with some of which it may have to communicate and synchronize. To model this essential aspect of concurrent computation within the actor model, we assume that every top level computation space is equipped with an **input** and an **output stream**. An actor computation may read from the input stream and write on the output stream. Agents in the outside world may write on the input stream and read from the output stream. We assume that the tokens communicated on the input and output streams are atoms.

There are four kinds of actors: Elaborators, conditionals, disjunctions, and solvers. Conditionals, disjunctions and solvers are called **proper actors**. While proper actors spawn local computation spaces, elaborators do not.

3.2 Elaboration of Expressions

Elaborators are actors that **elaborate** a class of **elaborable expressions** defined in Figure 3. Every constraint as defined by the Oz universe is an elaborable expression, *provided* it contains no names. There is the further side-condition that the formal arguments $\overline{y}$ of an abstractor expression $x:\overline{y}/E$ or $x:\overline{y}/\!\!/E$ be pairwise distinct.

$$
\begin{array}{lll}
E ::= & \phi & \text{constraint} \\
\mid & x:\overline{y}/E & \text{abstractor} \\
\mid & x:\overline{y}/\!\!/E & \text{once-only abstractor} \\
\mid & x:y & \text{cell creation} \\
\mid & E_1\,E_2 & \text{composition} \\
\mid & \textbf{local } \overline{x} \textbf{ in } E \textbf{ end} & \text{declaration} \\
\mid & \texttt{newName}[x] & \text{name creation} \\
\mid & \texttt{apply}[x\overline{y}] & \text{application} \\
\mid & \textbf{if } C_1 \,[]\, \ldots \,[]\, C_n \textbf{ else } E \textbf{ fi} & \text{conditional} \\
\mid & \textbf{or } C_1 \,[]\, \ldots \,[]\, C_n \textbf{ ro} & \text{disjunction} \\
\mid & \textbf{OR } C_1 \,[]\, \ldots \,[]\, C_n \textbf{ RO} & \text{nondistributing disjunction} \\
\mid & \texttt{solve}[x:E,y_1y_2y_3] & \text{solver} \\
\mid & \texttt{det}[x] & \text{determination} \\
\mid & \texttt{getDomain}[x,y] & \\
\mid & \texttt{input}[x] \mid \texttt{output}[x] & \\
\mid & \texttt{setThreadPriority}[x] & \\
\mid & \texttt{getThreadPriority}[x] & \\
C ::= & \overline{x} \textbf{ in } E_1 \textbf{ then } E_2 & \text{clause} \\
\end{array}
$$

$x,y,z ::= \langle \textit{variable} \rangle$

$\overline{x}, \overline{y} ::= \langle \textit{possibly empty sequence of variables} \rangle$

Fig. 3. Elaborable expressions.

An **abstraction** takes the form $\overline{y}/E$ or $\overline{y}/\!\!/E$, where the variables in $\overline{y}$ are called the **formal arguments** and the elaborable expression E is called the **body** of the abstraction. The formal arguments are required to be pairwise disjoint. An abstraction $\overline{y}/\!\!/E$ is called a **once-only abstraction** and can only be applied once.

Given an abstractor $x:\overline{y}/E$ or $x:\overline{y}/\!\!/E$, we call x the **designator** and $\overline{y}/E$ or $\overline{y}/\!\!/E$ the **abstraction** of the abstractor.

Given an application $\texttt{apply}[x\bar{y}]$, we call x the **designator** and $\bar{y}$ the **actual arguments** of the application.

Given a solver $\texttt{solve}[x\colon E, y_1 y_2 y_3]$, we call x the **root variable**, E the **guard**, and y_1, y_2, y_3 the **control variables** of the solver.

Given a clause $\bar{x}$ **in** E_1 **then** E_2, we call the variables in $\bar{x}$ the **local variables**, the expression E_1 the **guard**, and the expression E_2 the **body** of the clause.

The elaborable expressions come with the following variable binders:

- universal and existential quantification in constraints
- an abstractor $x\colon \bar{y}/E$ or $x\colon \bar{y}/\!/E$ binds its formal arguments $\bar{y}$ with scope E
- a declaration **local** $\bar{x}$ **in** E **end** binds its **declared variables** $\bar{x}$ with scope E
- a solver $\texttt{solve}[x\colon E, y_1 y_2 y_3]$ binds its root variable x with scope E
- a clause $\bar{x}$ **in** E_1 **then** E_2 binds its local variables $\bar{x}$ with scope E_1 and E_2.

Free and bound variables are defined accordingly. An elaborable expression is **closed** if it has no free variable.

Computation spaces also act as variable binders: They bind their local variables. Every variable occurrence must be bound either **statically** by a binder in an elaborable expression or a constraint, or **dynamically** by a computation space. In particular, all free variables of the elaborable expression of an elaborator must be bound dynamically.

Note that we heavily overload the term "binding". First, a blackboard can bind a name to a variable or an abstraction. Second, a blackboard can bind a variable x to a variable or constant s, which means that it entails the constraint $x \doteq s$. Third, a variable occurrence in an elaborable expression can be bound by a variable binder as defined above. Fourth, a variable occurrence can be bound by a computation space.

By **elaboration** of an expression E we mean the reduction of an elaborator for E. Elaboration of

- a constraint ϕ imposes ϕ on the blackboard of the computation space where the elaboration takes place. Recall that imposing a constraint on a blackboard means to impose it on all subordinated blackboards. Elaboration of a constraint in a space may result in the failure of some subordinated spaces.
- an abstractor $x\colon \bar{y}/E$ or $x\colon \bar{y}/\!/E$ chooses a fresh name a, binds a to the abstraction $\bar{y}/E$ or $\bar{y}/\!/E$, and imposes the constraint $x \doteq a$. Everything is done in the computation space where the elaboration takes place, which also acts as the home space of the fresh name a.
- a cell creation $x\colon y$ chooses a fresh name a, binds a to y, and imposes the constraint $x \doteq a$. The home space of a is the computation space where the elaboration takes place.
- a composition $E_1 \, E_2$ creates two separate elaborators for E_1 and E_2.
- a declaration **local** x **in** E **end** chooses a fresh variable y and creates an elaborator for the expression $E[y/x]$. The notation $E[y/x]$ stands for the expression that is obtained from E by replacing all free occurrences of x

with y. The home space of y is the space where the elaboration takes place. A multiple variable declaration **local** $x\,\overline{x}$ **in** E **end** is treated as a nested declaration **local** x **in local** $\overline{x}$ **in** E **end end**.

- **newName**$[x]$ chooses a fresh name a and imposes the constraint $x \doteq a$. The home space of a is the space where the elaboration takes place.
- **apply**$[x\overline{y}]$ must wait until there is a name a such that the blackboard entails $x \doteq a$. Then we distinguish three cases:

  1. If a is bound to an abstraction $\overline{z}/E$ by a superordinated blackboard and the number of the actual arguments $\overline{y}$ agrees with the number of the formal arguments $\overline{z}$, an elaborator for $E[\overline{y}/\overline{z}]$ is created (a copy of the body of the abstraction, where the actual arguments replace the formal arguments).

  2. If a is bound to an once-only abstraction $\overline{z}/\!\!/E$ by a superordinated blackboard and the number of the actual arguments $\overline{y}$ agrees with the number of the formal arguments $\overline{z}$, an elaborator for $E[\overline{y}/\overline{z}]$ is created. Moreover, a is rebound to the abstraction $\overline{y}/\bot$.

  3. If a is bound to a variable z by the blackboard of the space where the elaboration takes place and the actual arguments are $\overline{y} = y_1\,y_2$, then a is rebound to y_2 and the constraint $z \doteq y_1$ is imposed.

  In all other cases the elaborator for the application cannot reduce.

- a conditional **if** C_1 [] ... [] C_n **else** E **fi** creates a conditional actor spawning a local computation space for every clause $C_1, \ldots, C_n$ (see Figure 4). A local space for a clause $\overline{x}$ **in** E_1 **then** E_2 is created with a blackboard containing the constraint of the parent board, and a single elaborator for the expression **local** $\overline{x}$ **in** E_1 **end**. Moreover, the conditional actor carries the else expression E and associates with every local computation space the body E_2 of the corresponding clause. Since the scope of the local variables $\overline{x}$ includes both the guard E_1 and the body E_2 of the clause, the local variables $\overline{x}$ must be replaced consistently in the guard and in the body when **local** $\overline{x}$ **in** E_1 **end** is elaborated in the local space.

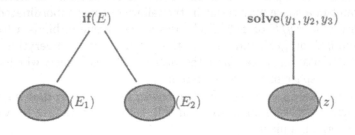

Fig. 4. A conditional actor with two local spaces and a solver.

- a disjunction **or** C_1 [] ... [] C_n **ro** or **OR** C_1 [] ... [] C_n **RO** creates a disjunctive actor spawning a local space for every clause $C_1, \ldots, C_n$. The local spaces are created in the same way as for conditionals. A disjunctive actor created by **or** ... **ro** is called **distributing**, and a disjunctive actor created by **OR** ... **RO** is called **nondistributing**.
- **solve**$[x: E, y_1 y_2 y_3]$ creates a solver actor spawning a single local computation space (see Figure 4). The local computation space is created with a blackboard containing the constraint of the parent blackboard, and a single elaborator for $E[z/x]$, where z is a fresh variable taking the local computation space as home. The solver actor carries the root variables z and the control variables y_1, y_2, y_3.
- **det**$[x]$ must wait until the blackboard entails $x \doteq c$ for some constant c of the signature of the Oz universe. When this is satisfied, the elaborator for **det**$[x]$ reduces without further action.
- **getDomain**$[x, y]$ must wait until there are nonnegative integers $n_1, \ldots, n_k$ such that the blackboard entails the disjunctive constraint $x \doteq n_1 \vee \ldots \vee x \doteq n_k$. When this is satisfied, the elaborator for **getDomain**$[x, y]$ reduces by imposing the constraint

$$y \doteq n_1 | \ldots | n_k | \texttt{nil}$$

where $n_1, \ldots, n_k$ is the shortest list in ascending order such that the blackboard entails $x \doteq n_1 \vee \ldots \vee x \doteq n_k$.
- **input**$[x]$ waits until there is an atom s on the input stream, consumes it, and imposes the constraint $x \doteq s$.
- **output**$[x]$ waits until the blackboard entails $x \doteq s$ for some atom s and then puts s on the output stream.
- **setThreadPriority**$[x]$ and **getThreadPriority**$[x]$ will be defined in Subsection 3.4.

We have now seen all reduction rules for elaborators.

3.3 Reduction of Proper Actors

We will now specify the reduction rules for proper actors. Recall that a proper actor is either a conditional, a disjunction, or a solver.

We say that a local computation space is **entailed** if it contains no actors anymore, and if the parent blackboard entails $\exists \overline{x} \, \phi$, where $\overline{x}$ are the local variables and ϕ is the constraint of the blackboard of the local space.

Reduction of Conditionals

A conditional actor can reduce if one of its local computation spaces is entailed, or if all its local computation spaces have failed.

If one of its local computation spaces is entailed, the conditional can reduce as follows: discard the other local spaces, merge the local blackboard with the global blackboard (there cannot be any conflicts), and create an elaborator for the associated clause body.

If several local computation spaces of a conditional are entailed, the conditional can choose with which one it reduces.

If all local computation spaces of a conditional have failed, it can reduce to an elaborator for the else expression.

Reduction of Disjunctions

A disjunctive actor can reduce if all but possibly one of its local computation spaces have failed, or if a local space whose associated clause body is the constraint $\top$ is entailed.

If all local computation spaces of a disjunction have failed, the disjunction can reduce to an elaborator for the constraint $\bot$.

If all but one local computation space of a disjunction have failed, the disjunction can reduce with the unfailed space. This is done by merging the unfailed local space with the global space (there cannot be any conflicts), and by creating an elaborator for the associated clause body.

If a local space with associated clause body $\top$ is entailed, the disjunctive actor can reduce without further action.

Reduction of Solvers

A local computation space is called **blocked** if it is unfailed and no actor in the space or a subordinated space can reduce. A local computation space is called **stable** if it is blocked and remains blocked for every satisfiable strengthening of the constraint of the parent blackboard.

A solver actor can reduce if its local computation space is either failed or stable.

If the local computation space of a solver is failed, the solver can reduce to an elaborator for the application $\texttt{apply}[y_1]$, where y_1 is the first control variable of the solver.

If the local computation space of a solver is stable and does not contain a distributing disjunctive actor, the solver can reduce to an elaborator for the expression

```
local x in
    x: z/F
    apply[y₂ x S]
end
```

where z is the root variable of the solver, F is an elaborable expression representing the stable local computation space, y_2 is the second control variable of the solver, and S (the so-called **status**) is either the atom **entailed** or **stable**, depending on whether the local space is entailed or not. That F represents the local computation space means that elaboration of $\text{solve}[z\colon F, y_1 y_2 y_3]$ will recreate the local space up to renaming of local variables and names by reduction of elaborators only. The transformation of a computation space into an elaborable expression is called **reflection**.

If the local computation space of a solver is stable and contains a distributing disjunctive actor **or** C_1 [] ... [] C_n **ro**, the solver can reduce to an elaborator for

```
local x1 x2 in
    x1: z // local ȳ in F or C1 ro end
    x2: z // local ȳ in F or C2 [] ... [] Cn ro end
    apply[y3 x1 x2 S]
end
```

where **local** $\overline{y}$ **in** F **or** C_1 [] ... [] C_n **ro end** is an elaborable expression representing the stable local computation space, z is the root variable of the solver, y_3 is the third control variable of the solver, and S (the so-called **status**) is either the atom **last** or **more**, depending on whether $n = 1$ or not. The alternatives are returned as once-only abstractions to allow for an efficient implementation.

For distributing disjunctive expressions and actors the order of clauses and local computation spaces is significant and preserved by elaboration and reflection.

3.4 Reduction Strategy

So far we have not made any assumptions about the order in which actors are reduced. Such assumptions are needed, however, so that one can write fair and efficient programs. Without such assumptions a single infinite computation could starve all other computations.

Oz's reduction strategy organizes actors into threads, where every thread is guaranteed to make progress if it can reduce and has sufficient priority. Threads are equipped with priorities to provide for asynchronous real time programming.

A **thread** is a nonempty sequence of actors. Every actor belongs to exactly one thread. When a computation space fails or is discarded, its actors are discarded, which includes their removal from the threads they reside on. The actors on a thread may belong to different computation spaces.

Every thread has a **priority** that can be changed. The priority is an integer, where a larger integer means a higher priority.

Threads are scheduled by means of a **priority queue**, which is served by one or several **workers**. A free worker picks the first thread from the queue and starts reducing it. If the thread cannot reduce anymore, or the worker has spent more than a given time limit reducing it, the worker puts the thread back into the queue, at the position determined by the current priority of the thread.

Although there may be several workers, only one actor can reduce at a time. Thus reductions performed by different workers are interleaved into a sequence of single reductions (so-called **interleaving semantics**).

A thread can reduce by reducing one of its actors, or by moving its first actor to a new thread. If possible, a thread reduces a proper actor. If it contains no reducible proper actor, the thread must reduce with its first actor. Every thread that contains more than one actor is reducible.

To reduce an actor on a thread means to reduce the actor and replace it with the possibly empty sequence of actors it has reduced to. Proper actors reduce to a single elaborator or no actor at all. Elaborators may reduce to more than one actor. For them the order of the replacing actors is defined as follows:

- For the elaborator of a composition $E_1 \, E_2$, the elaborator for E_1 goes before the elaborator for E_2.
- For the elaborator of a conditional [disjunction], the elaborators for the clauses $e_1, \ldots, e_n$ go before the conditional [disjunctive] actor a,

$$e_1 \ldots e_n \, a$$

where the order of the elaborators $e_1, \ldots, e_n$ is given by the order of the clauses in the conditional [disjunctive] expression
- For the elaborator of a solver, the elaborator of the local computation space goes before the solver actor.

Reduction of threads is defined as follows:

1. if a thread contains a reducible proper actor, reduce it
2. if a thread contains no reducible proper actor and the first actor is reducible, reduce the first actor
3. if a thread contains no reducible proper actor, the first actor is not reducible, and the thread contains further actors, move the first actor to a newly created thread; the newly created thread inherits the priority of the creating thread.

We say that the third rule **suspends** the first actor of a thread. Note that suspension of an actor creates a new thread, and that this is the only way to create a new thread.

The strategy gives priority to the reduction of proper actors, where the position in the thread does not matter. Since proper actors reduce to elaborators, a thread will quickly run out of reducible proper actors. Elaborators are reduced with a strategy reminiscent of sequential execution.

Elaboration of an expression

- `setThreadPriority[x]` must wait until there is an integer n such that the blackboard entails $x \doteq n$. When this is satisfied, the elaborator of `setThreadPriority[x]` can reduce by changing the priority of its thread to n. If the priority is not stricly increased, the worker must return the thread to the priority queue.
- `getThreadPriority[x]` imposes the constraint $x \doteq n$, where n is the current priority of the thread elaborating the expression.

Concerning solvers, there is a further assumption about order: When a solver reduces by distributing a disjunctive actor, the distributing disjunctive actor that was created last is distributed.

3.5 Computations

A computation space is called **irreducible** if no actor in the space or a subordinated space can reduce. Note that a space is irreducible if and only if it is either blocked or failed.

A **finite computation** issuing from a closed elaborable expression E is a sequence $S_1, \ldots, S_n$ of states of a top level computation space such that:

- The initial state S_1 consists of the empty blackboard and an elaborator for E.
- Every state S_{i+1} is obtained from its predecessor S_i by reduction of a single actor, possibly in a subordinated space.
- The final state S_n is irreducible.
- The state sequence respects the reduction strategy.

Since failure prevents further reduction, none of the states $S_1, \ldots, S_{n-1}$ can be failed.

A **infinite computation** issuing from a closed elaborable expression E is an infinite sequence $S_1, S_2, S_3, \ldots$ of states of a top level computation space such that:

- The initial state S_1 consists of the empty blackboard and an elaborator for E.
- Every state S_{i+1} is obtained from its predecessor S_i by reduction of a single actor, possibly in a subordinated space.
- The state sequence respects the reduction strategy.

Since failure prevents further reduction, none of the states in an infinite computation can be failed.

Example 1. There are both finite and infinite computations issuing from the closed elaborable expression

```
local X Y in
    X: / apply[X]
    if X≐Y then ⊤ [] X≐Y then apply[X] else ⊤ fi
    X≐Y
end
```

However, due to the reduction order imposed by threads, there are no infinite computations issuing from

```
local X Y in
    X: / apply[X]
    X ≐ Y
    if X ≐ Y then T [] X ≐ Y then apply[X] else T fi
end
```

3.6 Success, Failure, and Termination of Actors

The **direct descendants** of an actor A are the actors A creates when it reduces. The **descendants** of an actor are obtained by taking the reflexive and
transitive closure of the direct descendant relation. The actors in the local spaces
of a proper actor A are not considered descendants of A, and neither are their
reductions considered reductions of A.

We say that an actor has

- **succeeded** if all its descendants have reduced without failing the computation space
- **failed** if one of its descendants has failed the computation space
- **terminated** if all its descendants have reduced.

Note that an actor has terminated if and only if it has succeeded or failed.

4 Kernel Oz

This section defines Kernel Oz, a semantically complete sublanguage of Oz.
Every Oz program can be translated into an expression of Kernel Oz. In fact,
the meaning of Oz programs is defined by a reduction to Kernel Oz.

Kernel Oz consists of a class of expressions whose semantics is defined by a
translation into the elaborable expressions of the actor model.

Kernel Oz restricts the elaborable constraints such that the actor model can
be implemented efficiently. This is necessary since properties such as satisfiability
and entailment of constraints are undecidable in general. Kernel Oz provides
most of the available constraints only indirectly through predefined procedures.
All predefined procedures are defined by an elaborable expression called prelude.

Although Oz is semantically defined by reduction to Kernel Oz, it cannot be
implemented efficiently this way. In particular, implementations are supposed to
realize objects and finite domains more efficiently than it is suggested by their
translation to Kernel Oz.

4.1 Syntax

The abstract syntax of Kernel Oz is defined in Figure 5. It introduces a class
of expressions called **kernel expressions**. The kernel expressions are less expressive than the elaborable expressions. Except for constraints, the missing
expressivity is regained by means of predefined procedures.

$$E ::= \textbf{false} \mid \textbf{true} \mid x\text{=}s \qquad\qquad\qquad \text{constraints}$$

$\mid$ **proc** $\{x\ \overline{y}\}\ E$ **end**	procedure definition
$\mid$ $\{x\ \overline{y}\}$	procedure application
$\mid$ $E_1\ E_2$	composition
$\mid$ **local** $\overline{x}$ **in** E **end**	declaration
$\mid$ **if** C_1 [] $\ldots$ [] C_n **else** E **fi**	conditional
$\mid$ **or** C_1 [] $\ldots$ [] C_n **ro**	disjunction
$\mid$ **OR** C_1 [] $\ldots$ [] C_n **RO**	nondistributing disjunction

$$C ::= \overline{x}\ \textbf{in}\ E_1\ \textbf{then}\ E_2 \qquad\qquad\qquad \text{clause}$$

$$x, y ::= \langle variable \rangle$$

$$\overline{x},\ \overline{y} ::= \langle possibly\ empty\ sequence\ of\ variables \rangle$$

$$s ::= x \mid \langle atom \rangle \mid \langle number \rangle$$

Fig. 5. Kernel expressions.

A concrete syntax for kernel expressions is inherited from the concrete syntax of Oz (defined in [4]).

Every kernel expression can be rewritten into an elaborable expression by applying the following rules:

- A procedure definition **proc** $\{x\ y_1\ \ldots\ y_n\}\ E$ **end** rewrites into

      local A R in
          A: y₁ ... yₙ/E
          R≐rec(abstraction: A, arity: n)
          x≐ChunkLabel(Proc: R)
      end

- A procedure application $\{x\ y_1\ \ldots\ y_n\}$ rewrites into

      if R in subtree(x, Proc, R)
      then
          local A in
              subtree(R, arity, n)
              subtree(R, abstraction, A)
              apply[A y₁ ... yₙ]
          end
      else false fi

- The constraint expressions **false**, **true**, $x\text{=}s$ rewrite into the constraints $\perp$, $\top$, and $x \doteq s$, respectively.

The symbol *Proc* is a variable that must not occur in kernel expressions. Whenever possible, we use Oz's lexical syntax [4]; for instance, **abstraction**, arity and rec are atoms, and A, R, and ChunkLabel are variables. Moreover, subtree(R, arity, n) is a constraint, and R$\doteq$rec(abstraction: A, arity: n) and $x \doteq$ ChunkLabel(*Proc*: R) abbreviate constraints (see Section 2).

The variable binders of the kernel expressions are clear from the translation to the elaborable expressions. It is understood that the declarations of A and R introduced by the above translation rules do not capture variables.

By providing abstractors and applications only indirectly through procedure definitions and applications, Kernel Oz establishes a recognizable class of first-order values acting as procedures (see the definition of the kernel procedure IsProcedure).

A kernel expression E is **admissible** if its free variables are among the **kernel variables**, which are the following:

```
ChunkLabel  NewName  NewCell  Exchange  Det  SolveCombinator
IsInt  IsFloat  IsNumber  IsAtom  IsName  IsLiteral
IsProcedure IsCell  IsChunk  IsTuple  IsRecord  IsNoNumber
Label  Width  Subtree  ExtendTuple  Adjoin  AdjoinAt  Arity
AtomToString  StringToAtom  ProcedureArity
'=<'  '+'  '-'  '*'  '/'  Pow Abs
FloatToInt  IntToFloat  Ceil  Floor
Exp Log Sqrt Sin Cos Tan Asin Acos Atan
FiniteDomainBound  FiniteDomain  FiniteDomainNE
GetFiniteDomain 'Input'  'Output'
'SetThreadPriority'  'GetThreadPriority'
```

4.2 Semantics

The semantics of an admissible kernel expression E is defined as the semantics of the closed elaborable expression

```
local Proc ⟨Kernel Variables⟩ in
    newName[ChunkLabel]
    newName[Proc]
    ⟨Prelude⟩
    ⟨E rewritten into an elaborable expression⟩
end
```

where the elaborable expression ⟨Prelude⟩ is defined in the next section.

computation issuing from an admissible kernel expression E is a computation issuing from the closed elaborable expression obtained from E by the above translation.

4.3 Prelude

Below we define several elaborable expressions that composed together yield the expression ⟨Prelude⟩ needed for the semantic translation above. The procedures defined in the prelude are called **kernel procedures**. We use Oz's lexical syntax for variables and atoms (with the exception of the variable *Proc*, which has no concrete syntax), and Kernel Oz's syntax for procedure definitions and applications (to be expanded as defined in Section 4.1). Moreover, we write E_1 **then** E_2 for a clause $\overline{x}$ **in** E_1 **then** E_2 whose variable prefix $\overline{x}$ is empty.

Names, Determination, Procedures, and Cells

```
proc {NewName X}
   newName[X]
end

proc {Det X}
   if isInt(X) then det[X] else true fi
end

proc {IsProcedure P}
   if R in subtree(P,Proc,R) then true else false fi
end

proc {ProcedureArity P N}
   if R in subtree(P,Proc,R) then subtree(R,arity,N)
   else false fi
end

local Cell in
   {NewName Cell}
   proc {NewCell X C}
      local Z in
         Z: X
         C≐ChunkLabel(Cell:Z)
      end
   end
   proc {IsCell X}
      if Z in subtree(X,Cell,Z) then true else false fi
   end
   proc {Exchange C X Y}
      if Z in subtree(C,Cell,Z) then apply[Z X Y]
      else false fi
   end
end
```

Procedures and cells are modelled as special records called chunks, where a field holds the name bound to an abstraction or variable. Procedures and cells cannot be faked since their features *Proc* and `Cell`, respectively, cannot be accessed by admissible kernel expressions. This means that every value that qualifies as a procedure or cell must have been introduced by a procedure definition or an application of the kernel procedure **NewCell**, or must have been derived from such a value by possibly repeated adjunction.

Classification Predicates

The classification predicates classify the values of Kernel Oz according to the hierarchy shown in Figure 6. The classes value, number, noNumber, and literal are obtained by union of their subclasses. All leaf classes are disjoint. The classification predicates for procedures and cells were already defined in Section 4.3.

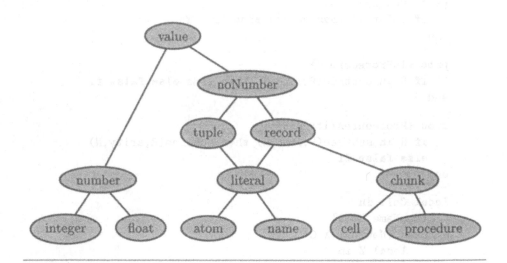

Fig. 6. Classification of values in Kernel Oz.

```
proc {IsInt X}
   if isInt(X) then det[X] else false fi
end

proc {IsFloat X}
   if isFloat(X) then true else false fi
end

proc {IsNumber X}
   if {IsInt X} then true else {IsFloat X} fi
end
```

```
proc {IsAtom X}
   if isAtom(X) then true else false fi
end

proc {IsName X}
   if isName(X) then true else false fi
end

proc {IsLiteral X}
   if {IsAtom X} then true else {IsName X} fi
end

proc {IsTuple X}
   if isTuple(X) then true else false fi
end

proc {IsRecord X}
   if isRecord(X) then true else false fi
end

proc {IsChunk X}
   if {IsRecord X} then label(X,ChunkLabel) else false fi
end

proc {IsNoNumber X}
   if {IsTuple X} then true else {IsRecord X} fi
end
```

Order

```
proc {'=<' X Y}
   if {IsInt X} {IsInt Y} then intLE(X,Y)
   [] {IsFloat X} {IsFloat Y} then floatLE(X,Y)
   [] {IsAtom X} {IsAtom Y} then atomLE(X,Y)
   else false fi
end
```

Tuples, Records, and Atoms

```
proc {Label X L}
   if {IsNoNumber X} then label(X,L) else false fi
end

proc {Width X N}
   if {IsNoNumber X} then width(X,N) else false fi
end
```

```
proc {Subtree X F Y}
   if {IsRecord X} {IsLiteral F} then subtree(X,F,Y)
   [] {IsTuple X} {IsInt F} then subtree(X,F,Y)
   else false fi
end

proc {ExtendTuple X Y Z}
   if {IsTuple X} then extendTuple(X,Y,Z) else false fi
end

proc {Adjoin X Y Z}
   if {IsRecord X} {IsRecord Y}
   then if {IsChunk X} then false else adjoin(X,Y,Z) fi
   else false fi
end

proc {AdjoinAt X F Y Z}
   if {IsRecord X} {IsLiteral F}
   then if {IsChunk X} then false else adjoinAt(X,F,Y,Z) fi
   else false fi
end

proc {Arity X L}
   if {IsRecord X} then arity(X,L) else false fi
end

proc {AtomToString A L}
   if {IsAtom A} then atomString(A,L) else false fi
end

local ListDet in
   proc {StringToAtom L A}
      if {ListDet L} then  atomString(A,L) else false fi
   end
   proc {ListDet Xs}
      if X Xr in Xs≐'|'(X,Xr) {Det X}
      then {ListDet Xr} else Xs=nil fi
   end
end
```

Arithmetic

```
proc {'+' X Y Z}
   if {IsInt X} {IsInt Y} then intPlus(X,Y,Z)
   [] {IsFloat X} {IsFloat Y} then floatPlus(X,Y,Z)
   else false fi
end
```

```
proc {'-' X Y Z}
   if {IsInt X} {IsInt Y} then intPlus(Y,Z,X)
   [] {IsFloat X} {IsFloat Y} then floatMinus(X,Y,Z)
   else false fi
end


proc {'*' X Y Z}
   if {IsInt X} {IsInt Y} then intTimes(X,Y,Z)
   [] {IsFloat X} {IsFloat Y} then floatTimes(X,Y,Z)
   else false fi
end


proc {'/' X Y Z}
   if {IsFloat X} {IsFloat Y} then floatDiv(X,Y,Z)
   else false fi
end


proc {Pow X Y Z}
   if {IsInt X} Y=0 then Z=1
   [] {IsInt X} Y>0 then
       local A B in {'-' Y 1 A} {Pow X A B} {'*' X B Z} end
   [] {IsFloat X} {IsFloat Y} then floatPow(X,Y,Z)
   else false fi
end


proc {Abs X Y}
   if {IsInt X} then if X<0 then {'-' 0 X Y} else X=Y fi
   [] {IsFloat X} then floatAbs(X,Y)
   else false fi
end


proc {FloatToInt X Y}
   if {IsFloat X} then floatToInt(X,Y) else false fi
end


proc {IntToFloat X Y}
   if {IsInt X} then intToFloat(X,Y) else false fi
end


proc {Ceil X Y}
   if {IsFloat X} then floatCeil(X,Y) else false fi
end
```

The remaining kernel procedures for floating point arithmetic

Floor Exp Log Sqrt Sin Cos Tan Asin Acos Atan

are defined analogously to Ceil.

Finite Domains

```
finiteDomainBound(FiniteDomainBound)

proc {FiniteDomain X}
   isInt(X) ∧ intLE(0,X) ∧ intLE(X,FiniteDomainBound)
end

proc {FiniteDomainNE X N}
   if {FiniteDomain X} {IsInt N} then ¬(X≐N) else false fi
end

proc {GetFiniteDomain X L}
   if {FiniteDomain X} then getDomain[X,L] else false fi
end
```

Solve Combinator

```
proc {'SolveCombinator' Query Answer}
   local Failed Solved Distributed in
      Failed:/
         Answer≐failed
      Solved:X S/
         local P Q in
            proc {P Y} apply[X Y] end
            adjoinAt(P,status,S,Q)
            Answer≐solved(Q)
         end
      Distributed:X Y S/
         local P Q L R in
            proc {P Z} apply[X Z] end
            proc {Q Z} apply[Y Z] end
            adjoinAt(P,status,last,L)
            adjoinAt(Q,status,S,R)
            Answer≐distributed(L,R)
         end
      solve[X: {Query X}, Failed Solved Distributed]
   end
end
```

Thread Priorities

The kernel procedures 'SetThreadPriority' and 'GetThreadPriority' must only be used in system programs.

```
proc {'SetThreadPriority' N}
    if {IsInt N} then setThreadPriority[N] else false fi
end

proc {'GetThreadPriority' N}
    getThreadPriority[N]
end
```

Input and Output

The kernel procedures 'Input' and 'Output' serve as a semantic model for the higher-level input-output functions provided by Oz implementations. They are not meant for real use. When applied in a local computation space, 'Input' and 'Output' fail.

```
local IsTopLevel TopLevelCell in
    proc {'Input' X}
        {IsTopLevel} input[X]
    end
    proc {'Output' X}
        if {IsAtom X} then {IsTopLevel} output[X]
        else false fi
    end
    {NewCell top TopLevelCell}
    proc {IsTopLevel}
        local X in
            {ExchangeCell TopLevelCell X X}
            if X=top then true [] true then false
            else false fi
        end
    end
end
```

4.4 Normal Computation Spaces

Kernel Oz restricts the elaborable constraints such that failure, entailment, and stability of local computation spaces become efficiently decidable. This is done by providing the necessary constraints in weakened form through predefined procedures, where the weakened forms can be defined by elaborable expressions.

In the following we define a property called **normality** that is satisfied by all computation spaces occurring in computations issuing from admissible kernel expressions. For normal computation spaces, satisfiability, entailment, and stability can be decided efficiently.

A **determinant** for a variable x is a constraint that has one of the following forms:

1. $x \doteq s$, where s is an atom, a name, an integer, or a float
2. $x \doteq l(l_1 : y_1, \ldots, l_n : y_n)$, where l and $l_1, \ldots, l_n$ are literals and $y_1, \ldots, y_n$ are variables
3. $x \doteq l(y_1, \ldots, y_n)$, where l is a literal and $y_1, \ldots, y_n$ are variables.

We say that a constraint ϕ **determines** a variable x if ϕ entails a determinant for x.

In the following it will become clear that the kernel procedure **Det** is defined such that an elaborator for {Det X} succeeds if and only if X is determined by the constraint of the blackboard.

A **normal constraint** for a variable x is either a determinant for x or a disjunction $x \doteq n_1 \vee \ldots \vee x \doteq n_k$, where $n_1, \ldots, n_k$ are $k > 1$ integers between 0 and the upper bound for finite domains.

A **solved constraint** is a constraint of the form

$$x_1 \doteq y_1 \wedge \ldots \wedge x_k \doteq y_k \wedge \phi_{k+1} \wedge \ldots \wedge \phi_n$$

where there exist variables $x_{k+1}, \ldots, x_n$ such that

- $x_1, \ldots, x_n$ are pairwise distinct
- $\phi_{k+1}, \ldots, \phi_n$ are normal constraints for $x_{k+1}, \ldots, x_n$
- the variables $x_1, \ldots, x_k$ are different from the variables $y_1, \ldots, y_k$ and do not occur in the normal constraints $\phi_{k+1}, \ldots, \phi_n$.

Proposition 1. *Every solved constraint is satisfiable in the Oz universe.*

Theorem 2. *The conjunction of two solved constraints is either unsatisfiable or logically equivalent (in the Oz universe) to a solved constraint. Moreover, entailment between two possibly existentially quantified solved constraints can be decided in quasi-linear time.*

Proof. Follows from the results in [15].

A computation space S is **normal** if all its subordinated spaces are normal, and if it satisfies one of the following conditions:

1. S is failed.
2. The constraint of S's blackboard is solved.
3. S contains no actors and the constraint of its blackboard is a conjunction of a solved constraint and an atomic formula obtained with one of the following constraint predicates: **subtree**, **isInt**, **IsFloat**, **IsAtom**, **IsName**, **IsTuple**, **IsRecord**.

Claim 3 *Every computation space occurring in a computation issuing from an admissible kernel expression is normal (up to logical equivalence of constraints in the Oz universe).*

4.5 Logical Semantics

A pair of a constraint ψ and n pairwise distinct variables $x_1, \ldots, x_n$ is called a **logical semantics** of a procedure p taking n arguments if the following two conditions are satisfied:

- If an elaborator for an application $\{p\ x_1\ \ldots\ x_n\}$ fails, where no actors but the descendents of the elaborator are reduced, then the initial constraint of the blackboard entails $\neg\psi$.
- If an elaborator for an application $\{p\ x_1\ \ldots\ x_n\}$ succeeds, where no actors but the descendents of the elaborator are reduced, then the equivalence

$$\phi_1 \wedge \psi \leftrightarrow \exists \overline{y}\, \phi_2$$

is valid in the Oz universe, where ϕ_1 is the initial constraint of the blackboard, ϕ_2 is the final constraint of the blackboard, and $\overline{y}$ are the new local variables created during the reduction.

With the exception of

```
NewName  NewCell  Exchange  SolveCombinator  GetFiniteDomain
'Input'  'Output'  'SetThreadPriority'  'GetThreadPriority'
```

all predefined kernel procedures have a logical semantics. A logical semantics for, say '=<', is

$$\mathtt{intLE}(x, y) \ \vee \ \mathtt{floatLE}(x, y) \ \vee \ \mathtt{atomLE}(x, y).$$

4.6 Interactive Programming

So far we have assumed that computation starts from a single admissible kernel expression. It is straightforward to generalize to an incremental regime elaborating expressions arriving on a stream. To be useful, the arriving expressions must be allowed to share variables.

A **kernel program** is a kernel expression with a hole • defined as follows:

$$\mathcal{E} ::= \ \bullet \ | \ E\,\mathcal{E} \ | \ \mathbf{local}\ \overline{x}\ \mathbf{in}\ \mathcal{E}\ \mathbf{end}$$

Kernel programs are compositional in that we can obtain from two programs $\mathcal{E}_1$ and $\mathcal{E}_2$ a composed program $\mathcal{E}_1[\mathcal{E}_2]$ by replacing the hole of $\mathcal{E}_1$ with $\mathcal{E}_2$. The idea is now to replace the initial expression E by a stream

$$\mathcal{E}_1[\mathcal{E}_2[\ldots \mathcal{E}_n[\mathbf{true}]\ldots]]$$

of nested programs, where elaboration of the hole • must wait until the next program arrives. To work as expected, a substitution must be maintained for the hole • mapping the statically bound variables to their dynamic replacements. (Recall that elaboration of **local** x **in** E **end** creates an elaborator for $E[y/x]$, where y is a fresh variable replacing x within its static scope.)

A convenient syntax for entering a program is

> **declare** $\overline{x}$ **in** E

which stands for

> **local** $\overline{x}$ **in** E • **end**

5   The Oz Calculus

Oz has been designed hand in hand with a formal model consisting of the Oz universe and the Oz calculus. It is fair to say that Oz could not have been conceived without a formal model. This becomes evident, for instance, with the notion of constraint entailment, or the semantics of solvers. As Oz evolved, its formal model evolved. Ideas for new combinators evolved by trying different formulations in the calculus, which provided the ground for arguing their simplicity and generality. The solve combinator was the one that came last and took longest to evolve.

It takes intuition and effort to understand a new formal system, even if it is mathematically seen simple. This is the reason for presenting the calculus last, although it certainly comes first in our understanding of Oz. The actor model can be seen as a computational metaphor for the calculus providing motivation and intuition.

The Oz calculus models concurrent computation as rewriting of a class of expressions modulo a structural congruence. This set-up, which is also employed in more recent presentations of the π-calculus [8, 7], proves particularly useful for Oz since constraint propagation and simplification can be accommodated elegantly by means of the structural congruence.

The Oz calculus is not committed to a particular constraint system; instead, it is parameterized with respect to a general and straightforward notion of constraint system. This divide and conquer approach simplifies things considerably since we can now deal with the complexities of the Oz universe separately and independently.

In the interest of a smooth presentation, the calculus is somewhat simplified. It will be extended with the missing expressivity when the connection with the actor model is made. The extended calculus formalizes all aspects of the actor model, with the exception of the reduction strategy and input and output. Not specifying the order in which actors are reduced greatly simplifies the formal machinery.

The expressions of the Oz calculus model the computation spaces of the actor model. Thus their purpose is different from the purpose of elaborable expressions, which can only occur within elaborators. While the elaborable expressions model only static aspects of the actor model, the expressions of the calculus model both the dynamic and static aspects of the actor model. Elaborators are not modelled explicitly but are expressible with the other primitives of the calculus.

The study of the Oz calculus should be prepared by reading [13], which introduces a simplified calculus not covering constraints and search.

5.1 Constraint Systems

We base our notion of constraint system on first-order predicate logic with equality. A **constraint system** consists of

1. a signature Σ (a set of constant, function and predicate symbols)
2. a satisfiable theory Δ (a set of sentences over Σ having a model)
3. an infinite set of constants in Σ called **names** satisfying two conditions:
   (a) $\Delta \models \neg(a \doteq b)$ for every two distinct names a, b
   (b) $\Delta \models \phi \leftrightarrow \psi$ for every two sentences ϕ, ψ over Σ such that ψ can be obtained from ϕ by permutation of names.

The Oz universe defines a constraint system as follows: take its signature and its names as they are, and let the constraint theory Δ be the set of all sentences valid in the Oz universe. It is not difficult to verify that the two conditions for names are satisfied. Note that the second condition on names prevents us from having an order on names; this explains why the predicate $\text{arity}(x, y)$ ignores those features of x that are names.

Given a constraint system, we will call every formula over its signature a **constraint**. We use $\perp$ for the constraint that is always false, and $\top$ for the constraint that is always true. We say that a constraint ϕ **entails** a constraint ψ if $\Delta \models \phi \rightarrow \psi$, and that a constraint ϕ is **equivalent** to a constraint ψ if $\Delta \models \phi \leftrightarrow \psi$. We say that a constraint is **satisfiable** if it does not entail $\perp$.

5.2 Syntax

Figure 7 defines the syntax of the Oz calculus. The definition assumes that a constraint system is given, which fixes infinite sets of variables, names and constraints. Variables and names are jointly referred to as **references**.

We use $\overline{u}$ to denote a possibly empty sequence of references. A sequence $\overline{u}$ is called **linear** if its elements are pairwise distinct. If $\overline{u} = u_1 \ldots u_n$, we often write $\exists \overline{u} \, E$ for $\exists u_1 \ldots \exists u_n E$.

Although our notation suggests the contrary, we do distinguish between a composition $\phi_1 \wedge \phi_2$ and a conjunction $\phi_1 \wedge \phi_2$, and also between a declaration $\exists x \phi$ and an existential quantification $\exists x \phi$. If we want to make the distinction explicit, we will use the symbols $\dot\wedge$ for conjunction and $\dot\exists$ for existential quantification.

Both variables and names can be declared. Declaration of names provides for reference to fresh names.

An expression $a : \overline{x}/E$ models a binding of the name a to the abstraction $\overline{x}/E$. For convenience, we call the entire expression $a : \overline{x}/E$ an abstraction. We call a

Symbols

x, y, z	:	variable
a, b, c	:	name
u, v, w	$::= x \mid a$	reference

Expressions

ϕ, ψ	:	constraint	
E	$::= \phi$	constraint	
	$\mid E_1 \wedge E_2$	composition	
	$\mid \exists u E$	declaration	
	$\mid a: \overline{x}/E$	abstraction	($\overline{x}$ linear)
	$\mid a: u$	cell	
	$\mid u\overline{v}$	application	
	$\mid$ **if** D **else** E	conditional	
	$\mid$ **or** (D)	disjunction	
	$\mid$ **solve**$(x: E, uvw)$	solver	
D	$::= C \mid \bot \mid D_1 \vee D_2$	collection	
C	$::= E_1$ **then** $E_2 \mid \exists u\, C$	clause	

Fig. 7. Syntax of the Oz calculus.

the **designator**, $\overline{x}$ the **formal arguments**, and E the **body** of the abstraction. We sometimes write $a: A$, where $A = \overline{x}/E$.

Given a cell $a: u$, we call a the **designator** and u the **reference** of the cell. A cell models a binding of a name to a reference.

Given an application $u\overline{v}$, we call u the **designator** and $\overline{v}$ the **actual arguments** of the application.

Given a solver **solve**$(x: E, uvw)$, we call x the **root variable**, E the **guard**, and u, v, w the **control references** of the solver.

Given a clause $\exists \overline{u}\,(E_1$ **then** $E_2)$, we call $\overline{u}$ the **local references**, E_1 the **guard**, and E_2 the **body** of the clause.

The syntactic category D represents multisets of clauses, where $\bot$ stands for the empty multiset and $\vee$ for multiset union.

The Oz calculus has the following binders for references:

- A declaration $\exists u E$ binds the **declared reference** u with scope E.
- An abstraction $a: \overline{x}/E$ binds its formal arguments $\overline{x}$ with scope E.
- A clausal declaration $\exists u C$ binds the local reference u with scope C.
- A solver **solve**$(x: E, uvw)$ binds its root variable x with scope E.
- Universal and existential quantification in constraints.

The **free and bound references** of expressions are defined accordingly. An expression is **closed** if it has no free variable.

The notation $E[u/x]$ stands for the expression that is obtained from E by replacing every free occurrence of x with u. The notation $E[\overline{u}/\overline{x}]$ is defined accordingly, where the elements of the sequence $\overline{x}$ are replaced simultaneously, and $\overline{x}$ is assumed to be linear.

A context is an expression having a hole • at a reducible position. **Contexts** are defined as follows:

$$\mathcal{E} ::= \bullet \mid \mathcal{E} \wedge E \mid E \wedge \mathcal{E} \mid \exists u\,\mathcal{E} \mid \textbf{if } \mathcal{D} \textbf{ else } E \mid \textbf{or}\,(\mathcal{D}) \mid \textbf{solve}(x{:}\mathcal{E}, uvw)$$
$$\mathcal{D} ::= \mathcal{C} \mid \mathcal{D} \vee D \mid D \vee \mathcal{D}$$
$$\mathcal{C} ::= \mathcal{E} \textbf{ then } E \mid \exists u\,\mathcal{C}.$$

We write $\mathcal{E}[E]$ for the expression obtained by replacing the hole in the context $\mathcal{E}$ with the expression E (capturing of free variables in E is OK). An expression E is called **free for a context** $\mathcal{E}$ if no free reference of E is captured at the position of the hole in $\mathcal{E}$.

5.3 Structural Congruence

A **congruence** is an equivalence relation on the expressions of the Oz calculus (i.e., the syntactic categories ϕ, E, D, and C) that is compatible with all syntactic combinators (e.g., if $E_1 \equiv E_1'$ and $E_2 \equiv E_2'$, then $E_1 \wedge E_2 \equiv E_1' \wedge E_2'$). The **structural congruence** $E_1 \equiv E_2$ of the Oz calculus is defined as the least congruence satisfying the congruence laws in Figure 8.

Proposition 4. *Given two constraints ϕ_1 and ϕ_2, the composition $\phi_1 \wedge \phi_2$ is congruent to the conjunction $\phi_1 \dot\wedge \phi_2$.*

Proof. We have $\phi_1 \wedge \phi_2 \equiv \phi_1 \wedge (\phi_1 \dot\wedge \phi_2) \equiv (\phi_1 \dot\wedge \phi_2) \wedge \phi_1 \equiv (\phi_1 \dot\wedge \phi_2) \wedge \top \equiv \phi_1 \dot\wedge \phi_2$ by relative simplification, commutativity of composition, relative simplification, and neutrality of $\top$.

For declaration and existential quantification an analogous proposition does not hold.

An expression E is called **failed** if $E \equiv \bot \wedge E$. A clause $\exists \overline{u}\,(E_1 \textbf{ then } E_2)$ is called **failed** if E_1 is failed. A collection D is called **failed** if D is $\bot$, or D is a failed clause, or $D = D_1 \vee D_2$, where both D_1 and D_2 are failed.

An expression E is called **nilpotent** if it has the form

$$\exists \overline{x} \exists \overline{a} \exists \overline{b} \exists \overline{c}(\phi \wedge \overline{a}{:}\overline{A} \wedge \overline{b}{:}\overline{u})$$

where $\Delta \models \exists \overline{x}\phi$. (The notation $\overline{a}{:}\overline{A}$ stands for a composition $a_1{:}A_1 \wedge \ldots \wedge a_n{:}A_n$ of abstractions, and $\overline{b}{:}\overline{u}$ stands for a composition of cells.)

Renaming

- $E_1 \equiv E_2$ if E_1 and E_2 are equal up to renaming of bound references

Composition and Collection

- $\wedge$ is associative, commutative and satisfies $E \wedge \top \equiv E$
- $\vee$ is associative, commutative and satisfies $D \vee \bot \equiv D$

Declaration

- $\exists u \exists v E \equiv \exists v \exists u E$
- $\exists u E_1 \wedge E_2 \equiv \exists u (E_1 \wedge E_2)$ if u does not occur free in E_2

Relative Simplification

- $\phi_1 \wedge \mathcal{E}[\phi_2] \equiv \phi_1 \wedge \mathcal{E}[\phi_2']$ if ϕ_1 is free for $\mathcal{E}$ and $\Delta \models \phi_1 \wedge \phi_2 \leftrightarrow \phi_1 \wedge \phi_2'$

Equality

- $x \doteq u \wedge E \equiv x \doteq u \wedge E[u/x]$ if u is free for x in E

Fig. 8. Structural congruence in the Oz calculus.

5.4 Induced Constraints

The Relative Simplification Law makes it possible to propagate constraints in an expression downward, provided no free variables of the constraint are captured. Given a context, whose bound references are renamed apart, there is a strongest constraint (unique up to equivalence) that can be propagated to the hole. Below we define this induced constraint for a class of contexts that is exhaustive modulo structural congruence.

An expression is called **basic** if it is no constraint, composition or declaration.

The following defines a partial function from constraints and contexts to constraints:

$$\text{Ind}_\phi (\bullet) = \phi$$
$$\text{Ind}_\phi (\psi \wedge \mathcal{E}) = \text{Ind}_{\phi \wedge \psi} (\mathcal{E})$$
$$\text{Ind}_\phi (E \wedge \mathcal{E}) = \text{Ind}_\phi (\mathcal{E}) \qquad \text{if } E \text{ basic}$$
$$\text{Ind}_\phi (\exists u \mathcal{E}) = \text{Ind}_\phi (\mathcal{E}) \qquad \text{if } u \text{ is not free in } \phi$$
$$\text{Ind}_\phi (\text{if } \mathcal{D} \text{ else } E) = \text{Ind}_\phi (\mathcal{D})$$
$$\text{Ind}_\phi (\text{or } (\mathcal{D})) = \text{Ind}_\phi (\mathcal{D})$$

$$\text{Ind}_\phi\left(\textbf{solve}(x\!:\!\mathcal{E},uvw)\right) = \text{Ind}_\phi\left(\mathcal{E}\right) \qquad \text{if } x \text{ is not free in } \phi$$
$$\text{Ind}_\phi\left(\mathcal{C}\vee D\right) = \text{Ind}_\phi\left(\mathcal{C}\right)$$
$$\text{Ind}_\phi\left(\mathcal{E}\textbf{ then }E\right) = \text{Ind}_\phi\left(\mathcal{E}\right)$$
$$\text{Ind}_\phi\left(\exists u\mathcal{C}\right) = \text{Ind}_\phi\left(\mathcal{C}\right) \qquad \text{if } u \text{ is not free in } \phi.$$

If $\text{Ind}_\phi\left(\mathcal{E}\right)$ is defined, we call $\text{Ind}_\phi\left(\mathcal{E}\right)$ the constraint **induced by** $\mathcal{E}$ **under** ϕ. If $\text{Ind}_\top\left(\mathcal{E}\right)$ is defined, we call $\text{Ind}_\top\left(\mathcal{E}\right)$ the constraint **induced by** $\mathcal{E}$.

Proposition 5. *If $\mathcal{E}$ induces ψ under ϕ, then $\mathcal{E}[\psi]\wedge\phi \equiv \mathcal{E}[\top]\wedge\phi$.*

The next proposition says that our definition of induced constraints is exhaustive on contexts modulo structural congruence. Structural congruence on contexts is the least congruence on contexts satisfying all congruence laws in Figure 8 rewritten for contexts. Note that $\mathcal{E}\equiv\mathcal{E}'$ does not imply $\mathcal{E}[E]\equiv\mathcal{E}'[E]$ (because of the Renaming Law).

Proposition 6. *For every context $\mathcal{E}$ and every constraint ϕ there exists a context $\mathcal{E}'$ such that $\mathcal{E}\equiv\mathcal{E}'$ and the induced constraint of $\mathcal{E}'$ under ϕ is defined.*

We say that a context $\mathcal{E}$ is **admissible** if $\mathcal{E}[\bot]\not\equiv\mathcal{E}[\top]$.

Proposition 7. *A context $\mathcal{E}$ is admissible if and only if there exists a context $\mathcal{E}'$ and a satisfiable constraint ϕ such that $\mathcal{E}\equiv\mathcal{E}'$ and $\mathcal{E}'$ induces ϕ.*

5.5 Reduction

The reduction relation $E \to E'$ of the Oz calculus is defined by the inference system in Figure 9 and the following definitions:

- An expression E is called **reducible** if there exists an expression E' such that $E \to E'$.
- An expression E is called **stable** if, for every abstraction and for every satisfiable constraint π, the expression $\pi \wedge E$ is neither reducible nor failed. (The definition is by induction on the number of nested solvers in E.)
- An expression E is called **distributable** if there exist $\overline{u}$, E' and D such that $E \equiv \exists\overline{u}\left(E'\wedge\textbf{or}\left(D\right)\right)$.

A **finite computation** issuing from a closed expression E_1 is a sequence $E_1,\ldots,E_n$ of closed expressions such that the final expression E_n is irreducible and $E_i \to E_{i+1}$ for all i. Since failure prevents further reduction, none of the expressions $E_1,\ldots,E_{n-1}$ can be failed.

An **infinite computation** issuing from a closed expression E_1 is an infinite sequence $E_1, E_2, E_3, \ldots$ of closed expressions such that $E_i \to E_{i+1}$ for all i. Since failure prevents further reduction, none of the expressions E_i can be failed.

As one would expect of a concurrent computation model with indeterministic choice, there are closed expressions that permit both finite and infinite computations. For instance:

$$\exists a\,(a\!:\!/a \wedge \textbf{if }\top\textbf{ then }a \vee \top\textbf{ then }\top\textbf{ else }\top).$$

Structure

- $$\frac{E \equiv \mathcal{E}[E_1] \quad E_1 \stackrel{\phi}{\Rightarrow} E_1' \quad \mathcal{E}[E_1'] \equiv E'}{E \to E'} \qquad \text{if } \mathcal{E} \text{ is admissible and induces } \phi$$

- $$\frac{E \Rightarrow E'}{E \stackrel{\phi}{\Rightarrow} E'}$$

Application

- $\mathcal{E}\,[a\bar{u}] \,\wedge\, a{:}\,\bar{x}/E \stackrel{\phi}{\Rightarrow} \mathcal{E}\,[E\,[\bar{u}/\bar{x}]] \,\wedge\, a{:}\,\bar{x}/E$

  if $\mathcal{E} \wedge \phi$ is admissible, $\bar{x}$ and $\bar{u}$ have equal length,
  $\bar{u}$ is free for $\bar{x}$ in E, and $a{:}\,\bar{x}/E$ is free for $\mathcal{E}$

Exchange

- $avw \,\wedge\, a{:}u \,\Rightarrow\, v \dot{=} u \,\wedge\, a{:}w$

Conditional

- $\textbf{if } \exists\bar{u}\,(E_1 \textbf{ then } E_2) \vee D \textbf{ else } E_3 \,\Rightarrow\, \exists\bar{u}\,(E_1 \wedge E_2) \qquad \text{if } \exists\bar{u}\,E_1 \text{ nilpotent}$
- $\textbf{if } D \textbf{ else } E \,\Rightarrow\, E \qquad \text{if } D \text{ failed}$

Disjunction

- $\textbf{or}\,(\exists\bar{u}\,(E_1 \textbf{ then } E_2) \vee D) \,\Rightarrow\, \exists\bar{u}\,(E_1 \wedge E_2) \qquad \text{if } D \text{ failed}$
- $\textbf{or}\,(\exists\bar{u}\,(E \textbf{ then } \top) \vee D) \,\Rightarrow\, \top \qquad \text{if } \exists\bar{u}\,E \text{ nilpotent}$

Solver

- $\textbf{solve}(x{:}E, uvw) \,\Rightarrow\, u \qquad \text{if } E \text{ failed}$
- $\textbf{solve}(x{:}E, uvw) \,\Rightarrow\, \exists a \exists b (vab \wedge a{:}\,x/E_2 \wedge b{:}\,x/E_3)$

  if $\exists x E$ is stable, $E = \exists\bar{u}\,(E_1 \wedge \textbf{or}\,(C \vee D))$,
  $\quad E_2 = \exists\bar{u}\,(E_1 \wedge \textbf{or}\,(C))$, and $E_3 = \exists\bar{u}\,(E_1 \wedge \textbf{or}\,(D))$

- $\textbf{solve}(x{:}E, uvw) \,\Rightarrow\, \exists a(wa \wedge a{:}\,x/E) \qquad \text{if } \exists x E \text{ stable and not distributable}$

Annulment

- $E \,\Rightarrow\, \top \qquad \text{if } E \text{ nilpotent and } E \not\equiv \top$

Fig. 9. Reduction in the Oz calculus.

The following proposition says that conditionals can reduce with clauses whose guards are entailed.

Proposition 8. *Suppose ϕ_1 is satisfiable and entails $\exists \overline{x} \phi_2$. Then*

$$\phi_1 \wedge \text{ if } \exists \overline{x}(\phi_2 \text{ then } E_1) \text{ else } E_2 \;\; \rightarrow \;\; \phi_1 \wedge \exists \overline{x}(\phi_2 \wedge E_1).$$

Proof. It will be convenient to use the congruence relation (on constraints)

$$\phi \vDash\!\!\!\dashv_\Delta \psi : \Longleftrightarrow \;\; \Delta \vDash \phi \leftrightarrow \psi.$$

Because of the Renaming Law we can assume without loss of generality that no variable in $\overline{x}$ occurs in ϕ_1. It suffices to show that there exists a constraint ϕ_3 such that $\phi_1 \wedge \phi_2 \vDash\!\!\!\dashv_\Delta \phi_1 \wedge \phi_3$ and $\exists \overline{x} \phi_3 \vDash\!\!\!\dashv_\Delta \top$ since

$$
\begin{aligned}
\phi_1 \wedge \text{ if } \exists \overline{x}(\phi_2 \text{ then } E_1) \text{ else } E_2 &\equiv \phi_1 \wedge \text{ if } \exists \overline{x}(\phi_3 \text{ then } E_1) \text{ else } E_2 \\
&\rightarrow \phi_1 \wedge \exists \overline{x}(\phi_3 \wedge E_1) \\
&\equiv \phi_1 \wedge \exists \overline{x}(\phi_2 \wedge E_1).
\end{aligned}
$$

by the Relative Simplification Law, the first reduction rule for conditionals, and once more the Relative Simplification Law. Let $\phi_3 := \phi_1 \rightarrow \phi_2$ (here $\rightarrow$ is implication, not reduction). Then $\phi_1 \wedge \phi_2 \vDash\!\!\!\dashv_\Delta \phi_1 \wedge \phi_3$ is obviously satisfied. Moreover, $\exists \overline{x} \phi_3 \vDash\!\!\!\dashv_\Delta \exists \overline{x}(\phi_1 \rightarrow \phi_2) \vDash\!\!\!\dashv_\Delta \phi_1 \rightarrow \exists \overline{x} \phi_2 \vDash\!\!\!\dashv_\Delta \top.$

5.6 Examples

The following examples give a first impression of how the Oz calculus models concurrent computation.

Example 2. Consider the expression

$$\exists x \exists y (\exists a(x \doteq a) \wedge \exists a(y \doteq a) \wedge \text{ if } x \doteq y \text{ then } E_1 \text{ else } E_2)$$

and suppose that x and y are distinct variables that do not occur free in E_1 and E_2. We will show that this expression reduces in four steps to E_2.

First we move the left declaration of the name a to the outside of the expression using the congruence laws for declarations and compositions.

$$\equiv \exists a \exists x \exists y(x \doteq a \wedge \exists a(y \doteq a) \wedge \text{ if } x \doteq y \text{ then } E_1 \text{ else } E_2)$$

This is of course only possible if a does not occur free in E_1 or E_2. Should this be the case, renaming a within its scope as justified by the Renaming Law is necessary. Next we apply the Equality Law to $x \doteq a$.

$$\equiv \exists a \exists x \exists y(x \doteq a \wedge \exists a(y \doteq a) \wedge \text{ if } a \doteq y \text{ then } E_1 \text{ else } E_2)$$

Now we move the declaration of x inside using the laws for composition and declaration (we exploit that x does not occur free in E_1 and E_2 and that x is different from y).

$$\equiv \exists a \exists y(\exists x(x \doteq a) \wedge \exists a(y \doteq a) \wedge \text{ if } a \doteq y \text{ then } E_1 \text{ else } E_2)$$

Since $\exists x(x \doteq a)$ is nilpotent, we can delete $\exists x(x \doteq a)$ using the Annulment Rule and the laws for compositions (in particular $E \wedge \top \equiv E$).

$$\to \exists a \exists y(\exists a(y \doteq a) \wedge \text{ if } a \doteq y \text{ then } E_1 \text{ else } E_2)$$

Next we rename the inner name a to the different name b using the Renaming Law.

$$\equiv \exists a \exists y(\exists b(y \doteq b) \wedge \text{ if } a \doteq y \text{ then } E_1 \text{ else } E_2)$$

This brings us in a position where we can eliminate $\exists b(y \doteq b)$ in the same way we did it before for $\exists a(x \doteq a)$.

$$\to \exists a \exists b(\text{if } a \doteq b \text{ then } E_1 \text{ else } E_2)$$

Now, since $a \doteq b$ is failed, we obtain

$$\to \exists a \exists b E_2$$

using the second rule for conditionals. It remains to get rid of the declarations of the names a and b. This can be done using the Annulment Rule together with the laws for compositions and declarations:

$$\equiv \exists a \exists b(\top \wedge E_2) \equiv (\exists a \exists b \top) \wedge E_2 \to \top \wedge E_2 \equiv E_2.$$

Example 3. Nilpotence and relative simplification model entailment of clauses in the presence of local abstractions and cells. For instance, consider the reduction

$$y \doteq b \wedge \text{ if } \exists x \, (\exists a(x \doteq a \wedge y \doteq b \wedge a{:}y/y \doteq x) \text{ then } E_1) \text{ else } E_2$$
$$\to y \doteq b \wedge \exists x \, (\exists a(x \doteq a \wedge a{:}y/y \doteq x) \wedge E_1)$$

which is justified by relative simplification, the first rule for conditionals, and the fact that $\exists x \exists a(x \doteq a \wedge a{:}y/y \doteq x)$ is nilpotent.

5.7 Relationship with the Actor Model

The expressions of the Oz calculus model the computation spaces of the actor model, provided we take the Oz universe as the constraint system underlying the calculus. Conditionals, disjunctions, and solvers model the respective proper actors. However, we need to extend the calculus so that it

- can express nondistributing disjunctions
- can express once-only abstractions
- captures solvers fully (need to provide status and to return alternatives as once-only abstractions)
- can express elaborators.

Nondistributing disjunctions are incorporated easily: they have the same reduction rules as distributing disjunctions, but they are not distributed by solvers.

Once-only abstractions are incorporated by extending the expressions of the calculus with the form $a{:}\overline{x}/\!\!/E$ and the reduction relation with the rule

$$- \ \mathcal{E}\,[a\overline{u}] \ \wedge \ a\colon\overline{x}/\!\!/ E \ \overset{\phi}{\Rightarrow} \ \mathcal{E}\,[E\,[\overline{u}/\overline{x}]] \ \wedge \ a\colon\overline{x}/\!\!/\bot$$

if $\mathcal{E} \wedge \phi$ is admissible, $\overline{x}$ and $\overline{u}$ have equal length,
$\overline{u}$ is free for $\overline{x}$ in E, and $a\colon\overline{x}/E$ is free for $\mathcal{E}$.

Moreover, it is necessary to strengthen the notion of nilpotence to all expressions of the form

$$\exists\overline{x}\exists\overline{a}\exists\overline{b}\exists\overline{c}\exists\overline{d}(\phi \wedge \overline{a}\colon\overline{A} \wedge \overline{b}\colon\overline{u} \wedge \overline{c}\colon\overline{B})$$

where $\Delta \models \exists\overline{x}\phi$ and $\overline{c}\colon\overline{B}$ stands for a conjunction of once-only abstractions.

Now it is easy to modify the second and third reduction rule for solvers such that the solvers of the actor model are faithfully modelled.

To model elaborators, we first extend the expressions of the calculus with $\mathbf{det}(u)$ and $\mathbf{getDomain}(u, v)$. The semantics of $\mathbf{det}(u)$ is captured by the reduction rule

$$- \ \mathbf{det}(u) \ \overset{\phi}{\Rightarrow} \ \top$$

if there exists a constant c such that ϕ entails $u \doteq c$.

The semantics of $\mathbf{getDomain}(u, v)$ is captured by

$$- \ \mathbf{getDomain}(x, u) \ \overset{\phi}{\Rightarrow} \ u \doteq n_1|\dots|n_k|\mathbf{nil}$$

if $n_1, \dots, n_k$ is the shortest list of nonnegative integers in ascending order such that ϕ entails $x \doteq n_1 \vee \dots \vee x \doteq n_k$.

How do we model an elaborator for a constraint ϕ? It cannot be modeled by the constraint ϕ itself since this would impose ϕ immediately (consider the inconsistent constraint $\bot$). However, the conditional $\mathbf{if}\ \top\ \mathbf{then}\ \phi\ \mathbf{else}\ \top$ behaves exactly like an elaborator for ϕ: Only when it is reduced, the constraint ϕ is imposed.

In the following we write $\langle E \rangle$ for $\mathbf{if}\ \top\ \mathbf{then}\ E\ \mathbf{else}\ \top$.

An elaborable expression is called **translatable** if it does not contain subexpressions of the form $\mathbf{input}[x]$, $\mathbf{output}[x]$, $\mathbf{setThreadPriority}[x]$, or $\mathbf{getThreadPriority}[x]$.

The function $[\![E]\!]$ translates a translatable elaborable expression E into an expression of the extended Oz calculus. The translation is such that $[\![E]\!]$ models an elaborator for E.

$$[\![\phi]\!] \ = \ \langle \phi \rangle$$

$$[\![x\colon\overline{y}/E]\!] \ = \ \langle \exists a (x \doteq a \wedge a\colon\overline{y}/[\![E]\!]) \rangle$$

$$[\![x\colon\overline{y}/\!\!/E]\!] \ = \ \langle \exists a (x \doteq a \wedge a\colon\overline{y}/\!\!/[\![E]\!]) \rangle$$

$$[\![x\colon y]\!] \ = \ \langle \exists a (x \doteq a \wedge a\colon y) \rangle$$

$$[\![E_1 \ E_2]\!] \ = \ \langle [\![E_1]\!] \wedge [\![E_2]\!] \rangle$$

$$[\![\mathbf{local}\ \overline{x}\ \mathbf{in}\ E\ \mathbf{end}]\!] \ = \ \langle \exists\overline{x}\,[\![E]\!] \rangle$$

$$[\![\mathbf{newName}[x]]\!] \ = \ \langle \exists a (x \doteq a) \rangle$$

$$[\![\mathtt{apply}[x\overline{y}]\!]] = x\overline{y}$$

$$[\![\mathtt{if}\ C_1\ []\ \ldots\ []\ C_n\ \mathtt{else}\ E\ \mathtt{fi}]\!] = \langle \mathtt{if}\ [\![C_1]\!] \vee \ldots \vee [\![C_n]\!]\ \mathtt{else}\ [\![E]\!]\rangle$$

$$[\![\mathtt{or}\ C_1\ []\ \ldots\ []\ C_n\ \mathtt{ro}]\!] = \langle \mathtt{or}\,([\![C_1]\!] \vee \ldots \vee [\![C_n]\!])\rangle$$

$$[\![\mathtt{OR}\ C_1\ []\ \ldots\ []\ C_n\ \mathtt{RO}]\!] = \langle \mathtt{OR}\,([\![C_1]\!] \vee \ldots \vee [\![C_n]\!])\rangle$$

$$[\![\mathtt{solve}[x\colon E, y_1 y_2 y_3]\!]] = \langle \mathtt{solve}(x\colon [\![E]\!], y_1 y_2 y_3)\rangle$$

$$[\![\mathtt{det}[x]\!]] = \mathtt{det}(x)$$

$$[\![\mathtt{getDomain}[x, y]\!]] = \mathtt{getDomain}(x, y)$$

$$[\![\overline{x}\ \mathtt{in}\ E_1\ \mathtt{then}\ E_2]\!] = \exists \overline{x}\,([\![E_1]\!]\ \mathtt{then}\ [\![E_2]\!]) \qquad \text{if } E_2 \neq \top$$

$$[\![\overline{x}\ \mathtt{in}\ E\ \mathtt{then}\ \top]\!] = \exists \overline{x}\,([\![E]\!]\ \mathtt{then}\ \top)$$

The special treatment of the constraint $\top$ in clause bodies is needed so that reduction of disjunctions by clause entailment is modelled correctly.

We can now state the relationship between the actor model and the Oz calculus. For every closed and translatable elaborable expression E we have the following:

- If there is a finite computation issuing from E in the actor model, then there is a finite computation issuing from $[\![E]\!]$ in the extended Oz calculus.
- If there is an infinite computation issuing from E in the actor model, then there is an infinite computation issuing from $[\![E]\!]$ in the extended Oz calculus.

The converse of each of the two statements is wrong in general. This is because the reduction strategy employed by the actor model excludes some of the computations of the calculus.

References

1. Hassan Aït-Kaci, Andreas Podelski, and Gert Smolka. A feature-based constraint system for logic programming with entailment. *Theoretical Computer Science*, 122(1–2):263–283, January 1994.
2. Rolf Backofen and Gert Smolka. A complete and recursive feature theory. *Theoretical Computer Science*. To appear 1995; a preliminary version is available as DFKI Research Report RR-92-30, German Research Center for Artificial Intelligence (DFKI), Stuhlsatzenhausweg 3, D-66123 Saarbrücken, Germany.
3. Rolf Backofen and Ralf Treinen. How to win a game with features. In Jean-Pierre Jouannaud, editor, *1st International Conference on Constraints in Computational Logics*, Lecture Notes in Computer Science, vol. 845, pages 320–335, München, Germany, 7–9 September 1994. Springer-Verlag.
4. Martin Henz. The Oz notation. DFKI Oz documentation series, German Research Center for Artificial Intelligence (DFKI), Stuhlsatzenhausweg 3, D-66123 Saarbrücken, Germany, 1994.
5. Martin Henz and Martin Müller. Programming in Oz. DFKI Oz documentation series, German Research Center for Artificial Intelligence (DFKI), Stuhlsatzenhausweg 3, D-66123 Saarbrücken, Germany, 1994.

6. Carl Hewitt. Viewing control structures as patterns of passing messages. *Artificial Intelligence*, 8:323–364, 1977.

7. Robin Milner. The polyadic π-calculus: A tutorial. ECS-LFCS Report Series 91-180, Laboratory for Foundations of Computer Science, University of Edinburgh, Edinburgh EH9 3JZ, October 1991.

8. Robin Milner. Functions as processes. *Journal of Mathematical Structures in Computer Science*, 2(2):119–141, 1992.

9. Tobias Müller, Konstantin Popow, Christian Schulte, and Jörg Würtz. Constraint programming in Oz. DFKI Oz documentation series, German Research Center for Artificial Intelligence (DFKI), Stuhlsatzenhausweg 3, D-66123 Saarbrücken, Germany, 1994.

10. Christian Schulte and Gert Smolka. Encapsulated search in higher-order concurrent constraint programming. In Maurice Bruynooghe, editor, *Logic Programming: Proceedings of the 1994 International Symposium*, Ithaca, New York, USA, November 1994. MIT-Press. To appear.

11. Christian Schulte, Gert Smolka, and Jörg Würtz. Encapsulated search and constraint programming in Oz. In A.H. Borning, editor, *Second Workshop on Principles and Practice of Constraint Programming*, Lecture Notes in Computer Science, vol. 874, Orcas Island, Washington, USA, 2-4 May 1994. Springer-Verlag.

12. Gert Smolka. A calculus for higher-order concurrent constraint programming with deep guards. Research Report RR-94-03, German Research Center for Artificial Intelligence (DFKI), Stuhlsatzenhausweg 3, D-66123 Saarbrücken, Germany, February 1994.

13. Gert Smolka. A foundation for higher-order concurrent constraint programming. In Jean-Pierre Jouannaud, editor, *1st International Conference on Constraints in Computational Logics*, Lecture Notes in Computer Science, vol. 845, pages 50–72, München, Germany, 7-9 September 1994. Springer-Verlag.

14. Gert Smolka. An Oz primer. DFKI Oz documentation series, German Research Center for Artificial Intelligence (DFKI), Stuhlsatzenhausweg 3, D-66123 Saarbrücken, Germany, 1994.

15. Gert Smolka and Ralf Treinen. Records for logic programming. *Journal of Logic Programming*, 18(3):229–258, April 1994.

16. Ralf Treinen. Feature constraints with first-class features. In Andrzej M. Borzyszkowski and Stefan Sokołowski, editors, *Mathematical Foundations of Computer Science*, Lecture Notes in Computer Science, vol. 711, pages 734–743, Gdańsk, Poland, 30 August-3 September 1993. Springer-Verlag.

Remark. Papers of authors from the Programming Systems Lab of DFKI are available through anonymous ftp from `ps-ftp.dfki.uni-sb.de` or through WWW from `http://ps-www.dfki.uni-sb.de/`.

Design, Implementation, and Evaluation of the Constraint Language cc(FD)

Pascal Van Hentenryck[1] and Vijay Saraswat[2] and Yves Deville[3]

[1] Brown University, Box 1910, Providence, RI 02912 (USA) Email:
pvh@cs.brown.edu
[2] Xerox Palo Alto Research Center, 3333 Coyote Hill Road, Palo Alto, CA 94304
Email: saraswat@parc.xerox.com
[3] Université Catholique de Louvain, Pl. Ste Barbe, 2 B-1348 Louvain-La-Neuve,
Belgium Email: yde@info.ucl.ac.be

Abstract

This paper describes the design, implementation, and applications of the constraint logic language cc(FD). cc(FD) is a declarative nondeterministic constraint logic language over finite domains based on the cc framework [28], an extension of the CLP scheme [17]. Its constraint solver includes (non-linear) arithmetic constraints over natural numbers which are approximated using domain and interval consistency. The main novelty of cc(FD) is the inclusion of a number of general-purpose combinators, in particular cardinality, constructive disjunction, and blocking implication, in conjunction with new constraint operations such as constraint entailment and generalization. These combinators significantly improve the operational expressiveness, extensibility, and flexibility of CLP languages and allows issues such as the definition of non-primitive constraints and disjunctions to be tackled at the language level. The implementation of cc(FD) (about 40,000 lines of C) includes a WAM-based engine [37], optimal arc-consistency algorithms based on AC-5 [35], and incremental implementation of the combinators. Results on numerous problems, including scheduling, resource allocation, sequencing, packing, and hamiltonian paths are reported and indicate that cc(FD) comes close to procedural languages on a number of combinatorial problems. In addition, a small cc(FD) program was able to find the optimal solution and prove optimality to a famous 10/10 disjunctive scheduling problem [24], which was left open for more than 20 years and finally solved in 1988.

1 Introduction

Constraint Logic Programming (CLP) is a new class of declarative programming languages combining nondeterminism and constraint solving. The fundamental idea behind these languages, to use constraint solving instead of unification as the kernel operation of the language, was elegantly captured in the CLP scheme [17]. The CLP scheme can be instantiated to produce a specific language by defining a constraint system (i.e. defining a set of primitive constraints and providing a constraint solver for the constraints). For instance, CHIP contains constraint systems over finite domains [31], Booleans [3] and rational numbers [15, 36], Prolog III [9] is endowed with constraint systems over Booleans, rational numbers, and lists, while CLP($\Re$) [18] solves constraints over real numbers. The CLP scheme was further generalized into the cc framework of concurrent constraint programming [28, 29, 30] to accommodate additional constraint operations (e.g. constraint entailment [22]) and new ways of combining them (e.g. implication or blocking ask [28] and cardinality [33]).

CLP languages[4] support, in a declarative way, the solving of combinatorial search problems using the global search paradigm. The global search paradigm amounts to dividing recursively a problem into subproblems until the subproblems are simple enough to be solved in a straightforward way. The paradigm includes, as special cases, implicit enumeration, branch and bound, and constraint satisfaction. It is best contrasted with the local search paradigm, which proceeds by modifying an initial configuration locally until a solution is obtained. These approaches are orthogonal and complementary. The global search paradigm has been used successfully to solve a large variety of combinatorial search problems with reasonable efficiency (e.g. scheduling [5], graph coloring [19], Hamiltonian circuits [8], microcode labeling [13]) and provides, at the same time, the basis for exact methods as well as approximate solutions (giving rise to the so-called "anytime algorithms" [11]).

CLP languages over finite domains (e.g. CHIP [14, 31]) have been applied to numerous discrete combinatorial problems, including graph coloring, cutting stock, microcode labeling, warehouse location, and car-sequencing. For many problems, they allow a short development time and an efficiency which compares well with procedural languages implementing the same approach. For other problems however, the CLP scheme appears to lack flexibility and operational expressiveness since it only offers constraint solving over a fixed set of predefined constraints. As a consequence, many problems lose their natural formulation and need to be recasted in terms of more basic variables and constraints, inducing a significant loss in efficiency.

The research described in this paper is an attempt to overcome some of the limitations of CLP languages while preserving their benefits: short development time and referential transparency. It describes cc(FD), an instance of the cc framework over finite domains.

The main novelty in the design of cc(FD) is the inclusion of a number of general purpose combinators, i.e. cardinality, constructive disjunction, and blocking implication. The combinators are *general-purpose* in the sense that they apply to any constraint system and are not tailored to the constraint system of cc(FD) and *declarative* since they preserve referential transparency. In conjunction with new constraint operations such as constraint entailment and generalization, the new combinators significantly enhance the operational expressiveness and efficiency of CLP languages and enable us to address issues such as the definition

---

[4] In the following, we use the term *CLP languages* generically to denote both CLP and cc languages.

of non-primitive constraints and the handling of disjunctions at the language level. As a consequence, the combinators, together with a small and natural set of constraints over integers, preclude the need for many ad-hoc extensions which were introduced for efficiency reasons but were difficult to justify from a theoretical standpoint. cc(FD) preserves or improves the efficiency of problems previously solved by CLP languages over finite domains but also allows the solving of problems that were previously out of scope for CLP languages, e.g. resource allocation and disjunctive scheduling problems. In particular, we were able, using cc(FD), to find the optimal solution, and prove its optimality, to a famous 10/10 scheduling problem [24], which was left open for more than 20 years and finally solved in 1988 [5].

The key novelties in the implementation of cc(FD) (about 40,000 lines of C) are the inclusion of optimal consistency algorithms based on AC-5 [35], dynamic specializations of data structures and constraints, and incremental algorithms for the combinators.

The contributions of this paper are as follows:

1. it presents cc(FD), a simple, uniform, and clean declarative nondeterministic constraint logic language over finite domains;
2. it demonstrates, by means of simple examples, programming idioms to design non-primitive constraints and pruning techniques without resorting to ad-hoc extensions;
3. it discusses how cc(FD) can be implemented to obtain a efficient performance;
4. it gives experimental results which indicate the viability of this approach, even for very complex problems such as the famous 10/10 scheduling problem.

The rest of this paper is organized as follows: the first section presents a motivating example, the perfect square problem, to acquaint the reader with the programming style in cc(FD). The next section discusses the design of cc(FD), including the constraint solver, the combinators, and some higher-order predicates. Section 4 discusses the implementation while the last section reports a large number of experimental results.

2 A Motivating Example

To illustrate several features of cc(FD), we present a program to solve the so-called perfect square problem. The purpose of the program is to build a square, called the *master square*, out of a number of given squares. All the squares must be used and they all have different sizes. The squares are not allowed to overlap and no empty space is permitted in the master square. The sizes of the squares (i.e. the size of their side) and the size of the master squares are given and are depicted in Figure 1. This problem is very combinatorial and there is no hope to solve it using simple backtracking approaches. An interesting fact is that 21

```
sizeMaster(112).
sizeSquares([50,42,37,35,33,29,27,25,24,19,18,17,16,15,11,9,8,7,6,4,2]).
```

Fig. 1. The Data for the Perfect Square Problem

is the smallest number of squares, all of different sizes, which can be packed to produce a master square.

Most programs in cc(FD) follow the following schema

```
solveProblem(...) :-
    generateVariables(...),
    stateConstraints(...),
    stateSurrogateConstraints(...),
    makeChoices(...).
```

The first goal in the body simply creates the problem variables and specifies their ranges. The second goal states the problem constraints. Since, in general, the constraint solver only approximates the constraints, the last goal makes nondeterministic choices to obtain a solution. The third goal states surrogate constraints, i.e. constraints expressing properties of the solutions. These constraints are redundant from a semantic standpoint but are fundamental from an operational standpoint since they may dramatically reduce the search space. This is a traditional technique in operations research. For the perfect square problem, the top-level predicate is as follows:

```
packSquares(Xs,Ys) :-
    generateSquares(Xs,Ys,Sizes,Size),
    stateNoOverlap(Xs,Ys,Sizes),
    stateCapacity(Xs,Sizes,Size), stateCapacity(Ys,Sizes,Size),
    labeling(Xs), labeling(Ys).
```

The first goal generates the lists of variables Xs and Ys of x and y coordinates of all squares, a list Sizes with the given sizes of all squares, and the given size Size of the master square. The goal stateNoOverlap states the no-overlapping constraints while the goals stateCapacity state surrogate constraints exploiting the fact that there is no empty space. The last two goals are nondeterministic goals to generate values for the coordinates. We now study these procedures in more detail.

Each square i is associated with two variables X_i and Y_i representing the coordinates of the bottom-left corner of the square. Each of these variables ranges between 0 and S - S$_i$ where S is the size of the master square and S$_i$ is the size of square i. The following procedure describes the creation of the two lists of variables as well as the list of the sizes.

```
generateSquares(Xs,Ys,Sizes,Size) :-
```

```
sizeMaster(Size), sizeSquares(Sizes),
generateCoordinates(Xs,Ys,Sizes,Size).

generateCoordinates([],[],[],_).
generateCoordinates([X|Xs],[Y|Ys],[S|Ss],Size) :-
    MaxCoord := Size - S, X ~∈ 0..MaxCoord, Y ~∈ 0..MaxCoord,
    generateCoordinates(Xs,Ys,Ss,Size).
```

The no-overlap constraint between two squares (X1,Y1,S1) and (X2,Y2,S2) where (X1,Y1) and (X2,Y2) are the positions of the squares and S1 and S2 are their respective sizes can be expressed using constructive disjunction, one of the combinators of cc(FD):

```
nooverlap(X1,Y1,S1,X2,Y2,S2) :-
    X1 + S1 ≤~ X2 ∨ X2 + S2 ≤~ X1 ∨ Y1 + S1 ≤~ Y2 ∨ Y2 + S2 ≤~ Y1.
```

The disjunction simply expresses that the first square must be on the left, on the right, below, or above the second square. Operationally, cc(FD) removes all values not satisfied by any of the disjuncts (in conjunction with the accumulated constraints) from the domain of the variables.

There is no need to state the no-empty space constraint thanks to the domain of the coordinates, the no-overlap constraint and the hypothesis that the surface of the master square is equal to the sum of the areas of the squares.

A traditional technique to improve efficiency in combinatorial search problem amounts to exploiting properties of all solutions by adding redundant or surrogate constraints. In the perfect square problem, the sizes of all squares containing a point with a given x-coordinate (resp. y-coordinate) must be equal to S, the size of the master square, since no empty space is allowed. These surrogate capacity constraints can be stated using cardinality and linear equations. For a given position P, the idea is to associate with each square i a boolean variable Bi (i.e. a 0-1 variable) that is true iff square i contains a point with x-coordinate (resp. y-coordinate) P. The boolean variable is obtained using the cardinality operator of cc(FD), i.e.

```
#(Bi,[Xi ≤~ P #& P ≤~ Xi + Si - 1 ],Bi).
```

A cardinality formula $\#(l, [c_1, \ldots, c_n], u)$ states that the number of formula which are true in $\{c_1, \ldots, c_n\}$ is no less than l and no more than u. Operationally, the cardinality uses constraint entailment to find out if there is a way to satisfy the constraint and constraint solving when there is a unique way to satisfy the formula. The surrogate constraint for position P and the x coordinate can now be stated as a simple linear equation:

```
B1 * S1 + ... + Bn * Sn =~ Size.
```

The program to generate a surrogate constraint is as follows:

```
capacity(Position,Coordinates,Sizes,Size) :-
   accumulate(Coordinates,Sizes,Position,Summation),
   Summation =~ Size.

accumulate([],[],_,0).
accumulate([C|Cs],[S|Ss],P,B*S + Summation) :-
   B ~∈ 0..1,
   #(B,[ C <~ P ## P <~ C + S - 1],B),
   accumulate(Cs,Ss,P,Summation).
```

The generation of places for the squares requires to give values to the x and the y coordinates of all squares. We use the idea of [1] for the labeling of a coordinate, exploiting the fact that no empty space is allowed. At each step, the program identifies the smallest possible coordinate and select a square to be placed at this position. On backtracking, another square is selected for the same position. The labeling is as follows:

```
labeling([]).
labeling([Coord|Coords]) :-
   minlist([Coord|Coords],Min),
   selectSquare([Coord|Coords],Min,Rest),
   labeling(Rest).

selectSquare([Coord|Coords],Min,Coords) :-
   Coord =~ Min.
selectSquare([Coord|Coords],Min,[Coord|Rest]) :-
   Coord >~ Min,
   selectSquare(Coords,Min,Rest).
```

The first goal in the labeling finds the smallest position for the remaining squares while the second goal chooses a square to assign to the position. Since no empty space is allowed, such a square must exist.

This concludes our motivating example. As is easily shown, the program is rather small and about one page long. It packs 21 or 24 squares in a master square in about 30 seconds on a Sun Sparc Station, illustrating the expressiveness and efficiency of the language.

3 The Design of cc(FD)

We now turn to the design of cc(FD). cc(FD) is a small and uniform language, based on a small constraint system (from a conceptual standpoint) and a number of general-purpose combinators. The key contribution is of course the inclusion of the new combinators and their associated constraint operations. The novelty in the constraint solver is its simplicity and the explicit distinction between domain and interval reasoning, two techniques that were previously hidden in the implementation. This section reviews the various aspects of the design of cc(FD).

3.1 The Constraint System

Syntax and Semantics In this section, we describe the functionality of the constraint system of cc(FD). We focus on finite domains and omit the traditional constraints on first-order terms.

Primitive constraints in cc(FD) are built using variables, natural numbers, the traditional integer operators $+, -, *, div, mod$ and the relations

$$\tilde{>}, \tilde{\geq}, \tilde{=}, \tilde{\neq}, \tilde{\leq}, \tilde{<}, \quad \text{and} \quad >\tilde{}, \geq\tilde{}, =\tilde{}, \neq\tilde{}, \leq\tilde{}, <\tilde{}$$

div and mod represent the integer division and remainder. The arithmetic relations are duplicated to make explicit the two forms of reasoning used in the constraint solver: domain consistency (operators prefixed by tilde) quote) and interval consistency (opeartors postfixed by tilde). The former are called *domain* constraints and the latter *interval* constraints. Variables appearing in constraints are assumed to take values from a finite set of natural numbers, e.g. the set of natural numbers that can fit in a memory word. For convenience, cc(FD) also provides the range constraints

$$x\tilde{} \in [a_1, \ldots, a_n], \quad x\tilde{} \in l..u, \quad x\tilde{} \notin [a_1, \ldots, a_n], \quad x\tilde{} \notin l..u$$

and

$$x \in\tilde{} [a_1, \ldots, a_n], \quad x \in\tilde{} l..u, \quad x \notin\tilde{} [a_1, \ldots, a_n], \quad x \notin\tilde{} l..u$$

although they can easily be obtained from the previous constraints in conjunction with the combinators. Note that the negation of a constraint is also a constraint. In the following, we use the term *constraint store* to denote a conjunction of constraints and use σ possibly subscripted to denote constraint stores. It should be clear that a computation state in cc(FD) is a pair $\langle B, \sigma \rangle$ where B is a conjunction of goals that remain to be solved and σ is a constraint store representing all constraints accumulated up to that point. The above constraints are also called primitive constraints. We will see that the combinators allow us to define new (non-primitive) constraints.

Constraint Operations As mentioned previously, the combinators of cc(FD) are general-purpose and not tailored to the above constraint system.[5] They use three operations on a constraint system C:

1. **constraint solving**: deciding the consistency of a constraint store σ, i.e. $C \models (\exists)\sigma$;
2. **constraint entailment**: deciding whether a constraint c is entailed by a constraint store σ, i.e. $C \models (\forall)(\sigma \Rightarrow c)$;

---

[5] Our current design and implementation efforts are devoted to build cc(Q) and cc(B), two instances of the same framework for rational linear arithmetics and Boolean algebra.

3. **constraint generalization**: finding a generalization σ of a set of constraint stores $\{\sigma_1, \ldots, \sigma_n\}$, such that

$$C \models (\forall)(\sigma_i \Rightarrow \sigma) \quad (1 \leq i \leq n) \qquad (1)$$

For constraint generalization, we would like in general the strongest constraint σ satisfying property (1). This is given, for instance, by the *lub* operation when the constraint system is a complete lattice with respect to the implication order on constraints. Many constraint systems do not enjoy the existence of a *lub* but any constraint store satisfying property (1) is sufficient.

Constraint Processing in cc(FD) Constraint solving and constraint entailment are decidable problems for cc(FD) (since only a finite set of integers is considered) but they are NP-complete problems. For this reason, cc(FD) approximates them by using domain and interval reasoning. The main idea behind domain reasoning is to use constraints to remove values ¿from the domains, to use the domains to decide constraint entailment, and to generate membership constraints during generalization.[6] The main idea behind interval reasoning is to use constraints to reduce the lower and upper bounds on the domains, to use the bounds to detect entailment, and to generate new bounds during generalization. The purpose of the next two sections is to describe the solver of cc(FD) in a precise way. For simplicity, we assume that all constraints are implicitly defined on a set of variables $\{x_1, \ldots, x_n\}$.

Domain Reasoning Domain reasoning is applied on the domain constraints $\tilde{>}, \tilde{\geq}, \tilde{=}, \tilde{\neq}, \tilde{\leq}, \tilde{<}$. Instead of checking consistency of these constraints, cc(FD) checks domain satisfiability, i.e. it enforces domain consistency and checks if none of the domains is empty. The key idea is to associate with each variable its possible set of values. We now define the three operations for domain reasoning: domain consistency, domain entailment and domain generalization.

Definition 1. A constraint c is *domain-consistent* wrt $D_1, \ldots, D_n$ if, for each variable x_i and value $v_i \in D_i$, there exist values $v_1, \ldots, v_{i-1}, v_{i+1}, \ldots, v_n$ in $D_1, \ldots, D_{i-1}, D_{i+1}, \ldots, D_n$ such that $c(v_1, \ldots, v_n)$ holds. A constraint store σ is *domain-consistent* wrt $D_1, \ldots, D_n$ if any constraint c in σ is domain-consistent wrt $D_1, \ldots, D_n$.

In cc(FD), domain consistency is achieved in an incremental way by reducing the domains of the variables at each computation step.

Definition 2. The *reduced domains* of a constraint store σ are the largest domains $D_1, \ldots, D_n$ such that σ is domain-consistent wrt $D_1, \ldots, D_n$, i.e. for all domains $D'_1, \ldots, D'_n$ such that σ is domain-consistent wrt $D'_1, \ldots, D'_n$ we have $D'_1 \subseteq D_1 \& \ldots \& D'_n \subseteq D_n$.

---

[6] The use of domain consistency in programming language was suggested first by Mackworth [21].

Definition 3. A constraint store σ is *domain-satisfiable* iff none of its reduced domains is empty.

It is easy to show that the reduced domains of a constraint store σ exist and are unique and that all the solutions of σ are in its reduced domains. Domain consistency is thus a sound approximation of consistency.

Constraint entailment is replaced by the notion of domain entailment. Intuitively, a constraint is entailed by the constraint store if it is satisfied for all possible combinations of values that are still in the domains of the variables.

Definition 4. A constraint $c(x_1, \ldots, x_n)$ is *domain-entailed* by $D_1, \ldots, D_n$ iff, for all values $v_1, \ldots, v_n$ in $D_1, \ldots, D_n$, $c(v_1, \ldots, v_n)$ holds.

Definition 5. A constraint store σ *domain-entails* a constraint c iff c is domain-entailed by the reduced domains of σ.

Domain entailment is a sound relaxation of entailment: domain entailment implies entailment.

Finally generalization is replaced by the notion of domain generalization. Intuitively, the generalization of a set of constraint stores are range constraints obtained by taking the pointwise union of the reduced domains of the constraint stores.

Definition 6. The *generalization* of a set of constraint stores $\{\sigma_1, \ldots, \sigma_m\}$ is the constraint store

$$x_1 \,\tilde{\in}\, \bigcup_{j=1}^{m} D_1^j \ \& \ \ldots \ \& \ x_n \,\tilde{\in}\, \bigcup_{j=1}^{m} D_n^j$$

where $D_1^j, \ldots, D_n^j$ are the reduced domains of σ_j.

The definition of generalization satisfies property (1). It is not the strongest, but provides a practical compromise between efficiency and expressiveness.

Interval Reasoning Interval reasoning is applied on the interval constraints $>\tilde{\ }, \geq\tilde{\ }, =\tilde{\ }, \neq\tilde{\ }, \leq\tilde{\ }, <\tilde{\ }$. Instead of checking consistency of these constraints, cc(FD) enforces interval consistency. The basic difference compared to domain consistency is that the reasoning is only concerned with the minimum and maximum values in the domains. We now define the three operations for interval reasoning: interval consistency, interval entailment and interval generalization. In the following, we use D^* to denote the set $min(D)..max(D)$ where $min(D)$ and $max(D)$ denote respectively the minimum and maximum values in D.

Definition 7. A constraint c is *interval-consistent* wrt $D_1, \ldots, D_n$ if, for each variable x_i and value $v_i \in \{min(D_i), max(D_i)\}$, there exist values $v_1, \ldots, v_{i-1}, v_{i+1}, \ldots, v_n$ in $D_1^*, \ldots, D_n^*$ such that $c(v_1, \ldots, v_n)$ holds.

Note how only the lower and upper bounds are considered for variable x_i. The remaining definitions for interval satisfiability are modelled after those of domain satisfiability. Existence and uniqueness of the reduced domains for interval constraints can easily be shown as well as the soundness of interval satisfiability.

The first definition for interval entailment becomes as follows.

Definition 8. A constraint $c(x_1, \ldots, x_n)$ is *interval-entailed* by $D_1, \ldots, D_n$ iff, for all values $v_1, \ldots, v_n$ in $D_1^*, \ldots, D_n^*$, $c(v_1, \ldots, v_n)$ holds.

The remaining notions are defined in a similar way as for domain-reasoning. Finally, the generalization is computed as follows.

Definition 9. The *generalization* of a set of constraint stores $\{\sigma_1, \ldots, \sigma_m\}$ is the constraint store

$$x_1 \in\tilde{}\, \left(\bigcup_{j=1}^m D_1^j \right)^* \ \& \ \ldots \ \& \ x_n \in\tilde{}\, \left(\bigcup_{j=1}^m D_n^j \right)^*$$

where $D_1^j, \ldots, D_n^j$ are the reduced domains of σ_j.

The Constraint Solver Given a set of domain constraints S_d and interval constraints S_i, the constraint solver in cc(FD) checks if S_d and S_i are simultaneously domain-satisfiable and interval-satisfiable with respect to the same domains. It also reduces the domains accordingly.

Example 1 Domain Consistency. The goal

```
?- X ˜∈ 1..2, Y ˜∈ 0..10, X ˜= Y mod 3
```

produces the reduced domains $D_X = 1..2$ and $D_Y = \{1, 2, 4, 5, 7, 8, 10\}$. Adding the constraint Y ˜∉ {2,5,8} would produce the domains $D_X = \{1\}$ and $D_Y = \{1, 4, 7, 10\}$.

Example 2 Interval Consistency. The goal

```
?- X ˜∈ 1..2, Y ˜∈ 0..10, X =˜ Y mod 3
```

produces the reduced domains $D_X = 1..2$ and $D_Y = 1..10$. Adding the constraint Y ˜∉ {2,5,8} would produce the domains

$$D_X = 1..2 \ \& \ D_Y = \{1, 3, 4, 6, 7, 9, 10\}$$

3.2 The Cardinality Combinator

Motivation The constraint solver in cc(FD) is only concerned with conjunction of constraints. Many practical applications however contain disjunctive information and an adequate processing of disjunctions is often a prerequisite to obtain a satisfactory solution. Consider, for instance, a disjunctive scheduling problem where two tasks i and j cannot be scheduled at the same time. The no-overlap constraint between these two tasks can be expressed as

```
disjunctive(S_i,D_i,S_j,D_j)  :- S_i + D_i ≤~ S_j.
disjunctive(S_i,D_i,S_j,D_j)  :- S_j + D_j ≤~ S_i.
```

assuming that S_i, S_j are the starting dates of i and j and D_i, D_j their respective durations. The main problem with this formulation comes from the fact that the no-overlap constraint is only used for making choices and never to reduce the search space. However, when it is known that the constraint "task i precedes task j" is not consistent with the constraint store, the other alternative "task j precedes task i" must hold and hence can be added to the constraint store achieving early pruning of the search space. This handling of disjunctions requires constraint entailment as a primitive constraint operation and treats constraints locally. It enables the system to deduce constraints from disjunctions and is the key idea behind the cardinality operator which, in addition, generalizes this idea to threshold operators. The cardinality operator has been used in numerous applications including car-sequencing, disjunctive scheduling, hamiltonian path, and DSP scheduling to name a few.

Description In its most primitive form, the cardinality combinator is an expression of the form $\#(l, [c_1, \ldots, c_n], u)$ where l, u are integers and $c_1, \ldots, c_n$ are primitive constraints. Declaratively, it holds iff the number of true constraints in $[c_1, \ldots, c_n]$ is no less than l and no more than u. The cardinality operator generalizes the usual logical connectives. $c_1 \wedge \ldots \wedge c_n$ is equivalent to $\#(n, [c_1, \ldots, c_n], n)$, $c_1 \vee \ldots \vee c_n$ to $\#(1, [c_1, \ldots, c_n], n)$ and $\neg c$ to $\#(0, [c], 0)$. Other connectives can then be obtained easily.

The key feature of the cardinality combinator is its operational semantics. The main idea is that constraint entailment is used in a local manner to determine if the cardinality expression has a solution. When only one way of satisfying the cardinality is left, the appropriate constraints are added to the constraint store. More precisely, the two basic cases are:

1. a cardinality $\#(n, [c_1, \ldots, c_n], \_)$ requires $c_1, \ldots, c_n$ to be true; $c_1, \ldots, c_n$ are then added to the constraint store;
2. a cardinality $\#(\_, [c_1, \ldots, c_n], 0)$ requires $\neg c_1, \ldots, \neg c_n$ to be true; $\neg c_1, \ldots, \neg c_n$ are then added to the constraint store.

Assuming that σ is the constraint store at some computation step, the two reduction cases are:

- $\#(l, [c_1, \ldots, c_n], u)$ reduces to $\#(l-1, [c_1, \ldots, c_{i-1}, c_{i+1}, \ldots, c_n], u-1)$ if $\mathcal{C} \models (\forall)(\sigma \Rightarrow c_i)$;
- $\#(l, [c_1, \ldots, c_n], u)$ reduces to $\#(l, [c_1, \ldots, c_{i-1}, c_{i+1}, \ldots, c_n], u)$ if $\mathcal{C} \models (\forall)(\sigma \Rightarrow \neg c_i)$.

In practice, entailment is approximated through domain and interval entailment, depending on c_i. cc(FD) offers various extensions to the primitive form: l and u can be any arithmetic terms and the c_i can also be cardinality combinators. The last case is handled by means of a simple rewriting rule [33]. Logical connectives (prefixed with $\#$) can also be used freely in cc(FD) and are interpreted as abbreviations for cardinality formulas. Finally, when only one bound is relevant, special forms such as U $\#\geq$ $[c_1,\dots,c_n]$ and L $\#\leq$ $[c_1,\dots,c_n]$ can be used. The implementation exploits the special forms to obtain better performance as discussed in the implementation section.

Example 3 Disjunctive Constraints. The no-overlap constraint mentioned in the motivation can be expressed as

```
disjunction(Sᵢ,Dᵢ,Sⱼ,Dⱼ) :-
    1 #≤ [Sᵢ + Dᵢ ≤˜ Sⱼ, Sⱼ + Dⱼ ≤˜ Sᵢ]).
```

It achieves the pruning described previously. When the negation of one of the constraints is implied by the constraint store, the other constraint is automatically added to the store. For instance, the goal

```
?- S₁ ˜∈ 1..6, S₂ ˜∈ 1..10, disjunction(S₁,7,S₂,6).
```

produces the reduced domain S_1 $\tilde{\in}$ $1..3$, S_2 $\tilde{\in}$ $8..10$. The no-overlap constraint is an important part of the disjunctive scheduling programs reported in the experimental results.

Example 4 Communication Constraints. An interesting application of the cardinality combinator occurs in the Digital Signal Processing (DSP) application of [7, 32], whose results are also reported in the experimental results. The purpose of the application is to allocate tasks to processors in an architecture combining pipeline processing and master-slave processing in order to minimize the total delay of the DSP application. To solve the problem, it is necessary to express a communication constraint between each two successive tasks in the task graph of the application. The delay between two tasks is 0 when both tasks are assigned to the same processor, 1 when one of them is assigned to the master processor or if the processor of the second task follows the processor of the first task in the pipeline, and 2 otherwise (the communication goes through the master). It is expressed in cc(FD) by

```
delay(S₁,P₁,S₂,P₂) :-
    Delay ˜∈ 0..2,
    Delay ˜= 0 #⇔ P₁ ˜= P₂,
    Delay ˜= 1 #⇔ P₁ ˜≠ P₂ #∧ (P₂ ˜= P₁ + 1 #∨ P₁ ˜= 1 #∨ P₂ ˜= 1
    S₂ ˜≥ S₁ + Delay.
```

In the above constraint, S_1, S_2 are the starting dates of tasks 1 and 2 and P_1, P_2 are their associated processors. The master processor is processor 1. This constraint is a key component of our solution which compares very well with a specific branch and bound algorithm written in C.

Example 5 Capacity Constraints. The motivating example contains a third use of cardinality for the capacity constraints. The main technique here is to associating a boolean with a constraint using cardinality

`B ~∈ 0..1, #(B,[c],B).`

Arbitrary constraints on the boolean can now be expressed and two-way propagation takes place between the boolean and the constraint. This technique is used in the perfect square application.

3.3 Constructive Disjunction

Motivation Constructive disjunction was motivated by the need to achieve a more global pruning for disjunctions than the one offered by cardinality. Consider, for instance, the definition of `maximum(X,Y,Max)` which holds iff `Max` is the maximum of X and Y. Using cardinality, it can be expressed as

```
maximum(X,Y,Max) :-
    X ≤~ Max,
    Y ≤~ Max,
    Max =~ X #∨ Max =~ Y.
```

Unfortunately, the above implementation produces no pruning on the maximal value of `Max`. For instance, the goal

`?- X ~∈ 5..10, Y ~∈ 4..11, Max ~∈ 0..20, maximum(X,Y,Max).`

produces the reduced domains $D_X = 5..10, D_Y = 4..11, D_{Max} = 5..20$ because both constraints in the cardinality are treated locally and are consistent with the constraint store. Constructive disjunction makes sure to produce $D_{Max} = 5..11$.

Description A constructive disjunction is an expression of the form $\sigma_1 \vee \ldots \vee \sigma_n$ or $\sigma_1 \vee \ldots \vee \sigma_n$. The difference between $\vee$ and $\vee$ comes from the two forms of generalizations available in `cc(FD)`: domain generalization and interval generalization. `cc(FD)` allows also the presence of cardinality formulas and constructive disjunctions in the disjuncts by using simple rewriting rules.

Declaratively, a constructive disjunction can be read as a simple disjunction. The operational behaviour is however the important feature. If any of the disjuncts is entailed by the current constraint store σ, then the constructive disjunction is clearly satisfied. Otherwise, the new constraint store is simply $\sigma \wedge \Gamma$ where Γ is the domain or interval generalization of $\{\sigma \wedge \sigma_1, \ldots, \sigma \wedge \sigma_n\}$.

Of course, the generalization is computed incrementally (and added to the constraint store) each time the constraint store is modified. In other words, the idea is to extract, at any computation step, common information from the disjuncts in conjunction with the constraint store. In `cc(FD)`, the common information takes the form of range constraints.

Example 6 Maximum Constraints. The maximum constraint is expressed as

```
maximum(X,Y,Max) :-
    X ≤~ Max,
    Y ≤~ Max,
    Max =~ X ∨ Max =~ Y.
```

The goal

```
?- X ~∈ 5..10, Y ~∈ 4..11, Max ~∈ 0..20, maximum(X,Y,Max).
```

leads to the reduced domains $D_{Max} = 5..10, D_X = 5..10$ for the first disjuncts and to $D_{Max} = 5..11, D_Y = 5..11$ for the second disjunction. The generalization produces the domains $D_{Max} = 5..11, D_X = 5..10, D_Y = 4..11$. The maximum constraint is an important component of the solution to disjunctive scheduling problems.

Example 7 Distance Constraints. Another example of constructive disjunction is the handling of constraints of the form $|X - Y| \geq I$. This is used in the applications referred to as satel1 and satel2 in the experimental results. The implementation is simply

```
absolute_distance(X,Y,I) :-
    X - Y ~≥ I ∨ Y - X ~≥ Y.
```

Contrary to the maximum constraint which only makes pruning on the bounds of the domains, the above constraint removes values in the middle of the domains. For instance, the query

```
?- X ~∈ 1..10, Y ~∈ 1..10, absolute_distance(X,Y,8).
```

produces the reduced domains $D_x = \{1, 2, 9, 10\}, D_y = \{1, 2, 9, 10\}$.

Example 8 Disjunctive Scheduling. In the previous examples, the disjuncts were simple primitive constraints but in cc(FD) they can be any constraint store, i.e. any conjunction of primitive constraints. For instance, in disjunctive scheduling, one often need conditional expressions of the form

$$(\text{Min} \geq^\sim X_1 , X_1 \sim= \text{Entry}) \vee \dots \vee (\text{Min} \geq^\sim X_n , X_n \sim= \text{Entry}).$$

Operationally, the intention is that Min be greater than at least one of the X_i that can be equal to Entry.

3.4 The Implication Combinator

Motivation Blocking implication [22, 28, 16] is a combinator generalizing corroutining mechanisms in logic programming. The main idea behind coroutining mechanisms is to postpone execution of a goal until some conditions on its variables are satisfied. The main idea behind blocking implication is to use constraints for the conditions. As a consequence, blocking implication is a convenient tool to implement local propagation of values, pruning rules, and algorithm animation. It is used in many applications including hamiltonian circuits, test generation, and disjunctive scheduling. All graphical animations also use blocking implication.

Description In its simplest form, a blocking implication is an expression of the form $c \rightarrow B$ where c is a primitive constraint and B is a body. Declaratively, it can be read as an implication. The key feature is once again the operational semantics. The body of the implication is executed only if c is entailed by the constraint store. If $\neg c$ is entailed by the constraint store, the implication simply succeeds. Otherwise, the implication suspends and the body will be executed only when a latter constraint store entails c due to the addition of other constraints.

cc(FD) also allows cardinality formulas instead of the constraints since once again the operational semantics can be given by simple rewrite rules. It also allows expressions such as fixed(T) with T being an arithmetic term to be used instead of c. An expression fixed(T) $\rightarrow$ B executes B as soon as T is constrained to take a unique value by the constraint store and is an abbreviation of the constraint #(1, [T ~= min_int, T ~= $min\_int + 1$, ..., T ~= max_int], 1) where min_int and max_int are a lower and upper bound of the finite set of natural numbers that can fit in a memory word.

Example 9 Local Propagation. Local propagation can be implemented in a simple way using blocking implication. For instance, a logical and-gate using local propagation techniques would be:

```
and(X,Y,Z) :-
     X ~= 0 → Z ~= 0,
     Y ~= 0 → Z ~= 0,
     Z ~= 1 → ( X ~= 1 , Y ~= 1 ),
     X ~= 1 → Y ~= Z,
     Y ~= 1 → X ~= Z,
     X ~= Y → X ~= Z.
```

The first rule says that, as soon as the constraint store entails X = 0, the constraint Z = 0 must be added to the constraint store. Note that the last three rules which actually do more than local value propagation; they also propagate symbolic equations and one of them is conditional to a symbolic equality.

Example 10 Disjunctive Scheduling. In disjunctive scheduling, a number of tasks are required not to overlap. A typical pruning technique amounts to establishing which tasks can be entry of the disjunction (i.e. can be scheduled first) and which tasks can be exit of the disjunction (i.e. can be scheduled last). To determine the entry, a typical rule is

$$S_i + \text{TotalDuration} \text{ ~> ExitDate} \rightarrow \text{Entry} \text{ ~} \neq i$$

where S_i represents the starting date of a task, TotalDuration the summation of the durations of all tasks in the disjunction, and ExitDate is the maximum end date of the tasks which can be exits of the disjunction. It simply expresses that if the constraint store implies that the starting date of task i added to the total duration is greater than the maximum end date, then task i cannot be an entry of the disjunction.

Example 11 Algorithm Animation. Blocking implication is the main tool to produce graphical algorithm animation. For instance, in a n-queens problem, the animation would show the queens already placed and the values removed from the remaining queens. The animation is obtained by using blocking implications of the form

```
fixed(Q2) → show_queens(Q2,2)
```

to display the queen associated with column 2 and

```
Q2 ~≠ 4  → show_removed(4,2)
```

to show that the value 4 is no longer possible for queens 2. The appeal of this approach is that the graphical animation is completely separated from the program and runs in coroutining.

3.5 Higher-Order Predicates

cc(FD) contains also a number of higher-order predicate for optimization purposes. The basic forms are

```
minof(Goal,Function,Res)
maxof(Goal,Function,Res)
minof_r(Goal,Function,Res)
maxof_r(Goal,Function,Res)
```

The purpose of these predicates is to obtain an optimal solution to a goal with respect to an objective function (i.e. an arithmetic term). Two versions of the predicates are given. The first version uses a depth-first branch and bound algorithm while the second version uses a restarting strategy. Special care is taken in the depth-first branch and bound when a new solution is found to backtrack to a point where the solution can potentially be improved upon. The restarting strategy may be of interest when heuristics are strongly influenced by the value of the best solution found so far [27]. The typical technique to solve optimization problems amounts to embedding the choice part in the higher-order predicate:

```
solve_problem(...) :-
    create_variables(...),
    state_constraints(...),
    minof(make_choice(...),Function,Res).
```

Finally, cc(FD) also contains a number of non-logical predicates giving access to the domains. These predicates should only be used for defining heuristics in the choice process (e.g. choosing the next variable to instantiate as the one with the smallest domain).

4 Implementation

As mentioned previously, the implementation of cc(FD) includes a version of the WAM [37], suitably enhanced with constraint processing facilities. The introduction of constraints is almost exclusively achieved by a set of built-in predicates, keeping the interface between the two parts to a strict minimum. In particular, no new instructions have been added to WAM apart from those necessary to achieve the coroutining facilities required by the implication combinator. As a consequence, cc(FD) preserves the simplicity and speed of the WAM. Note also that the implementation does not sacrifice the efficiency of constraint solving as our experimental results indicate. The specialization of constraints simply does not occur at the WAM level but inside the constraint solver. In the rest of this section, we concentrate on the main features of the constraint system and of the combinators.

4.1 Constraint System

Domain representation is an important aspect of the constraint system. cc(FD) uses different domain representations depending on the application. When the implementation only needs interval reasoning for a given domain variable, the domain representation is simply two integers: a lower and an upper bound. When some values are removed ¿from the middle of the domain, a more explicit representation, an array of booleans, is constructed to indicate the presence or the absence of the element. This is completely transparent to the user.

Constraints are attached directly to parts of the domain representation. For instance, inequalities are attached to the lower and upper bounds of the domains; $X \leq Y$ is attached to the lower bound of X (to update the lower bound of Y) and to the upper bound of Y (to update the upper bound of X). Disequations are attached to the domain as a whole and are only considered when one variable is instantiated. Finally, constraint entailment (e.g. entailment of $X \neq 3$) also attaches constraints to elements of the boolean array. This enables the system to check entailment of unary constraints (a very frequent case) in constant time over the whole execution. Once again, the representation is adapted depending on the need of the application.

Modifications to the domains are trailed by remember pairs

<address,old value>.

Time stamps are used to avoid trailing twice the same address in between two choice points.

4.2 Constraint Algorithms

Constraints are also classified depending upon their complexity. cc(FD) has specialized algorithms for nonlinear, linear, binary, and unary constraints. Once again, this is fully transparent to the user. The specialization is performed at run-time in the present implementation but global flow analysis should allow us to move most of the work at compile-time in the next version of the system.

The constraint-solving algorithms are based on (non-binary) generalization of the AC-5 algorithm [35] using a breath-first strategy. In particular, domain-consistency of any combination of binary functional (e.g. $X \tilde{} = Y$), anti-functional (e.g. $X \tilde{} \neq Y$), monotonic (e.g. $X \tilde{} > Y$), and piecewise constraints (e.g. $X \tilde{} = Y$ mod 7), require $O(cd)$ amortized time, where c is the number of constraints and d is the size of the largest domain [35]. Once again, the system (dynamically) compiles constraints differently depending on their properties. For instance, a constraint such as $X \tilde{} = Y$ mod c will be compiled into expressions of the form

$$\forall \; \alpha: Y \neq \alpha \rightarrow X \neq \alpha \text{ mod } c$$
$$\forall \; \alpha: X \neq \alpha \rightarrow Y \neq N * C + \alpha$$

when the constraint is recognized as functional due to the domains of the variables. Operationally these expressions can be seen as abbreviations for a finite number of blocking implications. The implementation however uses constant space to represent them. When the above constraint is not functional, it behaves operationally as a set of cardinality formulas of the form

$$X \tilde{} = \alpha \; \# \Leftrightarrow Y \tilde{} \in S$$

where S is the set of values supporting α. At the implementation level, the space requirement is proportional, not the size of the domains, but rather to the number of groups in the piecewise decompositions.

Interval consistency of non-binary monotonic constraints requires $O(cdn^2)$ amortized where n is the number of variables in the largest constraints. An optimal algorithm of complexity $O(cdn)$ exists [34] for linear constraints but our preliminary experimentations indicate that its overhead may reduce its interest.

The breath-first strategy makes sure that domain consistency of monotonic constraints has a complexity which is quadratic in the number of variables and constraints independently of the domain sizes contrary to a depth-search strategy which may be exponential.

4.3 The Cardinality Operator

A cardinality operator of the form $\#(l, [c_1, \ldots, c_n], u)$ is implemented by keeping two counters for the number of formulas which are true and false respectively. In addition, the system spawns n constraint-entailment procedures checking if the c_i or their negations are entailed by the constraint store. When the true-counter reaches the upper bound, all remaining constraints are forced to false, i.e. their negations are added to the constraint store. When the false-counter reaches $n - l$, all remaining constraints are forced to be true, i.e. they are added to the constraint store. Specific optimizations are possible for various specialized forms. For instance, when the lower bound is unimportant (e.g. $u \; \#\geq [c_1, \ldots, c_n]$), entailment needs only to be checked for the constraints $c_1, \ldots, c_n$ and not their negations.

Note also that our implementation of cardinality enables to implement arc-consistency on arbitrary binary constraints within the optimal (time and space) bounds of the AC-4 algorithm [23].

4.4 Constructive Disjunction

Constructive disjunction in cc(FD) is implemented in terms of constraint solving in order to obtain an incremental behaviour. The key idea is to rename the variables in each disjunct independently and to add the renamed disjuncts to the constraint store. In doing so, the implementation reuses the algorithms available for constraint solving, achieving both efficiency and reuse of existent code. The astute reader would have noticed that special care is needed in case of failures. The connections between the renamed variables and the original variables is achieved through a number of (internal) constraints which are essentially of two types

1. **subsumption constraints:** these constraints force the domain of a variable to be a subset of the domain of another variable;
2. **union constraints:** these constraints force the domain of a variable to be a subset of the union of the domains of other variables.

Subsumption constraints have been investigated previously by Parker [25] as a language extension. In cc(FD), they are only used inside the implementation since their directed nature is somewhat in contradiction with the multi-directional philosophy of constraint logic programming. Many optimizations are present in the system to handle efficiently the cases where some variables appear only in a subset of the disjuncts. For instance, these optimizations make sure that constructive disjunction comes close to cardinality for the case where both apply and constructive disjunction does not produce more pruning.

4.5 Blocking Implication

Blocking implementation is a generalization of the traditional if-then-else construct. The compilation schema is simply

```
< check entailment of the constraint >
JUMPIFNOTTRUE labelfalse
     < execute body >
     JUMP next
labelfalse: JUMPIFFALSE next
     < handle suspension >
next:
```

The handling of suspension amounts to creating an entailment procedure for the constraint and attaching the body to the procedure. Whenever a constraint is entailed, its associated body is inserted in a list of bodies which are executed as soon as possible, i.e. after a built-in procedure or at the neck of a user-defined procedure. The list is executed in a depth-first manner for simplicity and closely follows the traditional implementation of delay mechanisms (e.g. [6]).

5 Experimental Results

Problem	Search Time	Total Time	Search Space	Variables	Constraints	lines
Bridge	3.9	4.6	2^{77}	46	445	140
Car	0.92	9.37	20^{100}	600	12390	225
Cutting	7.8	11.3	4^{72}	72	79	303
Satel1	9.8	41.6	24^{200}	5158	6678	338
Satel2	8.1	13.09	$44^{98}36^{102}$	1362	2911	338
square	38.15	60.66	21^{224}	9366	52584	105
hamilton	1.45	4.61	$2^{92}3^{40}$	64	6560	166
donald	0.05	0.06	10^{10}	15	63	50
sendmory	0.00	0.01	8^{10}	8	38	46
queens8	0.02	0.04	8^{8}	8	92	52
queens8all	0.63	0.65	8^{8}	8	92	52
queens96	0.80	2.94	96^{96}	96	13776	52
magic11	0.14	0.25	11^{11}	11	165	58
magic16	0.39	0.57	16^{16}	16	320	58
magic21	0.77	1.12	21^{21}	21	525	58

Table 1. Experimental Results of cc(FD)

In this section, we report a number of experimental results of cc(FD). All times are for a Sun Sparc Station I (Sun 4/60). Table 1 shows the search time, the total time, the potential search space, the number of variables, and the number of constraints for a number of problems, and the number of lines of the program. The search time is the time spent in the nondeterministic part of the program while the total time includes reading of data, creating the variables, and stating the constraints. The number of variables and constraints are taken just before the nondeterministic part of the program although, in some cases, constraints are generated during the choice process as well. The potential search space does not always reflect the difficulty of the problem but should provide some more indication on the sizes of the problems dealt with by cc(FD). The number of lines (which includes blank lines and comments) gives also an idea of the compactness of the programs which enables a short development time. Bridge is a disjunctive scheduling problem ¿from [2], car is a car-sequencing problem [12, 26], cutting is the numerical statement of a cutting-stock problem taken from [10], satel1, satel2 are two resource allocation problems with distance constraints, square is the perfect packing problem, hamilton is the Euler knight problem, donald, sendmory are two cryptarithmetic problems, queens8, queensall, queens96 are n-queens programs to find respectively the first solution to the 8-queens problem, all solutions to the 8-queens problem, and the first solution to the 96 queens problems. magic11, magic16, magic21 are various instances of the magic series problem taken from [33, 31] for sizes 11, 16, and 21.

Table 2 compares cc(FD) with a specialized branch and bound algorithm

Problem	Size	Processors	Topology	Total Delay	cc(FD)	Specialized BB
RDAD01	9	3	Pipeline	3	0.78	0.016
RDAD02	9	3	Pipeline	3	0.72	0.016
RDAD03	6	5	Architecture-like	5	0.22	0.000
RDAD04	19	6	Parallel Pipelines	3	1.66	51.700
RDAD05	12	4	Pipeline	3	1.12	0.016
RDAD06	16	5	Parallel Pipelines	3	2.68	6.300
RDAD07	12	4	Parallel Pipelines	2	0.56	0.050
RDAD08	15	5	Merging Tasks	3	3.23	963.13
RDAD09	9	6	Many Generators	2	0.18	0.016
RDAD10	15	5	Parallel Pipelines	4	3.90	0.033
RDAD20	13	5	Architecture-like	3	0.99	0.016
RDAD40	25	8	Parallel Pipelines	5	54.40	?????
RDAD41	25	8	Parallel Pipelines	4	4.24	0.100

Table 2. Results on Actual DSP Applications

written in C on a number of DSP problems [7, 20]. Both algorithms were run on the same machine. As can be seen from the data, cc(FD) compares very well with the specialized program especially for the largest problems. The cc(FD) program is about 200 lines long.

Nb. of Machines	Nb. of jobs	Nb. of tasks	cc(FD)	Specialized BB
5	11	55	26	4
4	13	52	27	2
5	12	60	11	7
4	14	56	81	24
6	10	60	620	158
9	8	56	578	209
7	7	49	246	37

Table 3. Results on Disjunctive Scheduling Application

Table 3 compares cc(FD) with a specialized scheduling algorithm [4]. These are very difficult scheduling problems, requiring sophisticated handling of disjunctions. The potential search space of a 6/10 problem is 2^{330}. cc(FD), in its present state, cannot compete in pure speed with the specialized program but the difference is mainly a constant factor, showing that the pruning techniques of cc(FD) are quite effective. The cc(FD) program is about 440 lines long. Finally, it is interesting to point out that the cc(FD) program is able to solve optimally and prove optimality of a famous 10/10 job shop scheduling which was posed in 1963 [24] and left open for 25 years before being solved in [5]. The algorithm in [5] is very involved including relaxation techniques to preemptive scheduling. This problem requires about 90 hours of computation.

The above results seem to indicate that cc(FD) is a step in closing the gap between declarative constraint languages and procedural languages. Very difficult problems are now in the scope of cc(FD), which comes close in efficiency to specialized algorithms written in procedural programs.

6 Conclusion

In this paper, we have presented the design, implementation, and applications of cc(FD), a declarative nondeterministic constraint language over finite domains. cc(FD) is a small and uniform language based on a conceptually simple constraint solver and a number of general-purpose combinators. The key novelty in cc(FD) is the availability of the combinators which enable to address, at the language level, issues such as the handling of disjunctions, the definition of non-primitive constraints, and the control of the search exploration. The implementation of cc(FD) (about 40,000 lines of C) includes optimal consistency algorithms, adaptable data structures, and incremental techniques for the combinators. The experimental results indicate that cc(FD) can tackle very difficult problems with an efficiency which comes close to procedural languages in many cases. Future work on cc(FD) will be devoted to the generalizations of the combinators to arbitrary goals and to global flow analysis to specialize constraints and data structures at compile time. These extensions may further improve expressiveness and efficiency. Finally, instantiations of the framework to Boolean algebra and rational numbers are currently developed.

Acknowledgements

Discussions with Alain Colmerauer and Michel Van Caneghem help simplifying the design and solving the motivating example. This research was partly supported by the National Science Foundation under grant number CCR-9108032 and the Office of Naval Research under grant N00014-91-J-4052 ARPA order 8225.

References

1. A. Aggoun and N. Beldiceanu. Extending CHIP To Solve Complex Scheduling and Packing Problems. In *Journées Francophones De Programmation Logique*, Lille, France, 1992.

2. M. Bartusch. *Optimierung von Netzplaenen mit Anordnungsbeziehungen bei Knappen Betriebsmitteln*. PhD thesis, Fakultaet fuer Mathematik und Informatik, Universitaet Passau (F.R.G), 1983.

3. W. Buttner and H. Simonis. Embedding Boolean Expressions into Logic Programming. *Journal of Symbolic Computation*, 4:191–205, October 1987.

4. J. Carlier. Ordonnancement à Constraintes Disjonctives. *RAIRO Operations Research*, 12(4):333–351, November 1978.

5. J. Carlier and E. Pinson. Une Méthode Arborescente pour Optimiser la Durée d'un JOB-SHOP. Technical Report ISSN 0294-2755, I.M.A, Angers, 1986.

6. M. Carlsson. Freeze, Indexing and Other Implemenation Issues on the WAM. In J-L. Lassez, editor, *Fourth International Conference on Logic Programming*, pages 40–58, Melbourne, Australia, 1987.

7. J.W. Chinneck, R.A. Goubran, G.M. Karam, and M Lavoie. A Design Approach for Real-Time Multiprocessor DSP Applications. Report SCE-90-05, Carleton University, Ottawa, Canada, February 1990.

8. N. Christofides. *Graph Theory: An Algorithmic Approach*. Academic Press, New York, 1975.

9. A. Colmerauer. An Introduction to Prolog III. *CACM*, 28(4):412–418, 1990.

10. M.C. Costa. Une Etude Pratique de découpes de Panneaux de Bois. *RAIRO Recherche Operationnelle*, 18(3):211–219, August 1984.

11. T. Dean and M. Boddy. An Analysis of Time-dependent Planning. In *Proceedings of the Seventh National Conference On Artificial Intelligence*, pages 49–54, Minneapolis, Minnesota, August 1988.

12. M. Dincbas, H. Simonis, and P. Van Hentenryck. Solving the Car Sequencing Problem in Constraint Logic Programming. In *European Conference on Artificial Intelligence (ECAI-88)*, Munich, W. Germany, August 1988.

13. M. Dincbas, H. Simonis, and P. Van Hentenryck. Solving Large Combinatorial Problems in Logic Programming. *Journal of Logic Programming*, 8(1-2):75–93, January/March 1990.

14. M. Dincbas, P. Van Hentenryck, H. Simonis, A. Aggoun, T. Graf, and F. Berthier. The Constraint Logic Programming Language CHIP. In *Proceedings of the International Conference on Fifth Generation Computer Systems*, Tokyo, Japan, December 1988.

15. T. Graf. Extending Constraint Handling in Logic Programming to Rational Arithmetic. Internal Report, ECRC, Munich, Septembre 1987.

16. T. Graf, P. Van Hentenryck, C. Pradelles, and L. Zimmer. Simulation of Hybrid Circuits in Constraint Logic Programming. In *International Joint Conference on Artificial Intelligence*, Detroit, Michigan, August 1989.

17. J. Jaffar and J-L. Lassez. Constraint Logic Programming. In *POPL-87*, Munich, FRG, January 1987.

18. J. Jaffar and S. Michaylov. Methodology and Implementation of a CLP System. In *Fourth International Conference on Logic Programming*, pages 196–218, Melbourne, Australia, May 1987.

19. M. Kubale and D. Jackowski. A Generalized Implicit Enumeration Algorithm for Graph Coloring. *CACM*, 28(4):412–418, 1985.

20. Marco Lavoie. Task Assignment in a DSP Multiprocessor Environment. Master's Thesis, Department of Systems and Computer Engineering, Carleton University, Ottawa, Ontario, August 1990.

21. A.K. Mackworth. Consistency in Networks of Relations. *Artificial Intelligence*, 8(1):99–118, 1977.

22. M.J. Maher. Logic Semantics for a Class of Committed-Choice Programs. In *Fourth International Conference on Logic Programming*, pages 858–876, Melbourne, Australia, May 1987.

23. R. Mohr and T.C. Henderson. Arc and Path Consistency Revisited. *Artificial Intelligence*, 28:225–233, 1986.

24. J.F. Muth and G.L. Thompson. *Industrial Scheduling.* Prentice Hall, Englewood Cliffs, NJ, 1963.
25. R.G. Parker and R.L. Rardin. *Discrete Optimization.* Academic Press, London (England), 1988.
26. B.D. Parrello. CAR WARS: The (Almost) Birth of an Expert System. *AI Expert,* 3(1):60–64, January 1988.
27. H.M. Salkin. On the Merit of the Generalized Origin and Restarts in Implicit Enumeration. *Opns. Res.,* 18:549–554, 1970.
28. V.A. Saraswat. *Concurrent Constraint Programming Languages.* PhD thesis, Carnegie-Mellon University, 1989.
29. V.A. Saraswat and M. Rinard. Concurrent Constraint Programming. In *Proceedings of Seventeenth ACM Symposium on Principles of Programming Languages,* San Francisco, CA, January 1990.
30. V.A. Saraswat, M. Rinard, and P. Panangaden. Semantic Foundations of Concurrent Constraint Programming. In *Proceedings of Ninth ACM Symposium on Principles of Programming Languages,* Orlando, FL, January 1991.
31. P. Van Hentenryck. *Constraint Satisfaction in Logic Programming.* Logic Programming Series, The MIT Press, Cambridge, MA, 1989.
32. P. Van Hentenryck. Scheduling and Packing in the Constraint Language cc(FD). Technical Report CS-92-43, CS Department, Brown University, 1992.
33. P. Van Hentenryck and Y. Deville. The Cardinality Operator: A New Logical Connective and Its Application to Constraint Logic Programming. In *Eighth International Conference on Logic Programming (ICLP-91),* Paris (France), June 1991. Also to appear in *Constraint Logic Programming: Selected Research,* The MIT Press, 1992.
34. P. Van Hentenryck, Y. Deville, M.L. Chen, and C.M. Teng. New Results in Consistency of Networks. Technical report, CS Department, Brown University, 1992. Forthcoming.
35. P. Van Hentenryck, Y. Deville, and C.M. Teng. A Generic Arc Consistency Algorithm and its Specializations. *Artificial Intelligence,* 57(2-3), 1992.
36. P. Van Hentenryck and T. Graf. Standard Forms for Rational Linear Arithmetics in Constraint Logic Programming. *Annals of Mathematics and Artificial Intelligence,* 5(2-4):303–320, 1992.
37. D.H.D Warren. An Abstract Prolog Instruction Set. Technical Report 309, SRI, October 1983.

Springer-Verlag
and the Environment

We at Springer-Verlag firmly believe that an international science publisher has a special obligation to the environment, and our corporate policies consistently reflect this conviction.

We also expect our business partners – paper mills, printers, packaging manufacturers, etc. – to commit themselves to using environmentally friendly materials and production processes.

The paper in this book is made from low- or no-chlorine pulp and is acid free, in conformance with international standards for paper permanency.

Lecture Notes in Computer Science

For information about Vols. 1–831
please contact your bookseller or Springer-Verlag

Vol 867: L. Steels, G. Schreiber, W. Van de Velde (Eds.), A Future for Knowledge Acquisition. Proceedings, 1994. XII, 414 pages. 1994. (Subseries LNAI).

Vol. 868: R. Steinmetz (Ed.), Multimedia: Advanced Teleservices and High-Speed Communication Architectures. Proceedings, 1994. IX, 451 pages. 1994.

Vol. 869: Z. W. Raś, Zemankova (Eds.), Methodologies for Intelligent Systems. Proceedings, 1994. X, 613 pages. 1994. (Subseries LNAI).

Vol. 870: J. S. Greenfield, Distributed Programming Paradigms with Cryptography Applications. XI, 182 pages. 1994.

Vol. 871: J. P. Lee, G. G. Grinstein (Eds.), Database Issues for Data Visualization. Proceedings, 1993. XIV, 229 pages. 1994.

Vol. 872: S Arikawa, K. P. Jantke (Eds.), Algorithmic Learning Theory. Proceedings, 1994. XIV, 575 pages. 1994.

Vol. 873: M. Naftalin, T. Denvir, M. Bertran (Eds.), FME '94: Industrial Benefit of Formal Methods. Proceedings, 1994. XI, 723 pages. 1994.

Vol. 874: A. Borning (Ed.), Principles and Practice of Constraint Programming. Proceedings, 1994. IX, 361 pages. 1994.

Vol. 875: D. Gollmann (Ed.), Computer Security – ESORICS 94. Proceedings, 1994. XI, 469 pages. 1994.

Vol. 876: B. Blumenthal, J. Gornostaev, C. Unger (Eds.), Human-Computer Interaction. Proceedings, 1994. IX, 239 pages. 1994.

Vol. 877: L. M. Adleman, M.-D. Huang (Eds.), Algorithmic Number Theory. Proceedings, 1994. IX, 323 pages. 1994.

Vol. 878: T. Ishida; Parallel, Distributed and Multiagent Production Systems. XVII, 166 pages. 1994. (Subseries LNAI).

Vol. 879: J. Dongarra, J. Waśniewski (Eds.), Parallel Scientific Computing. Proceedings, 1994. XI, 566 pages. 1994.

Vol. 880: P. S. Thiagarajan (Ed.), Foundations of Software Technology and Theoretical Computer Science. Proceedings, 1994. XI, 451 pages. 1994.

Vol. 881: P. Loucopoulos (Ed.), Entity-Relationship Approach – ER'94. Proceedings, 1994. XIII, 579 pages. 1994.

Vol. 882: D. Hutchison, A. Danthine, H. Leopold, G. Coulson (Eds.), Multimedia Transport and Teleservices. Proceedings, 1994. XI, 380 pages. 1994.

Vol. 883: L. Fribourg, F. Turini (Eds.), Logic Program Synthesis and Transformation – Meta-Programming in Logic. Proceedings, 1994. IX, 451 pages. 1994.

Vol. 884: J. Nievergelt, T. Roos, H.-J. Schek, P. Widmayer (Eds.), IGIS '94: Geographic Information Systems. Proceedings, 1994. VIII, 292 pages. 19944.

Vol. 885: R. C. Veltkamp, Closed Objects Boundaries from Scattered Points. VIII, 144 pages. 1994.

Vol. 886: M. M. Veloso, Planning and Learning by Analogical Reasoning. XIII, 181 pages. 1994. (Subseries LNAI).

Vol. 887: M. Toussaint (Ed.), Ada in Europe. Proceedings, 1994. XII, 521 pages. 1994.

Vol. 888: S. A. Andersson (Ed.), Analysis of Dynamical and Cognitive Systems. Proceedings, 1993. VII, 260 pages. 1995.

Vol. 889: H. P. Lubich, Towards a CSCW Framework for Scientific Cooperation in Europe. X, 268 pages. 1995.

Vol. 890: M. J. Wooldridge, N. R. Jennings (Eds.), Intelligent Agents. Proceedings, 1994. VIII, 407 pages. 1995. (Subseries LNAI).

Vol. 891: C. Lewerentz, T. Lindner (Eds.), Formal Development of Reactive Systems. XI, 394 pages. 1995.

Vol. 892: K. Pingali, U. Banerjee, D. Gelernter, A. Nicolau, D. Padua (Eds.), Languages and Compilers for Parallel Computing. Proceedings, 1994. XI, 496 pages. 1995.

Vol. 893: G. Gottlob, M. Y. Vardi (Eds.), Database Theory – ICDT '95. Proceedings, 1995. XI, 454 pages. 1995.

Vol. 894: R. Tamassia, I. G. Tollis (Eds.), Graph Drawing. Proceedings, 1994. X, 471 pages. 1995.

Vol. 895: R. L. Ibrahim (Ed.), Software Engineering Education. Proceedings, 1995. XII, 449 pages. 1995.

Vol. 896: R. N. Taylor, J. Coutaz (Eds.), Software Engineering and Human-Computer Interaction. Proceedings, 1994. X, 281 pages. 1995.

Vol. 897: M. Fisher, R. Owens (Eds.), Executable Modal and Temporal Logics. Proceedings, 1993. VII, 180 pages. 1995. (Subseries LNAI).

Vol. 898: P. Steffens (Ed.), Machine Translation and the Lexicon. Proceedings, 1993. X, 251 pages. 1995. (Subseries LNAI).

Vol. 899: W. Banzhaf, F. H. Eeckman (Eds.), Evolution and Biocomputation. VII, 277 pages. 1995.

Vol. 900: E. W. Mayr, C. Puech (Eds.), STACS 95. Proceedings, 1995. XIII, 654 pages. 1995.

Vol. 901: R. Kumar, T. Kropf (Eds.), Theorem Provers in Circuit Design. Proceedings, 1994. VIII, 303 pages. 1995.

Vol. 902: M. Dezani-Ciancaglini, G. Plotkin (Eds.), Typed Lambda Calculi and Applications. Proceedings, 1995. VIII, 443 pages. 1995.

Vol. 903: E. W. Mayr, G. Schmidt, G. Tinhofer (Eds.), Graph-Theoretic Concepts in Computer Science. Proceedings, 1994. IX, 414 pages. 1995.

Vol. 904: P. Vitányi (Ed.), Computational Learning Theory. EuroCOLT'95. Proceedings, 1995. XVII, 415 pages. 1995. (Subseries LNAI).

Vol. 905: N. Ayache (Ed.), Computer Vision, Virtual Reality and Robotics in Medicine. Proceedings, 1995. XIV, 567 pages. 1995.

Vol. 906: E. Astesiano, G. Reggio, A. Tarlecki (Eds.), Recent Trends in Data Type Specification. Proceedings, 1995. VIII, 523 pages. 1995.

Vol. 907: T. Ito, A. Yonezawa (Eds.), Theory and Practice of Parallel Programming. Proceedings, 1995. VIII, 485 pages. 1995.

Vol. 908: J. R. Rao Extensions of the UNITY Methodology: Compositionality, Fairness and Probability in Parallelism. XI, 178 pages. 1995.

Vol. 910: A. Podelski (Ed.), Constraint Programming: Basics and Trends. Proceedings, 1995. XI, 315 pages. 1995.